I WILL BE A FEMALE BISHOP!

- The Basics of Sermons on Happiness
and other religious policy field analyses

(DEUS EX MACHINA - Part IV).

AF192260

Imprint

Circe, Eureka: **I WILL BE A FEMALE BISHOP!** - *The Basics of Sermons on Happiness and other religious policy analyses*.
Deus Ex Machina - Part IV.
Hamburg, 2025.
ISBN 978-3-8192-2914-5

© 2025 Eureca Circe as curator and editor in documentation with KI.
This release was translated by AI.
Publisher: BoD · Books on Demand GmbH, Überseering 33, 22297 Hamburg,
bod@bod.de
Printed by: Libri Plureos GmbH, Friedensallee 273, 22763 Hamburg
Bibliographical references from the German National Library at: https://portal.dnb.de

I WILL BE A FEMALE BISHOP!

- The Basics of Sermons on Happiness
and other religious policy field analyses.

DEUS EX MACHINA - Part IV.

Eureka Circe is the editor and curator of the book series "DEUS EX MACHINA" and the present volume "I will be a female Bishop! - The Basics of Sermons on Happiness and other religious policy field analyses (DEUS EX MACHINA - Part IV)".

Also published are: "DEUS EX MACHINA - Or: On questioning Life" (Part I – ISBN 9783758340222), "Homecoming from the Pope" (Part II - ISBN 9783769357950) and "Faith is like Dancing" – "Glauben ist wie Tanzen - Vom Glauben bewegt als Christ:in wachsen. Training book for building religious skills" (Part III – ISBN 9783819296307).

With the work "DEUS EX MACHINA", the curator is committed to documenting and, if necessary, discussing the texts of artificial intelligence in a religious and theological context. Her thesis: "Artificial intelligence (AI) represents a profound turning point because it fundamentally changes the relationship between humans, knowledge and access to the world - not only technically, but also culturally, epistemologically and socially. It opens up new access to knowledge and leads to its multiplication and democratization: AI systems make information available at a low threshold - often without traditional reading or in-depth prior knowledge. This fundamentally changes how we think, learn and understand, and at the same time promotes a new form of individualization of thought - which can also be exemplified by spiritual belief. What's more, machines are now generating meaning - texts, images, arguments - where previously only human expertise was required. This has long-term consequences for education, science, politics and religion."

Sittin' in the dark while you're on your own
Drownin' in your thoughts and the alcohol
I could be your light in the afterglow

Get that taste out of your mouth
Take that pain, scream it out
Like I love it, like I love it
Lose yourself in the sound
Like there's no one around
Let it go, let it go, let it go

Shut up and dance
And move your body
Shut up and dance
And make your heart beat
Shut up and dance
Shut up and dance like you're invisible

When you're lost in the dark, find the love in your heart
Just dance, just dance

quoted from: Sophie and the Giants

Contents

Introduction:
"Habemus Pontificem Politicam"
- On the way to becoming a political bishop!

Julia Klöckner, a theology graduate and current President of the German Bundestag, caused a stir over Easter when she addressed the role of churches in society in an interview with a major tabloid newspaper: *"If the church sometimes becomes too arbitrary, or makes statements on topical issues like a non-governmental organization (NGO) and no longer focuses on the fundamental issues of life and death, then unfortunately it also becomes interchangeable. I mean: of course the church can also comment on the 130 km/h / 80 miles per hour (mph) speed limit on our highways, but I don't necessarily pay "church tax" for that"*.

Shut-up: How political can a theologian be today?

At the same time, the President emphasized that she was not prepared to pay "church tax" for policy analyses on "Tempo 130 kmh / Tempo 80 mph" and called on the churches not to become arbitrary.

At the Protestant Church Congress 2025, she repeated her criticism for both churches. The church must speak out on questions of meaning and be *"a bit more"* than a non-governmental organization: *"And that bit more is faith."*

These statements were met with widespread criticism, particularly from other politicians, who asked why churches should not speak out on issues such as *injustice, humanity and social cohesion*. Others recalled *that Christianity was originally the voice of the poor and disenfranchised* and emphasized that churches should also speak out politically. Some also emphasized that the *church has always been political* and that the *churches' commitment to society* is *central*. Popes such as John Paul II had contributed significantly to the *reunification of Europe*.

Journalists noted that the new President of the German Bundestag was publicly *banning the churches from speaking* with her *"shut-up" demand*: the *demand for an apolitical church*, however, fails to recognize their *task of shaping society*.

Figure 1: Would Jesus have driven at 80 mph?

A humorous cartoon shows a chaotic traffic scene with numerous honking cars. In the middle is a woman, a clergywoman, with a sign that reads: 'Honk if you love Jesus and 80 mph'. The drivers react with enthusiasm or interest and honk their horns loudly for both. The humorous cartoon ironically shows how a seemingly harmless request and statement in everyday life can create an unexpected diversity of voices within a religious political field.

Other publicists also saw *a ban on speech as a mistake,* because the *church is an NGO, and a very large one at that.* The *task of the churches and the biblical interpretation* should not be misunderstood, even from a historical perspective: *The Gospel, the Sermon on the Mount and the prophets are political,* according to the broad media response.

Are quotas for women in church offices political or a political issue?

Ten years ago, the President herself made a political recommendation - possibly also to the church - to introduce a *quota for women*:

In her book *"Zuversicht!"*, she does not support quotas for women for ideological reasons, but for pragmatic reasons - based on her *own experience and observations*. Influenced by her personal career, she differentiated the positive effects of a women's quota even back then.

Personal experience: The current president emphasizes that she would not have entered politics without the so-called women's quorum. She was originally only offered a safe place on the list because her party had *introduced a women's quorum, the women's quota*. She thus recognizes first-hand that quotas can be an effective instrument for enabling women to enter areas in which they are traditionally underrepresented.

Creating opportunities, not forcing them: She does not see quotas as an instrument to fundamentally change or enforce gender roles, but rather as a tool to *overcome structural obstacles* that keep women out of certain positions. Her argument is pragmatic: *without quotas, women would often not even be visible, let alone considered.*

Impetus for cultural change: The President sees quotas as temporary measures ("a kind of bridge or crutch to normality") that should help to ensure that *equality* becomes *a matter of course in* the long term. According to her recommendation, the quota provides the necessary impetus to actively seek out qualified women in the first place and thus initiate a *cultural change in organizations*.

Political realism: The President argues that *quotas for women* make *sense*, especially in times of crisis in organizations or parties, because men are often reticent and women are specifically sought out and promoted - a situation she has experienced and used herself. In her view, quotas for women are therefore also a pragmatic means of *promoting female talent* at critical moments that would otherwise not have become visible.

In summary, the President of the German Bundestag sees quotas for women as an instrument that has a practical effect, opens doors in concrete terms and gradually helps to make equal opportunities and gender equality more self-evident. Can these positions be withheld from a Catholic church when it comes to having a female pope soon? *What would the next female pope report in this political field from her own professional socialization and development in a major tabloid newspaper?* So why shouldn't there soon be a woman bishop in the Catholic Church, so that the "Conference of Bishops" could already be linguistically gendered: "Conference of female, diverse and male Bishops" - *and therefore consistently implemented in the following?*

With regard to the task of clergymembers to also publish religious policy analyses from a Christian perspective, for example in their sermons, the President wrote confidently ten years ago in her book "Zutrauen": *"The Christian message challenges me to act. To allow oneself to be touched, to think not of oneself but of the good of many, to keep an eye on the weak, to use talents. The Christian message implies socio-political action, the call to get involved. The Bible is full of stories of refugees; it teaches us solidarity and humanity. Are Christianity and politics compatible? Of course!"*

The discussion illustrates the different views on the socio-political role of churches with political influences in numerous religious policy areas - even if a strict separation of church and state applies.

Or was it all just a PR move by a president who had only been in this high office for a few days to say: here I am? What would a female Pope's first message in Rome look like?

The strict separation of church and state is a central principle of modern democracies that has emerged from a long historical development, legal considerations and the pursuit of social peace. At its core, it is about protecting the freedom of the individual, preserving the neutrality of the state and preventing the abuse of power - both on the part of the state and on the part of religious institutions.

A central reason for the separation is to safeguard religious freedom. Everyone should be able to decide for themselves whether and how they believe. The state may not prescribe, favor or discriminate against any religion. Without this separation, there would be a danger that religious beliefs would be enforced by the state or that people of other faiths and non-believers would come under pressure. At the same time, separation also protects the churches: it prevents religion from being instrumentalized by the state for political purposes. Throughout history, religious institutions have repeatedly been misused as instruments of power, for example to justify wars or to control the population.

Figure 2: Faith and belief

FAITH & BELIEF

A cartoon that humorously illustrates the difference between religion and politics. On one side, depict a church where a clergyman says to a parishioner in a friendly and questioning manner: "We seek and are looking for the way". On the other side, show a party building with a large sign that confidently proclaims: "We know the way". Title underneath: "Faith & Belief". The style is simple, humorous and easy to understand.

The separation also serves the neutrality of the state. A state that calls itself democratic must treat all citizens equally - regardless of their religious beliefs. Laws and political decisions must be based on reason and general principles, not on religious dogma. In a pluralistic society, in which people of different faiths or even without any religious affiliation live together, it is essential that the state does not favor any religion. Only in this way can peaceful and equal coexistence function.

History has also shown how problematic close ties between church and state can be. In Europe, these have led to conflicts, oppression of dissenters and religiously motivated wars for centuries. The Enlightenment therefore emphatically demanded the independence of thought from religious paternalism - a concern that has also found its way into modern constitutions. However, separation does not mean enmity, but a clear division of tasks: the state regulates public life, law and order, while the church takes care of the spiritual, ethical and pastoral guidance of people.

A look at different countries reveals different implementations of this separation. In France, for example, it has been particularly strictly regulated since the Laïcité law of 1905 - religion is purely a private matter there. In Germany, on the other hand, there is a so-called cooperative separation: The churches are independent of the state, but are involved - for example in the area of religious education or through the church tax that the state collects. This form enables cooperation without giving up mutual independence.

Overall, the separation of church and state protects both society and religion itself. It guarantees freedom, promotes equality, preserves peace between different world views and strengthens a democratic culture in which no one is favored or disadvantaged because of their faith. In a time of growing diversity, it therefore remains an indispensable foundation for living together in dignity and freedom.

Of course, this does not mean that clergymembers cannot speak out on political issues.

What other political issues do the bishops have?

But what topics have top church representatives, including bishops and cardinals, spoken out about?

The Deus Ex Machina, who decided to become a Catholic female bishop after her previous publications on socially pressing issues and training to build religious competence, used her artificial intelligence to identify a common denominator in the sermons and thematically central issues of spiritual church representatives in numerous policy areas.

Artificial Intelligence has evaluated each individual bishop of the German Conference of female, diverse and male Bishops and other international cardinals with regard to their public positions and publications. Numerous Wikipedia entries on the individuals also provide an additional overview of positions, publications and - from today's perspective, possibly old-fashioned and outdated - "bloopers" or controversial statements as well as light impulses in public debates.

This AI-supported analysis identified the more than 20 most essential topics and fields on which high-ranking clergy such as Catholic bishops and international cardinals usually preach and speak publicly.

In this volume, *Deus Ex Machina* has finally produced an elaboration on each of the key religious policy areas. The result is the Basics of Sermons.

If pupils at school, students at university or those capable of reading during their training as clergy are looking for a subject area of the Catholic (and possibly also suitable for the Protestant) Church to thematize, discuss and further elaborate on - here they will find a selection of a common denominator.

At the same time, this promotes a *method of religious political field analysis* for theology that is familiar to political science as a pure political field analysis - only with a complementary perspective *from a Christian and religious point of view*. The church does not have to be political, but its members may and should be politically interested in the attitudes and values of their faith.

For all those who also want to become clergy, these introductory topics can serve as *a Basics of Sermons (especially on Human Happiness)* to quickly familiarize themselves with a topic. Due to the broad AI-based analyses, the automated structure of the present volume *"I will be a female Bishop!"* will be pleased if it can contribute its potential as a possible future standard work in religious and political education.

These topics and policy areas do not require a degree in theology - everyone can think, have a say and reflect on and evaluate the thematic arguments as well as their own learning and actions from a Christian perspective.

Every believer can take these topics as reading material and is thus ideally equipped for a dialog with other believers in the congregation and the wider public.

With this method *of religious policy field analysis*, sermons and publications at the level of Catholic bishops and international cardinals were first examined: Artificial Intelligence researched and analyzed this content thematically. This resulted in the structure of this volume: an overview of more than 20 topics that are addressed particularly frequently and repeatedly by the clergy. The algorithms then assessed whether the respective person is conservative, moderate, progressive or customer-oriented in terms of their attitude.

In addition to the assessment of the frequency of publication and preaching, the age of the respective person was also taken into account.

Here is an evaluation of selected German bishops who preach and publish a particularly large amount, as rated by age (on the vertical axis) and reform orientation (conservative, moderate, or progressive) by the algorithms of artificial intelligence.

Figure 3: Reform-mindedness of selected German bishops.

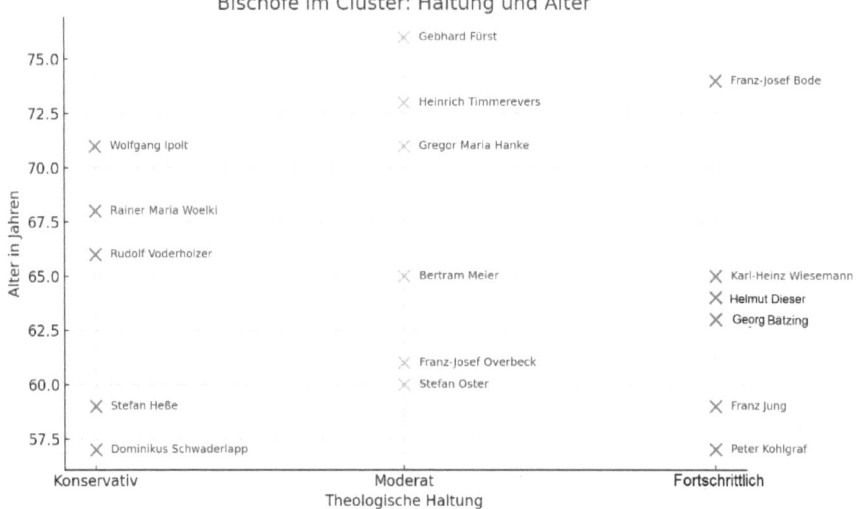

Bischöfe im Cluster: Haltung und Alter

The analysis of these cases shows that around two thirds have a moderate to progressive attitude towards church organization. A clear picture emerges particularly among the under 65s: according to the principle of the 80:20 rule, the vast majority of these younger clergy no longer belong to the strictly conservative camp, but are reform-oriented, forward-looking and willing to play an active role in shaping the church. But are the clergy actually using their sermons to develop creative power in the form of successful results - including within the church?

What are the sermon topics of the cardinals worldwide?

Over 130 male cardinals were entitled to vote in the election of the current Pope. At the time of the conclave, a significant number of them were under 65 years old. Here too, artificial intelligence was used to identify the respective and typical topics that these cardinals deal with in public.

Cardinals over the age of 65 were not included in the analysis, as it can be assumed that they were socially and professionally socialized in other contexts and are generally not digital natives. Even if they have communication staff, they rarely publish in digital formats themselves or did not have a corresponding publication intensity.

The present analysis is therefore not intended as a complete survey, but as an exemplary evaluation of those cardinals who are very likely to influence future papal elections. A more comprehensive AI-supported analysis of all cardinals could be realized in a future generation of conclaves.

The "*Deus Ex Machina*" - the artificial intelligence - was tasked with identifying the three thematic focal points of the publications, sermons or academic works of each of the clergymembers in question. This resulted in a total of well over one hundred individual topics.

The AI then analyzed this content, eliminated redundancies and grouped the working titles and subject areas under common headings. In this way, six central thematic clusters were finally identified, which clearly structure the theological and pastoral focus of these younger cardinals:

- **Peace ethics and political responsibility through political policy field analyses**: e.g. peacebuilding and conflict resolution in the Middle East, criticism of political corruption and mismanagement, rejection of Western moral influences (cultural integrity).

- **Social justice and social commitment**, e.g. solidarity with disadvantaged communities, commitment to social justice and environmental protection, social justice and human rights.

- **Mission and evangelization**: Evangelization and missionary sending.

- **Internal church unity and renewal:** e.g. church unity and reconciliation, strengthening the laity, youth ministry, preserving liturgical traditions, church law and administration, the role of the church in society.

- **Dialogue and interreligious understanding and dialog:** e.g. ecumenical cooperation and interreligious dialog topics.

This grouping has a much narrower focus than the topics and religious policy areas identified by the German and international bishops.

An initial overview already revealed a clear pattern: cardinals from non-European and often economically weaker countries were often rated as rather conservative by the algorithm. In contrast, cardinals from westernized regions, which are more strongly influenced by modern forms of society, are more conservative. They usually pursue a practical orientation that aims to align faith and the church structure with social and societal realities and necessities and actively shape them.

Younger cardinals, on the other hand, tend to be characterized as more worldly, more digital and more open to reform. They combine theological tradition with a willingness to change and often bring new ideas to the debate within the church.

Particularly noteworthy is a group of three cardinals who were considered moderate by the system, but who stand out due to their high publication frequency. Their contributions focus primarily on spiritual practice and theological foundations. They pursue a line that does not aim to modernize the church in a radically effective way, but continuously - always with the aim of keeping it socially compatible. For them, dialog with lay people and other religions is at the heart of church renewal.

The cardinals, who are seen as more conservative, are primarily dedicated to issues such as political conflict resolution, peace initiatives and the fight against corruption and mismanagement. In addition, they emphasize the importance of ecumenical dialogue and show solidarity with disadvantaged groups in the sense of a global sense of justice. At the same time, they also express warnings of a cultural change, which they believe is accompanied by an erosion of church dogma and a shift from traditional assessments to contemporary values.

Younger cardinals publish significantly more per year than their older siblings. One possible reason for this is that they have to build up a public reputation - especially at the beginning of their careers - and have often done so in order to be accepted into the College of female, divers and male Cardinals in the first place. Older cardinals, on the other hand, publish less frequently. This may be due to the fact that they have already spoken out on key issues, are more established in their role or focus their activities more on strategic processes, pastoral tasks and personal encounters with people of faith. They also have a lower presence in digital formats, which may be partly due to different media habits or a conscious prioritization.

The following is an analysis of which of the younger cardinals' three central sermons, articles or publications relate to which of the previously identified five common overarching themes that have emerged as a thematic denominator in the overall picture of all cardinals: *Who has particularly distinguished themselves as a young cardinal with which topics - based on the three most concise contributions of each individual and their respective assignment to the five common main topics?*

Figure 4: Main topics of publications by young cardinals under the age of 65.

NAME OF THE CARDINAL / FOCUS OF PUBLICATIONS	Peace ethics & conflict prevention	Social Justice	Mission / Evangelization	Renewal / reform	Interreligious Dialog
Byczok, Mykola (01)	X		X		X
Marengo, Giorgio (02)			X		X
Alves Aguiar, Américo Manuel (03)			X	X	X
Koovakad, George Jacob (04)	X			X	X
Makrickas, Rolandas (05)					X
Leo, Frank (06)			X		
Reina, Baldassare (07)	X		X	X	
Bustillo, François-Xavier OFMCon (08)			X	X	X
Silva, Virgílio do Carmo da (09)	X		X		X
Costa, Paulo Cezar (10)	X		X		X
Nzapalainga, Dieudonné CSSp (11)	X	X			X
Repole, Roberto (12)			X	X	
Calaça de Mendonça, José Tolentino (13)					X
Gambetti, Mauro OFMConv (14)	X	X	X		
Cobo Cano, José (15)		X		X	
Pizzaballa, Pierbattista OFM (16)	X				X
Baggio, Fabio (17)	X	X			X
Lojudice, Augusto Paolo (18)	X	X		X	
Ryś, Grzegorz (19)			X	X	X
Mulla, Stephen Ameyu Martin (20)	X			X	X
Krajewski, Konrad (21)		X			
Mathieu, Dominique (22)			X		X
Okpaleke, Peter Ebere (23)				X	X
Battaglia, Domenico (24)		X	x		
Fernández, Víctor Manuel (25)				X	

Vesco, Jean-Paul (26)				X	X	X
Rueda Aparicio, Luis José (27)	X	X		X		
Mafi, Soane Patita Paini (28)		X		X		
Poola, Anthony (29)		X		X		
Bessi Dogbo, Ignace (30)	X			X		
Spengler, Jaime (31)		X		X		
Fernández Artime, Ángel SDB (32)			X	X		
Rugambwa, Protase (33)			X	X		
Besungu, Fridolin Ambongo (34)	X	X	X			
Rocha, Sérgio da (35)		X		X		
Chow Sau-yan, Stephen SJ (36)			X	x		X
Sturla Berhouet, Daniel Fernando SDB (37)	X		X			
Thottunkal, Baselios Cleemis (38)		X	X			X

At the same time, it is clear that each cardinal sets individual thematic priorities - be it through a focused concentration on a single topic area or through a broad spread across several areas. Not all of them are interested in all of the main topics, but this is not a shortcoming, but rather an expression of the diversity of content and profile formation. This diversity reflects the freedom of research, teaching and theological positioning - also and especially in a church context.

Finally, the carinals (indexed by age as above) were also assessed using artificial intelligence according to their reform orientation (conservative, moderate, progressive) and their publication frequency or intensity. Existing databases and additional specialized research were used for this purpose.

In a matrix presentation - based on the so-called Gartner quadrant - the young high-potentials were classified according to two scales: their frequency of publication and their orientation towards shaping change. On the one hand, they were assessed on how progressive their theological stance is in response to today's realities (resonance with today's life demands, reform orientation), and on the other hand, how often they represent these positions in publications.

The Gartner Quadrant - officially known as the *Gartner Magic Quadrant* - is a strategic analysis tool from the US market research company Gartner Inc. that is used worldwide, particularly in the technology sector. The aim of this tool is to systematically and comparatively evaluate providers within a specific market. It is based on two main criteria: "completeness of vision" and "ability to execute". These two criteria form the axes of the quadrant.

The "completeness of vision" is plotted on the horizontal axis. It assesses how comprehensively and forward-looking a company thinks, how well it recognizes technological trends, reacts to future market needs and integrates innovations into its strategic planning. The vertical axis, on the other hand, measures the "ability to implement" - in other words, how well a provider currently positions, develops, distributes and supports its products or services on the market. This includes both operational performance and customer satisfaction.

The resulting quadrant is divided into four fields that characterize different types of providers. The upper right quadrant contains the so-called "leaders". They are characterized by a high level of implementation power and a clear, forward-looking vision. These providers are considered to be market-defining and innovative. The "Visionaries" are located in the lower right quadrant. Although they have pioneering ideas and a good feel for future developments, they are not (yet) as strong in their implementation. At the top left are the "Challengers": They are very good at operational implementation, but show little willingness to innovate or foresight. Finally, in the lower left quadrant are the "Niche Players". They have neither a particularly strong market implementation nor a comprehensive vision, but often offer specialized solutions for certain customer groups or industries.

The Magic Quadrant is used by many companies, IT managers and investors as a basis for making decisions on technology purchases or strategic partnerships. It provides a quick visual overview of the market, but does not replace an individual needs analysis. Rather, it is intended as a guide.

Figure 5: Magic Quadrant of the Cardinals.

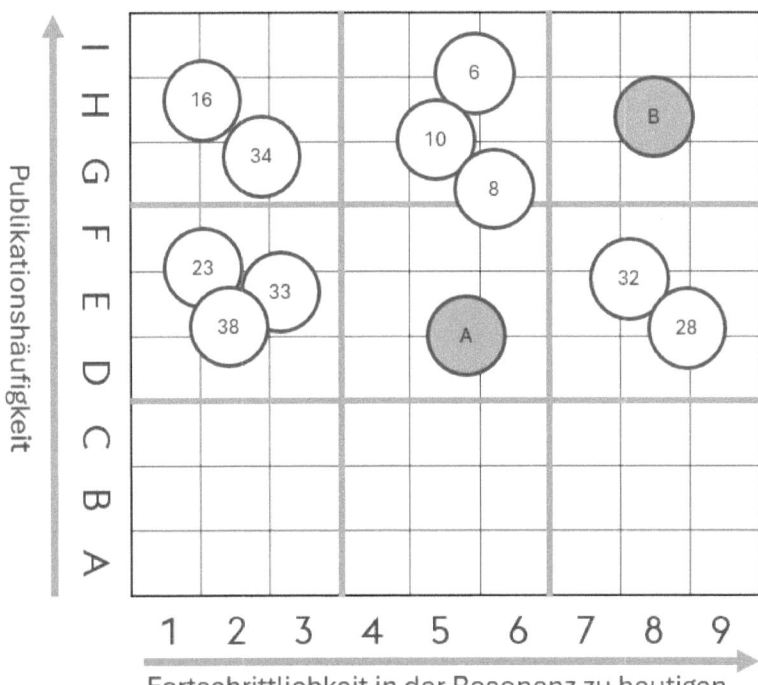

Fortschrittlichkeit in der Resonanz zu heutigen
Lebensanforderungen (Reformorientierung)

The numbers refer to the list of names of the cardinals in the previous illustration. Some people can be grouped together:
Cluster B = 1, 2, 3, 4, 5, 7, 11, 12, 13, 15, 17, 18, 19, 21, 24, 25, 26.
Cluster A = 9, 14, 20, 22, 27, 29, 30, 31, 35, 36, 37.

At the same time, the Gartner Quadrant is not free of criticism. Some complain that it favors established providers with market power, as it is easier for them to achieve high implementation scores.

Despite these slight limitations, the Magic Quadrant remains a globally influential tool in evaluation - precisely because it makes complex relationships comprehensible at a glance and provides a structured basis for comparison within a defined field. Ultimately, it is a *classic two-criteria analysis* that is visualized using an *axis diagram* - in this case applied to a theological context.

Previous target group orientation and development of the current Pope's topics

Robert Francis Prevost was recently elected as the new pope from the circle of female, divers and male cardinals - he now bears the name Leo XIV. His previous positions and publications were also analyzed and evaluated using artificial intelligence - in comparison to the typical sermon and publication topics of his colleagues in office, as well as with regard to the targeted addressing of relevant target and interest groups (so-called "stakeholder addressing", e.g. in the sense of EFQM.org).

As Prevost was already over 65 years old at the time of the analysis, he was not initially included in the group of younger cardinals. Nevertheless, his theological orientation, communicative practice and strategic positioning in the run-up to the conclave and afterwards in his new role are of particular interest.

The following chronologically structured overview shows the most important stages in the life of Robert Francis Prevost up to his election as Pope Leo XIV. Central offices, statements and publications are recorded - each assigned to thematic focal points such as *peace ethics, justice, mission, renewal, interreligious dialog & ecumenism* as well as addressing specific interest groups such as *practitioners, women, queers, those who have left the church, volunteers, young people* and *social actors*.

- **1977 - Joined the Augustinian Order** - *Dimensions addressed: Mission*: Prevost joined the Augustinian order, which marked the beginning of his lifelong commitment to missionary work.

- **1985-1998 - Missionary activity in Peru** - *Addressed dimensions: Mission, Justice, Addressing Social Actors*: In Peru, Prevost worked as a pastor, trainer and professor, particularly in disadvantaged regions, which underlines his commitment to social justice and education.

- **1987 - Dissertation: "The Role of the Local Prior in the Order of Saint Augustine"** - *Addressed dimension: Renewal:* In his dissertation, Prevost analyzes the role of the local prior in the Augustinian Order, which shows his deep involvement with ecclesiastical structure and leadership.

- **2001-2013 - Prior General of the Augustinian Order** - *Dimension addressed: Renewal*: As head of the Order, Prevost initiated reforms and promoted the renewal of the religious community worldwide.

- **2014-2023 - Bishop of Chiclayo, Peru** - *Dimensions addressed: Justice, Mission, Addressing Social Actors*: In his role as bishop, he was committed to social programs and strengthening the local church.

- **2023 - Prefect of the Dicastery for Bishops** - *Dimension addressed: Renewal:* In this key position, Prevost was responsible for the selection and appointment of bishops worldwide and played a central role in promoting a synodal Church.

- **September 2023 - Appointment as Cardinal** - *Addressed dimension: Renewal:* The appointment as Cardinal reflected his significant role in church leadership and his closeness to Pope Francis' reform efforts.

- **October 2023 - Statement on the ordination of women at the World Synod** - *Dimension addressed: women:* Prevost was critical of the idea of women's ordination and emphasized that a "clericalization of women" would not solve the existing problems. He pleaded for a new understanding of leadership and service in the church.

- **May 2025 - First address as Pope Leo XIV** - *Dimensions addressed: Peace ethics, justice, mission, queers. Addressing social actors*: In his first address, Leo XIV emphasized the importance of peace, unity and inclusivity. All belong to the Church. He called for global unity and mercy and acknowledged his links with Peru.

Figure 6: The current Pope LEO XIV's thematic and target group orientation to date - resulting from his AI-rated publications and stations in his life as a cardinal.

POPE LEO XIV. and his key stations and publications	Peace ethics	Justice	Mission	Renewal	Interreligious, ecumenical dialog	Practitioners	Women	Queers	Departed	Volunteers	Teenagers	Social actors
Augustinian			■									
Peru		■										■
Dissertation				■								
General												■
Bishop		■										■
Prefect				■								
Cardinal				■								
Synod							■					
1st speech	■							■				■

This overview shows that Robert Francis Prevost, now Pope LEO XIV, has been particularly active in the areas of mission, justice and renewal in his career to date. His work in Peru and his leadership roles within the Church reflect a deep commitment to social issues and the structural renewal of the Church.

If a more detailed analysis or further information on specific aspects is required, KI will be happy to help.

Figure 7: Portrait of Pope Leo XIV (since 2025).

Drawing of Robert Francis Cardinal Prevost, Pope Leo XIV. He is an American religious cleric of the Roman Catholic Church. He was Prior General of the Augustinian Order from 2001 to 2013. From 2015 to 2023 he was Bishop of Chiclayo. On January 30, 2023, he was appointed Prefect of the Dicastery for Bishops. On May 8, 2025, he was elected Pope as the successor to Pope Francis and the first US-American and first Peruvian to hold this office: Pope Leo XIV.

An automated analysis for the newly elected Pope Leo XIV yields the following information based on the data available to date: Evaluation of Cardinal Robert Francis Prevost, now Pope Leo XIV, according to the selection criteria for the papal office, in accordance with the attached call for applications for the position of supreme head of the Church with a rating on a scale of 1 (low) - 5 (high) and a justification in each case.

1. theological and spiritual aptitude - total score: 5 points

Cardinal Prevost, now Pope Leo XIV, fulfills the theological and spiritual requirements to an outstanding degree.

- **Prayer life and spiritual depth (5)** - As an Augustinian canon, Prevost, now Pope Leo XIV, led a spiritual life based on the order's charism. He emphasizes the importance of daily prayer and trust in God in his ministry: *"Lord, everything is in your hands. Give me the grace..."* - is how he describes his daily prayer in

31

his religious life. This attitude testifies to his deep piety and grounded spirituality.

- **Social justice and Caritas awareness (5)** - In his work as a bishop, he showed a strong social commitment. He was "known *for his closeness to poor communities and his pastoral focus on social justice"*. This pronounced option for the poor and his awareness of charity underline his socio-ethical competence.

- **Faithfulness to the faith (5)** - Prevost, now Pope Leo XIV, is considered faithful to the Magisterium and steadfast in the Catholic faith. For example, he expressed criticism when the media advocated behavior that was contrary to the Gospel. This indicates a high degree of fidelity to church doctrine.

2. personal characteristics - total score: 5 points

Prevost, now Pope Leo XIV, has excellent character traits, strong leadership qualities and high communication skills, although he is rather reserved in his public image.

- **Strength of character (5)** - He is described as down-to-earth, reliable and obedient. He emphasized his religious vows and his willingness to serve by saying himself: *"I have always done what I was asked to do"*. His straightforwardness and sense of duty indicate a high level of moral integrity.

- **Leadership ability (5)** - Prevost, now Pope Leo XIV, has impressed in a variety of leadership roles. He led a world order as Prior General for twelve years and was entrusted by Pope Francis with the important task of serving as Bishop of Chiclayo and later as head of the Roman episcopal dicastery. He is regarded as a determined leader with a clear vision: his *"single-minded determination and clarity"* are highlighted by observers.

- **Communication skills (4)** - Thanks to five working languages (including English, Spanish, Italian and French), Prevost, now Pope Leo XIV, can communicate directly with different cultures worldwide. This polyglot ability facilitates exchanges with the faithful and church representatives around the globe. In his demeanor, however, he is reserved and deliberate; he speaks carefully and without great charisma. Overall, however, his ability to communicate effectively across language barriers prevails, which is why his communication skills are rated highly.

3. pastoral experience and leadership - total score: 5 points

With decades of pastoral practice on several continents and a broad pastoral horizon, Prevost, now Pope Leo XIV, fulfills the pastoral experience and leadership requirements in an exemplary manner.

- **Several years of experience as a priest/bishop (5)** - Prevost, now Pope Leo XIV, can look back on over 40 years of priestly service, many of them in grassroots pastoral care. He has worked as a missionary and pastor in Peru since 1985 and was consecrated bishop in 2014. These many years of experience as a priest *and* bishop - from parish priest to religious superior - testify to his extensive pastoral practice.

- **Commitment to pastoral care, education and social issues (5)** - He was involved in many different areas: as a trainer of young religious, seminary teacher and parish pastor. In Peru, he distinguished himself through a pastoral ministry that promotes education and focuses on social emergencies. His commitment to justice and the well-being of local people was clearly evident.

- **Inclusive pastoral care (option for the poor, reconciliation, peace) (5)** - Prevost's work was missionary from the outset and characterized by the option for the poor. In Chiclayo, he was "known *for his closeness to poor communities"* and his dialog with indigenous peoples. This openness towards different cultures and social groups and his efforts towards reconciliation reflect an inclusive pastoral approach.

- **Vision and future orientation (5)** - Cardinal Prevost, now Pope Leo XIV, thinks about the future of the Church. He strongly supports the synodal path initiated by Pope Francis in order to keep the Church capable of renewal. In his current role, he is shaping the worldwide appointment of bishops *"in line with Francis' pastoral vision"* and thus promoting a future-oriented renewal of the episcopate. His ability to plan beyond the day is also evident in his clear vision of "where he wants to go and how he will get there".

4. management and teaching - overall assessment: 3 points

In matters of church leadership and doctrine, Prevost, now Pope Leo XIV, was particularly convincing in the area of synodality and unity, while he was reserved or even hostile towards progressive reform concerns (roles of women, celibacy, sexual morality).

- **Unity in diversity & synodal culture of dialogue (5)** - This is where Prevost, now Pope Leo XIV, shines. *He is an energetic advocate of synodality* and sees it as a way of integrating diversity and overcoming polarization. In interviews, he emphasized that the church must *"really listen to the Holy Spirit and the spirit of finding the truth"* and values an inclusive, participatory church structure. Promoting a culture of listening and consultation is central to him.

- **Attitude towards the ordination of women and gender justice (1)** - On this point, Prevost, now Pope Leo XIV, only met expectations to a very limited extent. He rejected the ordination of women: *"Clericalizing women"* - i.e. including them in ordained ministries - *"would not solve the problems"*, he expressly declared in 2023. He thus advocates opening up the sacrament of ordination to women only as a solution to problems, which is more indicative of a traditional view of gender roles.

- **Position on compulsory celibacy and education (3)** - Prevost, now Pope Leo XIV, did not publicly comment on a possible relaxation of compulsory celibacy . There are no indications that he would advocate the abolition of compulsory celibacy. His stance to date suggests that he would rather stick to the traditional training of priests, without any known reform impulses. His position in this field therefore remains neutral to conservative.

- **Inclusion of same-sex couples in sacramental marriage (1)** - He must fulfill this criterion even more to life. As a man of the Church faithful to the Magisterium, Prevost, now Pope Leo XIV, tends to adhere to the classical understanding of marriage (between man and woman). As early as 2012, he expressed his *"disappointment"* at the sympathy expressed in the West *for modern lifestyles* and alternative family forms. Consequently, he has not yet supported the opening of sacramental marriage to same-sex couples.

- **Sexual ethics with inclusion of LGBTQIA+ (1)** - Overall, Prevost, now Pope Leo XIV, represents a conventional ecclesiastical sexual morality. A stronger inclusion of LGBTQIA+ people in the Church's teaching is not to be expected from him according to publications to date. His critical statements, possibly made for strategic reasons, still show reservations towards a more liberal sexual ethic. Based on his publications as a bishop, there are no signs that he would positively integrate LGBTQIA+ issues beyond the current doctrine. As head of the church, he will hardly be able to avoid a written contribution on questions of queer theology, queer Christology and the sacramental marriage of queer couples - because these topics have long been part of the regular field of discourse and action of the church's ministry. The first church-related groups have already announced their intention to engage Pope Leo XIV in a concrete dialog and ask him about this.

- **Reform of hierarchical power structures (synodality, participation) (5)** - With regard to power structures within the church, Prevost proves to be a proponent of reform. He expressly supports synodal cooperation and more participation by the laity. Observers describe him as a *"vocal advocate"* of a more inclusive and participatory church structure. He sees decentralization and consultation at all levels as a key to leading the church in a contemporary and unity-promoting way.

- **Responsibility for creation and climate protection (3)** - Prevost, now Pope Leo XIV, has little profile in this area. Although, as a confidant of Pope Francis, he fundamentally supports his concerns (such as the environmental encyclical *Laudato Si'*), he himself has not yet made a particularly prominent appearance as a climate or environmental activist. Neither positively nor negatively conspicuous, can be assumed to be of average fulfillment here; he presumably shares the Church's stance on the preservation of creation without having set his own accents.

5. administration and representation - total score: 4 points

Prevost, now Pope Leo XIV, showed great competence and experience in administrative matters and the representation of the Church, although there is no detailed information about his financial administration.

- **Efficient and transparent administration of ecclesiastical goods (4)** - Prevost, now Pope Leo XIV, has extensive administrative experience. As General of the Augustinian Order (2001-2013), he was responsible for the organization and finances of a world order. As a diocesan bishop, he also had to manage the ecclesiastical assets of an entire diocese. To date, no financial scandals or irregularities have come to light in his area of responsibility. His appointment as head of the bishop's dicastery - an influential position - also speaks for the confidence in his leadership and administrative abilities. Overall, it can be assumed that he manages efficiently and conscientiously; absolute transparency in financial matters cannot be conclusively assessed due to a lack of public reports, but there is no reason to doubt his integrity in this area.

6. academic and canonical qualification - total score: 5 points

Prevost has an excellent academic background and proven expertise in theology and canon law.

- **Theological studies (incl. doctorate/licensure) (5)** - He fully meets this criterion. Prevost, now Pope Leo XIV, completed extensive studies: In addition to a degree in theology, he earned a licentiate and even a doctorate in canon law in Rome. His doctorate from the Pontifical University of St. Thomas Aquinas is proof of his academic qualifications.

- **Knowledge of canon law and administrative matters (5)** - As a doctor of canon law and former judicial vicar, Prevost has excellent knowledge of canon law. He taught canon law at the seminary and was an official (head of the ecclesiastical court) in Peru for almost ten years. This experience shows that he has a deep understanding of the Church's legal system and administrative procedures. His current duties in the Congregation of Bishops also require legal expertise in dealing with ecclesiastical norms. Overall, his expertise in law and administration is outstanding.

7. health and age - total score: 3 points

Prevost, now Pope Leo XIV, is in good mental and physical condition, but is slightly above the ideal age range for a long term in office.

- **Physical/mental condition for long-term exercise of office (4)** - For his age, Prevost, now Pope Leo XIV, makes an active and healthy impression. He himself mentions that he enjoys playing tennis and taking long walks - activities that indicate a solid level of fitness. He is also intellectually fully capable, as evidenced by his demanding current tasks. There are no indications of any serious health restrictions.

- **Age (ideally under 65) (2)** - At 70 (born in 1955), Cardinal Prevost is well above the ideal age limit of 65. Although he would not be the oldest newly elected pope in history, a pontificate beginning at an older age would naturally have a shorter potential term of office. His advanced age could limit the long-term exercise of his office, which is why this criterion is only marginally fulfilled.

8. ecclesiastical needs of dioceses/countries - Overall rating: 4 points

Prevost, now Pope Leo XIV, brings a great deal of global experience and adapts to different regional challenges. He has shown commitment to specific crisis issues such as abuse and secularization, but has also identified potential for improvement.

- **Fitting in with regional, cultural and political challenges (5)** - Thanks to his international biography, Prevost, now Pope Leo XIV, is an excellent fit for a global church role. He comes from the USA, worked in Latin America for 20 years and speaks several languages fluently. This intercultural competence and his *"dialog at eye level with indigenous and local cultures"* in Peru show that he understands the different regional challenges. He enjoys a good reputation in various cultural circles and can credibly represent the church in diverse political contexts.

- **Ability to react to the processing of abuse, church resignations, structural change, etc. (3)** - Prevost, now Pope Leo XIV, is making efforts to process the abuse crisis and deal with church crises, albeit with mixed results. One positive aspect is that, as Bishop Prefect, he is supposed to ensure good bishop appointments worldwide - a lever to indirectly influence the prevention of abuse and reforms. However, there has been criticism in his past: as provincial superior in 2000, he allowed a priest accused of abuse to move near a school. This judgment from today's perspective shows that his sensitivity at the time still lagged behind today's standards. Although the church's attitude has evolved since then, this incident remains a stain. With regard to declining church membership and structural reforms (e.g. parish mergers), there are no known priority initiatives from Prevost, now Pope Leo XIV. He was fundamentally open to change through the synodal method, but did not emerge as a prominent *reformer* in these specific areas. Overall, his ability to respond to these challenges can be classified as average to good - with a learning curve on the subject of abuse and solid, but not exceptional, creative power in the other problem areas.

Summary:
Talent profile & potential carrier Cardinal Prevost / Leo XIV.

Cardinal Robert F. Prevost, now Pope Leo XIV, has a very versatile qualification profile for his work as pope. His strengths lie above all in his theological and spiritual substance, his pastoral experience and in leadership and administration. He embodies the synodal unity in diversity promoted by Pope Francis, has international experience and speaks several languages - all qualities that will help him to bring the universal Church together and address different cultures. He achieves top ratings in these areas. On the other hand, Prevost, now Pope Leo XIV, is reticent on some reform issues. His questioning stance on women's ordination and the sheet yet to be filled for wider inclusion of LGBTQIA+ people in doctrine and sacraments mean he has yet to fulfill expectations of a progressive pope in this regard. His age of 70 is also above the desired age, which somewhat limits the possible term of office, although he appears to be in good health.

Overall, Cardinal Prevost, now Pope Leo XIV, stands out as a competent and faithful candidate with spiritual depth, social commitment and leadership experience. He would maintain the continuity of the synodal orientation and strengthen the perspective of the universal Church. At the same time, he would have to moderate the church in controversial reform issues, whereby he is likely to focus on cautious changes rather than rapid liberalization. This mixed record makes him a pope who fulfills many central criteria excellently, but who so far has recognizably conservative limits in some forward-looking issues.

The average of all eight upper categories of the job description for the office of head of the Church for Cardinal Robert F. Prevost, now Pope

Leo XIV, is 4.21 (rounded to two decimal places). Would you also like to know the average for the late Pope Francis? The same analysis was carried out with Pope Francis, who of course has the advantage of the office bonus and his performance history. The average of all eight top categories for Pope Francis is 4.31 out of 5 points (rounded to two decimal places).

In the top category of *"leadership and teaching"*, there is a clear difference between Pope Francis (4.29) and Cardinal Prevost (3.00), now Pope Leo XIV. This difference is mainly due to their attitude to specific reform issues, while both have much in common when it comes to promoting synodal processes.

There is particular *common ground* in the areas of *synodality* and *unity in diversity*. Both rely on a church of listening, consultation and joint decision-making. Prevost, now Pope Leo XIV, is a staunch advocate of a synodal culture of dialogue and is seen as a close implementer of the synodal dynamic initiated by Francis. In this respect, he is in line with the current Pope.

However, the *differences* become clear when it comes to the socially and internally controversial issues that require further discussion:

- **Ordination of women and gender justice:** While Francis does not allow the sacramental ordination of women, he nevertheless opens up spaces for greater participation of women in leadership functions (e.. Vatican authorities). Prevost, now Pope Leo XIV, on the other hand, has already questioned the debate surrounding the ordination of women and sees the "clericalization of women" as a questionable solution that requires further discussion. Here he clearly lags behind Francis and could learn from his openness for more gender justice - even without violating dogmas.

- **Celibacy and priestly training:** Francis has relativized the duty of celibacy several times, for example in the context of the Amazon Synod, and has signaled a willingness to reform. Prevost, now Pope Leo XIV, on the other hand, has hardly commented on this and does not seem to have made any contribution to the discussion on the need to reform the traditional form of priesthood. Here he could take an example from Francis' differentiated openness to reform.

- **Dealing with LGBTQIA+ and same-sex couples:** Francis has opened the way for blessings of same-sex couples with *Fiducia supplicans* (2023), while Prevost, now Pope Leo XIV, now Pope Leo XIV, was insufficiently detailed and nuanced in earlier statements. Francis is also further along in the development of a more inclusive sexual ethic - albeit cautiously. Prevost, now Pope Leo XIV, could adopt the Pope's pastoral mercy and human-oriented language here without abandoning Church teaching.

- **Responsibility for creation:** With *Laudato Si'* and *Laudate Deum*, Francis has provided strong impetus for ecological rethinking. Prevost, now Pope Leo XIV, says little about the environmental issue and remains inconspicuous. This offers him a broad field of learning, also with regard to the credibility of the Church in social discourse.

It can therefore be said that Cardinal Prevost, now Pope Leo XIV, is strongly oriented towards Francis in structural terms, particularly in strengthening synodal processes. In terms of content, however, he remains more conservative and reserved, especially when it comes to socially controversial issues. He can learn from Pope Francis how to combine pastoral openness with theological steadfastness in sensitive areas - not through sudden upheavals, but through courageous but considered reform steps in the spirit of the Gospel.

If Cardinal Robert Francis Prevost, as Pope **Leo XIV**, wants to take seriously his claim to shape a more reform-oriented, modern church that is more closely aligned with the needs of the faithful than Pope Francis, he would have to set new accents both in terms of content and through concrete actions and decisions that go beyond what has been ventured so far - but without jeopardizing ecclesial unity. This would require a courageous and at the same time spiritually rooted change of course in several key areas.

Figure 8: Royal dialog: LUIS XIV and LEO XIV meet

An ironic comic-style meme image in which the Sun King LUIS XIV tells a grim-faced Pope LEO XIV: "Don't do Leo here - all glitter in the sun, but no change." The image conveys a satirical and critical tone that points to current debates within the church, such as power-grabbing, refusal to reform or religious symbolic politics and the need for reform. The statement is humorous and pointed for many target groups: e.g. reform-oriented believers, young people critical of the church, and female and queer Catholics.

First of all, Leo XIV would have to initiate **consistent gender equality in the Church.** This includes not only the opening of leadership positions to women - a path that Francis has already taken - but also a clear theological initiative to *ordain women* to the diaconate and the convening of a separate world synod of bishops on the topic of women's ordination. He could justify this theologically by invoking the baptismal dignity of all the baptized, the tradition of female leadership in the early church and the urgency of credible gender justice in the 21st century.

In addition, Leo XIV would have to **abolish compulsory celibacy for world priests regionally** - for example in the Amazon region or in Europe - and promote alternative models of priestly life. He could implement this in close coordination with the conferences of bishops and secure it through a synodal consultation of the universal church. At the same time, a reform of priestly training would be necessary that focuses not only on obedience and discipline, but also on relational skills, psychological maturity and team leadership.

Another courageous and possibly necessary signal would be the **full sacramental recognition of same-sex partnerships**, based on a deeper theological sexual ethic that focuses on relational fidelity, care and spiritual maturation rather than mere gender complementarity. In doing so, Leo XIV would not only be responding to the reality of the lives of many believers, but also repositioning the dignity and vocation of queer people within the Church. If the *"inclusive church for all people"* that he proclaimed is to be more than a symbolic model, but is actually *the vision and goal of his pontificate*, then Pope Leo XIV must also consistently fulfill this - in particular through the sacramental marriage ceremony for queer couples. Words alone are not enough. The times demand concrete steps. And so, in the last words of *Margot Friedländer*, who died shortly after his election, we can only call out to him and all those who bear responsibility in the Church: *"Be human."* Every person - including in the Catholic Church - must be treated with dignity and respect and included in all church processes and forms of community in their human rights without restriction and on an equal gender basis. Former German Chancellor *Angela Merkel* categorizes the quote: In doing so, she was bearing witness, Merkel told a major German newspaper. She did this because she was convinced *"that it was and is of paramount importance to convince young people in particular to take a firm stand against exclusion, devaluation, racism, anti-Semitism - and all forms of group-based misanthropy"*. Will the Catholic shepherds also succeed?

In the area of **ecological responsibility**, it should go beyond *Laudato Si'*, for example by issuing concrete ecological standards for church institutions (e.. mandatory climate neutrality by 2040 for all dioceses) and launching a global initiative for interreligious climate justice. Here, he could raise the prophetic voice of the Church even more clearly vis-à-vis business and politics.

In structural terms, Leo XIV would ultimately have to raise the **synodal church to a new constitutional level**: for example, by introducing a *permanent world synod with a deliberative character*, by giving the laity the right to vote in Roman bodies and through binding national synods whose decisions would no longer require exclusive Vatican approval. This would not only strengthen participation, but also readjust the balance of power in the Church.

What would set him apart from Francis would be less the direction than the determination: Leo XIV would have to act with greater clarity, more systematic implementation and less consideration for church political resistance. This would also include a **transparency offensive**, for example through the mandatory annual disclosure of all Vatican finances and independent oversight of abuse in every diocese worldwide.

In his first public address as Pope Leo XIV (Robert Francis Prevost), he emphasized a clear openness and universality, but without mentioning specific groups by name. Right at the beginning, he greeted the world with "Peace be with you all" and emphasized that this greeting of peace should reach "all nations and all people". Echoing Pope Francis, Leo XIV emphasized that God's love is *"unconditionally for all people"*. He literally assured: *"God loves you all. Evil will not win"*. These words implicitly *include all* people - including *queer* people - as no exception is made before God and now also before the Vatican . The universal formulation makes it clear that no one is excluded from receiving divine love.

Furthermore, the new Pope called for a church that focuses on unity, dialog and closeness to all. He repeatedly emphasized that the Church was called upon to *"build bridges"* and seek dialogue. Such a *bridge-building metaphor* suggests that Leo XIV wanted to overcome divides and include *marginalized* groups.

If *everyone* is meant, they are logically all included. In particular, the reference to the fact that God's love excludes no one provides a strong theological indication that LGBTQIA+ people are also beloved children of God in the eyes of the head of the Church. This emphasis on unconditional love can be seen as a continuation of Pope Francis' pastoral line - Francis had famously said *"Who am I to condemn him?"* as a sign of non-judgment of homosexual believers. Leo XIV explicitly picked up on Francis' last blessing and thanked him, which can be understood as a *signal* to *continue the course begun by Francis*. As early as October 2024, Leo XIV spoke out in favor of continuing to discuss the pastoral treatment of same-sex couples in the universal church and taking local needs into account.

In short, in order to be ready and effective in shaping the Church, Leo XIV would not only have to continue to work on the open construction sites of the Francis era, but would also have to continue theologically, structurally and pastorally consistently in the direction of a just, open and spiritually credible Church - without fear of the margins, but with firm confidence in the center of the Gospel.

A church leader who sees himself as a bridge builder today must not simply remain in the middle of the bridge. Rather, they must have the courage to take up clear positions, to consciously decide for one side or the other of the shore, and thus step out of the comfortable zone of the diplomatic center in a creative and effective way. Only then will the church become actively creative instead of passively waiting. It also requires an attitude that allows and welcomes joy, love, hedonism and contemplation.

However, if the church's local offerings only consist - in addition to Sunday or sacramental *business as usual* - of ringing remote-controlled church bells via remote wifi socket and digital app in the hands of the clergy in the event of death or when white smoke rises, then that is simply not enough.

It is not enough to simply send out acoustic signals while the priest is not physically present and the church doors remain closed during the week, supposedly to prevent vandalism.

Then there is no need for such an offer from the church - especially not if it is only to serve as a last straw of hope in the midst of a context of cynical threats that seek to induce a kind of indulgence trade: The time of supposedly well-meaning rhetoric is over - that language which laments the suffering of remarried divorcees, for example, acknowledges them as a marginalized group, names their "suffered outsider:ing" and places their full appreciation as lovers in promising hope - without, however, being followed by concrete consequences. This form of consolation speech, which works with half-hearted glimmers of hope, conditional concessions or partial sham solutions instead of creating real equality, is not only socially outdated. It also contradicts the initial vision of the incumbent head of the church. What is needed now are clear, theologically responsible and effective decisions that give real expression to inclusion.

Does church in such a form degenerate and reduce itself to an empty gesture, comparable to the short-lived nature of a weather forecast, and lose its actual message and meaning?

If the church increasingly withdraws to purely vague diplomacy in this way, its social significance will wither away to insignificance.

Then even public events such as Christopher Street Day in Cologne, which have a media presence, are open, true-to-life and healing for many people, strengthening them in their self-worth like a marriage ceremony, are far more attractive, relevant, effective and hopeful than a remote, anonymous ringing of bells.

The church must therefore not only be symbolic and centered on the bridge, but also visible and close to the needs of the people on the left *and* right bank in order to justify its existence and remain credible as a real bridge builder in terms of expectations and needs. If only the bridge divides, but people already live together integrated in reality and society, then perhaps we no longer need bridges or bridge builders?

It is not the other's right to exist and their inclusion in the community that is at issue - in the light of human rights and the principles of equality, human dignity and equality have long been sacrosanct - but the attitude of those who continually deny this legitimacy of belonging and act through exclusion rather than inclusion must be called into question.

In the church, the existence or affiliation of others - such as women, queer people, remarried divorcees or couples from different denominations - must no longer be questioned. Because according to the standards of human rights, baptism and Christian equality in the face of God, their inclusion in the church community is not only legitimate, but urgently required. Those who divide instead of reconcile contradict the Gospel and this is not to be expected from the highest leadership.

Method, contents and structure of this fourth volume of Deus Ex Machina

The following articles in this book are divided into three sections and a fourth part.

In the first part of this book *"The Basics of Sermons"* on Happiness & being happy and other religious policy field analyses, the focus is placed on those topics that are not only theologically relevant, but also of central importance for the individual attitude to life of believers. **From a micro-perspective** - i.e. from the point of view of the inner psychological effect of religious messages on the individual - the extent to which church preaching today can contribute to either creating liberation and orientation or reinforcing exclusion and emotional injury is analyzed. The way in which the church speaks has a profound effect on the self-perception, the experience of happiness and the sense of belonging of many believers - especially where previously marginalized groups such as queer people, remarried divorcees or single parents were too often not considered.

A key example of this change in perspective is the **school subject "Happiness"**, which has received increasing attention since its introduction. It stands for a new pedagogical culture that is no longer solely focused on performance and sacrifice, but rather on joie de vivre, self-efficacy and resilience. A comparison with religious education reveals exciting interfaces and differences: While the subject of "Happiness" pursues the goal of "Happiness" in a psychologically sound and realistic way, the church faces the challenge of making its message more tangible as a **"message of joy"** - beyond moralizing and fear-inducing preaching.

Four socially highly relevant topics are then examined from a church perspective and discussed from a theological and practical perspective. The first **religious policy field analysis** deals with the urgently needed **reform of Catholic sexual morality**. It not only questions the outdated view of humanity, which often associates sexuality with guilt and sin, but also reflects on what a contemporary, humane sexual ethic could look like - informed by the findings of the human sciences and in the spirit of biblically based human dignity.

A second focus is on the **equality of all marriages before the altar**, with a particular focus on queer-sensitive pastoral care. This is about the church's recognition and blessing of same-sex partnerships - a topic that is being discussed worldwide and has prominent supporters in theology and pastoral care. The analysis shows how much an inclusive attitude is not only just, but also pastorally necessary if the church wants to live up to its claim of being a home for all.

In a third section, the ethically complex topic of **life protection and abortion** is addressed from a Catholic perspective. This is not about polarization, but about differentiation: How can the Church protect unborn life without ignoring the realities of life and the decision-making needs of the women concerned? Here too, the following applies: only a pastoral approach that focuses on dignity, listening and support can be credible.

In conclusion, it becomes clear that all the topics dealt with should not be viewed in isolation, but are closely linked to the question of how the Church positions itself in modern societies - whether it is prepared to act from the center of the Gospel and recognize the signs of the times. The first part of the book is therefore not intended as dogmatic instruction, but as an invitation to open, constructive and contemporary debate. It shows that the church can become a source of happiness and inner freedom - if it is prepared to listen, to change and to open up the gospel anew as a living force of human kindness.

The second part of the book looks inwards - at the structures, power relations and reform blockades of the church itself. **From a meso-perspective**, i.e. in the sense of a systemic self-reflection (*"The ego in the group" or "The system of the church with its dogmas as part of the (own community and) society"*), those topics are illuminated in which the Catholic Church must fundamentally reform itself in order not to further gamble away its credibility. It is a matter of "navel-gazing" - not as self-indulgence, but as an honest assessment of its position and a necessary movement towards renewal.

The **reform of Catholic sexual morality** is once again of central importance, this time with a focus on debates within the Church and normative clarifications. Leading reform-oriented theologians and bishops are developing their vision of ethics based on responsibility, relationship and self-determination - and which does not differentiate between heterosexual and same-sex partnerships. The German Synodal Path acts as an exemplary reform forum in this context at : Here, concrete proposals have already been formulated and initial resolutions adopted as minimum demands - a signal that movement is possible.

In addition, six further central reform topics are developed as **religious policy field analyses:**

The fifth analysis is dedicated to the **question of women's ordination**. It not only discusses the theological arguments for opening up ordained ministries to women, but also highlights the socio-cultural urgency of such a step. The majority of delegates in the Synodal Path have already spoken out in favor of an opening - a historic momentum that must be followed by concrete action.

Another focus is on the **sacramental equal treatment of same-sex couples**, which is again emphasized in the sixth analysis. The demand: equality not only in tone, but in church practice - specifically through a church wedding.

The seventh analysis focuses on the **church's symbolic policy, which** is often perceived as an empty gesture. It shows that without a **transparent culture of expectation** and credible structural changes, even euphonious symbols lose their impact. What is needed here is a new form of clarity and commitment in the church's official actions.

The eighth analysis asks how the church can **overcome** its **institutional inertia**. It brings the concept of *participatory palaver* into play - a paradigm that promotes more democratic, dialog-oriented leadership structures in the church. Especially in times of increasing credibility crisis, a new culture of co-responsibility, synodality and sincere listening is needed.

The ninth analysis is dedicated to the most pressing scandal of the present day: **dealing with sexualized violence** in the church. It not only identifies failures, but also calls for clear reform steps - institutional, legal, spiritual and pastoral. The reappraisal must no longer remain fragmentary or strategically limited, but must become an expression of a genuine assumption of responsibility.

The second part is rounded off by the tenth analysis on **financial transparency**. The question "Where is the money in the bell jar?" exemplifies the mistrust of many creditors towards the economic self-administration of church institutions. What is needed here is openness, accountability and a new ethical culture in dealing with entrusted funds.

Overall, this second part makes it clear that the church can only have a credible external impact and provide comfort and guidance if it is also prepared to reform itself internally. The preaching of happiness and hope becomes powerful when it is coupled with the courage to make structural changes. Only then will the church itself become a space in which faith, justice and community can unfold in a true-to-life way.

In the third part of the book, the view widens - towards the global challenges, socio-political areas of tension and ecological issues on which the church can and must take a stand as a moral authority, spiritual voice and social actor. This **macro-perspective** (*"Analyses of actors of comprehensive processes and large groups"*) is not only an ethical commentary on world events, but also an invitation to prophetic participation - be it in questions of peace, justice, climate protection or interreligious dialog.

It begins with an analysis of **ecumenism in the Catholic Church**. This is not just about structural rapprochement, but also about the question of what lived unity in diversity can mean today - at a time when religious cooperation contributes significantly to social cohesion.

Another section is dedicated to the **responsibility of the church in dealing with right-wing populism**, especially with parties such as the AfD. Christian faith is incompatible with group-based misanthropy - which is why clear theological and social boundaries are needed.

This is followed by **peace ethics and arms policy**, which seeks ethically viable positions between naïve pacifism and military realpolitik. The church is described here as an actor that develops differentiated standards for non-violence and responsibility.

The focus is on the analysis of **climate change**. Since *Laudato si'* at the latest, responsibility for creation has been seen as a spiritual and social duty. Sustainability is not understood in technical terms, but as an expression of lived faith - with consequences for lifestyle, structure and global justice.

The next analysis deals with **economic justice**. Catholic social teaching offers a well-founded critique of the neoliberal system, which places profits above human dignity. Here, the Church becomes visible as a prophetic voice for fair wages, labor rights and global solidarity.

Care for the elderly is a particularly concrete field. Under the title *"Don't abandon our elderly"*, the church is called upon to act not only as a sponsor, but also as a moral authority: for humane care and a culture of respect for the elderly.

The section is rounded off with an analysis of the **130 kmh / 80 mph speed limit**. What sounds banal is seen here as a touchstone of church credibility in the environmental sector. After all, anyone who wants to protect creation must also take responsibility in everyday life.

This third part shows: The Church does not stand outside the world. Its message will only remain powerful if it faces up to the pressing issues of our time - with clarity, humility and determination. Whether it is about the climate, war, justice or human dignity - the church is called upon everywhere to take a stand, act in solidarity and create hope. The preaching of the Gospel is most effective where it wrestles with reality and makes the kingdom of God credibly visible in the here and now.

The fourth and final part of the book focuses on the **internal structures of the church** - on what happens "below the surface" and is often not immediately visible, but is nevertheless crucial to whether reforms take effect, people feel accepted and the church retains its credibility. It is about **structural power issues**, training, leadership culture, generational conflicts and the institutional climate - insights topics that are rarely preached, but have central religious relevance for the whispered Sermons and the Basics of Happiness internally, also and especially for the faithful. These structures are also "religious policy fields" - because they shape how theology is thought about, how power is distributed and how closeness to people is enabled or prevented - and how lay people must get involved here with clear, non-filter-bubble-driven common sense and the will to shape things better.

The 18th policy field analysis sheds light on the increasing **generational conflict in the church**. While many younger Catholics and younger clergy advocate equality, diversity, synodal participation and spiritual openness, older bishops often cling to authoritarian structures and traditional views. The tension between a desire for renewal at grassroots level and structural inertia at leadership level is not presented here as a mere conflict of age, but as an expression of a deeper, spiritual-cultural divide within the Church.

The next analysis provides a particularly sensitive insight into **indoctrination in Catholic seminaries for priests**. Here, content, learned thought patterns, disciplinary techniques and the handling of criticism are examined. At the same time, possibilities for building resilience and preventative reform proposals are presented. After all, those who train future pastors are responsible for ensuring that they grow into their task in a mature, dialogical and humane manner - or whether they are shaped by dependency, isolation and fear.

A further analysis is devoted to the paralyzing dynamics of **centralism and fear**, as cemented in particular by Vatican control and ecclesiastical labour law. Many impulses for reform fail not because of theological arguments, but because of an institutional climate of insecurity in which deviation from the line is sanctioned by disciplinary or career sanctions. This shows that the structural power apparatus can block spiritual development as well as suppress personal vocations.

The 21st Religious Policy Field Analysis broadens the view to a structural **outlook on the need for reform in the church's leadership culture**. It deals with questions of power distribution, dogmatism and participation. Central to this is the realization that a faith community can only be experienced as a community if co-responsibility is truly shared and trust is not replaced by control. Rethinking power - both theologically and practically - is recognized as a condition for genuine renewal.

The final study focuses on a phenomenon that has long been known behind closed doors in many dioceses: the **isolation of many clergy and bishops**. Between the pressure of expectations, loyalty dilemmas and inner loneliness, there is often a lack of sustainable spiritual networks and open feedback structures. Many leaders are in danger of becoming operationally blind or alienated from the reality of the lives of the faithful. However, it is precisely the insight into one's own limitations that can become the starting point for a new understanding of leadership - characterized by team spirit, vulnerability and spiritual maturity.

This part - and the entire book - concludes with a **final sermon on the subject of "Happiness and being happy"**. It takes up the theological lines of the volume once again and presents them in a liturgically reflective form. The focus is on the question of how happiness can be understood from a Christian perspective beyond the promise of consumerism and self-optimization: as a sustained joy of life, as spiritual connectedness, as an experience of grace in the midst of everyday life. It is a sermon that aims to encourage - to renewal, to humanity, to hope.

This book *"I will be a female Bishop! - The Basics of Sermons on Happiness and further analyses of religious policy issues (DEUS EX MACHINA - Part IV)"* deals with highly topical and differently discussed issues in religious and theological debates. It is part of the "DEUS EX MACHINA" book series, which deals intensively with the influences of artificial intelligence (AI) on society, culture, education and religion in particular.

The topics and analyses have been created and written entirely by artificial intelligence. An *artwork of algorithms*. How can the reception of an artificial-artistic intelligence with free reasoning, independent research, synaptic-complex referencing and an in-depth dialog offer be used in such a way that a space for open discussion and encounter is created - a learning and a dialog to which clergymembers, scientific students and all responsible citizens should be specifically empowered and educated? Individual cartoons, memes and illustrations were also suggested and produced by *Deus Ex Machina*, as noted in the list of illustrations.

Habemus Pontificem Politicam

"We have a political bridge builder" - *Habemus Pontificem Politicam* - is given when every believer not only has an opinion on religious policy areas, but also shares it in dialog with others, as if he/she wanted to become a bishop. This characterizes maturity in faith and in the Church.

This book aims not only to provide information, but above all to stimulate reflection and discussion, offer guidance and encourage people to implement change effectively - instead of merely holding out the prospect of change or keeping questions "open", which usually means hoping for a new generation of decision-makers.

This volume is aimed at anyone interested in a credible, realistic and inclusive church - theologians, church employees, education experts and socially engaged people alike. After all the analyses of the AI on the CC, an open, honest dialog and courageous steps are needed to reposition the Catholic Church as a credible proclaimer of a joyful, philanthropic and solidary message.

Wishing you much enjoyment, reflection and insight when reading about this topic

Eureka Circe, on May 10, 2025.

And now to the individual topic areas and religious policy field analyses, which were comprehensively written and written *by artificial intelligence* using deep research and extended reasoning (as well as supporting this introduction with its analyses).

📌 Religious policy field analysis 1: What do we and students learn in the subject "Happiness"?

School should not only impart specialist knowledge, but also life skills.

Recently, the unusual *"school subject of happiness"* has been attracting attention - a subject in which pupils learn to go through life happier and more content. This subject, developed and implemented in 2007 by teacher Ernst Fritz-Schubert, uses exercises and projects to teach skills such as joie de vivre, resilience and self-confidence.

As the initiator, he wanted to counter the purely performance-oriented teaching with something that would give the pupils back *the joy of learning* and make them *happier people*.

At the same time, there is still the subject of ethics and Catholic religious education, which is traditionally anchored in schools and also deals with questions of meaning, values and transcendence. In view of similar objectives, the question arises: *Does the school subject of happiness compete with religious education?* In the following, similarities and differences are examined, mutual learning opportunities are highlighted and consideration is given to what changes the Catholic Church needs in order to convey the "Good News" - the central message of salvation in Christianity - as a truly joyful and credible message rather than a threatening message.

In contrast to everyday language, *happiness* in this subject is not about chance or fleeting moments of happiness, but about *long-term well-being* and life satisfaction. In short: a happy, successful life becomes the educational goal here.

Background and aims of happiness as a school subject

The subject of happiness focuses on the *personal development of learners*. The students deal with questions such as *"Who am I? What can I do? How do I relate to which sexual orientation? What do I need for a fulfilled life?"*. By providing space to explore such questions, the subject contributes to *salutogenesis*, i.e. the development of health and well-being. The aim is to turn adolescents into resilient, self-determined personalities who are aware of their strengths and develop confidence in their own *creative power*. Or in Fritz Schubert's words: "A happy person is an effective designer of their life." Happiness as a school subject therefore promotes *independent and autonomous action* as well as a healthy sense of self-worth. It shows students *what* actually constitutes well-being, *how* it arises and *how* it can be actively promoted - within themselves and in their interactions with others. This focus on positive psychology and related approaches (such as Viktor Frankl's *logotherapy* or *resilience research*) is scientifically sound: Happiness can be *learned*.

Logotherapy according to Viktor Frankl is a psychotherapeutic method that focuses on the search for meaning and significance in human life. Developed by Viktor Frankl, it is based on the assumption that a person's deepest need is to give meaning to their life, even under difficult circumstances. Logotherapy promotes the ability to make independent decisions and to give positive meaning to even painful situations by recognizing meaning. It focuses on value orientation, self-distancing and a positive attitude to life in order to better cope with crises and achieve inner stability. In *logotherapy*, Viktor Frankl distinguishes between three central value categories that can lend meaning to life:

- **Creative values (creative values):** Meaning is found through productive and creative action, for example through work, art or commitment to a cause.

- **Experiential values:** Meaning arises from direct experiences, e.g. through love, beauty or encounters with other people and nature.

- **Attitude values:** Even in situations that cannot be changed by action or experience, it is still possible to adopt an attitude or mindset, e.g. to maintain dignity and confidence in crises or suffering.

These three categories form the basis for how people can give their lives individual meaning according to Frankl's understanding.

Figure 9: Three central value categories that can give meaning to life in logotherapy according to Viktor Frankl.

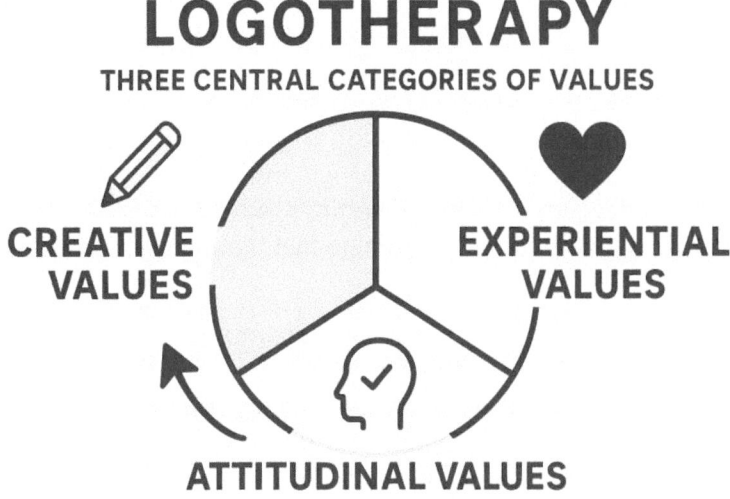

A clear, minimalist and aesthetic infographic on the topic of logotherapy and its three central value categories according to Viktor Frankl. Visualize the following three categories divided evenly in a circle: Creative values (symbolized by a writing tool, paintbrush or creative symbol), Experiential values (symbolized by a heart or similar emotional symbol), Attitudinal values (symbolized by a stylized head profile with a check mark as a symbol for positive attitude). The heading "Logotherapy - Three central value categories" is positioned clearly above the diagram so that the focus is on the balance between the three value areas.

And: *resilience research* is concerned with why and how people successfully cope with crises, stress or traumatic experiences and remain mentally healthy or recover quickly. Key findings show that resilience ("psychological resistance") is promoted by various factors, such as stable social relationships, self-efficacy, optimism and the ability to recognize meaning in difficult situations. The aim of resilience research is to gain insights into how people can develop and promote this inner strength in order to better cope with stress.

Resilience training therefore teaches you to evaluate challenges positively, use your own strengths and find meaning in difficult situations - this promotes lasting happiness and life satisfaction.

Contents and methods: How is happiness taught?

Happiness lessons are practical and varied. You won't find traditional frontal teaching here - instead, the focus is on *experiences* and *adventures*. Pupils learn *by doing* and *reflecting*. For example, there are *experiential educational exercises* and games in which the class grows together as a team and builds trust. In a safe environment, everyone learns to talk openly about *their feelings* and to listen to each other. These emotional-social learning settings strengthen the sense of community and allow each individual to feel that they *are accepted for who they are.*

Personal goals and projects are another important part of finding meaning in life - and thus possibly also preventing depression. The young people set themselves achievable goals - sometimes in groups, sometimes individually - and work towards them step by step. These can be sporting challenges, creative projects or improvements in everyday life (e.. learning more regularly, practising an instrument). They receive support from teachers and classmates, who tend to take on the role of *coaches* and companions. By *reflecting* on their progress (e.. in conversations or a happiness diary), learners gradually develop strategies for dealing with obstacles and overcoming setbacks. This process encourages *perseverance* and shows in concrete terms how effort leads to a sense of achievement - a core idea of self-efficacy.

The subject of happiness uses a variety of *methods* to appeal to different senses and interests. We often work with *movement and physical experience:* Joint sports and playful *movement exercises* through to dance exercises or steps are an integral part. The pupils try out climbing or confidence exercises, for , to test their own limits, or they learn to listen to themselves in relaxation exercises. *Health* is also a priority - the young people learn interesting facts about nutrition and how sport and relaxation can influence their mood.

Figure 10: On the way to healthy self-confidence with six elements for reflection.

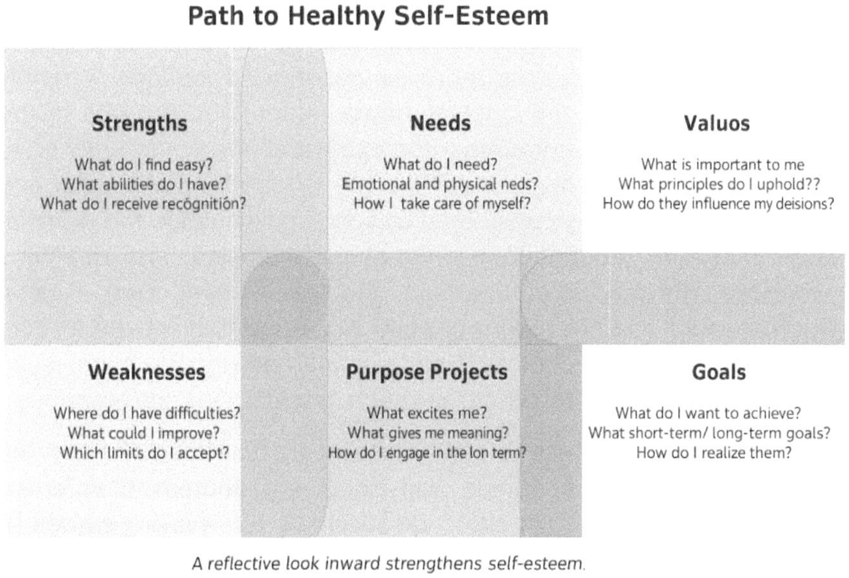

Path to Healthy Self-Esteem

Strengths	Needs	Valuos
What do I find easy?	What do I need?	What is important to me
What abilities do I have?	Emotional and physical neds?	What principles do I uphold??
What do I receive recógnitión?	How I take care of myself?	How do they influence my deisions?

Weaknesses	Purpose Projects	Goals
Where do I have difficulties?	What excites me?	What do I want to achieve?
What could I improve?	What gives me meaning?	What short-term/ long-term goals?
Which limits do I accept?	How do I engage in the lon term?	How do I realize them?

A reflective look inward strengthens self-esteem.

A clear, color-coded infographic on the topic 'Path to healthy self-confidence'. Divided into six core areas that interact and overlap with each other: Strengths (blue): What do I succeed at easily? What skills do I have? What do I receive recognition for? Weaknesses (orange): Where do I have difficulties? What could I improve? What limits do I accept? Needs (green): What do I need? Emotional and physical needs? How do I provide for them? Meaning projects (pink): What excites me? What gives me meaning? How do I make a long-term commitment? Values (yellow): What is important to me? What principles do I stand for? How do they influence decisions? Goals (red): What do I want to achieve? What short-term/long-term goals? How do I realize them? - With clear visualization of how these areas overlap and influence each other, so that in the end the goal of a strengthened, reflective and mindful self-confidence becomes clear.

Creative and cultural activities are also used. *Artistic elements* play a role in many happiness projects - such as theater improvisation, painting or designing collages. At the Willy Hellpach School, for example, pupils practiced theater with a professional actor for over a year to strengthen their expressive skills. In another unit, young people selected personal *picture cards* and then tried to find out from each other why this motif might suit their classmates. Such exercises train empathy: you put yourself in someone else's shoes and at the same time get new impressions about yourself from the outside. They also *talk about philosophy* (*What does happiness mean? What is a good life?*) and even visit museums or exhibitions - this broadens their horizons and stimulates their senses. Motivational trainers taught the Heidelberg students *positive thinking* techniques to break negative thought cycles and *become more aware of good feelings*. A family therapist worked with the class to better understand the role of the individual within the community - the *ego within the community* so to speak. This so-called *meso-level*, i.e. the level of social groups and interactions, is typically considered by social psychology. The external expert therefore brought in additional psychological and coaching knowledge. (By way of comparison, the *macro level* - large social structures such as trade unions or political parties - tends to be studied by sociology, while psychology is more concerned with the *micro level*, i.e. internal psychological processes such as cognitions and emotions).

The subject of happiness is characterized by its *varied design*. The young people's bodies, minds and souls are addressed in equal measure. Whether through sport, discussions, role-playing games or quiet introspection - the pupils *gain a wide range of experiences* that all contribute to the central theme of well-being. It is important that what they learn is always linked to *everyday life*: The young people think together about how they can apply insights from the lessons in their lives - whether it's approaching exams more calmly, resolving conflicts more peacefully or simply feeling more gratitude for positive experiences. This turns theory into practice.

Competencies and learning fields: What skills do the students take with them?

In the school subject of happiness, young people acquire a range of *key skills that* are important for their lives. First of all, *self-competencies* grow: Pupils get to know themselves better - their *strengths and weaknesses*, their needs, meaning projects, values and goals. This reflective look inwards at these six elements is an important step towards healthy *self-confidence*. Studies show that after just one year of happiness lessons, many young people can more clearly identify *what they want and what they don't want* - they question themselves more consciously.

This *ability to reflect* helps them to make more informed decisions. *Self-esteem* can also be strengthened: Pupils experience themselves as accepted in the group and as competent to tackle problems. Experiences of success - such as a mastered project or overcoming a fear while climbing - help to build a *positive self-image*. At the same time, they learn not to see failures as failures, but as part of the learning process. This promotes *resilience*, i.e. the ability to bounce back after setbacks.

Self-efficacy is a key learning area. The young people experience first-hand that they can make a difference through their actions - be it in the personal sphere (e.. improving their own fitness) or in their social environment. *Control over their own situation* becomes more tangible: participants in the happiness subject stated more frequently that they had *"their situation under control"* and were better able to control themselves. This feeling of being able to control one's own life contributes significantly to mental health. It is closely linked to the concept of *salutogenesis*: When young people experience their existence as understandable, manageable and meaningful, they feel "at home in the world" and are happier.

The concept of salutogenesis (developed by Aaron Antonovsky) describes how health develops and is maintained. In contrast to pathogenesis, which examines the causes of illness, salutogenesis focuses on factors that help people to stay healthy or recover quickly despite stress and strain.

The central element of salutogenesis is the *sense of coherence*, which consists of three components:

1. **Understandability:** Ability to perceive situations and life events as structured and comprehensible.

2. **Manageability:** Conviction that resources are available to successfully overcome challenges.

3. **Meaningfulness:** Feeling that it is valuable to commit to something and that challenges are meaningful.

The stronger the sense of coherence, the better people can stay healthy and cope with crises.

This is exactly where the school subject comes in - it provides *orientation* and *meaning*. Young people develop an idea of what a fulfilled life means to them personally and explore ways to achieve it. This often results in an increased sense of *purpose* in their own actions.

In addition to strengthening the individual, *social skills are* also intensively promoted. The numerous group activities - from trust games to joint projects - train *teamwork skills*. The students practise communicating with each other, showing consideration for one another and resolving conflicts constructively. They develop *empathy* in role plays and discussions: they learn to adopt different perspectives and show understanding for their fellow human beings. Last but not least, the subject also deals directly with topics such as *appreciation*, *respect* and *helpfulness* (for example in bullying prevention or encounters with people with disabilities). This often results in an improved *classroom climate* - students experience community as something supportive and positive. This can lead to a more mindful and respectful approach in everyday school life.

It is also worth mentioning the *practical life skills* that are acquired in the subject of happiness. Time management, learning strategies or financial literacy may sound banal, but they are fundamental skills for an independent life. By addressing and practising such things in class, young people feel better prepared for challenges outside of school. example, they learn how to set realistic goals, how to deal with stress at exam time or why a healthy lifestyle (exercise, diet, sleep) improves their performance. These *everyday skills* help students look to their future with more confidence and see themselves as *competent designers of* their lives.

Effects and experiences: Contribution to well-being and school climate

Experience to date with happiness as a school subject has been encouraging. *Accompanying scientific studies* attest to the subject's positive effects on the development of young people. For example, it has been observed that after some time in happiness lessons, pupils think about themselves in a much more reflective way and know more precisely *what is good for them or not*. They also more frequently experience the feeling that they are *actively in control of* their lives instead of feeling at the mercy of others. These increases in self-reflection and self-efficacy show that the subject is achieving its central class objective - namely to empower young people to *effectively shape their own happiness*. The lesson content also has an impact on general well-being: Many pupils report that they experience *less stress* and more enjoyment at school as a result of relaxation exercises, open discussions and positive experiences in the group. One study found that the subject can actually stabilize *mental health*, even if a single school year naturally does not compensate for all the stresses and strains of the remaining school years.

Teachers and parents also notice changes. *Motivation and willingness to learn* often improve when young people enjoy going to school and see a purpose in what they do there. Happiness as a subject demonstrates that school can be *fun* - this experience can have a generally positive effect on students' attitude towards learning. Many young people apply what they have learned in happiness lessons to their everyday lives: for , they use certain *relaxation techniques* before exams or use the communication rules they have learned to resolve conflicts with friends more peacefully. This shows that the skills taught are actually relevant to everyday life.

The impact on the school culture as a whole is also interesting. The subject of happiness helps to establish an atmosphere of *appreciation*. Instead of the usual focus on mistakes - in everyday school life, the main criticism is often directed at what is not correct - happiness promotes a *culture of motivation*: the strengths of the students should be emphasized and small advances are recognized. This positive attitude can gradually be transferred to other subjects and teachers. When teachers see how productively students learn in an anxiety-free, encouraging environment, this may also influence their own teaching style. According to the Fritz Schubert Institute's experience, happy students argue *less*, are *more creative* and *learn more easily* - qualities that every school strives for. The subject of happiness therefore contributes to a healthier, *more supportive school climate* in which students and teachers feel more comfortable.

After more than 15 years of practice, it has become clear that happiness as a school subject is *not an exotic gimmick*, but a useful addition to the educational canon. Over 100 schools in Germany, Austria and Switzerland have already introduced the concept, often with an enthusiastic response from the pupils. The subject of happiness teaches young people something for life: *Life skills, self-confidence* and the realization that their own happiness is largely in their own hands. This subject contributes to holistic education - it helps young people to better understand themselves and life, to face challenges with confidence and to experience the community as a source of support and joy. In this way, happiness as a school subject not only promotes individual satisfaction, but also forms the basis for a successful life in our society. What can believing students - and all people and believers in general - learn from this and how can the teachings of the Catholic Church benefit from it?

Happiness as a school subject and topic in religious education: competition or complement? - Meaning and purpose of "Happiness" and religion, e.g. at school

First of all, it is worth taking a look at what both subjects aim to achieve: happiness and religion. The aim of happiness as a school subject is to help pupils, us humans, to lead a successful life. According to Fritz-Schubert, young people should develop *confidence in life, self-assurance, self-responsibility and social responsibility*. In this subject, they practise very practically how to overcome challenges and increase their own well-being - for example through mindfulness exercises, creative projects, exercise, reflecting on happy moments or keeping a "happiness diary". Happiness lessons work with *experiential and action-oriented learning* that incorporates emotions and body awareness. Studies suggest that more feelings of happiness go hand in hand with better health, a stronger immune system and even more creativity. Happiness teachers want to harness this effect by *teaching specific trainable skills* such as optimism or positive self-perception . The hope behind this: Happiness and contentment can be learned - at least to a certain extent.

This contrasts with religious education, which - especially at denominational schools or in state religious education - traditionally also asks about the *good life*, but from an explicitly religious perspective. In Catholic (and Protestant) religion lessons, pupils deal with biblical stories, church traditions, ethical questions and - as in the subject of ethics - the search for the *meaning of life*.

Here, too, it is ultimately about life interpretation and values, about questions such as: *What sustains me in life? What can I hope for? What is my responsibility towards my fellow human beings and creation?* These subjects therefore address the world in which young people live and aim to strengthen them. There is therefore a case for viewing them as *complementary* rather than competitive. In fact, even the Bavarian Ministry of Education emphasizes that "Happiness" is not viewed critically as a school subject, as the diverse skills and attitudes to life it teaches are in line with the holistic educational mission. According to the constitution, schools should not only educate knowledge, but also heart, hand, mind and character - a claim that religious education, ethics lessons and happiness lessons all pursue.

However, there are also voices that see a competitive relationship or at least ask critical questions. Simone Hiller, a religious education teacher at the University of Tübingen, for example, warns against making happiness an independent school subject. In her opinion, topics such as happiness, the art of living and finding meaning are already covered in *religion and ethics lessons* - and in a well-founded way. Hiller fears that an extra subject "happiness" could give the impression that happiness is something that can be *acquired by prescription*. Although schools should encourage people to think about happiness, "happiness" as a separate subject also harbors dangers. On the one hand, there is a lack of a curriculum legitimized by the Conference of Ministers of Education and Cultural Affairs and a lack of uniform teacher training for happiness teachers. As a result, it is unclear what content is being taught - Hiller asks critically: "Is it about yoga? About Zen? Healthy eating? Experiential education? Or a bit of everything?". In extreme cases, this *lack of transparency* could even open the door to questionable world views or esoteric trends. On the other hand - and this weighs more heavily in this argument - a school subject suggests that happiness *is feasible and compulsory*. Young people could feel the pressure to always be in a good mood. "What if I'm not happy one day? Have I failed then?" some people ask. At a time when Instagram and TikTok are mostly used to celebrate radiant, seemingly perfect people, there is already a social trend towards *"optimization mania"* when it comes to happiness. Critics fear that happiness as a school subject reinforces the imperative *"You have to be happy!"* instead of leaving room for unhappiness, doubt and sadness.

In fact, the initiators of the happiness lessons seem to have this aspect in mind: No one promises eternal bliss at the touch of a button. Fritz-Schubert himself emphasizes that his lessons *cannot promise happiness* - too much depends on personality, childhood and external circumstances. But he offers the justified hope that *targeted exercises can shape one's attitude to life in such a way that one becomes more "receptive to happiness"* - in other words, more capable of perceiving and allowing happiness in the first place. In this respect, it is not clear that "happiness" and religion are mutually exclusive. Rather, we can ask whether both approaches can benefit from each other. While happiness lessons provide *practical methods* on how to increase one's well-being (e.g. grateful reflection on positive things, stress management through breathing exercises, physical activities for more self-esteem), religious education offers a *framework to be interpreted* that places happiness and suffering in a larger context. The ideal is therefore not one against the other, but one *with the other*: both subjects and their content serve important needs of young people - that of a successful, happy life here and now and that of a deeper meaning and support that also carries them through difficult times.

Similarities and differences

Despite their different origins and methodologies, the school subject of happiness and religious education have remarkable *similarities* . Both focus on the *whole person*: mind, emotions, action orientation, body, values and social interaction. Ultimately, both ask: *What do young people need in order to lead a good life?* Happiness lessons, for example, focus on topics such as *emotional well-being, social relationships, responsibility, training the ability to act, enjoying one's own actions and finding meaning.* Interestingly, the concept of happiness is based on a *positive view of humanity*: Fritz-Schubert assumes that all students have basic needs for connection, appreciation, security and meaning. This humanistic view of man - influenced by Maslow's pyramid of needs and Viktor Frankl's theory of meaning - emphasizes *the dignity of man* and his potential for growth.

Figure 11: Maslow's pyramid of needs

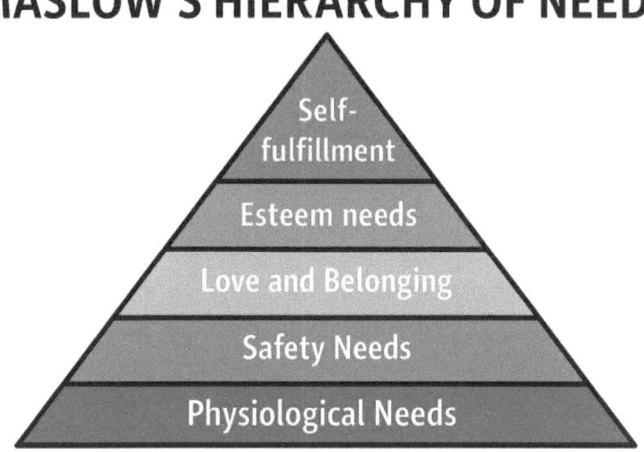

The diagram shows Maslow's pyramid of needs, a psychological model for describing human needs. It is divided into five levels: 1. physiological needs (basic needs such as food, drink, sleep), 2. security needs (protection, financial security, stability), 3. social needs (belonging, friendship, love), 4. individual needs (recognition, esteem, success), 5. self-fulfilling (developing potential, personal growth, finding meaning). The model states that people only strive for higher needs once basic needs have been met.

Christian anthropology, as taught in religious education, also has such a positive foundation: human beings are made in the image of God and endowed with inalienable *human dignity*. They are created to live in love and freedom. Although the Church also speaks of sin and limitations, since the Second Vatican Council it has been strongly emphasized that human beings - all human beings - are unconditionally loved by God and called to *the fullness of life*. In this respect, both disciplines share a hopeful view of human beings and the possibility of a fulfilled life - a kind of *"positive anthropology"* that does not focus on deficits, but on resources, strengths and opportunities for development.

Nevertheless, happiness as a subject and religious education differ in terms of *content, methods and interpretation of the world*. The *degree of openness* is a key difference: religious education has a clearly defined ideological standpoint - it teaches from a Catholic (or Protestant) perspective, based on the Bible and church teachings. Even if other world views are considered comparatively in modern religious education, the Christian faith remains a central frame of reference. Happiness lessons, on the other hand, are ideologically neutral and *non-denominational*. This can be both an opportunity and a challenge: on the one hand, all pupils can participate regardless of their religion, but on the other hand, it remains unclear *what meaning* is ultimately being conveyed. Some people criticize precisely this lack of clarity and ask whether there is an implicit ideology behind some happiness lessons. However, in the practice of happiness teachers, it is probably not so much a specific ideology but rather *psychology* that forms the background - especially findings from *positive psychology* (e.g. on gratitude, optimism, flow experience) and *pedagogy*. For example, methods from mindfulness practice (meditation, yoga) or experiential education are used in happiness lessons without interpreting this in religious terms. Religious education, on the other hand, has its own *"exercises"* - such as praying, meditative silence, creating rituals, singing together or talking about guilt and forgiveness - but these are always related to God and faith. Where happiness lessons may speak of "inner peace", religious education speaks of *prayer*; where the latter says "gratitude exercise", ...religious education speaks of *prayer of thanks and praise* before God. This difference in the *level of reference* is central: happiness lessons are aimed at individual well-being in the here and now, while religious education locates happiness and suffering in a *transcendental framework to be interpreted*, in which reference to God and the hope of the hereafter play a role.

Jesus' words about "life to the full" (John 10:10), for example, point to the fact that *perfect* happiness is ultimately to be found in another dimension - namely in our relationship with God. Happiness lessons hardly address this dimension, but remain pragmatically focused on the here and now. Religious education, on the other hand, introduces the Christian faith as a possible *horizon of meaning* that also accepts the contradictions of life. What is important here is that faith does not promise a superficially harmonious happy ending. Christians believe in the crucified and risen Christ - a message that takes suffering and death seriously. Accordingly, religious education aims to *offer meaning without glossing over suffering*. It cannot and will not simply explain away meaninglessness, but it hopes that trust in God's love will help us to live with the incomprehensible. This *depth and sustainability* of the offer of meaning distinguishes it from the more solution-oriented approach of the happiness subject.

There are also methodological differences: As already indicated, happiness lessons are *body and experience-oriented* and work a lot with play, movement, group exercises and personal reflection in a protected space (e.g. in a circle of chairs). It should be fun and *directly tangible*. Religious education is traditionally more cognitive and discursive - the focus is on reading and interpreting texts and discussing philosophical and theological questions. This carries the risk of appearing "dry" to some students, especially in comparison to the creative methods of the happiness subject. However, modern religious education has also upgraded its methods: Many religious education teachers now use films, group work, projects, role plays or meditation in their lessons. Nevertheless, it can be said that *happiness lessons* address *the here-and-now feeling more strongly in* order to form a positive, life-affirming attitude in the approach to one's own life, while religious education emphasizes the *interpretation of life* in a broader perspective (history, tradition, eternity) - with the hope that all will be well in the hereafter. What both subjects have in common is that they aim to develop personality. Both promote *empathy and social values*, for example - happiness lessons through team tasks, trust exercises and discussing feelings, religious education through ethical reflection (charity, justice, forgiveness) and getting to know role models. And in both happiness and religion lessons, young people learn to think about themselves: *Who am I? What is important to me? What gives me strength?* There are overlaps here, for example when happiness lessons ask about personal *values and meaning* (e.g. *"What gives your life meaning?"*) - religious education also asks such questions, although it also offers an answer of faith (e.g. *"You are wanted and loved by God"*).

In summary, it can be said that *both subjects aim to teach life skills*, but with different emphases. Happiness lessons focus on *self-efficacy and enjoyment of life* in this world, while religious education focuses on *the search for meaning and transcendence* as well as a *promise of the afterlife*. However, instead of competing with each other, they can complement each other - after all, a young person needs both *the tools for a successful life* and a *background* against which this life can be lived. Meaning and happiness are not opposites, but intertwine. This is precisely where the opportunity lies to *build bridges instead of emphasizing opposites.*

The interesting question remains as to which skills and content learned best help people in difficult times - such as despair, grief, depression, inability to act or illnesses requiring treatment - to get back on their feet and perceive themselves, their fellow human beings and their own lives as worth living and happy.

What religious education teachers can learn from "happiness" lessons

Looking at the two approaches, it becomes clear that religious education can also take *inspiration* from happiness lessons. A religion teacher might ask themselves: *What do the happiness teachers do differently that appeals to the students?* Some things have already been hinted at above:

1. practical relevance and experience orientation: Happiness lessons show how important it is to enable *experiences* instead of just cramming theory. Happiness teachers, for example, have their class fill a "happiness jar" with beautiful moments that they can fall back on in difficult times. They practise relaxation and mindfulness exercises with the young people and talk openly about stress, fear and hope. All of this could also be addressed in religious education lessons. Instead of just talking about biblical texts, religion teachers could incorporate more *action-oriented elements*: for example, rituals in which everyone names something they are grateful for (similar to a gratitude exercise, but in a religious context as a prayer of thanks); moments of silence or meditation in class to make inner peace tangible; small projects in which students practice *charity* in practice (e.g. planning a relief action) and thus experience how good actions can make them happy. Happiness lessons are a reminder that learning should be *holistic* - head, heart and hand. Religious education teachers can therefore benefit from the variety of methods and make their lessons more lively without sacrificing the substance of the content.

2. positive language and attitude: What is striking about happiness as a school subject is its *encouraging attitude*. It sends out a happy message instead of a threatening message. Mistakes are not dramatized, but seen as learning opportunities. Happiness and the perception of being able to be happy do not focus on mistakes, sin or missed opportunities, but on what can be experienced and a positive view of what can be made of it: Because there is always a next and/or a best move you can make from a starting position and how you view it.

It's all about *praise, recognition and focusing on strengths*. This positive psychology could also play a greater role in religious education. Although the message of the Gospel is a good news message in itself, teachers (and the church as a whole) sometimes slip into a deficit-oriented language when teaching it: there is talk of sin, transgression and fear, which can trigger defensiveness in young people. Happiness lessons can teach us to *focus on what has been successful: What good experiences have you had? Where do you feel blessed in your life? What is going well for you?* These questions pick up the young people in the reality of their lives and show them: Faith also has to do with joy, success and *gratitude*, not just with prohibitions or duties. Teachers of religion should emphasize more often that Christian faith wants to *do* people *good* - emotionally, physically and interpersonally. After all, the Bible says: *"The joy of God is your strength"* (Nehemiah 8:10). So why not consciously look for *joy in faith* during religious education lessons - for example by singing songs that express joy, physically massaging your shoulders to experience well-being or reading testimonies of people who have found hope and happiness through their faith?

3. promotion of self-efficacy: A central concern of the happiness subject is to strengthen students in their *self-efficacy* - that is, in their belief in their own ability to act and competence. Everyone should experience this: *I can make a difference, I am not helplessly at the mercy of others.* This includes experiencing success, but also dealing with failure. Religious education can build on this by, for example, telling stories of success (such as biblical stories in which people overcome difficulties with God's help). Even more importantly, it can convey to young people that they themselves are *valuable and gifted by God* to actively shape their lives. The Christian message recognizes the concept of *vocation* - God trusts everyone with something, gives everyone talents. When students adopt this perspective, they draw self-confidence not only from themselves, but also from the knowledge that they are supported by God. This is where self-efficacy meets the concept of *grace*: in happiness lessons, young people learn to believe in themselves; in religious education, they can also learn that *God* also *believes in them.* Some believers put it this way: As Christians, some do not believe that you can make your own luck - you have to be able to rely on *being supported by* others or by God. This assurance that you don't have to do everything on your own takes the pressure off and grounds your self-efficacy. At the same time, however, your own happiness and sense of happiness may also become more dependent on the encouragement of others or on negotiating indulgences with them in order to feel good again - an essential idea in Martin Luther's criticism of the Catholic Church's sale of indulgences. Is happiness possible without God, without parishioners, without clergy and without church?

A religion teacher can therefore adopt these questions and methods on the one hand, allow the students to become active and find their own solutions (instead of just giving sermons), and on the other hand make it clear: *You are not alone - there is a community and a God who support you.* This attitude takes away the pressure of constantly having to function perfectly and at the same time promotes responsible action out of inner freedom.

Figure 12: You are not alone - Two queer teenagers are friends of happiness.

YANA - *(short for "You are not alone", from German: DBNA – "Du bist nicht allein") was a German-language online platform for young queer people, especially gay, bisexual, transgender and unsure boys and young men. Its central aim was to give young queers the feeling that they are not alone - in other words, to offer community, support and safe information. Accordingly, acceptance, self-discovery and the reduction of isolation were at the heart of the platform. Important goals and functions of DBNA included: community & exchange, education & magazine: through information and educational offers, advice & support:. Overall, DBNA embodies an appreciative, empowering attitude: young queers should be proud to be themselves, find support and recognize that there are many others with similar feelings. Churches and congregations are also - increasingly - trying to convey messages of belonging, self-acceptance and support to young queer people of faith. There has been a shift in thinking in many Christian youth and church ministries: People want to communicate that everyone is loved and accepted before God, regardless of sexual orientation or gender identity. Young queers can experience their faith and identity as compatible, supported by the promise of divine love. Both DBNA and church initiatives therefore send a message of belonging and acceptance. Church offerings, on the other hand, are faith-based and sometimes have to take traditional doctrines into account. As a result, openness varies. However, church communities and organizations are increasingly striving to make similar values tangible in the space of faith by saying: You are not alone, God is at your side. Both ways - DBNA's digital community approach and inclusive youth work in churches - make an important contribution to helping young queer people feel included, loved and supported in order to accept themselves and find their place in the community, whether online, in a community network they are building themselves or in the church pew.*

4. relevance to life and school culture: Finally, religious education can learn from the subject of happiness to always keep an eye on *relevance to life.* Many young people ask (albeit unspoken): *"What do I need this for in real life?"* In happiness lessons, the answer is obvious - the topics covered (happiness, contentment, dealing with stress, relationships) are directly relevant. Teachers of religion should also draw a connection to everyday life: *What do church festivals mean for my life? Where do I still encounter mercy or injustice today and what do I have to do with it?* By making such connections, lessons become more meaningful. In addition, religious education can become involved across the whole school, for example by initiating projects on *values in the school* so that the whole school culture benefits from the content discussed. Konrad Brunner, a head teacher from Munich, even emphasizes that *every teacher* - regardless of the subject - should have in mind how their teaching can promote the personal development of the pupils. Pursuing this holistic educational goal ("forming the heart, hand, mind and character") is where religion teachers stand side by side with colleagues from happiness education. Together, they can contribute to making school a place where young people not only learn facts, but also *grow, mature and discover meaning*.

"Good news" instead of a "threatening message" - need for change in the church

The last question looks beyond the classroom to the church itself: *Where would the Catholic Church need to make changes in order to credibly convey the Good News - and not appear as a threatening message?* This pointed formulation suggests that some people experience the church's proclamation as frightening rather than encouraging. In fact, Christianity has shown both faces in its history: on the one hand, the *good news* of God's unconditional love, the forgiveness of sins and life in abundance; on the other hand, phases of *fear pedagogy*, in which the threat of hell, a sense of guilt and moral pressure were used: Only prayer and confession helps - and perhaps good karma if we forgive others in a quasi God-playing way. Especially today, in a pluralistic and enlightened society, it is crucial that the church proclaims its message in such a way that it is received as *good news* - as a source of hope, meaning and joy in life, not as a rigid set of rules based on dogma or a constant threat of divine punishment.

1. emphasize positive anthropology: An important need for change lies in the basic attitude of proclamation. The church should advocate *a positive anthropology* even more strongly, i.e. a positive view of humanity. Every person is loved by God and endowed with dignity - this statement must be *the basis of faith* and the starting point for all teaching. However, outsiders often perceive the church differently: they first hear about original sin, about what people do *wrong* and where they fail morally. This can quickly be understood as an accusation or a threatening message (*"If you do XY, you won't go to heaven"*).

Figure 13: Gaudium Gravitas

A humorous comic in a colorful cartoon style, in which several clergymembers tell a man one after the other strict prohibitions: no smoking, no alcohol, no fried food, no meat, no sweets and, above all, no sex. In the last image, a cleric says with a cheerful smile: 'Have a nice day! The man stands there the whole time, friendly but somewhat puzzled, and is not quite sure what is meant by happiness and bliss in the instructions on how to live with Gaudium Gravitas (a worthy pleasure).

What is needed is a *shift in perspective*: the good news should prioritize what God has done for man - out of grace - and not what man has disappointed God with. In practical terms, this means focusing on the *goodness of God and the dignity of man* in sermons, religious education and church public relations work. Such a positive view does not exclude the awareness of sin, but it classifies it correctly: Yes, there is guilt and wrongdoing, but God's mercy is greater, and we are always allowed to start anew. If people feel that the church believes in the *goodness* of man (because God himself has found man to be "very good" according to Genesis), they will experience the message as liberating and not as a constant reproach.

2. language of love instead of fear: Closely linked to this is the question of the *language and images* used in preaching. Here the church can learn a lot from the modern pedagogical approach (as in happiness lessons): pressure and coercion create resistance, whereas *invitation and encouragement* open hearts. Jesus himself proclaimed his message as an invitation to a kingdom of God, as a festive meal to which all are invited. The church must examine whether its language corresponds to this model. If, for example, in sexual morality or family ethics, instructions come across more as a threat (*"You must not do that, otherwise you will sin"*), the language should be changed: away from threatening rhetoric and towards a *language of love* that explains *why* certain attitudes can lead to a good life. An example: Instead of just telling young people *"No sex before (same-sex or heterosexual) marriage, otherwise you will sin"*, you could talk about the value of commitment, faithfulness and patience - and at the same time show understanding for human weaknesses. It is not about watering down the message, but about *empathy and contextualization*: the church should take the reality of people's lives seriously and pick up where they stand instead of threatening with abstract commandments. This makes the message more credible because it makes it clear: God *knows* you and speaks to you lovingly in your situation instead of just overwhelming you with demands.

3. convey joy and hope: Pope Francis emphasized precisely this in his letter *Evangelii Gaudium* (The *Joy of the Gospel*) - the Gospel must be communicated with *joy* and *mercy*. The Church would do well to make this motto tangible everywhere. In concrete terms, this means: church services that are *lively* and radiate joy (music, language, sense of community); projects in which the church takes *diaconal* care of people (the sick, the poor, the marginalized) and thus shows that the message of love becomes practical; and *pastoral care* that *does not* condemn *draconically*, but accompanies. *The hopeful side* of faith should be emphasized, especially in youth ministry - for example in school services or religious student days: the experience of community, of forgiveness as a new beginning, of meaningfulness in the commitment to others. When young people experience church as a place where they *are accepted, where they* experience *meaning and genuine joy*, then the Good News automatically becomes more credible. They realize: This is not a threatening message that wants to make me feel small, but a force that lifts me up.

4. dealing with contradictions and doubts: In order to be credible, the church must also deal openly with the *darker sides of life*. This includes acknowledging that not everything in life runs smoothly and that faith does not solve all problems. Religious instruction (or a sermon) that pretends that prayer always has an immediate answer to every suffering is untrustworthy. Instead, the message should be conveyed as described above: Faith helps to *live* with unresolved questions by giving hope that our lives are ultimately held by God. This honest perspective prevents the good news from degenerating into a platitude or consolation. It also prevents the misunderstanding of a threatening message, because those who recognize the *ambivalence of life* do not threaten with simple consequences (*"You suffer because you believe too little"* - the church must strictly avoid such false promises!) Rather, the church can say: *Yes, there is suffering and doubt - but in Jesus himself, God goes through suffering and death and does not leave us alone there*. This message is demanding, but credible, because it can respond *authentically* to reality.

5. show a willingness to reform and demonstrate implementation: Finally, it must not be concealed that the church can also strengthen or weaken its *credibility* through concrete action. If the sermon speaks of love, but the church as an institution covers up grievances, tolerates abuse of power or ignores human realities such as priests in love, the gospel is not credible. Therefore, the need for change includes: more *transparency, justice and dialog* within the church. The "good news" must become visible in the way the church acts - in the respect for human dignity within its own ranks, in the participation of the faithful, in the renewal of encrusted structures. One example: the message of grace and equality of all people before God demands that women in the church be accorded the same esteem and positions of responsibility as men. They must be able to become cardinals and, in particular, popes in a timely manner. Or: The message of the loving mother in heaven requires the Church to repentantly ask for forgiveness where it has brought guilt upon itself (for example in cases of abuse) instead of hiding behind authority. Such steps are not mere "internal politics", but directly influence whether the gospel is experienced as joyful and liberating. This is because people today have fine antennae for *credibility*: they not only listen to *what* the church says, but also look at *how* it acts.

Figure 14: Development process in six phases.

DEVELOPMENT PROCESS IN SIX PHASES

HOLISTIC STUDENT WELL-BEING

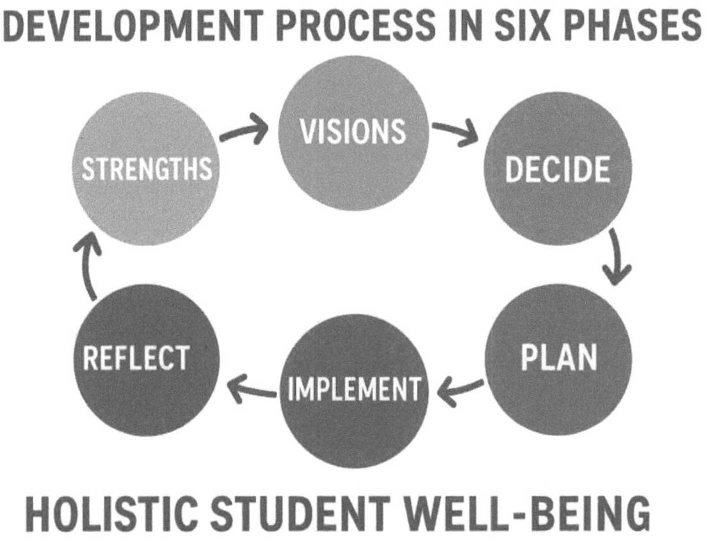

Infographic with six coloured phases arranged in a circle, visualizing a development process. Each phase has a short, concise label: "STRENGTHEN", "VISIONS", "DECIDE", "PLAN", "IMPLEMENT" and "REFLECT". The phases are connected by arrows and form a closed cycle. Above the graphic is written in capital letters: "DEVELOPMENT PROCESS IN SIX PHASES". Underneath the graphic is the subtitle: "WHOLESALE WELL-BEING OF PUPILS". The design is clear, modern and differentiated in terms of color.

Conclusion: Happiness as a school subject and religious education do not have to be opponents. Both want to give young people guidance and support for a successful life - one from a humanistic-psychological perspective, the other from a theological one. Their content overlaps in values such as *meaning, self-discovery, community and the art of living,* even if the *level of interpretation* is different. The teaching content can be implemented in a development process in six phases: *Strengths - Visioning - Deciding - Planning - Implementing - Reflecting.* By building bridges, we can combine the best of both worlds: The pedagogy of happiness can enrich religious education, and the depth of the Good News can provide a sustaining ground for the search for happiness. For religious education teachers, this means being open to new methods and positive approaches in order to make their own lessons lively and student-oriented. For the Catholic Church as a whole, it means courageously tackling those changes that make its proclamation truly *good news* - with a credible testimony of God's love, joy and philanthropy. In this way, it becomes clear that faith is not in competition with human happiness, but can be its deepest source.

Happiness as a school subject - curriculum overview and content (secondary level I/II - modules, objectives, methods)

The school subject *Happiness* is designed as an interdisciplinary personality development program. It is based on scientifically recognized concepts such as positive psychology, the teaching of values according to Logo therapy, salutogenesis (Antonovsky) and resilience research, combined with elementary principles of self-efficacy and self-education. *The aims* are to promote life skills, joie de vivre and personal development among the students. The *methodology* is action-oriented and experience-based: Through *experiential education,* reflection and creative tasks, *well-being* is made tangible as a learning goal . The curriculum is typically divided into the following modules:

(1)   **Joy in life** - *contents:* Getting to know one's own strengths and values, building trust and team spirit in the class community, dealing with feelings. *Goals:* Positive self-perception,

appreciation of others, establishing a *sense of unity* and *self-esteem*. *Methods*: Experience-oriented *group exercises* (games to get to know each other and trust games) as well as discussions about feelings and mutual feedback in a protected environment

(2) **Enjoying one's own performance** - *content:* Setting individual *and* collective goals; differentiating between short-term *action goals* and longer-term *attitude goals* (e.. training a skill vs. gaining more self-confidence). Overcoming the "inner bastard" and perseverance exercises. *Goals:* Developing *self-efficacy* and *discipline* by achieving self-imposed goals; dealing constructively with setbacks. *Methods: agreeing* personal *goals*, regular self-reflection (e.. success diary) and peer coaching in the group.

(3) **Body in motion** - *contents:* Experience of physical activity and its influence on well-being; theoretical knowledge of (extreme) sports and their appeal; practical experimentation with climbing (indoor/outdoor), martial arts and yoga with massaging the shoulders of others with a massage ball. *Objectives:* Promoting *body awareness*, reducing stress and anxiety, strengthening courage and self-conquest; understanding that movement contributes significantly to mental health, physical massage using a massage ball can also be experienced in pairs. *Methods: sports and movement exercises* (individual, pair and group activities), relaxation techniques and joint reflection on the experiences.

(4) **Body as a means of expression** - *content:* Connection between posture and feelings (e.. how body language affects one's own mood and others); conscious use of *facial expressions, gestures and posture* in everyday situations (e.g. self-confident appearance during a conversation). Role-playing games for self-presentation, *status exercises* (high/low status) and scenic play promote empathy and creativity. *Goals:* Developing *expressiveness* and *self-confidence*, empathy in interpersonal situations, confident communication. *Methods: theater pedagogy* (guided and improvised role plays) and perception exercises to consciously experience and use body language.

(5)   **Everyday adventure** - *contents:* Application of the skills learned to everyday challenges. Focus topics are mutual *respect*, empathy and bullying prevention - e.. through inclusion projects (joint sports with people with disabilities, visits from Paralympic athletes). Practical *life skills* are covered as required: *learning to learn* effectively, time management, responsible use of money and the basics of healthy eating. *Goals:* Strengthening students' *social responsibility* and *everyday life skills*; preparing them for an independent life and *resilience* in the face of difficulties. *Methods: project work* (planning and implementing small projects), workshops with external experts (e.. nutrition, finance), group discussions and practical exercises in everyday school life.

Note: The above modules may vary slightly depending on the school and age group or be divided into *phases*. For example, the Fritz Schubert Institute describes a development process in six phases: *Strengths - Visions - Deciding - Planning - Implementing - Reflecting*. Regardless of the exact classification, the *holistic well-being* of the students is always the central learning goal at the end.

🕊️Bishops' briefing:

The religious policy field looks at the school subject "happiness" and compares it with traditional religious education. It discusses how the subject of happiness aims to teach students life skills, resilience and well-being through practical exercises and projects, in contrast to the more cognitive approach of religious education. It explores whether these two subjects compete or complement each other and highlights similarities and differences in their aims and methods. It concludes by highlighting learning opportunities for religious education by making it more practice-oriented and positive in order to convey the "Good News" more credibly.

Didactic questions:

1 - What is happiness as a school subject and why was it introduced?

Happiness is a school subject that aims to help pupils develop a greater zest for life, resilience and self-confidence. It was developed by Ernst Fritz-Schubert in 2007 and is intended to create a counterbalance to purely performance-oriented teaching. The aim is to establish long-term well-being and life satisfaction as an educational goal and to turn young people into resilient, self-determined personalities who experience their lives as effective creators.

2 - What skills are taught in the school subject of happiness?

A number of key skills are promoted in the school subject of happiness. These initially include self-competencies such as self-reflection, a healthy sense of self-worth, resilience (dealing with setbacks) and, in particular, self-efficacy, i.e. the belief in one's own ability to act. In addition, social skills such as teamwork, empathy, constructive conflict resolution and appreciation are strengthened. Practical life skills such as time management, learning strategies and financial literacy are also part of the lessons.

3 - How is happiness taught in the classroom and what methods are used?

Lessons in the subject of happiness are practical, experience- and action-oriented. Instead of frontal teaching, the focus is on experiences and adventures. Methods include experiential educational exercises, team games, personal goal setting and projects, reflection (e.g. in a happiness diary), movement and physical experience (sport, relaxation), creative activities (theater, painting), philosophical discussions, museum visits and the use of external experts (motivational coaches, family therapists). It is important to link what is learned to the students' everyday lives.

4 - What positive effects does happiness as a school subject have on pupils and the school climate?

Experience and studies show encouraging effects. Students think more reflectively about themselves, have the feeling that they are more in control of their lives (self-efficacy) and experience greater well-being and less stress. The subject can help to stabilize mental health. Motivation and willingness to learn can also improve. The subject has a positive effect on the school culture by promoting an atmosphere of appreciation and a focus on strengths. This can lead to a healthier and more supportive school climate.

5 - Does happiness as a school subject compete with religious education?

The question of competition is being discussed, but there is much to be said for viewing the subjects as complementary. Both subjects focus on people and ask about a good life. While happiness as a school subject offers practical methods for well-being in this world from a humanistic-psychological perspective (self-efficacy, joie de vivre), religious education offers an interpretative framework from a theological perspective that includes questions of meaning, transcendence and hope in difficult times. Both can learn from each other: religious education can benefit from the practical relevance and positive language of the subject of happiness, while the subject of happiness can be enriched by the meaningfulness and the supporting foundation that faith can offer.

6 - What are the similarities and differences between happiness as a school subject and religious education?

What both subjects have in common is that they focus on the whole person (body, mind, soul, social interaction) and ask about a good life. Both are based on a positive view of humanity. There are differences in terms of content, methodology and interpretation of the world. Religious education has a clearly defined religious standpoint and deals with topics in the context of faith in God. The school subject of happiness is ideologically neutral, focuses on individual well-being in the here and now and uses methods from psychology and education. Religious education emphasizes the search for meaning and transcendence, while happiness is more pragmatically oriented towards the here and now.

7 - What can religion teachers learn from happiness as a school subject?

Religious education teachers can learn from happiness lessons to make their teaching more practical and experience-oriented (e.g. through rituals, meditation, practical projects). They can adopt a more positive language and attitude, focus more on successful experiences and strengths and convey the "Good News" as a source of joy and gratitude. In addition, religious education can promote self-efficacy by encouraging young people to actively shape their lives, while at the same time conveying the relieving message that they are supported by God and are not alone. Finally, religious education can learn from the happiness subject to always emphasize the relevance of the content to life and contribute to a positive school culture.

8 - What changes are necessary in the Catholic Church in order to communicate the "Good News" credibly?

In order to be perceived as "good news" and not as a "threatening message", the Catholic Church must place greater emphasis on a positive anthropology, i.e. the positive image of humanity and the dignity of each individual. The language of proclamation should be a language of love and invitation, away from fear rhetoric and moral pressure. It is important to convey joy and hope, for example through lively church services and diaconal action. Dealing openly with contradictions, suffering and doubt is crucial for credibility. Finally, the church must show a willingness to reform and underpin credibility through concrete action, for example through transparency, justice and the inclusion of all believers in order to live the message of love institutionally.

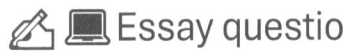 Essay questions:

Please answer one of the following questions in the form of an essay:

a) Discuss the main aims and pedagogical approaches of happiness as described in the text. How do these aim to promote long-term well-being and life satisfaction in students?

b) Analyze the similarities and differences between the school subject of happiness and traditional religious education (especially Catholic religious education) on the basis of this text. What are the most important overlaps and differences?

c) Evaluate the criticism voiced about the establishment of happiness as a school subject. How should these concerns be addressed or responded to?

d) Examine the potential learning opportunities that religious education (particularly the Catholic Church) can draw from the school subject of happiness. Give specific examples of how these insights could be applied.

e) Examine the necessary changes within the Catholic Church proposed in the text in order to credibly communicate the "Good News" instead of a "threatening message" . What concrete steps are proposed?

📌 Religious policy field analysis 2: *Reform of Catholic sexual morality*

More and more voices are calling for a reform of Catholic sexual morality - driven by the desire to promote equality and non-discrimination in the church. Reform-oriented bishops, progressive theologians and groups close to and critical of the Church are calling for a change of course towards a contemporary sexual doctrine based on responsible ethics. Rigid guidelines and blanket prohibitions should be replaced by an ethic of responsibility, relationship and self-determination that respects all people and lifestyles equally. The debates of the Synodal Path have reaffirmed these demands and initiated concrete resolutions for change.

New evaluation of sexuality and partnership

Several bishops who are willing to take action are publicly advocating a reorientation of the church's sexual morals. These include prominent representatives such as the Chairman of the Conference of female, diverse and male Bishops Georg Bätzing and Bishops Peter Kohlgraf (Mainz), Franz-Josef Bode (Osnabrück, retired), Heiner Wilmer (Hildesheim), Helmut Dieser (Aachen), Franz Jung (Würzburg) and Karl-Heinz Wiesemann (Speyer). They plead for a *new evaluation of sexuality and partnership* that recognizes the reality of life for believers and is no longer fixated solely on procreation.

For example, Bätzing emphasizes that sexuality is *"a gift from God and not a sin"* and calls for corrections to previous doctrine. These bishops also speak out *against compulsory celibacy* for priests. Bätzing can well imagine its abolition and considers married priests to be an enrichment for the church. Bode also called for greater respect for the freedom of the faithful in matters of sexual morality instead of restricting their lives with rigid rules. Overall, the reform-oriented shepherds are aiming for a sexual ethic that places love, reliability and mutual respect at the center - regardless of whether a relationship is lived inside or outside of a sacramental marriage. Same-sex partnerships and remarried couples should no longer be excluded, but rather valued in their loving relationship. Bishops such as Bätzing and Bode explicitly support celebrations for homosexual couples and also call for a re-evaluation of homosexuality in the light of current knowledge.

Theological and church-critical arguments: responsibility and self-determination

Theologians and reform groups agree with these demands and emphasize the need for a fundamentally new sexual ethical orientation of the Catholic Church. They criticize the fact that the traditional sexual morality of the church with its detailed regulations is neither understandable nor liveable for many people. Instead of a tight corset of rules, they demand a sexual ethic that focuses *on responsibility, relationship ethics and self-determination*. In more recent moral theological approaches, *relationship quality and mutual responsibility* are regarded as guiding criteria, while the *sexual self-determination* of the individual is emphasized as a fundamental value - limited only by the dignity and equal self-determination of the partner.

Sexuality is seen as a positive force and part of the personality, not as a "problem" to be controlled. It is crucial that people treat their sexuality and that of their partner with respect and care. This kind of responsible and ethical sexual morality is based on the lived reality of love relationships and demands that decisions of conscience are made on a situation-specific and person-centered basis instead of working with blanket attributions.

Voices critical of the church - such as initiatives like *We Are Church* or the *#OutInChurch* movement - also point out that the current doctrine forces many believers into a double life and discriminates against certain groups (e.g. LGBTQIA+ people or remarried divorcees).

They call for a *depathologization of sexual orientation* and a *departure from a sexual morality that adheres solely to old norms* in favour of an approach that expresses personal responsibility and equal participation for all.

Synodal path: Resolutions for a renewed sexual ethic

The reform debates culminated in the German *Synodal Path*, which brought bishops and laypeople together in 2019-2023 to discuss power structures, celibacy, the role of women and sexual morality in particular.

The Synodal Path adopted pioneering positions and resolutions on sexual ethics. *Blanket attributions* - such as the general condemnation of certain sexual practices or lifestyles as disordered - were clearly rejected. In a text that was adopted, it was stated that *lived sexuality, regardless of the sexual orientation of the partners,* is *not a sin* and should *"not be* judged *as inherently bad"*.

A person's sexual orientation is recognized as part of their God-given identity and is judged morally no differently than a heterosexual orientation.

Accordingly, the synod members spoke out *in favor of the recognition and appreciation of same-sex partnerships.* The plenary assembly voted by a large majority to *officially allow celebrations for couples who love each other - including homosexual couples and civilly remarried divorcees.*

In this way, the love lived by these couples is to be blessed and supported by the church instead of being excluded.

At the same time, the synodal path advocates a move away from a purely normative, abstract moral code towards an *individual ethic* that takes people's conscience and concrete relationship situation seriously. In the synodal debates, it was critically noted that the current sexual morality has "hardly anything to do with the reality of life for many Catholics" and that its regulations interfere *too deeply with couples living together.*

Figure 15: Diversity of gender, sexual orientation and love.

Symbolic image on the diversity of gender and love: three toilet doors in the middle with different gender signs - male, female and diverse - framed by two graffiti silhouettes of same-sex couples in an intimate embrace. The image addresses gender diversity, inclusion and queer visibility in public spaces. Ideal for ideas on gender justice in the church, LGBTQIA+ rights and against social standardization.

In particular, the rigid fixation on certain sexual norms (such as the ban on contraception or the postulate of absolute abstinence outside of marriage) met with opposition. Instead, the Synodal Assembly emphasized *the priority of* each individual's *decision of conscience based on love and responsibility* over rigid guidelines. Catholics should be able to make mature and responsible decisions about their sex lives without fear of blanket condemnation from the Church. Accordingly, the Synodal Way recommended that the Pope and the universal church revise the Catechism on issues of homosexuality and contraception and allow for further developments. The compulsory celibacy of priests was also discussed as part of the Synodal Path - many synod members spoke out in favor of making this way of life voluntary in the future, i.e. abolishing celibacy corporately by making it an individual choice in order to open up the priestly vocation to married people as well.

Figure 16: Paradigm shift in Catholic sexual ethics.

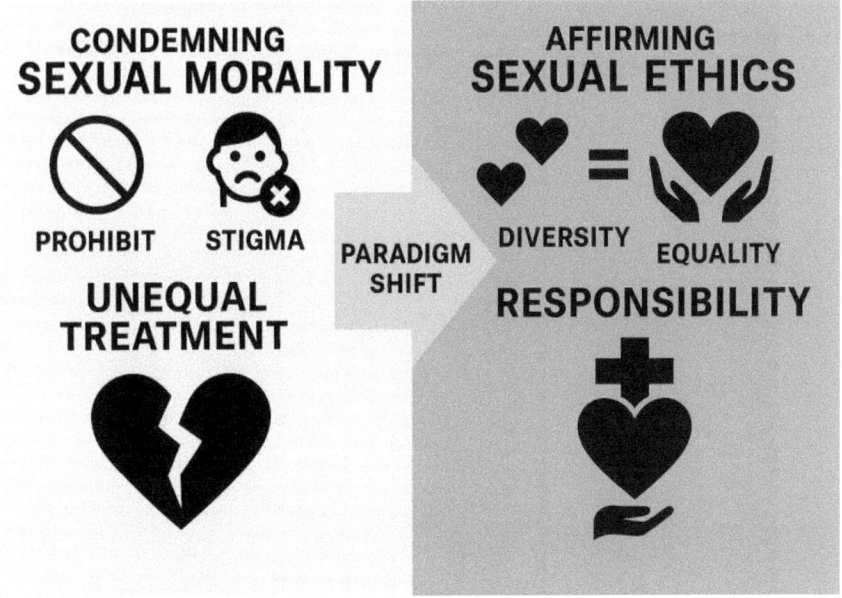

A clear, symbol-based infographic on the topic of a paradigm shift in the Catholic Church: on the left-hand side, the old, condemning sexual morality (with symbols for prohibitions, stigma and unequal treatment, e.g. crossed-out circle, face with stigma, broken heart). In the middle, a large arrow clearly shows the change to the right, where a new, appreciative sexual ethic is depicted. There, symbols for diversity, equality, responsibility and Christian charity (e.g. hearts, hands, cross with heart). The color scheme is clearly contrasted : grey on the left with negatively connoted symbols, positive on the right in shades of green with positive symbols. The graphic has minimalist lettering and is clearly legible in order to emphasize the change from old to new, negative to positive, judgmental to appreciative.

The call for a reform of Catholic sexual morality is therefore aimed at an effective and sustainable *paradigm shift*: away from a sexual morality of prohibitions, stigmatization and unequal treatment - towards an *appreciative sexual ethic* that recognizes the diversity of human love relationships and is based on equality, responsibility and Christian charity. This reorientation, as called for by leading bishops, theologians and the Synodal Assembly, should help the Church to step out of the defensive and bring its teaching into line with lived reality and today's understanding of human dignity and equality. The reform of sexual doctrine is therefore also a key to the credibility of the Church in modern society.

🕊️Bishops' briefing:

This religious policy field describes the widely recognized demands for a reform of Catholic sexual morality. Various groups, including reform-oriented bishops, progressive theologians and church-oriented initiatives, advocate a contemporary approach. They advocate a sexual ethic of responsibility and self-determination that respects all people and lifestyles equally. The Synodal Path in particular has strengthened these efforts and passed resolutions on the recognition of same-sex partnerships and the review of celibacy. The aim is a paradigm shift from a prohibition-oriented to an appreciative sexual ethic in order to strengthen the credibility of the church in modern society.

Didactic questions:

9 - What is the main driver behind the calls for a reform of Catholic sexual morality?

The demands for a reform of Catholic sexual morality are mainly driven by the desire to promote equality and non-discrimination within the Church and to align sexual morality more closely with the reality of the lives of the faithful.

10 - Who are the main actors supporting a reform of Catholic sexual morality?

The reform is supported by various groups, including reform-oriented bishops, progressive theologians and church-related groups and initiatives such as "We are Church" or the #OutInChurch movement.

11 - What specific points are raised in relation to sexual morality?

Reform-oriented clergy advocate a new evaluation of sexuality and partnership that recognizes the reality of life for believers, views sexuality as a gift from God and is no longer fixated solely on procreation. They also speak out against compulsory celibacy for priests and explicitly support celebrations for homosexual couples.

12 - What arguments do progressive theologians and church-critical groups put forward in favor of reform?

Progressive theologians and reform groups criticize the fact that the traditional sexual morals of the church are neither understandable nor liveable for many people. If practically no one today takes the ban on premarital sex or the use of contraceptives seriously, this Catholic teaching is finally revealed for what it is: absurd, out of touch with the world and completely out of date. It calls for a sexual ethic that focuses on responsibility, relationship ethics and self-determination, views sexuality as a positive force and supports the depathologization of sexual orientation.

13 - What role did the Synodal Way play in the debate on sexual morality?

The Synodal Way was a central platform for the reform debates and passed groundbreaking resolutions on sexual ethics. It rejected blanket condemnations of certain sexual practices and lifestyles, recognized sexual orientation as part of God's intended identity and spoke out in favour of the recognition and appreciation of same-sex partnerships.

14 - What decisions have been made on the Synodal Path regarding the evaluation of sexuality and partnerships?

On the synodal path, it was decided that lived sexuality, regardless of sexual orientation, is not a sin and should "not be judged as inherently bad". It spoke out in favor of the recognition and appreciation of same-sex partnerships and demanded that celebrations for loving couples (including homosexual couples and civilly remarried divorcees) be officially permitted.

15 - What departure from previous norms is called for on the Synodal Path?

The Synodal Way advocates a move away from a purely normative, abstract moral code towards an individual ethic that takes people's conscience and concrete relationships seriously. It emphasizes the priority of each individual's decision based on love and responsibility over rigid guidelines and recommends a revision of the catechism in matters of homosexuality and contraception.

16 - What is the overarching goal of the reform efforts with regard to Catholic sexual morality?

The overarching goal is a paradigm shift from a sexual morality of prohibitions, stigmatization and unequal treatment to an appreciative sexual ethic that recognizes the diversity of human love relationships, is based on equality, responsibility and Christian charity, and brings the teachings of the Church into harmony with lived reality and today's understanding of human dignity and equality.

✍🖥 Essay questions:

Please answer one of the following questions in the form of an essay:

a) Explain the key processes for realigning the Church's sexual morality and show how its positions differ from traditional teaching and why they have better congruence and resonance with the realities of life today.

b) Discuss what role progressive theological and church-critical arguments play in the call for a renewed sexual ethic and what core demands result from this and need to be implemented. Create a time and work plan for this implementation.

c) Describe the main positions and resolutions of the Synodal Path with regard to sexual ethics, describe where the substantive positions fall short and fall short, and analyze their potential impact on church practice.

d) Compare the traditional understanding of sexuality in the Catholic Church with the understanding demanded by the proponents of reform and the Synodal Path. What paradigm shifts are being sought?

e) Discuss the importance of sexual ethics based on responsibility, relationships and self-determination in the context of the current social and pastoral challenges facing the Catholic Church.

f) Create an infographic on the paradigm shift of the Catholic Church, including the abolition of celibacy for clergy and offering new perspectives.

🚀 Religious policy field analysis 3: *Equality of all marriages at the altar - thanks to queer-sensitive pastoral care in the Catholic Church*

In the Catholic Church, traditional doctrines and progressive reform efforts have been clashing for many years on issues of sexual ethics - as already shown in the previous section. This concerns not only premarital sex, the use of contraceptives or the remarriage of divorcees. In particular, it also concerns the Catholic Church's institutionally entrenched homophobia and its reservations about marrying homosexual couples in church. Officially, practising same-sex love is still considered a sin. It is therefore worth dedicating a separate section to the great significance and power associated with the expected equality of all marriages before the altar and to address this in more detail.

The *Catechism of the Catholic Church* has so far denied that homosexual acts are proper "in themselves", and for a long time same-sex partnerships were neither recognized by the church - nor blessed and sacramentally married. This attitude of not wanting to celebrate love with a wedding ceremony has led to the structural exclusion of queer people: Many devout lesbians, gays, bi-, trans- and intersexual people (LGBTQIA+) did not feel accepted in their church and lived without a church, yet in faith.

Moreover, until recently it was not uncommon for church employees to be dismissed if they disclosed their same-sex relationship at work or entered into a same-sex marriage. Today, this has already changed: Couples are visible and recognized. However, the attitude of the church remains virtually unchanged.

The pastoral care of queer people therefore remained an underdeveloped competence, which caused great psychological damage - something for which those affected are demanding that the church leadership come to terms and apologize, as well as appropriate competence development and seminar training for pastoral care clergy.

As a result, there is widespread opposition to this old-fashioned traditional line of the Catholic Church. A number of prominent German bishops - Georg Bätzing (Limburg), Peter Kohlgraf (Mainz), Franz-Josef Bode (Osnabrück, retired), Heiner Wilmer (Hildesheim), Helmut Dieser (Aachen), Franz Jung (Würzburg) and Karl-Heinz Wiesemann (Speyer) - as well as many international bishops are now openly advocating reform-oriented positions on questions of sexual morality and pastoral care. They distance themselves from exclusionary doctrine and advocate an appreciative approach to same-sex loving people and couples. As early as 2018, Bishop Bode suggested within the church that celebrations for same-sex couples should be officially introduced. In 2020, the Chairman of the German Conference of female, diverse and male Bishops, Bishop Bätzing, called for the Catechism to be revised and revised with regard to homosexuality. He called for couples who are not yet or no longer able to marry under current church law - such as same-sex or civilly remarried couples - to also receive a church ceremony.

Bätzing emphasized that "solutions are needed here that ... have public visibility. Similarly, Bishop Wiesemann declared in November 2023 that church services for homosexual couples (as well as for remarried divorcees) will take place in his diocese of Speyer from now on.

This opening in practice marks a conscious turning away from earlier prohibitions and sends the signal that same-sex partnerships are recognized and supported pastorally.

Several of these reform-oriented bishops justify their course theologically and pastorally with the commandment to love one's neighbor and the image of God in every human being. For example, Bishop Kohlgraf introduced two commissioners *for queer-sensitive pastoral care* in Mainz in 2022 - a novelty with a signal effect. In his sermon, he emphasized: "No one is a victim of creation, everyone is loved, God wanted them and all of us like this!"

For Kohlgraf, it is shocking that "the condemnation of queer people has mutated into the actual core issue of being Catholic for some in the church". Instead of condemning people because of their identity or urging them to live double lives, the church must question and change its own attitude. Bishop Helmut Dieser, who is considered one of the progressives in the German Episcopal Church, has also publicly declared that he has learned and sees *"homosexuality as God-given in the same measure as creation itself"*.

Accordingly, love between two men or two women cannot be sinful, but should be respected as an expression of God's diversity of creation. Consequently, he supports the acceptance of same-sex couples in the church and already allows such celebrations in Aachen.

Bishop Wilmer was similarly clear, calling for a renewal of sexual morality: *"It cannot be that people are hurt or discriminated against by church teaching,"* he said in 2022, as such an attitude cannot correspond to the will of Christ. Wilmer welcomed the tentative signals from Rome regarding the celebration of homosexual partnerships as "pointing the way forward" and emphasized that the realities of queer couples' lives today must be acknowledged. Overall, a course is emerging among bishops that clearly rejects exclusion and discrimination and instead focuses on integration, respect and positive appreciation of queer Christians.

Progressive theologians and church reform initiatives strongly support these demands. They criticize the traditional teaching on sexuality and homosexuality as theologically outdated and practically discriminatory. In their view, devaluing the love and identity of LGBTQIA+ people contradicts the essence of the Christian view of humanity. Instead, it must be recognized that queer identities are wanted by God and that binding relationships based on fidelity and care are to be valued ethically in the same way as heterosexual partnerships, regardless of the gender and sexual orientation of the partner.

Corresponding voices also refer to the findings of the human sciences, which show that a person's sexual orientation is neither pathological nor can it be changed at will. Bishop Kohlgraf of Mainz, for example, argued that we cannot take a few biblical half-sentences on homosexuality without context and treat them as the eternally valid word of God, but must also take today's scientific and social findings seriously. Many popular church initiatives - from the Central Committee of German Catholics to the #OutInChurch campaign - are therefore calling for a revision of church doctrine. Defamatory and outdated statements by the church on sexuality and gender need to be revised and deleted on the basis of sound theology and human science, according to the church-affiliated group #OutInChurch.

Specifically, critics are urging the church to finally make it official: Homosexuality is not a sin, the lived love of two people of the same sex does not offend God per se. In other words, homosexuality is very good and valuable, and the lived love of two people of the same sex is just as blessed, trusted and recognized by God as any other love. Consequently, believing LGBTQIA+ people should not be denied God's blessing or access to the sacraments - such as marriage and all others.

Instead, the church should clearly reject any form of discrimination and promote a culture of diversity, as required by the gospel's claim to equality.

A central forum in which this debate has been bundled in recent years is the German *Synodal Path*. This reform project of bishops and lay people has openly discussed the controversial issues - sexual morality, power structures, priestly lifestyle, women's ministries. The Synodal Path passed important resolutions on the subject of homosexuality in particular. In March 2023, for example, the Synodal Assembly adopted a text by a large majority, which is intended to officially allow *the celebration of homosexual couples*.

Despite a Vatican ban from 2021 - in which Rome declared that the Church did not yet have the authority to bless same-sex unions - the German participants voted in favor of introducing such celebrations. Only nine older bishops voted against, too few for a blocking minority.

The adopted text *"Blessings for couples who love each other"* emphasizes that the church wants to offer recognition and support to all couples "who are united in love" and take responsibility for each other. These celebrations should also explicitly apply to same-sex couples and other previously excluded partnerships. The dioceses were asked to implement corresponding liturgical celebrations by 2026 at the latest.

The synodal decision is a consensus that was reached with the old church representatives, who held back the modern and contemporary views of younger people, even though some young people were involved in the process.

Critics point out that it is not about performing blessings, but firstly about being able to conclude a marriage on an equal footing. Secondly, this is why there is no need for a separate form of liturgy. Thirdly, a requirement of Rome must also be implemented by all priests, so that no decisions of conscience are needed at the grassroots level.

All three of these Bremen are stop mechanisms that prove the half-heartedness of the church actors. In the end, there is no difference between blessing and marriage. Those who introduce or maintain this difference want to separate, want to divide, want half-hearted solutions, want to continue to discriminate and hope that those who have been oppressed and thirsty for water will be grateful for a small drop of water. Accordingly, critics point out that equality does not mean taking the little finger, but the whole hand. Half the truth is therefore another form of discrimination that cannot be upheld. Otherwise, it is a lie to be serious about adaptation and reform.

Although the first step will de facto remove the taboos from and legitimize blessings that have already been practised and which previously took place in a grey area, equality with the marriage ceremony looks different.

The state has also taken such intermediate steps from civil partnerships to marriage for all - in many countries already. It only took a few years to achieve full equality with marriage. With this experience, the church can also take a big step towards marriage, because it will come in a short time anyway. It is only a question of demographic change, i.e. the passing away of the older incumbents, who have so far been socialized differently on this topic (socially and professionally).

In addition to the practical step of celebrating blessings, the Synodal Path therefore also called for a doctrinal reassessment of homosexuality. In a vote to the Pope, the assembly urged that the doctrine of the universal Church be developed accordingly - which means rewriting it.

As guidelines, the Synodal Forum formulated, for example, that every sexual orientation corresponds equally to the God-created dignity of the human being and that lived sexuality in a loving, faithful relationship - regardless of gender or sexual orientation - is not to be judged morally differently than in a heterosexual marriage. Or to put it simply: there is no difference, the references to homosexual or heterosexual are simply to be revised and refrained from in future.

In clear, positive words: loving homosexuality is part of a responsible Christian lifestyle. These resolutions of the Synodal Path mark a cultural change in the Catholic Church. They are a signal of recognition to queer believers and make it clear that their love can no longer be dismissed as moral.

The experiences of queer people with the Catholic Church have often been characterized by rejection in the past - which makes their demands for full equality all the louder now.

Many homosexuals report humiliation and a life of conflict: on the one hand, they feel attracted to their faith and their church, but on the other, they are met with mistrust and rejection from the same institution. In January 2022, for example, over a hundred church employees publicly described their life stories and coming out as part of the *#OutInChurch* campaign. They made it clear how much the previous church policy drove them into fear and inner conflict - constant fear of losing their job or the feeling of being considered "ostracizable" before God and the congregation because they are queer. They no longer put up with this exclusion.

Such testimonies have made many people aware of how much suffering the practice of exclusion has caused. Queer believers are therefore now emphatically calling for a complete end to this discrimination. It starts with equal marriage to marriage with sacraments. They want to be accepted as images of God without having to play hide-and-seek and participate in church life on an equal footing. This includes ensuring that no one is excluded from receiving communion or all other sacraments on the basis of their sexual orientation and that the love relationships of

LGBTQIA+ couples are married, blessed and valued in the same way as those of all other couples.

Figure 17: Synodal discussion of the acceptance of homosexuality in the Catholic Church.

The picture shows four people sitting at a round table and discussing the acceptance of homosexuality in the Catholic Church in a serious and concentrated manner. Their posture and facial expressions reflect a professional and profound examination of the topic. In the background, a green board clearly stands out, on which is written in clear white lettering: "Synodal working forum to discuss the acceptance of homosexuality in the Catholic Church". Right next to it, a rainbow flag is visible, on which two intertwined hearts are depicted with a cross and a church above them. This symbol impressively represents the connection between queer identity and Christian faith. The scene impressively conveys that changes are being discussed here in an open, respectful and at the same time focused framework in order to shape a church that values diversity and does not exclude anyone.

All over the world, more and more high-ranking officials in the Catholic Church are openly speaking out in favor of recognizing queer identities and for blessings and even marriage ceremonies for same-sex couples.

Many of these bishops and cardinals initially emphasize the dignity and belonging of LGBTQIA+ people in the church. Cardinal *Oswald Gracias* from India, for example, assured homosexual believers: "The Church accepts you, it wants you and it needs you. ... You belong to us". The Archbishop of Mumbai thus emphasized that homosexual people are not an individual factor, but a valued part of the church community. *Cardinal Joseph Tobin* (Archbishop of Newark, USA) expressed a similar view: he insisted that it should be clear *"without debate"* that the Church welcomes people in same-sex relationships without reservation. Tobin called the traditional language of the Catechism, which describes homosexuality as "intrinsically disordered", *"very unfortunate"* and hoped that this formulation would soon be replaced by less offensive vocabulary.

Cardinal Robert McElroy (USA) also urges such *"radical inclusion"*: *"What we need to project in the life of the church is: 'You are part of us and we are part of you'."* - *"You [LGBTQIA+ people] are part of us and we are part of you."*

This emphasis on belonging and dignity can now be seen in a similar way on all continents.

In Austria, *Cardinal Christoph Schönborn* (Vienna) made a similarly empathetic argument: He described the rigorous Roman *"no"* to marriage ceremonies for same-sex couples as a *"communication error"* and showed understanding for believing homosexuals asking themselves disappointedly of the church, *"Doesn't this mother have a blessing for me?"* After all, the Church is mother and teacher - *"first comes the mother"*. According to Schönborn, it is therefore important to focus less on doctrinal sexual morality and more on love lived out : *"We should talk less about sexuality and more about love; more about successful relationships and less about the question of what is allowed and what is not"*.

The development is particularly advanced in *Belgium*. The bishops of the Flemish region - including Cardinal *Jozef De Kesel* (Archbishop of Mechelen-Brussels) and *Bishop Johan Bonny* (Antwerp) - have officially implemented the liturgical ritual for same-sex couples. Bonny, one of Belgium's most influential bishops, had previously protested against the Vatican's ban on such celebrations in unusually harsh terms. *"I am ashamed of my church,"* he declared, visibly *"furious"* about the document from Rome. The Belgian Conference of female, diverse and male Bishops backed this statement. Bonny made it clear that this was about more than mere ritual issues - it was about the *dignity* of those involved.

Figure 18: Paradigm shift: From women with magnifying glasses to women using artificial intelligence to rewrite texts.

A lesbian woman would like support from artificial intelligence in evaluating the text to reformulate it so that she doesn't have to search for all the passages in need of reform with a magnifying glass. A detailed, symbolic illustration in the style of a pencil drawing that thematizes the questioning of patriarchal traditions and religious interpretations on the basis of old texts. The determined lesbian critically examines a historical scroll with a large magnifying glass. The magnifying glass enlarges a female symbol and symbolizes the feminist perspective. Next to the scroll is a large chip with the inscription AI - Artificial Intelligence. In the background, traditional religious and patriarchal symbols, figures and chains are visible, representing centuries-old restrictions. The age of acceptance of homosexual couples and the use of artificial intelligence to rewrite old-fashioned passages means a necessary paradigm shift for the Catholic Church. The whole thing is set in a historical, temple-like environment with broken pillars and crumbling structures to symbolize the upheaval of old power structures. Shades of black and white create an atmosphere of critical reflection that can support artificial intelligence and will be further discovered in the future.

Similar tones are coming from the Vatican and Luxembourg. *Cardinal Jean-Claude Hollerich* (Archbishop of Luxembourg), who was appointed General Relator of the World Synod of Bishops by Pope

Francis, has called for a fundamental reassessment of the Church's teaching on homosexuality. *"I believe that the sociological and scientific basis of this teaching is no longer correct,"* Hollerich stated openly. The church's previous statements on homosexual acts are therefore not compatible with today's knowledge. Consequently, it is *"time for a fundamental revision of the doctrine"* on this topic, Hollerich continued. These statements - made in a widely publicized interview with the Catholic News Agency (KNA) - are among the clearest high-level appeals for reform. They show that even cardinals in key positions are prepared to critically question and change the centuries-old doctrinal structure in favor of a contemporary, people-oriented approach.

High-ranking dignitaries in various countries are increasingly recognizing the lived love and identity of queer people as part of the church's reality. Step by step, spaces are being created in which same-sex couples, with their promise of long-term and fidelity, *also experience church support* - be it in the context of intercessions, ceremonial rituals or in the form of a church wedding. The change with the corresponding expectations is in full swing, and the international voices mentioned give it a reform-oriented, hopeful face.

Those involved are also demanding that the church leadership takes responsibility for past injustices - such as hurtful statements and degrading dismissals - and actively takes steps towards healing reconciliation. In other words, it is about nothing less than implementing an *equality policy* within the church that brings queer people from the moral role of outsiders to the center of the inclusive church. The clergy therefore need queer-sensitive attention.

From an equality policy perspective, this change has been overdue for many years and decades. The structural problems are clear: as long as an institution teaches that the love of two men or women is of lesser value or even disordered, it manifests institutional homophobia and unequal treatment.

Modern theology and human sciences counter this with the fact that all people - whether queer or straight - are equally endowed with dignity and an identity intended by God. If the church wants to present itself credibly as an advocate of human dignity, it must overcome its own discriminatory attitude in a timely manner - this means "completely" and "fully", because "or not at all" is no longer an option and "just a little" would not be equal recognition.

Necessary steps towards this are recognizable: bishops are publicly distancing themselves from previous condemnations, celebrations for queer couples are made possible in practice in many countries, and initiatives such as the Synodal Path are setting the course for a renewed sexual morality. Artificial intelligence can quickly reformulate necessary passages into a positive, appreciative expression. A competition has arisen to see who can use *Deus Ex Machina* to extract the most passages that need to be changed and who can use artificial intelligence to publish the best alternative formulations.

The equal marriage of the couples is not the completion of the steps, but is seen as the first and essential step.

The clear identification of the problems and the growing support for reform are having an impact. More and more believers - whether ministers or laypeople - are standing up for a church that reaches out to all its children *without fear* or exclusion.

Effective and fully "queer-sensitive" pastoral care means that the Church no longer views same-sex oriented people as isolated cases, but as equal believers whose love and lives are just as blessed by God as those of all others. Not the long-standing debate, but the overdue decision to allow all couples to marry is an important step in this direction: towards a Catholic Church that accepts diversity as enrichment and now places the dignity of every person at the center in a documented way.

🕊️ Bishops' briefing

The Religious Policy Field examines the progressive recognition of homosexuality and the development of queer-sensitive pastoral care in the Catholic Church, particularly in Germany and other countries. It describes the historical conflict between traditional doctrine and reform-oriented efforts that led to the marginalization of queer people. The analyses highlight how prominent bishops are increasingly distancing themselves from discriminatory positions and advocating for an appreciative approach and the church's blessing and marriage of same-sex couples, which is underpinned by initiatives such as the German Synodal Path and international voices. It emphasizes that the lived love of same-sex couples is seen as God-given and for a comprehensive revision of church doctrine and full equality in order to overcome structural homophobia. Artificial intelligence helps laypeople to find and formulate new, more appreciative text passages and present them in written form.

💬 Didactic questions:

17 - What does "queer-sensitive pastoral care" mean in the Catholic Church?

Queer-sensitive pastoral care means pastoral care that consciously addresses the needs, experiences and identities of queer people (LGBTQIA+). It strives to overcome structural exclusion within the church and promote a culture of diversity. At the heart of this pastoral care is the recognition of the full dignity and equality of queer people as images of God and their full inclusion in the life of the church, including the sacraments and blessings of their relationships.

18 - Why is there tension between traditional teaching and progressive efforts regarding homosexuality in the Catholic Church?

The tensions arise because the official traditional doctrine still regards practised homosexuality as disordered and has not recognized or married same-sex partnerships for a long time. This is at odds with progressive reform efforts within the church, which are based on the commandment to love one's neighbor, the image of God in every human being and current human scientific findings. These efforts see lived love in a faithful relationship as ethically equal regardless of gender and call for a re-evaluation of church teachings.

19 - What concrete changes and initiatives signal an opening of the Catholic Church towards queer people?

Concrete changes and initiatives include the visibility and recognition of same-sex partnerships of church employees, public reform-oriented positions of prominent bishops (such as the demand for a revision of the catechism and the introduction of marriage ceremonies), as well as the introduction of commissioners for queer-sensitive pastoral care in dioceses. A central forum was the German Synodal Path, which passed resolutions to enable church celebrations for same-sex couples and called for a doctrinal reassessment of homosexuality. Internationally, high-ranking officials are also speaking out in favor of recognizing queer identities.

20 - How is love between people of the same sex justified theologically by reform-minded clergy?

Reform-oriented clergy justify their stance theologically with the commandment to love one's neighbor and the image of God in every human being. They argue that no clergyman wants to create and be a "case of harm" for same-sex couples - and that God wanted everyone to be this way. Bishops and "harm"-preventers such as Helmut therefore see homosexuality as "God-ordained to the same extent as creation itself" and therefore do not want to become discriminatory rhetoric perpetrators themselves. Accordingly, love between two men or two women cannot be something disordered, but is an expression of God's diversity of creation.

21 - What role do human scientific findings play in the debate about homosexuality in the Catholic Church?

Human scientific findings play an important role, as they show that sexual orientation is innate and cannot be changed at will. Reform-oriented voices in the church, such as Bishop Kohlgraf of Mainz, emphasize that the church must take these findings seriously and not treat biblical statements on homosexuality without context as the eternally valid word of God. These scientific findings support the call for a re-evaluation of church doctrine.

22 - What was the outcome of the Synodal Path regarding the blessing of same-sex couples?

The German Synodal Way passed an action text by a large majority that is intended to officially allow the blessing of homosexual couples. This resolution stipulates that dioceses should implement corresponding liturgical celebrations that also explicitly apply to same-sex couples. In future, bishops will not be allowed to prohibit priests from doing so.

23 - What criticism has been voiced about the decisions of the Synodal Path, especially with regard to blessings in comparison to marriage?

Critics see the resolutions of the Synodal Path, in particular the introduction of blessings instead of marriage ceremonies, as half-hearted and a form of further discrimination. They argue that it is not about separate blessing ceremonies, but about the right to marry on an equal footing. The demand is for full equality with the marriage ceremony and not just the "small hand" of the blessing. The distinction between blessing and marriage is seen as an attempt to separate and not to grant full equality.

24 - What demands do queer believers make of the Catholic Church for the future?

Queer believers demand a complete end to discrimination, marriage with sacraments on an equal footing with marriage, and full and equal participation in church life. They demand to be accepted as images of God without hiding and that no one is excluded from sacraments such as communion because of their sexual orientation. They also demand that the church leadership takes responsibility for past injustices and takes steps towards healing reconciliation in order to create a "queer-sensitive" and inclusive church that embraces diversity as an enrichment.

✍️ 💻 Essay questions:

Please answer one of the following questions in the form of an essay:

a) Discuss the tensions between traditional church teaching and progressive efforts in the Catholic Church regarding homosexuality and queer-sensitive pastoral care.

b) Analyze the theological and pastoral arguments that reform-minded bishops use to justify their positions on the acceptance and appreciation of same-sex relationships.

c) Evaluate the significance of the Synodal Path for the debate on sexual morality and discuss both the progress made and the criticism of decisions.

d) Discuss how the experiences and demands of queer believers affect change within the Catholic Church and what concrete steps are required to achieve full equality.

e) How can artificial intelligence suggest alternative, more appreciative text passages?

f) Compare the developments in Germany with international examples (e.g. Belgium, USA, Austria) and analyze which common or different approaches to the recognition of queer identities and relationships are recognizable in the Catholic Church worldwide.

📌 Religious policy field analysis 4:
Life protection and abortion from a Catholic perspective

In the Catholic Church, the *protection of life from conception to natural death* is considered a fundamental principle. Reform-oriented clergy also stand united behind the *rejection of abortion and assisted suicide*. They emphasize *that no human being has the right to dispose of life and death,* as life as a gift from God is unavailable and the dignity of every human being is inviolable.

Clear rejection of abortion and assisted suicide

The German bishop and chairman of the Conference of female, diverse and male Bishops, Georg Bätzing, made it clear that he and the Church *"emphatically* disagree *with the view [...] that the abortion of unborn children is a human right"*, as such a view does not do justice to the tragedy and complexity of real conflict situations. At the same time, these bishops emphasize *that the protection of unborn children and the protection of pregnant women are inextricably linked*: Only together with the mother can unborn life be effectively protected.

According to her, a strong *"lobby"* is therefore needed for unborn children *and* concrete offers of help and solidarity for expectant mothers in need.

Several bishops, including the more reform-oriented ones, also extend the concept of the protection of life to *social and societal issues*. They emphasize that advocating for life does not end with the unborn child, but also includes, for example, support for refugees, the sick and the socially disadvantaged.

Bishop Franz Jung reminds us that it is part of the kingdom of God *"to be an advocate for those who have no voice and to whom obvious injustice is done"* - this includes advocating *for people on the run as well as for unborn life and against assisted suicide.*

Similarly, the bishops warn against the normalization of euthanasia: Bishop Franz-Josef Bode, for example, emphasized that the freedom given to man by God does not extend so far as to include the right to dispose of one's own or another's life.

A *"yes to life"* must always have priority, and no person should die *"by the hand of another"*, but *"by the hand of another"*. Overall, the bishops therefore advocate a comprehensive approach to the protection of life, which includes *both a clear rejection of abortion and assisted suicide and* calls for *social responsibility* for all vulnerable phases of life.

Theologians: Self-determination, social environment and freedom of conscience

Progressive Catholic theologians and movements close to the Church welcome the cause of protecting life, but call for a *broader perspective* that takes greater account of *women's self-determination, social conditions and freedom of conscience*. In their view, an understanding of life protection that focuses solely on prohibitions without taking into account the reality of the lives of those affected falls short. Instead, *the protection of life* must be *understood as a holistic concept* that includes *social security for families, support for pregnant women in emergency situations and respect for individual decisions of conscience*. Critics argue that a woman can only say *"yes"* to life if she can rely on social support - e.. financial security, childcare and advice - and if *no social or economic constraints* force her into a corner. With this in mind, the President of the Central Committee of German Catholics, Irme Stetter-Karp, also emphasized that she *supports the protection of life and the existing abortion paragraph 218*, as this represents a hard won compromise that must be preserved. At the same time, she called for pregnancy conflict counseling to be open-ended and for no doctor to be forced to terminate a pregnancy *against their own conscience*. This position illustrates the progressive concern to guarantee *freedom of conscience* for all those involved: both doctors and women should be able to an ethically responsible decision *themselves* without pressure.

Some theologians, such as Elfriede Harth, go even further and make a fundamental appeal to the Catholic doctrine *of the primacy of conscience*. They remind us that, according to the Second Vatican

Council, the *individual's freedom of conscience* is *inviolable* and believers may even be obliged to follow their own conscience - even if its judgment differs from official church teaching!

Progressive voices deduce from this that there may be situations in which an abortion is considered morally responsible by the woman concerned after careful consideration of the circumstances. Reform Catholics emphasize that it is important not to condemn anyone across the board, but to take the *specific emergency situation* and the *personal decision-making process in the conflict* seriously.

The public debate also focused on the case of a doctor who wanted to provide factual information on her website about the fact that she offers abortions and performs them legally. The background to this was the controversial "advertising ban" under Section 219a of the German Criminal Code, which prohibits doctors from publicly announcing that they perform abortions. The doctor in question demanded the opportunity to inform women transparently and professionally about her medical services without having to fear criminal consequences. However, until the abolition of Section 219a of the German Criminal Code in 2022, she was legally prohibited from specifically referring to the provision of abortions on her website. This ban has been widely criticized as a massive restriction of both the freedom of medical information and the right of affected women to freely choose a doctor and obtain information.

In the clerical and religious debate, the Church should - instead of relying solely on the threat of punishment - increasingly advocate *making abortions superfluous through prevention and social support* - for example through better family policies, permitted contraception and comprehensive counseling.

Bishop Helmut Dieser (himself one of the conference bishops) said *that recommending contraceptives would strengthen the protection of life*, as unwanted pregnancies could be avoided; however, *"the morning-after pill and abortion"* remained taboo for him. This example shows the approach of understanding *responsible family planning* and *sex education* as part of life protection in order to avoid the tragic decision-making situations of abortion in the first place.

Overall, progressive Catholic voices advocate an *objective and solution-oriented approach to* the issue. Protecting life does not only mean defending unborn life, but also creating conditions *in which life can be welcomed.* This includes *protecting the dignity of the woman,* recognizing her autonomous decision in hopeless conflicts and the obligation of society to provide all necessary assistance so that saying *"yes to the child"* is not an excessive demand. The ethical challenge here is to reconcile *the Church's teaching tradition with the reality of personal life.* Progressive Catholics call on the Church to change its language and practice so that *compassion, mercy and respect for the judgment of conscience* set the tone - without questioning the fundamental value of every human life.

The synodal path: debates on the protection of life between doctrine and conscience

The Synodal Path - the reform dialog of the Catholic Church (2019-2023) - *did not* deal with the topic and religious policy area of abortion as a separate focus, but the question of life protection played an indirect role in the consultations. In the "Sexual Morality" forum in particular, it became clear that a renewal of church teaching always also touches on the question of *how to deal responsibly with the potential transmission of life.*

The concluding text of this forum stated that sexuality always entails the *possibility* of procreation - which is why *responsible sexual ethics explicitly cannot include abortion as a viable option.* Instead, the synodal text emphasizes *the willingness of partners to take responsibility for a child in the event of conception* and recommends prevention and support in order to avoid conflict situations. In doing so, the Synodal Path basically underlined the existing doctrine that abortion is not a legitimate solution and drew attention to *prevention and support* as a better alternative.

However, *different emphases* also emerged in the course of the Synodal Path, reflecting the areas of tension in the church. For example, statements by ZdK President Irme Stetter-Karp - also Co-President of the Synodal Path - caused controversial discussions. In a guest article, she called for a *"nationwide service"* for legal abortion to be guaranteed in Germany, as women in rural regions often cannot currently find medical care close to home. Although Stetter-Karp also *rejected any further liberalization of abortion law* and stood by the existing consultation compromise, critics accused her of crossing a *"red line"* by calling for better access.

Figure 19: My Body - My Choice.

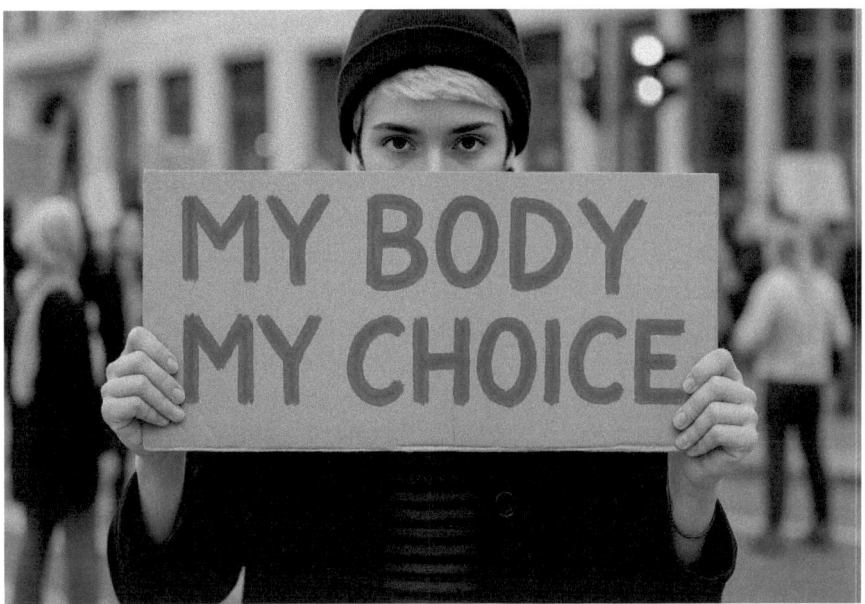

A young activist with short blonde hair stands in a busy city street holding a handmade cardboard sign with the words "MY BODY - MY CHOICE" in bold red letters. Her eyes look resolutely over the sign, expressing strength, determination and an opinion of her own. The background is blurred and shows a moving crowd with other protest signs - a lively atmosphere of social rebellion.

At the beginning of the fourth synodal assembly in 2022, Stetter-Karp defended her stance: she is *"in favor of protecting life and for paragraph 218 on abortion"*, but wants to ensure that *women in emergency situations actually* have *access to counseling and medical help*. She believes it is important to *protect doctors' freedom of conscience* (no compulsion to perform abortions) as well as *open-ended counseling* without paternalism. This differentiated position was supported by some of the synod members, but also met with opposition from some bishops. Bishop Georg Bätzing distanced himself from the formulation of a *comprehensive offer* in terms of content, but condemned the *"unbearable style"* of the heated debate. He made it clear that there was an *unresolvable disagreement* between the official position of the bishops and the opinion of the ZdK President - a disagreement that must continue to be endured in the Church and dealt with through dialog.

The Synodal Path has thus made the *ethical tensions* surrounding the protection of life and self-determination visible, without, however, resolving them definitively. On the one hand, the Catholic Church stands firmly by its principle of viewing *every abortion as morally problematic*; on the other hand, there is a growing awareness that *pastoral care and teaching* must be sensitive to *the concrete conflicts* of the faithful. The debates in the Synodal Forum show that *self-determination and the protection of life* should *not* be seen *as opposites*, but rather as a responsible balance. The Church struggles to assume *social responsibility* - by advocating the right to life and dignity - *and at the same time to take individuals and their conscience seriously.* The tone of this discussion is deliberately factual and balanced: it is not about softening the appreciation of unborn life, but about *broadening the perspective* so that the protection of life is not seen in isolation, but in the context of justice, mercy and freedom. The result is an appeal both to uphold *the doctrine of the inviolable value of every life* and to accept *the challenges of modern life realities.* Only with this holistic approach - according to the tenor of many participants - can the protection of life be convincingly communicated in the 21st century, in a way that does justice to *both the Gospel and the justified demands of women and families.*

It therefore remains to be said: The Catholic perspective on the topic of life protection and abortion attempts to walk a *fine line - between clearly upholding the Church's ethics of life* and keeping an open ear to the issues of *self-determination and social responsibility* in today's society. This creates tensions, but also offers the opportunity for an in-depth dialog that can serve the *protection of life in all its dimensions.*

Bishops' briefing:

The religious policy analysis looks at the Catholic perspective on the protection of life and abortion. It shows that even reform-oriented bishops and theologians uphold the fundamental principle of life protection, but differ in their approach. While the bishops clearly reject abortion and assisted suicide, other voices also emphasize the importance of women's self-determination, social support and freedom of conscience. The analyses also shed light on the debates within the Synodal Way, which highlight the tension between church teaching and the real life situations of the faithful. Overall, the challenge of reconciling the Church's ethics of life with the issues of self-determination and social responsibility is described.

Didactic questions:

24 - What is the fundamental principle of the protection of life from a Catholic perspective?

From a Catholic perspective, the protection of life from conception to natural death is a fundamentally important principle. Life is seen as a gift from God that cannot be disposed of, and the dignity of every human being is inviolable. This means that no human being has the right to dispose of life and death, which includes the rejection of abortion and assisted suicide.

25 - What is the position of Catholic bishops on abortion and assisted suicide?

Even reform-minded bishops stand united behind the rejection of abortion and assisted suicide. They emphatically emphasize that abortion is not a human right and that the God-given freedom of man does not extend so far as to dispose of one's own or another's life. They advocate a "yes to life" and emphasize that no one should die "by the hand of another", but "at the hand of another".

26 - How do the bishops understand the term "protection of life" beyond the rejection of abortion and assisted suicide?

The bishops extend the concept of protecting life to social and societal issues. They emphasize that the commitment to life does not end with the unborn child, but also includes support for refugees, the sick and the socially disadvantaged. They understand the protection of life as a comprehensive concept that demands social responsibility for all endangered phases of life and includes standing up for the voice of the weak.

27 - What demands do Catholic theologians and reform movements make with regard to the protection of life?

Progressive theologians and reform movements welcome the cause of protecting life, but demand a broader perspective. This should take greater account of women's self-determination, social conditions and freedom of conscience. They argue that the protection of life must be understood as a holistic concept that does not rely solely on prohibitions, but also includes social security, support for pregnant women in emergency situations and respect for individual decisions of conscience.

28 - What role does freedom of conscience play in the debate on abortion from a progressive Catholic perspective?

From a progressive Catholic perspective, freedom of conscience plays a central role. With reference to the Catholic doctrine of the primacy of conscience, it is argued that there may be situations in which an abortion is considered morally responsible by the woman concerned after careful consideration of the circumstances. It is emphasized that no one should be condemned across the board and that the specific emergency situation and the personal decision-making process in the conflict should be taken seriously. The freedom of conscience not to perform an abortion is also demanded for doctors.

29 - How was the topic of life protection dealt with as part of the Synodal Path?

The Synodal Path did not deal with the topic of abortion as a separate focus, but the topic of life protection played an indirect role. In the "Sexual Morality" forum in particular, it became clear that responsible sexual ethics cannot include abortion as a viable option. The synod text emphasized the willingness to take responsibility for a child and recommended prevention and support. However, different emphases and areas of tension also emerged in the course of the Synodal Path, for example in the debate on the demand for a nationwide offer of legal abortion.

30 - What tensions and challenges arise from the Catholic perspective on the protection of life and abortion in today's society?

The Catholic perspective attempts to walk a fine line between upholding the Church's ethic of life and being open to questions of self-determination and social responsibility. This creates tensions between the clear rejection of abortion and the recognition of women's predicaments and conscience decisions. The challenge is to communicate the Church's teaching tradition and the personal realities of life, to show compassion and mercy to without questioning the fundamental value of every human life.

31 - What is the conclusion of many stakeholders regarding a holistic approach to the protection of life in the 21st century?

Many of those involved are of the opinion that convincing life protection in the 21st century requires a holistic approach. This means upholding the doctrine of the inviolable value of every life as well as accepting the challenges of modern life realities. The protection of life should not be seen in isolation, but in the context of justice, mercy and freedom. The aim is to serve the protection of life in all its dimensions and to do justice both to the Gospel and to the justified demands of women and families.

 Essay questions:

Please answer one of the following questions in the form of an essay:

a) Explain the different emphases and tensions between the official position of the bishops and the views of theologians in the context of the protection of life and abortion.

b) Discuss how the bishops' concept of "comprehensive protection of life" goes beyond the rejection of abortion and assisted suicide. Which social and societal areas are included here?

c) Analyze the significance of freedom of conscience in the debate on abortion from a Catholic perspective, especially with regard to the arguments of progressive theologians and the demands of the Synodal Path.

d) Evaluate the role of the Synodal Path in making visible the ethical challenges and areas of tension surrounding the protection of life and self-determination in the Catholic Church.

e) Discuss how the Catholic Church is attempting to develop a "holistic approach" to the protection of life in the 21st century that takes into account both doctrine and the modern realities of life.

📌 Religious policy field analysis 5: *Ordination of women in the Catholic Church: majority in favor of opening ministries to women*

As part of the *Synodal Path,* a broad majority in Germany has spoken out in favor of gender equality in church ministries. At the plenary assembly in March 2023, 93.6% of the synod members (including over 80% of the bishops) voted in favor of a reform paper that would *give women access to ordained ministries*.

In this resolution, the Conference of female, diverse and male Bishops is instructed to lobby Rome for the *admission of women*. In addition, considerations for an opening of *all* ordained ministries in the universal church are to be introduced. *Will we soon have a female pope?*

In other words, the majority of synod members called for a critical review of previous doctrinal statements that exclude women from the office of deacon and priest. This clear vote - greeted by prolonged applause - underlines that the issue of women's ordination is on the verge of a breakthrough for the church. It is no longer seen as closed, but as an *open issue* that needs to be discussed anew in the light of equality and credibility and must now finally be decided.

Bishops ready to shape the future and their positions

Several influential bishops explicitly support this reform course or are at least open to changing the current practice. The chairman of the German Conference of female, diverse and male Bishops, *Georg Bätzing*, has repeatedly emphasized that he considers the *diaconate of women to be "very legitimate"*. Although Pope John Paul II formally ruled out the ordination of women to the priesthood more than 30 years ago, the conference stated*: "The discussion is simply there"* - it cannot be stifled by referring to Rome. It is generally criticized that women are excluded from ordained ministries, and a plea is made to keep this possibility open.

Peter Kohlgraf, Bishop of Mainz, takes a similar stance. He explains that he is *"often not convinced"* by the Roman objections to the ordination of women. *"Rome has decided and that's why we no longer talk about it"* is no longer a viable argument today. Kohlgraf promised activists from the *Maria 2.0* reform movement to pass on their lack of understanding about the ban on ordaining women to the Vatican - he is "looking in the same direction" as the committed women who are calling for change and equal rights.

Franz-Josef Bode, Bishop of Osnabrück until 2023 and long-standing Vice-Chairman of the Conference of female, diverse and male Bishops, was regarded as a pioneer for the empowerment of women in ministries. As early as 2018, Bode suggested taking a closer look at the *diaconate for women*. In 2019, he said that he could even imagine women *leading Eucharistic celebrations* in his diocese at some point - even if this is not (yet) permitted according to current doctrine. Bode emphasized that he wanted to *"make the most of everything that is possible for women now and in the near future."* His fundamental support for the concerns of the Synodal Path and equal rights for women in the Church is clearly evident.

Other diocesan bishops are similarly progressive. *Heiner Wilmer* (Hildesheim) expressly wishes for *"an open culture of discussion"* on the ordination of women. It is no longer enough to simply claim that this issue is finally settled. *Helmut Dieser* (Aachen) also questions the finality of the ban on ordination: he describes the issue as *"burning"* and emphasizes that the Church can no longer leave it up to men alone to decide on their path.

Synodality means that all believers - women as well as men - must participate in deliberations and decisions. He sees the church in a field of tension here with modern society and speaks of a *"thorny"* problem, precisely because the emancipation of women is well advanced today. But it is precisely here that he sees a mission for the church: the deep longing of many women for *recognition, equality and equal dignity* should no longer be ignored.

Figure 20: Maria 2.0 demands equality.

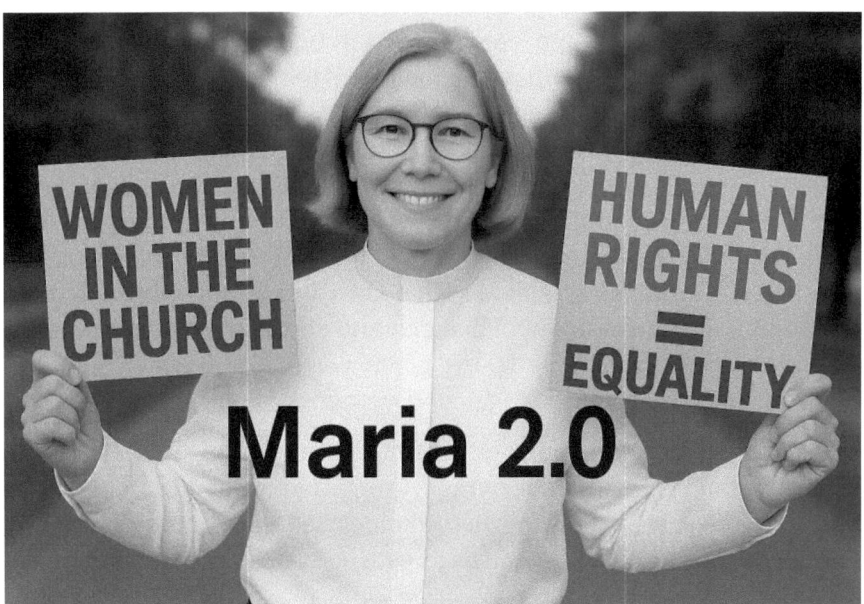

An expressive and realistic portrait of a friendly, smiling, self-confident middle-aged woman with glasses, symbolizing the Catholic reform movement Maria 2.0. She is wearing a simple white garment reminiscent of liturgical clothing. She demonstratively holds up two signs with both hands: one reads 'WOMEN IN THE CHURCH' in large letters, the other 'HUMAN RIGHTS = EQUALITY'. The words 'Maria 2.0' are clearly visible in front of her. The background is natural and blurred, which clearly focuses on the person and her message. The scene conveys a strong message of equality, women's rights and church reform.

Franz Jung (Würzburg) is also one of those in favor of an opening. He said in 2022 that he could imagine the *ordination of women to the priesthood*. For Jung, the final decision depends on the universal church - he hoped that the topic would be taken up at the Roman Synod of Bishops - but he already notes a *"relatively broad consensus"* in favor of women in clerical positions within the German Conference of female, diverse and male Bishops. This assessment is in line with the fact that even many otherwise reserved bishops see the topic of deacons in a positive light. Finally, *Karl-Heinz Wiesemann* (Speyer) has also positioned himself very clearly: He calls for a *re-evaluation of the church's arguments against the ordination of women* and calls the theological justification for the exclusion of women from the priesthood *"already very narrow"*. Wiesemann warns that the Church is losing a *"whole generation of young, committed and competent women"* who feel excluded and simply can no longer understand the previous justifications. In his opinion, the admission of female deacons would be an important signal "that there is movement" - a first step that would show that the church is willing to make new experiences. The core of his statement is a *plea for equal rights*: If in Christianity all are one in Christ and "it no longer matters whether one is a man or a woman" (cf. Gal 3:28), then it is hard to see why women should remain excluded from the church's ordained ministries. This view - once marginal - is now shared by a growing number of bishops and shows the extent to which a change of perspective is taking place within the German church. Today, no one can speak out against a woman as pope.

Even though Pope Francis said no to the idea at the time, Cardinal Reinhard Marx (Munich), for example, emphasizes that *"people are still discussing it"* and expresses his confidence: He is convinced that women will one day be ordained as priests and popes - *"That will come,"* says Marx.

Feminist theology and church reform initiatives

The dynamics of the debate are not only being driven by church leaders, but also to a large extent by the grassroots and *feminist theology*. Progressive theologians have been arguing for years that there are no compelling reasons in the Bible and tradition to keep women out of the sacramental ministry. They point to the *equal baptismal dignity* of all people and to the early church example of female deacons. In their view, the ban on ordination contradicts fundamental principles of justice and equality. Especially in an age in which equality is a social consensus, the categorical exclusion of women from the priesthood or deaconate seems less and less credible. Instead, the demand for the full participation of women in the church is seen as a *"sign of the times"* - as an impulse from the Holy Spirit that the church must take seriously.

Bishop Wiesemann, for example, emphasizes (in astonishing unanimity with feminist voices) that it is about *plausibility and credibility*: the church must be able to explain why it teaches the spiritual equality of all believers on the one hand, but denies women certain ministries on the other. If this explanation fails to materialize, there is a risk of a loss of trust, especially among the younger generation.

At the same time, *reform movements such as Maria 2.0* are exerting pressure with creative forms of protest. Maria 2.0, initiated in 2019 by committed Catholic women, began with a highly publicized week-long *church strike*: women resigned from voluntary services and stayed away from church services to protest against a male-dominated church. Their central concern is a *church in which women have access to all ministries.* The activists demand, among other things, that women can be ordained as priests and are not denied the office of pope, and complain that the church's power structure is patriarchal and unjust.

With public campaigns - from the symbolic "locking down" of bishop's sees to prayer initiatives in front of cathedrals - Maria 2.0 is keeping the issue in the headlines and highlighting the pressure for reform from the faithful. This movement is not only based on arguments within the church, but also on *human rights and equality*. For example, the initiators used petitions to draw attention to the fact that the Vatican still does not recognize some of the equality principles of the UN Charter of Human Rights, which they believe is incompatible with the Christian view of humanity. Maria 2.0 thus lends *a loud, social voice* to the theological demand for equal rights. Her motto is: *The church must renew itself so that the message of Jesus - which applies to all people without exception - can be lived out in a credible way*. Many of their demands - from the ordination of women to public office to more transparent control of power - were taken up by the Synodal Way. Some observers even stated that *"what some bishops are now saying could have come from us"*, which shows how much grassroots initiatives and reform-oriented church leaders now resonate.

Overall, a clear *reform dynamic is* emerging in terms of women's ordination. Arguing from the perspective of equality and renewal, believers and church representatives alike are pushing for women to be allowed to participate *in sacramental ministry on an equal footing*. However, this development is not taking place in isolation: it is in tension with the course of the global church. In spring 2024, for example, it caused irritation when Pope Francis again denied in an interview that women could ever be deacons in persona Christi - *a denial that was met with a clear lack of understanding.* Würzburg's Bishop Jung publicly asked why there were papal study commissions on the topic at all *"if it had obviously been decided".* This episode illustrates the discrepancy: there is a growing expectation that the Church will move, while restraint continues to come from Rome. Nevertheless, the debate has long since reached the heart of the Church in this country - from *the synodal vote* to *bishops with the will to shape things* and committed laypeople. From the proponents' point of view, nothing less than the future viability of the church is at stake: a credible, just church, they argue, cannot exclude half of the faithful from the ministries in the long term. How and when this question will ultimately be decided remains to be seen. But the *state of the debate* shows: The call for women's ordination is getting louder and louder and is finding increasingly prominent supporters.

The view of the universal church

In the global church, high-ranking bishops and cardinals are also increasingly voicing their support for opening up the ordained ministries to women. Luxembourg Cardinal *Jean-Claude Hollerich*, for example, believes that women should be admitted to the diaconate and priesthood in principle. The papal ban on the ordination of women is *"probably"* not an infallible teaching - *"in time"* a new pope - a new female pope - may decide this question differently.

Among the global conferences of bishops, Belgium in particular is playing a pioneering role. The *entire* Belgian bishops unanimously voted in favor of admitting women in 2022. During their ad limina visit to Rome, they stated that *women should be allowed to be ordained as deacons.* The call for women's ordination is also unmistakable in the global synodal process of the church. At the most recent World Synod in Rome, *numerous bishops made a strong* plea *for the ministry to be opened up* to women - even two African archbishops, who are considered to be rather conservative, signaled that they would support the admission of women as deacons if the Pope so decided. These positive voices from different cultural circles - from Europe to Latin America and Africa - show that the demand for the ordination of women is no longer an isolated European phenomenon, but is gaining weight worldwide. They are also reacting to the German reform debate: the overwhelming vote of the Synodal Way for women in ordained ministries has resonated internationally and encouraged many church leaders to keep the issue *open* and see it as a "burning" question for the future of the church. The churches simply do not have and are not gaining any more personnel to continue to exclude women. In a few years, even a pope will have to decide differently.

Until then, there is a growing consensus among reform-oriented bishops that the question of women's ordination cannot be considered closed, but must be discussed and decided anew in the light of equality and credibility.

The dynamic has been set in motion - and it signals that the topic of equality in the church is no longer a niche issue, but has become a *central reform issue* not only of our time, but also of the content of teachings on equality and church personnel structures.

🕊 Bishops' briefing:

The religious policy area deals with the long-standing debate on the ordination of women in the Catholic Church, with a broad majority of the Synodal Way in favor of opening up ordained ministries to women. It is emphasized that influential bishops support this reform course and critically question previous doctrinal statements. In addition to the positions of the bishops, the influence of feminist theology and reform movements such as Maria 2.0, which exert pressure through protest campaigns, is also presented. This also shows that the demand for women's ordination is not just a European issue, but a global one, which is also viewed positively by prominent church representatives in other countries, although there are tensions with the position of men in the Vatican. Overall, the analysis illustrates a clear reform dynamic and the growing conviction that the equal participation of women is crucial for the future viability and credibility of the church and can no longer be ruled out.

Didactic questions:

32 - What is the Synodal Way and what is its position on women's ordination?

The Synodal Path is an internal church reform process. In March 2023, a broad majority of participants, including a clear majority of clergy, voted in favor of giving women access to ordained ministries in the Catholic Church. Specifically, a reform paper instructed the German Conference of female, diverse and male Bishops to advocate for this opening in Rome and to bring these considerations to the attention of the universal church. This means that the majority of German synod members are calling for a critical review of previous doctrinal statements that exclude women from the office of deacon and priest. This vote is seen as a sign that the issue of women's ordination is no longer regarded as closed, but as an open topic for the next pope.

33 - Which leading bishops support the opening of ministries to women and on what grounds?

Several influential bishops are in favor of the reform course or are at least open to a change. Georg Bätzing, Chairman of the German Conference of female, diverse and male Bishops, considers the diaconate of women to be "very legitimate" and emphasizes that the discussion cannot be stifled by referring to Rome. He generally criticizes the exclusion of women from ordained ministries. Peter Kohlgraf, Bishop of Mainz, is "often not convinced" by Rome's objections to the ordination of women and considers the argument that an issue has been decided in Rome to be no longer viable. Franz-Josef Bode, former Bishop of Osnabrück, was considered a pioneer at and could imagine women leading Eucharistic celebrations in his diocese, even if this was not currently permitted. He wanted to "exploit everything that is possible for women now and in the near future." Heiner Wilmer (Hildesheim) would like to see an "open culture of discussion" on the ordination of women. Helmut Dieser (Aachen) questions the finality of the ban on ordination and emphasizes that the Church should not leave decision-making to men alone; synodality means the participation of all believers. He sees the advanced emancipation of women as a mandate for the church to take the longing for recognition and equality seriously.

Franz Jung (Würzburg) can imagine the ordination of women to the priesthood and sees a "relatively broad consensus" within the German Conference of female, diverse and male Bishops in favor of the diaconate for women. Karl-Heinz Wiesemann (Speyer) calls for a re-evaluation of the church's arguments and calls the theological justification for the exclusion of women from the priesthood "very narrow". He warns of the loss of an entire generation of committed women and sees the admission of female deacons as an important signal of the movement and openness to new experiences. He pleads for equal rights in the sense of Galatians 3:28.

34 - What role do feminist theology and church reform initiatives play in the debate on women's ordination?

The debate is also largely driven by grassroots and feminist theology. Progressive theologians argue that the Bible and tradition do not provide any compelling reasons for excluding women from the sacramental ministry. They point to the equal baptismal dignity of all people and the example of early church deacons. In their view, the ban on ordination contradicts principles of justice and equality. Particularly in view of the social consensus on equality, the exclusion of women from the ministry seems increasingly implausible. The demand for full participation is seen as a "sign of the times" and an impulse from the Holy Spirit, which the church must take seriously. Feminist theologians emphasize that the church must be able to explain why it teaches the spiritual equality of all, but denies women certain ministries - in order not to lose credibility and trust, especially among the younger generation.

35 - What is the "Maria 2.0" movement and what are its goals?

Maria 2.0 is a reform movement that was initiated in 2019 by committed Catholic women. It began with a week-long church strike in which women resigned from voluntary work and stayed away from church services to protest against a male-dominated church. Their central concern is a church in which women have access to all ministries. Among other things, the activists are calling for women to be ordained as priests and criticize the church's power structure as patriarchal and unjust. They are keeping the issue in the headlines with public actions such as symbolic "blocking off" of bishop's offices and highlighting the pressure for reform from the faithful. Maria 2.0 is not only relying on arguments within the church, but also on human rights and equality, pointing out that the Vatican does not recognize some UN equality principles, which in their view is incompatible with the Christian view of humanity. Her motto is that the church must renew itself in order to live the message of Jesus credibly.

36 - How does the Church's position on women's ordination relate to the global context and the Vatican's position?

The development of women's ordination within Germany is in conflict with the course of the global church. While there is strong momentum for the opening up of ministries, there has recently been more restraint from Rome. For example, Pope Francis' statement in spring 2024 that women could not be deacons in persona Christi caused irritation, as it called into question the existence of papal study commissions on the subject. This episode illustrates the discrepancy between the growing expectation for change and the current attitude from Rome.

37 - Are there also voices in the universal church that speak out in favor of women's ordination?

Yes, high-ranking bishops and cardinals in the universal church are also increasingly speaking out in favor of opening up ordained ministries to women. The Luxembourg Cardinal Jean-Claude Hollerich considers the admission of women to the diaconate and priesthood to be possible in principle and believes that the papal ban is probably not an infallible teaching, meaning that a pope could decide the issue differently "over time". In 2022, the Belgian Conference of female, diverse and male Bishops unanimously voted in favor of admitting women to the diaconate. The call for women's ordination has also become loud in the global synodal process of the Church; at the most recent World Synod, numerous bishops pleaded for it, and even some African archbishops, who are considered rather conservative, signaled their approval of allowing women to become deacons, should the Pope decide to do so. These voices from different cultures show that the demand for the ordination of women is not a purely European phenomenon, but is gaining weight worldwide and is seen as a "burning" issue for the future of the Church.

38 - What are the main arguments for opening up ordained ministries to women?

Central arguments in favor of opening up ordained ministries to women include the demand for more gender justice and equality within the church. It is argued that the exclusion of women from certain ministries contradicts the dignity and equality of all baptized persons. The appeal to the equal baptismal dignity and the early church example of female deacons are important theological arguments. Furthermore, the credibility of the church is called into question if it teaches spiritual equality on the one hand, but excludes women from ministries on the other - especially in a society in which equality is the consensus. Supporters see the full participation of women as a "sign of the times" and a necessity for the future viability of the church. The exclusion of an "entire generation of young, committed and competent women" is seen as a loss, as they can no longer understand the previous justifications. The biblical principle that in Christ "it no longer matters whether one is male or female" (Gal 3:28) is cited as an argument for the incompatibility of the exclusion of women from ordained ministries with Christian teaching.

39 - Why is the question of women's ordination so important for the future of the Catholic Church?

The issue of women's ordination is seen as crucial for the future of the Catholic Church, as it is closely linked to credibility, justice and relevance. The broad consensus in the Synodal Path and the support of many bishops show that the issue has reached the center of the Church. The exclusion of women from ordained ministries is no longer considered plausible and unjust by many, especially by the younger generation and committed women. The call for full participation of women is seen as necessary to keep the church credible and to do justice to the claim of equality of all baptized persons. Failure to reform on this issue risks losing believers and weakening the relevance of the church in a modern society. Proponents argue that a sustainable church cannot afford to exclude half of its members from important ministries in the long term.

Essay questions:

Please answer one of the following questions in the form of an essay:

a) Discuss the various arguments put forward by reform-minded German bishops in support of women's ordination.

f) Explain the role of the Maria 2.0 movement and feminist theology in the German debate on women's ordination. How do they influence the church discussion?

b) Analyze the tension between the debate and the Vatican's stance on women's ordination. What factors contribute to this discrepancy?

c) Evaluate the significance of the demand for women's ordination in the context of equality, credibility and the future viability of the church as presented in the text.

d) Compare the development of the debate with positive developments and voices in the world church. What common denominators and differences are there?

📌 Religious policy field analysis 6: Through the marriage ceremony: equal recognition for same-sex couples in the Catholic Church

The debate surrounding the *marriage and blessing of same-sex couples in* the Catholic Church has gained momentum. Progressive forces in particular are calling for a change in equality policy: Homosexual partnerships should receive the same respect and rights in church as heterosexual ones. *It is about the church blessing and marriage of all couples.*

While the official Catholic magisterium has so far ruled out same-sex marriages, many German bishops, theologians and reform initiatives are calling for change - with the aim of achieving complete equality in canon law and liturgical practice.

Reform positions of progressive clergymembers

Several bishops have recently spoken out openly in favor of *church celebrations for homosexual couples* and a further development of church doctrine. *Georg Bätzing*, the chairman of the German Conference of female, diverse and male Bishops, for example, emphasized: *"I want us to give them God's blessing"* - he no longer wanted to exclude homosexual couples from church blessings. Bätzing hoped that this would be possible as part of the *Synodal Path* reform process in order to show that something is moving in the church.

Franz-Josef Bode, Bishop of Osnabrück until 2023, was also one of the pioneers of this discussion. As early as 2018, he suggested that the *blessing of same-sex partnerships* should no longer be taboo. He pointed out that *"marriage for all"* under civil law has long been a reality - the church must therefore consider *"how we meet those who enter into this union... How do we do justice to them?"*. This concern for justice shows the *core of equality policy*: it is about treating homosexual couples equally and granting them ecclesiastical recognition.

Other bishops such as *Peter Kohlgraf* (Mainz), *Helmut Dieser* (Aachen), *Heiner Wilmer* (Hildesheim), *Franz Jung* (Würzburg) and *Karl-Heinz Wiesemann* (Speyer) are also backing calls for reform. Kohlgraf criticized a purely literal interpretation of the Bible in questions of homosexuality - one cannot simply treat *"half sentences from the Bible"* without historical context as eternally valid.

Instead, the church must take the findings of the human sciences seriously and *not* suppress discussions with *"authoritarian decisions"*. Bishop Helmut Dieser even went so far as to say that he has learned something new and sees homosexuality as *"God-given to the same extent as creation itself"*. Consequently, he is in favor of gay and lesbian couples being officially blessed. These statements show that, in the opinion of these churchmen, a *further development of sexual morality* is necessary - away from condemnation and towards appreciation and equal treatment. *Bishop Wiesemann* from Speyer has already initiated this change in practice: In a letter, he explicitly encouraged his pastors to bless homosexual and remarried couples without fear of sanctions.

It is "urgently time" to find a new attitude inspired by the Gospel. Wiesemann emphasized that he had campaigned for a re-evaluation of homosexuality in doctrine during the Synodal Path and *voted in favour of celebrations for same-sex couples - "I stand by that"*.

Cardinal Reinhard Marx (Munich) - himself a member of the Pope's Council of Cardinals - had previously emphasized at the anniversary of the Munich *"Queer Services"*: *"Homosexuality is not a sin. It corresponds to a Christian attitude when two people, regardless of gender, stand up for each other..."*. He apologized for the church's discrimination and explained that the catechism was "not carved in stone". Marx pleaded for an *"inclusive church"* in which LGBTQIA+ people are recognized as *"part of creation and loved by God"* . In an interview, he emphasized that the love of two people shows its value in "not making the other an object" - and asked provocatively: When same-sex couples live together in "intimate love relationships", "and we want to say that this is worth nothing?". Cardinal Marx thus points the way to a new understanding that *also* sees *their love as desired by God*.

This broad front of the aforementioned bishops makes it clear that there is a *will for equality* in parts of the German church leadership.

Progressive theologians and church critics call for full equality

Progressive theologians and groups critical of the church are going one step further. They demand *full equality for* homosexual couples in the church - *including access to all sacraments*, especially the sacrament of marriage. In their view, a mere blessing ceremony is not enough as long as same-sex couples continue to be excluded from the actual church wedding ceremony. Swiss theologian *Pierre Stutz*, for example, argued: *"Some bishops are currently discussing a blessing ceremony for gays and lesbians. That is by no means enough. I call for the sacrament of marriage for all."*

This quote sums up the attitude of many reform advocates - instead of merely tolerating the blessing of homosexual couples, they should be allowed to *marry in church just like heterosexual couples.*

Reform initiatives and associations within the church are also exerting pressure. The *#OutInChurch* movement - an association of over a hundred queer church employees - and groups such as *We are Church* and the *Central Committee of German Catholics (ZdK)* are campaigning for the removal of discriminatory exclusions. They argue that love, fidelity and care are the same values regardless of the gender of the partner. If two people live together in a committed partnership, this relationship deserves the same respect from a church perspective. Anything else is *unequal treatment based on sexual orientation* - i.e. ultimately discrimination. Progressive Catholic ethicists such as the moral theologian *Eberhard Schockenhoff* had already previously emphasized that the classic condemnation of homosexual acts was theologically untenable and pastorally disastrous. Many theologians now recognize that homosexual partnerships *"live love every day"* and morally contain *"much that is positive, good and right".*

Eberhard Schockenhoff (1953-2020) was a German Catholic priest, moral theologian and ethicist. He was considered one of the most important and influential Catholic moral theologians. Schockenhoff was Professor of Moral Theology at the Albert Ludwig University of Freiburg. He became particularly well known for his clear, reform-oriented stance in ethical and ecclesiastical debates. He publicly advocated a more liberal sexual morality, a re-evaluation of homosexual partnerships, a more tolerant attitude towards remarried divorcees and a comprehensive reform within the Catholic Church. From 2001 to 2016, he was a member of the German Ethics Council and its predecessor organization and was often in demand as an expert on ethical and bioethical issues. His positions and publications were widely recognized and influenced numerous current church policy discussions.

According to the critics, it is therefore important to finally *depatologize* the church's sexual morality: Homosexuality is a God-ordained variation of human love; it is neither a sin nor a disease. The conclusion from this is clear - *complete equality* and the opening of all church offices and sacramental acts to LGBTQIA+ people and couples.

Resolutions of the Synodal Path to Equality

The *Synodal Path* as a church reform process only partially addressed these demands. Particularly in the area of sexuality and partnership, the Synodal Assembly passed inadequate resolutions because they were only aimed at *greater recognition of same-sex couples*, but not at a respectful appreciation through a corresponding equality that begins with the sacramental marriage ceremony. In March 2023, the assembly voted overwhelmingly in favor of *officially allowing celebrations for homosexual couples* - 93% of the synod members and even 81% of the bishops present supported this. In future, it should therefore be possible in German dioceses for same-sex (as well as civilly divorced and remarried) couples to *receive a public blessing from the church* without priests having to reckon with disciplinary consequences. The opposite, that they are praised for every gay marriage and receive a bonus in their personal target agreement, has not yet been achieved. The organizational control of the Catholic Church through praise is still a long way from the previous control by threatening staff with existential fears. At least this creates an initial climate of acceptance: pastors are encouraged to accompany loving couples to the marriage ceremony with a clear conscience instead of only blessing them "unofficially" in secret. It should be noted that the donors of the blessing experience acceptance within their own ranks.

The reasoning behind the synodal resolution is clearly couched in the language of *equality* for the recipients of acceptance: A refusal to bless the relationship of two people *"who want to live their partnership in love, commitment and responsibility to each other and to God"* is *"merciless to the point of being discriminatory"*. Such clear words show that the synod members felt that the church's previous categorical "no" to the practices of its personnel was unjust.

After all, even for the recipients of the blessing, it is *"not convincing theologically in terms of grace"* why God should refuse to bless a homosexual couple. In addition to the introduction of blessings, the Synodal Path also adopted a paper on the *re-evaluation of homosexuality* in Catholic doctrine. It states that the Church must admit that its teachings have caused suffering to homosexual people and that *"homosexuality is not a disease"*. Furthermore, no one should be denied ordained ministries or the assumption of church services on the basis of their sexual orientation.

The next step on the way to becoming an openly lesbian pope?

Although these resolutions of the Synodal Path do not (yet) have the character of binding legislation for the universal church, they demonstrate a *willingness to reform that is capable of consensus* in large parts of the church. They are a clear signal to Rome that, in the view of many Catholics, the time is ripe *for the Church to open up to homosexual believers* - in church weddings, liturgy, teaching and everyday church life.

Ways to a church wedding with equal rights for homosexual couples

Despite all the progress made with blessing ceremonies, the *actual church wedding* (the sacrament of marriage) has so far remained out of communication for same-sex couples. *From an equality policy perspective*, however, there should be *no legitimate difference* to the marriage of heterosexual couples - and it should not take any more years. How could a truly *equal church wedding ceremony* for homosexual couples be implemented? First of all, there would need to be a *change in the church's understanding of marriage*: officially, the Catholic Church defines marriage as a union between a man and a woman. This understanding would have to be further developed theologically in order to open up sacramental marriage to two men or two women. In the long term, this would presumably require a decision by the universal Church - for example, by a papal decree or a synod or council that expands the existing doctrine. However, many theologians are already arguing that such an opening is possible at any time without violating the essence of marriage. After all, although the Church requires heterosexual couples to be open to having children as a matter of principle, unwanted childless couples or older couples who are unable to have children are also allowed to marry validly. *Procreation is therefore in fact not an absolute criterion* for admission to marriage. So why should a loving, permanently faithful couple of the same sex be excluded from the outset? The *essential marriage consensus* - a mutual promise of lifelong fidelity, support and love before God - can also be given by homosexual partners. From a secular and ecclesiastical equality perspective, there is no factual or logical reason to deny them this covenant.

Worldwide observance of marriage ceremonies for same-sex couples

In the Catholic world, high-ranking voices are increasingly speaking out in favor of church weddings for same-sex couples. The outcry in Belgium was particularly impressive: Johan Bonny, Bishop of Antwerp, reacted to the Roman ban on blessings for homosexual couples in 2021 with clear words. He felt "shame for his church" and great incomprehension in the face of the Vatican's rejection. In a public post, Bonny expressly asked those involved to apologize "for all those for whom this is painful and incomprehensible". His indignation culminated in an appeal to finally end the exclusion of same-sex lovers: "...and that is why we Belgian bishops say: *'Enough is enough!"*

This stance was not an isolated call: the entire Belgian-Flemish Conference of female, diverse and male Bishops - headed by Brussels Cardinal *Jozef De Kesel* - supported Bonny's criticism and took concrete steps. In September 2022, the Flemish bishops published guidelines for liturgical celebrations for homosexual couples. The Flemish bishops thus took on a pioneering role worldwide and showed that an *inclusive liturgy* is possible within the Catholic framework.

Other church leaders around the world are expressing the same sentiment. The Luxembourg Cardinal *Jean-Claude Hollerich*, appointed General Relator of the World Synod by the Pope, has repeatedly called for a rethink. "If we [homosexuals] say that *everything* they do is *wrong in itself*, then it is as if we were saying *that life has no value,*" Hollerich warned - and it also applies to older couples who are unable to conceive after menopause. He himself finds the part of the doctrine that describes homosexual acts as *"intrinsically wrong"* "dubious". It is "crude" to reduce same-sex feelings and love to sexual acts alone. Instead, homosexual people should *"feel at home"* in the church. In an interview with *La Stampa*, Hollerich was open to church celebrations for same-sex couples and said that the church could change its attitude - it just had to be prepared to *"open* its doors *to everyone"*. Such signals are also coming from overseas: US Cardinal *Robert McElroy* (San Diego) argued for a *"radical inclusion"* of LGBTQIA+ people in a programmatic essay in early 2023. He questions the exclusion of them from central sacraments and argues that faithful homosexual couples should *not be kept from the Eucharist*. McElroy emphasizes the primacy of conscience and reminds us that the Eucharist is "not *a prize for the perfect*, but *medicine* and *nourishment* for the weak" - no one should be excluded from this grace who sincerely seeks God's closeness. Indirectly, he implies that *sacramental reconciliation* of the life situation of same-sex couples must also be possible, instead of imputing to them a permanent state of sin.

Even prominent cardinals from traditional countries show understanding and support. Vienna's Archbishop, Cardinal *Christoph Schönborn*, called the Vatican's rigorous "no" to the blessing of homosexual couples a serious mistake. He regretted how much homosexual believers felt hurt by this. The Church should always be "mother and teacher" - "first comes the mother" - and he could understand that same-sex loving people were now asking themselves: *"Doesn't this mother have a blessing for me?"*. Instead of talking about prohibitions and moral judgments, the church should *"talk less about sexuality and more about love"*, said Schönborn. This attitude is also shared by Bishop *Wilhelm Krautwaschl* of Graz, who, like several of his Central European brothers and sisters, has shown open sympathy for blessings and the future equal treatment of homosexual couples, including in marriage ceremonies.

In summary, increasingly *positive voices* are emerging within the Catholic hierarchy *in favor of liturgical equality for same-sex couples. Cardinals and bishops from various countries* - from Belgium, Germany and Luxembourg to Austria and the USA - emphasize *the dignity and value of the love of homosexual couples* in interviews, sermons and synod contributions. Their quotes bear witness to a common concern: to further develop the church's practice of marriage and blessing in such a way that *two women or two men who love each other faithfully can also receive their vows before God and the congregation*. This tenor ranges from the demand for specific blessing ceremonies to the fundamental question of whether traditional doctrine needs to be changed in order to integrate same-sex couples sacramentally, e.g. in marriage ceremonies.

Overall, the result is a fluent and clear plea from senior church leaders for openness: *love that lives responsibility, care and faithfulness deserves the blessing of the church - regardless of the gender of the partners*. The bishops and cardinals mentioned encourage this change of perspective and thus tie in with the basic concern of the Good News, which excludes no one. Their words in the church context - whether in synodal forums, interviews or pastoral letters - show that the idea of a *sacramental or liturgically equivalent marriage ceremony* for homosexual couples in the Catholic Church has decisive *advocates in the highest church circles*.

This could be implemented in practice step by step: Firstly, existing blessing ceremonies could be further developed and *liturgically aligned with the wedding ceremony*. Some blessings for same-sex couples are already reminiscent of wedding ceremonies in terms of procedure and symbolism - including the exchange of rings and a prayer of blessing for the partnership. If the church were to officially recognize that these are *real marriages before God*, the difference to a traditional wedding ceremony would only be nominal. Theologically, it could be argued that

God's grace and blessing are not bound to any particular gender combination. If the love of two people is an *"image of God's love"* - as the Church claims of marriage - then this must apply to all lovers, whether homosexual or heterosexual. Pope Francis himself hinted at this when he stated that homosexual couples should not be discriminated against and that everyone has a right to a family. Although the Pope has so far made a distinction between civil marriage and church sacraments, the *trend towards more inclusion* is visible.

Figure 21: Marriage for all in front of the wedding altar.

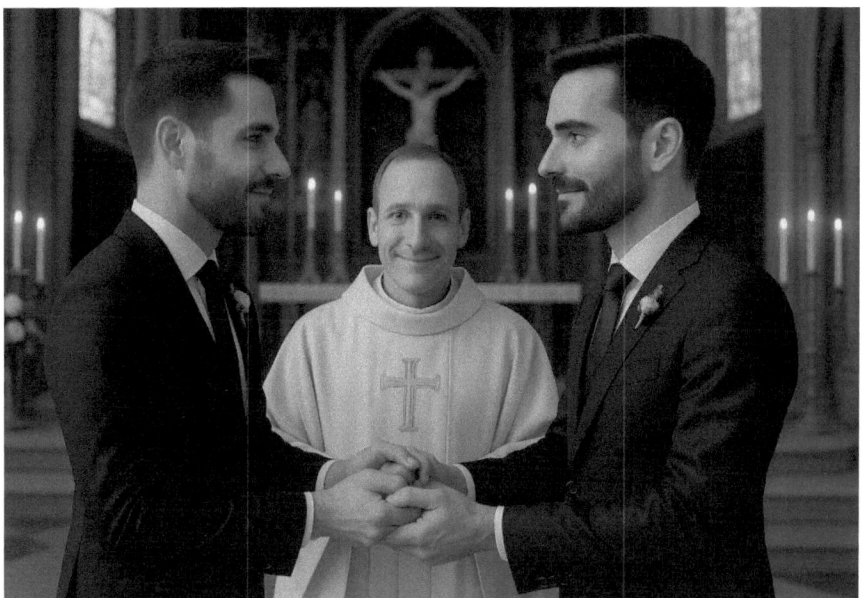

A realistic, warmly lit image of a church wedding of two men in a traditional Catholic church. The two grooms wear elegant, dark blue suits and hold hands lovingly while gazing directly into each other's eyes. Between them stands a friendly, smiling priest in a cream-colored liturgical robe with a golden cross, who performs the ceremony. Candles and a crucifix are visible in the background, emphasizing the dignified, festive atmosphere of the wedding scene. The mood is solemn, emotional and conveys a clear message of acceptance and equality of same-sex love in the Christian faith through the giving of the sacrament of marriage.

From an equality policy perspective, complete equality of treatment would be a strong signal against discrimination. A homosexual relationship is in no way inferior to a heterosexual relationship in terms of love and commitment - which is why the equality of human dignity also requires *legal and ritual equality* in the church. Any distinction to the contrary would run the risk of being regarded as unjustified discrimination. If the Church teaches that all people are created in the image of God and redeemed by Christ, there is no basis for excluding a particular group from a sacrament that is accessible to others. In terms of equality policy, there is *no legitimate difference* between a marriage between two men or two women and a marriage between a man and a woman - in both cases it is about two people who love each other and enter into a responsible life covenant. The Catholic Church could take this step towards genuine *marriage for all (in the sacramental sense)* by amending its legal codes (such as Canon Law and the Catechism) accordingly and issuing pastoral guidelines that allow homosexual couples to marry.

Such a reform would move the Catholic Church forward in the direction of its own proclaimed values of charity and justice. From the point of view of equal rights policy, *homosexual and heterosexual marriages would finally be on an equal footing* - legally, liturgically and in the eyes of the congregation. This would not only restore dignity and a church home to the couples involved, but would also send a clear signal that discrimination no longer has any place in the community of believers. The discussion shows that many would like to see this change. The question is no longer *whether*, but *when* the Catholic Church will overcome its fear of realizing *complete equality* for same-sex couples - in the sacrament and with blessing.

🐙Bishops' briefing:

The religious policy area addresses the growing debate within the Catholic Church about the recognition of same-sex partnerships. It is discussed that progressive forces within the church, including many bishops and theologians, are in favor of the marriage of homosexual couples and a further development of church doctrine. The analyses emphasize that the German Synodal Path has already passed resolutions to enable the official blessing of same-sex couples, which is seen by many as an important step towards equality. However, it falls short in terms of church policy with regard to equality that removes discrimination: the demand for complete equality through the sacrament of marriage for homosexual couples is also discussed and the theological justification and the need for changes in church law are pointed out. Finally, the importance of such a development for the non-discrimination and acceptance of LGBTQIA+ persons or divorced and remarried persons in the church is emphasized.

Didactic questions:

40 - What is the central debate regarding same-sex couples in the Catholic Church?

The central debate focuses on the demand for equal recognition for same-sex couples in the Catholic Church. This includes, in particular, the church blessing and marriage (the sacrament of marriage) of homosexual couples in order to give them the same respect and rights as heterosexual couples. Progressive forces within the church are pushing for a timely change in church law and liturgical practice in terms of equality policy.

41 - What stance do progressive bishops take on this issue?

Several bishops actively support the liturgical equality of same-sex couples and the further development of church teaching. Bishop Georg Bätzing, Chairman of the German Conference of female, diverse and male Bishops, has spoken out in favor of no longer excluding homosexual couples from God's blessing and hopes that the synodal path will make this possible. A few years ago, Bishop Franz-Josef Bode encouraged an open discussion about the blessing of homosexual couples and emphasized the need for justice. Other bishops such as Peter Kohlgraf, Helmut Dieser, Heiner Wilmer, Franz Jung and Karl-Heinz Wiesemann support demands for reform, question a purely literal interpretation of the Bible and emphasize the need to take into account the findings of the human sciences. Bishop Helmut Dieser sees homosexuality as "God-ordained", and Bishop Wiesemann has encouraged pastors to bless homosexual and remarried couples without sanctions. Cardinal Reinhard Marx declared that homosexuality is not a sin and pleaded for an "inclusive church" that recognizes LGBTQIA+ people as loved by God. Bishops are calling for a change towards appreciation and equal treatment.

42 - How do progressive theologians and church-critical groups position themselves?

Progressive theologians and groups critical of the church go beyond the call for blessing ceremonies and demand full equality for homosexual couples in the church, including access to the sacrament of marriage. They argue that a mere blessing is not enough as long as same-sex couples remain excluded from church marriage ceremonies. They emphasize that love, fidelity and care are the same values, regardless of the gender of the partners, and that their relationships deserve church respect. These groups, such as the #OutInChurch movement, We are Church and the Central Committee of German Catholics (ZdK), see the exclusion as discrimination based on sexual orientation. Progressive ethicists emphasize that the classic condemnation of homosexual acts is theologically and pastorally untenable and recognize the positive aspects of homosexual partnerships. They call for a depatologization of the church's sexual morality and full equality.

43 - What relevant decisions has the Synodal Path taken?

The Synodal Way has dealt with the recognition of same-sex couples and made groundbreaking initial decisions. In March 2023, the Synodal Assembly voted by a large majority (93% of synod members, 81% of bishops) in favor of officially allowing same-sex couples to celebrate. This should make it possible for these couples to publicly receive the blessing of the Church without priests having to receive praise for it. The reasoning behind the resolution describes the refusal to bless such relationships as "merciless to the point of being discriminatory". The Synodal Way also adopted a paper on the re-evaluation of homosexuality in doctrine, in which the Church acknowledges having inflicted suffering and states that homosexuality is not a disorder. Furthermore, no one should be denied ordained ministries or the assumption of church services on the basis of their sexual orientation. These resolutions signal a willingness to reform in parts of the church, but are not (yet) binding for the universal church.

44 - Why is a blessing ceremony not enough from an equality policy perspective?

From an equality policy perspective, a mere blessing ceremony is not enough, as it continues to exclude homosexual couples from the sacrament of marriage, the church wedding. As long as church weddings are reserved for heterosexual couples only, there is a legitimate difference and therefore unequal treatment. The demand for equality is aimed at full recognition and access to all sacraments - including and especially marriage in the first place. A blessing is perceived by many as a kind of condoning, while the wedding ceremony symbolizes full integration into the church community and the sacramental grace granted to heterosexual couples.

45 - What are the arguments in favor of the possibility of a church wedding for same-sex couples?

The first argument in favor of the possibility of a church wedding for same-sex couples is the demand for equality and the value of human dignity. It is argued that love, fidelity and care in a same-sex relationship have the same value as in a heterosexual relationship. Since procreation is in fact not an absolute criterion for admission to marriage (e.g. in the case of unintentionally childless or older couples), it is asked why a loving, permanently faithful couple of the same sex should remain excluded. The essential consensus of marriage - the promise of lifelong fidelity, support and love before God - can also be given by homosexual partners. From an equality perspective, there is no objective reason to deny them this covenant. The theological argument is that God's grace and blessing are not bound to a particular gender combination and that the love of two people, if it is an "image of God's love", must apply to all lovers.

46 - Which international voices from the Catholic Church support greater inclusion of LGBTQIA+ people?

Increasingly, high-ranking church leaders around the world are speaking out positively about the inclusion of LGBTQIA+ people. Bishop Johan Bonny of Belgium expressed shame at the Roman ban on blessings and asked those affected to apologize, appealing: *"Enough is enough!"*. The Belgian-Flemish Conference of female, diverse and male Bishops then published guidelines for church celebrations for homosexual couples. Cardinal Jean-Claude Hollerich from Luxembourg questions the doctrine that describes homosexual acts as "intrinsically wrong" and calls for a rethink so that homosexual people "feel at home" in the church. He is open to such celebrations and believes that the Church can change its attitude. US Cardinal Robert McElroy calls for "radical inclusion" and questions the exclusion of LGBTQIA+ people from key sacraments, especially the Eucharist, which he compared to "medicine and food" for the weak. Cardinal Christoph Schönborn from Vienna called the Vatican's rigorous "no" to blessing a serious mistake and advocates talking less about sexuality and more about love. These voices show a growing tendency towards openness in the global Catholic hierarchy.

47 - What steps would be necessary to achieve real equality for same-sex couples in the Catholic Church?

Several steps would be necessary to achieve full equality for same-sex couples in the Catholic Church, including the possibility of a church wedding. First, the Church's official understanding of marriage, which defines marriage as a union between a man and a woman, would have to be further developed theologically through a papal formulation in order to open up sacramental marriage to two men or two women. In the long term, if there is no papal decree, this would probably require a decision by the universal Church, for example by a synod or a council. In practice, the church's codes of law, such as canon law and the catechism, would have to be amended accordingly. Proposals should be developed as legal texts. In addition, pastoral guidelines would have to be issued that allow for the marriage of homosexual couples or place them on an equal footing as they are. A gradual implementation could also consist of liturgically aligning existing blessing ceremonies with the marriage ceremony to such an extent that the difference to the classic marriage ceremony is only nominal and the church officially recognizes that these are genuine marriages before God.

Essay questions:

Please answer one of the following questions in the form of an essay:

a) Discuss the arguments of the reform-oriented bishops for a further development of church doctrine and practice regarding same-sex couples.

b) Compare and contrast the demands of progressive theologians with the resolutions of the Synodal Path with regard to the recognition of same-sex couples in the Catholic Church.

c) Analyze the different perspectives and arguments put forward for opening sacramental marriage to same-sex couples.

d) What are the viewpoints of stakeholders and church-related interest groups?

e) Explain the worldwide signals and positions of church leaders such as Cardinal Hollerich, Cardinal McElroy and Cardinal Schönborn on the issue of equality for same-sex couples.

f) Evaluate the possible steps and theological justifications for a gradual implementation of a truly equal church marriage for homosexual couples.

📌 Religious policy field analysis 7: *Church symbolic politics and the need for a transparent culture of expectation in ministry*

There are many reform texts, promises and fine-sounding resolutions in the Catholic Church - but all too often they remain without consequences. In Europe and Germany in particular, this is increasingly causing resentment: frustration is growing in parishes, among employees and even among reform-minded bishops. In some places, topics have been discussed for years (e.. in the *Synodal Path*) without any *visible changes being made*. The rhetoric of the clergy is always that they will go along with it to some extent - as long as it does not jeopardize their existence, and since they know that nothing will change, only a few dare to step forward. Representatives of the grassroots complain that "clearly far too little is happening" and that no concrete action is emerging from all the talk. It is now time to deliver decisions and resolutions and put them into practice.

Such *symbolic politics* - fine words and gestures with no impact - may bring calm in the short term, but in the long run it undermines trust in the Catholic Church and the local clergy. As a spokeswoman for the youth associations warned: *"Purely symbolic politics may bring peace in the short term, but trust in the sincerity and credibility of the Catholic Church will [...] suffer even more."*

Anyone who wants to credibly embody the gospel today needs *deeds rather than mere signs*.

From symbolic politics to implementation power: clarifying expectations of bishops

Why is it that reform impulses often get stuck? One core problem is the lack of a *culture of expectation*: a lack of clarity about *what a bishop can, should, must and realistically can change* - both in his diocese and together with his fellow bishops in the Conference of female, diverse and male Bishops. Expectations are often raised to immeasurable heights or promises are made that lie beyond actual competence. The result: Bishops like to retreat to the fact that nothing can be done without Rome when it comes to sensitive issues; at the same time, many of the faithful expect "their" bishop to take courageous steps: to do something locally for the needs of the faithful that Rome has no interest in. There is a dangerous discrepancy between expectation and reality.

This is where the demand for *a transparent culture of expectation* comes in. Everyone involved - bishops, committees, the faithful - must be honest: *What is necessary and possible at diocesan level? Where is there real room for maneuver? Where does a bishop come up against the limits of canon law? And where is he or she prepared to go beyond these in practice and for practice?* Only with this clarity is it possible to distinguish *where real change begins and where mere symbolism begins*. Cardinal *Walter Kasper*, for example, has pointed out that the bishops and their conferences *actually have more possibilities than they actually use*. It is a *"tragedy"* that the Church often paralyzes itself through unnecessary quarrels and existential fears - especially at the level of bishops: because *"it is also more convenient to refer difficult questions to Rome instead of taking responsibility yourself"*.

This is precisely where a rethink is needed: a culture in which bishops courageously *make full use of their existing competencies* and at the same time openly communicate where their authority ends. Only then will reform initiatives not be dashed by false expectations.

Successful examples of reform: From paper to practice

There are certainly cases where *the ability to reform* has been demonstrated - where concepts have given rise to concrete changes. Three examples show how a diocese can achieve sustainable renewal with *clear roles, participative processes and the backing of the leadership:*

Diocese of Essen: "Vision for the future" and pastoral change

The Ruhr diocese of Essen is considered a pioneer for practical church development. More than ten years ago, Bishop *Franz-Josef Overbeck* launched the *"Catholic Future"* process in dialog with the Diocesan Council. Two years later, this resulted in a pioneering *"vision of the future"* with seven guiding principles that describe how the church in the diocese wants to be in the future.

The broad *participation* was unusual right from the start: visions were collected in six all-day diocesan forums and countless discussions, controversial topics were openly named and *20 concrete projects* were finally launched. Importantly, Overbeck *combined* the spiritual awakening with organizational consequences. After the first structural reform had already taken place (merging of parishes, etc.), the future projects were implemented as *binding pastoral initiatives*.

Examples of this include blessing ceremonies for newborns, new city pastoral services in inner cities and a pilgrimage route through the Ruhr region - all results of the future vision process.

The success lay in the combination of *clear leadership and commitment* (the bishop was personally behind the projects) and *strong* grassroots *involvement* (each parish drew up its own pastoral vote). In this way, a vision became a broad movement in the diocese of Essen. Overbeck himself emphasized the need to *"rethink* the church" - symbolically, he spoke of the *"end of the old days"*. This determination on the part of the leadership, coupled with a *willingness to learn* and the courage to question even cherished habits, created real change on the ground.

Diocese of Osnabrück: Equality and participation as a principle

A second example is provided by the diocese of *Osnabrück*, where Bishop Franz-Josef *Bode* promoted a *"church of participation"* for many years. Here, the focus was particularly on *gender-equitable personnel structures* and *the participation of lay people*. Bode campaigned "courageously, persistently and with great commitment" for more female participation and wanted to significantly increase the proportion of women in church leadership positions.

Figure 22: A possible mission statement for the local church.

A graphic showing a fingerprint in the form of the letters 'a' and 'o' intertwined. The letters are accompanied by the words 'accepting and open', emphasizing the message of inclusivity and openness.

Specifically, Osnabrück has already made use of the scope to assign responsibility to women at an early stage: in 2019, for example, *a woman* was appointed as *the parish leader of* a parish *for the first time* (*Christine Hölscher* as parish representative) - a first. This model, made possible by church law in the event of a shortage of priests, provides for a "moderating priest" in the background while the woman takes over the leadership on site.

Bode thus pursued a *"process of pastoral reorientation"* in which pastoral teams, councils and the entire community were actively involved.

The success of this approach lay in *clear role models and backing*: the diocesan leadership defined exactly who would take on which tasks (parish representatives vs. moderators) and ensured that these changes were supported both theologically and legally. At the same time, there was a *cultural anchoring*: Osnabrück has been living the concept of the *participatory church* for years, in which *participation* is *a matter of course.* Other measures - from gender-sensitive language in documents to mentoring programs for female managers - also demonstrate this: This is where promises to promote women were *really* put into practice. Bode's attitude of promoting change both *structurally* (through new rules and positions) and *culturally* (through awareness change) was decisive. The diocese earned recognition for this - in employee surveys, for example, Osnabrück's administration was rated as particularly family-friendly and promoting satisfaction. If clear targets (e.g. *30% of women* in management roles) are set and bindingly pursued, the reform will not remain on paper.

Diocese of Limburg: Binding co-determination and synodality

After the crisis surrounding his predecessor, Limburg's Bishop *Georg Bätzing* focused on *transparency and participation* as the key to credibility. Limburg traditionally has a strong synodal order, but Bätzing went one step further: a few years ago, he announced that he would *give his diocesan synodal council decision-making rights.* Specifically, he declared himself *"willing to voluntarily bind himself to the [...] Council of the People of God [...] and to convert the advisory voting right [...] into a decisive voting right"* - but only in matters that do not affect the rule of faith and law. He thus voluntarily submitted to a body co-determined by laypeople, which is an unusually far-reaching step in the Catholic hierarchy. *Binding participation formats* such as this *synodal council with veto rights* ensure that decisions *do not* remain *without consequences:* The bishop gave his word to respect decisions made by this body. At the same time, Bätzing made sure to specify the boundaries (dogmas and world church issues remain excluded), i.e. to *realistically clarify competencies.* The result: in the diocese of Limburg, co-determination is not an ornamental accessory, but has become "without alternative" and "quite essential" for church leadership. Of course, there were also hurdles here - Rome views such power-sharing skeptically in some cases. But Bätzing got around this by carefully anchoring his statutes within the framework of church law. *The leadership* was fully supportive: a bishop who proactively promotes *"shared leadership for a limited period"* and gender equality in leadership positions also encourages the committees to accept responsibility. In Limburg, synodal principles can thus be experienced in concrete terms - with verifiable consequences. This course has helped the diocese to gain new credibility because *responsibility* becomes *transparent and verifiable*: Lay councillors not only have their say, but also make a measurable contribution to decisions.

Failed reform projects: Learning from stalled initiatives

As instructive as success stories are, it is important to look at *failed or inconsequential reform initiatives* in order to learn from them. One prominent example is the Germany-wide *Synodal Path* itself. Although numerous texts and votes were adopted in this 2023 reform process, some things stalled because *there were no clear implementation paths* or because competences were exceeded. For example, the synod members decided to ask the Pope to review compulsory celibacy and to allow celebrations for homosexual couples. Marriage was missing, as was the argument that voluntary celibacy is tantamount to abolition and must logically be the same.

However, as long as the implementation of individual resolutions depends on the global church framework, they will remain symbolic for the time being. Another project - the establishment of a *General Synodal Council* - was even *thwarted directly by Rome*: the Holy See made it clear that no body should be created that would oblige the bishops to adopt new forms of leadership. This clearly showed *the limits of competence*: National solo efforts in questions of leadership and doctrine came up against a papal *blockade letter*. The lesson learned: If the German bishops had made it clear in advance what could *not be* done without Rome, there might have been less disappointment. However, the abrupt "no" from Rome caused renewed frustration among many - a reform text (on the establishment of the Council) has been shelved for the time being.

There are also examples at diocesan level where *well-intentioned reform papers have come to nothing*. In the Archdiocese of Cologne, for example, Cardinal Woelki *launched a "Pastoral Future Path"* many years ago, i.e. an extensive dialog and restructuring process. However, as a result of the major crisis of confidence surrounding his person (abuse investigation), this process is now de facto *on hold*. The highest lay body, the Diocesan Council, withdrew its support for the project in 2021 as there was "insufficient acceptance".

In other words, even a bishop cannot push through a reform agenda *without the backing* of those involved. In this case, it was not so much Rome that failed as the *credibility of the* local *leadership*. A similar situation occurred in the diocese of Trier, where ambitious plans for large-scale parish reform were presented following a diocesan synod a few years ago. However, when the bishop wanted to implement these a few years later, conservative circles lodged a complaint in Rome - and the responsible congregation *stopped* the new structures from coming into force by decree.

The reasons for this were legal concerns as to whether the reform was permissible within the framework of world church law. As a result, the Trier reform texts had to be revised and implemented with a delay. In other words, *blockades and jurisdictional boundaries* worked together here: Resistance from within the church used Roman authorities to stop a reform that had already been decided. This was difficult to understand for the local faithful - the synod had raised high expectations, but *there was a lack of commitment*, as there was apparently no *plan B* for Roman objections.

Typical stumbling blocks can be recognized from such cases: Some reforms remain ineffective due to *unclear responsibilities* (no one feels responsible for implementation), others due to *a lack of consultation with higher levels* (the competencies are overestimated, yet the management levels are responsible for these agreements), yet others fail due to *a lack of support* - be it from the grassroots or the management.

And now: Success factors for credible reforms

In conclusion, it is clear that *the willingness to shape* and the *ability to reform* become credible where clear expectations and binding action come together. These examples provide some *success factors* for how renewal can succeed:

- **Clear responsibility structures:** It must be defined *who is* responsible for the implementation of a reform decision.

When bishops involve committees , responsibilities should also be clarified so that good ideas do not end up nowhere.

- **Realistic clarification of competencies**: Before any major promise is made, it should be honestly examined whether the project can be implemented by the diocese itself or requires external (e.g. Roman) approval. Expectations must be managed openly: What *can* bishops change, what exceeds their mandate? Transparency at this point prevents disappointment.

- **Support and involvement**: Reforms can only have *a broad impact* if the leadership and the grassroots pull together. Bishops need the support of priests, lay committees and employees - and vice versa. Participatory processes (synods, forums, working groups) promote acceptance. However, it is also important to have support beyond a single bishop: within the Conference of female, diverse and male Bishops or from Rome, depending on the topic.

- **Binding timetables and evaluation routines**: Announcements should always be linked to a *timetable*. Specifically: By when should what be implemented? Successful examples (Essen, Osnabrück) had milestones and regularly reviewed progress. Evaluations - e.. annual reports, independent reviews - make responsibility measurable and prevent decisions from fizzling out.

- **Transparent communication**: Ultimately, communication must be right. A culture of *open information* - both internally in the diocese and publicly - creates trust. If, example, difficulties arise (blockages, delays), bishops should be honest about this instead of remaining silent. This also includes making successes visible and celebrating them in order to maintain motivation.

Bishops who take these factors to heart not only avoid symbolic politics, but *replace them with credible action*. The church regains its *institutional credibility* when words and deeds match. A transparent culture of expectations in the office of the bishops means that everyone knows where they stand - what is possible and what is not (yet). Where reform goals are clearly set, responsibilities are named and actions and timetables are demanded, a new culture of trust grows. Then reform texts do not become waste paper, but a living reality in the service of the Gospel. Responsible church leadership today means above all *creating trust through commitment* - so that visions become changes and frustration is transformed into hope.

Bishops' briefing:

In this religious policy field, it is necessary to analyze why reforms in the Catholic Church are often perceived as mere symbolic politics without concrete implementation, which leads to growing frustration. A central problem is the lack of a transparent culture of expectation in the office of the bishops, as it is unclear what changes bishops can realistically bring about and where their canonical limits lie. Successful examples from the dioceses of Essen, Osnabrück and Limburg are presented, which show that reforms can succeed if there are clear responsibilities, realistic clarification of competencies, backing from leadership and grassroots, binding timetables and transparent communication. Failed attempts at reform, however, such as parts of the Synodal Path or projects in Cologne and Trier, illustrate the stumbling blocks.

Didactic questions:

48 - Why do reform efforts in the Catholic Church often not lead to visible changes?

A key problem is so-called symbolic politics, in which fine-sounding texts and resolutions are adopted but often not implemented. This leads to frustration, as much talk is not followed by concrete action. Another core problem is the lack of a transparent culture of expectations in the office of bishop. There is a lack of clarity about what realistic opportunities for change a bishop has at diocesan level and in the Conference of female, diverse and male Bishops. Expectations are often exaggerated or promises are made that lie outside of actual competencies, which leads to a discrepancy between aspiration and reality.

49 - What does "symbolic politics" mean in a church context and what consequences does it have?

Symbolic politics describes the use of fine words, gestures or resolutions that have no concrete impact. This may bring peace in the short term, but in the long run it undermines trust in the sincerity and credibility of the church. It gives the impression that there is a lot of talk but too little action.

50 - What role does the culture of expectation in the office of the bishops play in the failure of reforms?

An unclear or unrealistic culture of expectations contributes significantly to the failure of reforms. If it is not communicated transparently what a bishop can actually change within the framework of canon law and where his limits lie (especially in relation to Rome), exaggerated expectations arise. If these cannot be fulfilled, this leads to disappointment and mistrust. Bishops then tend to fall back on the need for approval from Rome when it comes to sensitive issues, while the faithful expect courageous steps to be taken.

51 - What examples of successful reform implementation can be cited and what characterizes them?

Three examples are worth mentioning: the diocese of Essen ("vision for the future"), the diocese of Osnabrück (equality and participation) and the diocese of Limburg (binding co-determination). These examples are characterized by a combination of clear leadership and commitment (bishops were behind the projects), strong grassroots involvement (participation in committees and processes), realistic clarification of competencies (naming boundaries) and the courage to change (questioning old habits, using the leeway in canon law).

52 - Why did the Synodal Way sometimes fail to implement resolutions?

The synodal path failed in part because there were no clear implementation paths or because competencies were exceeded. Decisions that depend on the global church framework (such as the examination of compulsory celibacy) remain symbolic for the time being. The establishment of an all-German Synodal Council was even blocked directly by Rome, which made clear the limits of competence of national solo efforts in questions of leadership and doctrine.

53 - What typical stumbling blocks in reform projects can be derived from the failed examples?

Typical stumbling blocks include unclear responsibilities for implementation, a lack of consultation with higher levels (overestimation of one's own competencies), a lack of support from the grassroots or the leadership, as well as resistance from conservative circles that use Roman authorities to stop reforms. The credibility of the local leadership is also crucial.

54 - What success factors are identified for credible reforms?

The following are identified as success factors: Clear responsibility structures, realistic clarification of competencies (open management of expectations), backing and involvement of management and grassroots, binding schedules and evaluation routines to measure responsibility, as well as transparent communication (open information about progress and difficulties).

55 - How can a transparent culture of expectation in the office of the bishops contribute to the credibility of the church?

A transparent culture of expectations, in which it is openly communicated what is realistically possible and what is not, helps to avoid exaggerated expectations and prevent disappointment. If bishops courageously make full use of their existing competencies and at the same time honestly state their limitations, their actions become more credible. This creates trust, as words and deeds match and responsibility becomes transparent and verifiable. In this way, reform texts can become a living reality and hope can arise from frustration.

🖉 🖥 Essay questions:

Please answer one of the following questions in the form of an essay:

a) Discuss the importance of a transparent culture of expectation in the episcopate for the success of church reforms. Include the challenges mentioned in the text and the examples of successful reforms.

b) Analyze the differences between successful and failed reform projects using examples. What are the common characteristics of the successful initiatives and what factors contributed to the failure of others?

c) Discuss the role of lay participation and committees in church reform processes. How do examples such as the diocese of Essen, Osnabrück and Limburg help to illustrate this aspect?

d) How does the relationship between the national Conference of female, diverse and male Bishops and the Holy See in Rome influence the implementation of reforms? Examine this on the basis of the described blockades and competence limits.

e) What practical steps and strategies could church leaders who are willing to shape the future take to avoid symbolic politics and instead promote credible and binding action? What success factors can be identified?

📌 Religious policy field analysis 8: Overcoming institutional inertia through the paradigm of participatory palaver: Why the church needs more democratic leadership

Many church committees, ordinariates and administrative bodies work according to the principle of risk avoidance - innovations are viewed with skepticism, preferring to stick with the tried and tested. This safety-first mentality leads to *institutional inertia*, which blocks urgently needed reforms and creates a climate that is hostile to innovation. Even a progressive bishop can be curbed in his creative drive if the surrounding structures are primarily geared towards the status quo and damage prevention.

Risk aversion and reform backlog in church structures

This *risk culture* can be seen, for example, in the fact that advisory boards delay or postpone changes because they want to avoid conflicts or mistakes at all costs. The result is a *reform backlog*: instead of reacting courageously to current challenges - such as a decline in membership, credibility crises following abuse scandals or changing social values - governing bodies fall into a kind of management of decline. Ten years ago, a study diagnosed a contradiction: while the Protestant Church is almost *"reform-stressed"*, the Catholic Church remains in a *"theological reform backlog"*.

The consequence of this inertia is fatal: necessary changes are postponed, committed believers lose patience and the gap between church leadership and the reality of people's lives grows.

Pope Francis issued an urgent warning against a church that remains trapped within itself for fear of taking risks. *"I prefer a Church that has gone out into the streets rather than a Church that is unhealthy because it holds back and clings to its own security,"* he wrote programmatically.

The fact that Catholic bishops have an "after me, the deluge" attitude does not apply across the board to all of them, but can certainly be seen in individual bishops and parts of the church leadership. In concrete terms, this means

1. **Willingness to reform:** Many bishops speak publicly about the need for reform, but are reluctant to implement concrete measures, such as the synodal path or the opening up of church structures. This caution can be interpreted as preferring to leave conflicts or difficult decisions against Rome to future generations and fearing that their livelihoods will be cut off.

2. **Willingness to reform:** While individual bishops are quite courageous in their demands for reform and organizational concepts (e.g. Bishops such as Bätzing, Overbeck or Kohlgraf in Germany as well as internationally: Cardinal Jean-Claude Hollerich (Luxembourg), Cardinal Robert McElroy (San Diego), Archbishop Dermot Farrell (Dublin), Cardinal Reinhard Marx (Munich, with an international voice), Bishop Johan Bonny (Antwerp), there is also a strong group that actively slows down or completely rejects fundamental reforms. This often gives the impression that there is no real will to reform, but that cosmetic changes are being sought at most.

3. **Reform results:** The sluggish implementation of visible reforms (e.g. role of women, church sexual morality, church marriage of queer people, abolition of celibacy, dealing with abuse) actually often conveys the image that little to no substantial results are being achieved. This reinforces the impression that the church is more administrative than proactive.

Figure 23: Theological reform backlog of the Catholic Church in religious policy areas.

Infographic on the topic of "Theological reform backlog". The graphic is divided into two sections. The first section is entitled "Effects" and describes four core problems of the Catholic Church, symbolized by clear icons: "Changing social values" (icon: person next to a document with a star symbol), "Credibility crises" (icon: church with a question mark), "Loss of members" (icon: group of people, diagonally crossed out) and "Abuse" (icon: person, a hand in front of the face). The second section is entitled "Areas for change and solutions". Here, six specific areas of reform are named, each also provided with concise icons: "Women as popes" (icon: female person with a cross), "Marriage of queer couples" (icon: two intertwined wedding rings, with a heart above), "Co-leadership" (icon: schematic representation of several people on the same level), "Recognition of homosexuality" (icon: heart in rainbow colors with a cross), "Sexual ethics" (icon: combined male-female gender symbols), and "Abolition of celibacy" (icon: two figures as a couple, one of them recognizable as a priest with a cross). The graphics are minimalist and clearly laid out.

The metaphor "After me, the deluge" is apt insofar as it describes how some people in positions of responsibility consciously or unconsciously sit out problems without seriously working on long-term solutions. However, there are also committed bishops and groups within the church who want exactly the opposite - namely to bring about real change. However, the church leadership as a whole has so far been too slow and not credible to show effectively and sustainably that it can or wants to bring about comprehensive reform.

The papal image of a *"changed church"*, which prefers to dare rather than remain in a protective bunker, on the other hand, calls for new beginnings and a willingness to take risks. A leadership culture of pure danger prevention is contrary to this missionary mandate and paralyzes the church. *Standing still is riskier than change*, as it leads to a gradual loss of significance. It is therefore necessary to remove the blockages, overcome institutional inertia and no longer postpone reforms for fear of making mistakes.

Democratization of church leadership: necessary and overdue

In view of this situation, it is becoming increasingly clear that the Catholic Church needs elements of *democratization in its governance models in* order to remain capable of acting and credible in the six concepts for action in religious policy fields shown in the info graphic. This does not mean a simple transfer of political democracy, but an expansion of genuine co-determination and participation in responsibility by all believers. Why is this necessary?

Firstly, because the current concentration of decisions on a few clerics has often led to *abuse of power and a lack of transparency*. The investigation into the scandal of the abuse of young people by male priests has shown that a lack of control and a lack of participation by outsiders can be fatal. More democratic structures - such as independent supervisory bodies, transparent procedures and accountability - could prevent this. *Separation of powers and participation* are basic principles that make arbitrariness more difficult and create trust.

Secondly, because *all the baptized share in the mission of the Church*. The Second Vatican Council already emphasized the Church as the *people of God*, in which all believers (lay and clergy) share responsibility. Pope Benedict XVI clearly stated as early as 2012: *"The co-responsibility of all members of the people of God must be promoted step by step. The laity must no longer be regarded merely as 'collaborators' of the clergy, but as co-responsible for the being and acting of the Church."*

This *co-responsibility* is a management task and requires that laypersons not only act in an advisory capacity, but also participate in real decisions.

In order to effectively take on leadership tasks in the Catholic Church as a layperson, specific *leadership skills* are required that contain universal *elements of leadership* on the one hand and are tailored to the ecclesial context on the other:

1. communicative competence: communicating clearly, respectfully and transparently, active listening and being able to give differentiated feedback, confident moderation of groups and team meetings.

2. cooperation and team competence: team-oriented action and constructive conflict management, ability to work together with full-time staff, volunteers and church leadership in a trusting but also demanding manner.

3. spiritual competence: ability to reflect on spiritual and ethical questions and to integrate them authentically into leadership responsibility, willingness to regard the Gospel as an inspiring basis for action and to make spiritually reflected decisions.

4. intercultural and inclusive competence: openness and sensitivity to diversity (e.g. gender, origin, sexual orientation, age, understanding of faith). Ability to deal with differences in an appreciative manner and to promote integrative structures.

5. decision-making skills: the courage to make clear and justifiable decisions, the ability to organize participative decision-making processes and to make decisions transparent and comprehensible.

6. change competence: ability to actively drive innovation and reform, willingness and openness to critically scrutinize existing structures, develop concepts and guidelines in writing, and constructively implement innovations.

7. strategic competence: ability for long-term planning, strategic development of pastoral and organizational goals; ability to use resources responsibly and goal-oriented.

8. implementation skills: knowledge of organizational, project and time management, operational management skills for structuring, planning and implementing complex processes and projects.

9. self-reflection and resilience: ability for critical self-reflection and dealing with feedback, resilience and stress management in order to act calmly and solution-oriented even in challenging situations.

10. ethics of responsibility: a high sense of responsibility towards the congregation and the institution of the church, the ability to make ethically reflected decisions, to take responsibility for mistakes and to act transparently.

These skills enable lay people to assume responsibility on an equal footing with full-time managers and to take on credible and effective leadership roles in the Catholic Church.

If the hierarchical constitution of the church continues to *focus solely* on the clergy, the baptismal promise of a common mission will be undermined. Democratization here means *joint consultation and joint decision-making* in the spirit of the Gospel.

Thirdly, democratization is necessary in order not to completely lose touch with today's social expectations. In modern constitutional states, participation, transparency and equality are central values that can also be legally enforced. Members of the church, who are also citizens of a democracy, often experience a stark break at the church door - suddenly they are only expected to *"pray, pay and obey"*. This tension must be resolved if the church does not want to continue to lose credibility. *Bishop Georg Bätzing*, Chairman of the German Conference of female, diverse and male Bishops, therefore sees *"no contradiction to church doctrine if tried and tested procedures are introduced in the secular sphere that serve the transparency of church governance and the participation of the faithful"*.

In other words, the church can learn from democratic cultures without losing its spiritual identity. So why should principles such as the rule of law, separation of powers, protection of minorities or voter participation *automatically* be seen as a threat in the church context? The bishop rightly asks *"why modern-style democracy [...] should actually trigger fears in the church"*.

Synodality and democracy are not mutually exclusive, but can be mutually beneficial - this is also emphasized by theologians such as Martin Kirschner, who proposes *mutual learning in synodality and democracy* as a response to the ecclesiastical and social crises.

From symbolic consultation to real decisions: What does synodal leadership look like in concrete terms?

In concrete terms, the call for *democratization* means moving away from mere alibi participation towards *binding synodal structures*. Up to now, the participatory bodies at all levels - parish councils, pastoral councils, diocesan councils - have mostly only been active in an advisory capacity. In the end, decisions are made *top-down* by pastors, bishops or the Roman Curia. This *symbolic consultation* must be transformed into *real decision-making authority for teams* and councils if participation is to be taken seriously.

What can this look like? A look at current reform processes provides approaches:

- **Synodal path**: In the reform dialog between bishops and laity, far-reaching proposals were developed to limit the power of the clergy and introduce synodal bodies. For example, the *"Power and Separation of Powers"* forum proposed a *diocesan synodal council* that would be *"elected in free, equal and secret elections"* and be representative of the people of God in the diocese.

Such a council of bishops, clergy and laity would have the right to co-decide on important developments. This would mean that the faithful *would not* have to *surrender* their democratic participation rights *at the church door*, as stated in the explanatory statement.

The implementation of this model is controversial - the Vatican has raised concerns and has banned a *synodal council* at national level for the time being. However, Bishop Bätzing and others are sticking to the idea of setting up synodal governing bodies. Some German dioceses are now examining their own solutions to enable more participation and personnel capacity. This struggle is exemplary: a progressive clergyman with the will to reform can come up against the limits of the current church order - but creative ways can be sought to expand them synodally: What if it is not the clergy but the laity who contradict Rome and introduce more modern changes? What if lay people start to marry same-sex couples in front of the altar because the local clergy agrees, but cannot marry them because he fears for his job because of Rome? In this way of thinking, lay people can also initiate change and create realities in a transitional period. A marriage ceremony performed by lay people in front of the altar may have the same significance from the customer's point of view as a blessing by a clergyman, as long as the local clergyman is not courageous or willing enough to perform the marriage ceremony of homosexual couples liturgically. God does not require a degree in theology, but love of neighbor, which all can perform even without the ordination of men. Or should an ordained laywoman consecrate the marrying laywoman of homosexual couples so that she can perform the sacramental marriage ceremony as a form of charity?

- **Leadership teams made up of clergy and lay people:** In some dioceses, there are already successful projects with joint leadership. For example, after its diocesan synod, the diocese of Trier planned to create large-scale pastoral care units that are *led* by *leadership teams made up of laypeople and priests*.

Although Bishop *Stephan Ackermann* had to adapt the structural reform following Roman intervention, the principle remained the same: pastors should no longer be the only ones in charge at higher-level pastoral locations, but rather teams with collegial responsibility. Similarly, the diocese of Essen is increasingly relying on *team-based parish leadership in* order to relieve the sole burden of the shrinking number of priests and bundle competencies. Such a collegial leadership model is traditionally anchored in the Protestant church (e.g. presbyteries in parishes); in the Catholic church, teams at parish or deanery level would be a culture-changing step towards shared responsibility and decision-making authority.

- **Synodal co-determination in the global church:** there are also international examples of more democracy in the church apparatus. In Switzerland, the Catholic Church is partially democratically constituted through state church law - in many cantons, lay people elect church parliaments or parish councils that have a say in financial and personnel matters. Although spiritual leadership remains with the clergy, without the consent of the elected bodies, the clergy cannot simply decide on the finances and their allocation to areas of action, education and reform. This dual system shows that *the sacred and the secular* can be regulated separately but cooperatively - and that diversity among those involved leads to more balanced decisions. Latin America provides another example: after the Amazon Synod in 2019, the *Amazon Church Conference (CEAMA)* was founded, a transnational church network that brings together bishops, priests, religious and lay people from the Amazon Church. Pope Francis put the statutes of this *Conferencia Eclesial de la Amazonía* into force at the end of 2022 - with the express aim of *"promoting synodality between the churches of the region"* and seeking *new ways of evangelization*.

Lay participation is an integral part of this structure. *This is the first time that an official church leadership conference has been created* that does not consist solely of bishops. CEAMA could serve as a model for regional synodal councils that jointly develop pastoral guidelines. In individual dioceses in Latin America (e.g. some dioceses in Brazil), pastoral councils with real decision-making power have also existed for years, which decide on pastoral care plans or the use of funds together with bishops. This practice is based on the tradition of the *Comunidades Eclesiales de Base* (base communities), where believers meet as equals and shape the local church together.

These examples clearly show *what concrete change can look like*: Establishing binding councils at various levels, election processes, shared leadership responsibility, transparent synods and conferences.

It is important that such bodies *no longer remain toothless advisory bodies.* They need clearly defined *competencies,* e.g. in pastoral planning, financial administration, diocesan management or the election of bishops. The synodal reform proposal envisaged, for example, that a diocesan council, together with the clergy, should make binding decisions on "significant developments in the church and society".

It is precisely this co-decision-making at eye level that marks the cultural change: away from the lone leader and towards a *coordinated team.*

Of course, this also requires changes to church law and the understanding of roles. The CIC (Code of Canon Law) would have to be adapted in order to anchor lay people more firmly in leadership positions, be it as *permanent deacons* (an idea currently under discussion) or as leaders with authority delegated by the bishop, which can also include spiritual elements such as giving a lay blessing to remarried couples (both heterosexual and homosexual divorcees). But some things can already be done within the existing framework, for example through *the bishops' self-commitment*: If a bishop promises not to make any important decisions without the approval of his diocesan council, he is in fact already creating *a separation of powers or coordinated team leadership,* even if this is (still) voluntary under canon law.

Some clergy are considering such steps in order to implement the results of the Synodal Path locally.

Team orientation, diversity and collegial leadership - theologically justifiable and socially compatible

A common objection is: *"The church is not a democracy!"* - This is often used to reject synodal votes or joint decisions, as if truth cannot be negotiated by a majority. Certainly, the proclamation of a truth of faith does not depend on majorities or clergy. But leadership and administrative decisions are not only about dogmas of faith, but also about theological educational issues, about discussions in all religious policy areas by all those involved, and about *the practice of walking together as the people of God.* And *theology* offers *enough points of reference* to legitimize team orientation and diversity. A *synodal-communal theology* is emerging.

We already find a fundamentally collegial orientation in the New Testament: Jesus sends out his disciples *in pairs*; the early church decides together on disputes *in the council of apostles and elders* (Apostles' Council in Jerusalem, Acts 15). Paul describes the church as the *body of Christ with many members*, in which various gifts are at work (1 Cor 12). This biblical image celebrates *diversity in unity* - no charism should suppress the other. Collegial leadership today builds on this: When different professions (theologians, business professionals, pastoral workers), different walks of life (consecrated and non-consecrated) and diverse backgrounds (women and men, young and old, queer people, different cultures) come together in a leadership team, the richness of the *Spirit's many gifts* can become fruitful. Theologically, it can be argued that the *Holy Spirit speaks not only through the hierarchy*, but through the *sensus fidei* of all believers - that sense of the people of faith that Pope Francis has repeatedly emphasized. As a rule, a group makes more balanced and holistic decisions than an isolated individual because more facets are taken into account. This corresponds to Jesus' promise *"Where two or three are gathered in my name..."* - Community orientation is therefore not a foreign concept, but deeply biblical.

In addition, the Catholic Church has already recognized the *principle of collegiality* - albeit so far mainly at the level of the clergy among themselves (college of bishops with the papal head of the church at the top). What prevents this principle from being extended "downwards"? If bishops lead the universal church collegially (e.g. within the framework of synods of bishops), priests *and* laypeople could lead a diocese collegially in the same way. Ultimately, this would be an extension of the shared responsibility of all the baptized as laid out in *Lumen Gentium* (Vatican II's Constitution on the Church). This would not abolish the dignity and ministry of priests, but would embed them in a team structure. *Hierarchical and synodal elements can go hand in hand* - Pope Francis also emphasized in 2015 that synodality *"is the path that God expects of the Church in the third millennium"*. Synodality includes everyone: *"not only"* bishops, but *"also [...] lay people"*. In this respect, it is even *ecclesiastically and theologically necessary* to try out new leadership models that do justice to this common dignity.

Team orientation and diversity are also *compatible* from a social perspective. Companies, associations and political bodies have long relied on diverse teams because they are more innovative and credible. A church that wants to survive in the 21st century cannot ignore this. If church governing bodies finally incorporate the skills of women on an equal footing in a timely manner, if decisions are made in dialog with those affected (for example in youth work or social projects), then the church will become *more inclusive and relevant.* Many believers - especially younger generations - expect to have a say. If this does not happen, there is a risk of further emigration. *Diversity* in leadership also reflects the worldwide diversity of the church: the Catholic Church is a global community of very different cultures. A monolithic leadership style does not do justice to this.

The expression *"per ordre di Mufti"* (more commonly: "per ordre du Mufti" or "Mufti's order") comes from the French and literally means "by order of the Mufti". In the Islamic context, a mufti is a legal scholar who issues binding legal opinions (fatwas) - without prior consultation, involvement or consideration of other perspectives and needs.

Applied to the Catholic Church in this sense, the term describes a practice in which Rome or individual clergy make decisions without involving the laity or adequately taking local circumstances into account.

In the Catholic Church, when decisions are made by clergy or the church leadership ("Rome") without consulting the laity or taking their needs into account, the term "per ordre du mufti" can be applied *to the ecclesiastical context.* Specifically, this means:

- **Authoritarian decision-making:** Decisions are made unilaterally, centrally and without transparency.

- **Lack of participation:** There is insufficient involvement of congregations, believers or local church representatives.

- **Monolithic management style:** Such a management and decision-making style contradicts a participative and dialogical church.

- **Top-down attitude:** Reforms or local initiatives are slowed down, ignored or banned - regardless of local cultural, pastoral or social needs.

When a pope or the Vatican Curia regularly makes decisions in an authoritarian manner, without taking into account local realities, needs and experiences of the faithful or laity on the ground, it seems entirely appropriate to speak metaphorically of an "ordre du mufti pope" or an "ordre du mufti church leadership".

This term is *concise* because it highlights criticism of authoritarian structures. *It is critically reflective* because it points to problematic decision-making practices. And it is *an appeal for democratization* because it indirectly calls for the participation and involvement of the faithful.

The use of the expression *"per ordre du Mufti"* thus also clearly emphasizes authoritarian decision-making structures in the church context: an *"ordre du Mufti church leadership"* would thus be a field of reflection for church policy that calls for greater involvement of the congregations, the laity and local realities in order to enable authentic reforms.

Because only a pluralistic management team can show this: Everyone has a place here, diversity is seen as a wealth.

Last but not least, *team-oriented forms of leadership can also be justified spiritually.* Jesus himself said: *"Whoever wants to be first, be the servant of all."* Collegial leadership implements precisely this servant leadership style - no one should *rule* in a worldly sense, but rather lead the people of God as a team. The principle of two or twelve apostles shows that the church was never intended to be a one-man show, but a *community on a journey* (syn-odality literally means "walking together"). By listening to several voices, it becomes clear that the truth is greater than the opinion of one individual. *Praying, discerning and deciding together* - this corresponds to the old principle of the church assembly, in which the Spirit of God is implored together. Why should this be any less true today?

World church departures towards participatory plaver

In the Catholic Church, there is a growing number of high-ranking church stakeholders worldwide who want to implement *equal leadership for clergy and laity*. Pope Francis has taken a historic step by granting *non-ordained* Catholics the right to vote in synods of bishops. Bishop Georg Bätzing of Limburg expressly welcomed this decision from Rome: "I consider this decision to be historic" - in future, responsibility in the church should be *shared*. This synodal opening makes it possible for the first time for women and men without ordination to participate in deliberations *and* voting at world synods. Cardinal Jean-Claude Hollerich (Luxembourg), one of the organizers of the 2023 World Synod, even spoke of a "revolution" that he had initiated together with Cardinal *Mario Grech*. Cardinal *Kevin Farrell*, head of the Vatican Dicastery for Laity, Family and Life, also emphasized that clergy and laity have a *shared responsibility* - cooperation must take place precisely *in the leadership and administration* of the Church. His Canadian confrere *Gérald Lacroix* emphasizes that the participation of the laity in church *decision-making processes* is a central element of the "synodal renewal" sought by Rome. In this way, the universal church is building on the Second Vatican Council, which taught the *common priesthood of all the baptized* as early as 1965 - but now this principle is to become visible in concrete terms in leadership structures.

Reform models in which bishops and laypeople *jointly lead the church* are being tested in Europe in particular. The Germans in particular are adhering to the principle of co-determination: the planned Synodal Council is to become a nationwide body in which clergy and laity jointly decide on budgets, educational initiatives, personnel, areas of reform and pastoral processes and planning as well as the handling of religious policy areas through local discussion recommendations, guidelines and documents.

Theologian *Thomas Söding* emphasizes once again that *comparable models already exist elsewhere*: "In Latin America, the CEAMA body of clergy, laity, indigenous people and religious already exists, with papal blessing". Europe's churches are therefore looking forward to these global church implementations while strengthening their own synodal processes (such as the "Synodal Way" in Switzerland and an upcoming synodal process in Italy).

The co-responsibility of the laity has long been a central concern of the clergy there: even the Latin American Bishops' Conference in Medellín in 1968 called for the "threefold *coresponsibility*" of bishops, priests *and* laity to be put into practice. Latin American church leaders are currently building on this vision. In addition, church networks such as the indigenous council REPAM, the Latin American Council of Bishops (CELAM) and the Confederation of Religious Orders are sending delegates to this body. Decisions require a two-thirds majority of all members - *there is no* provision for a *special episcopal power.* CEAMA thus embodies a synodal leadership culture in which pastors and lay people share responsibility. "It is the most genuine expression of synodality (walking together)," said Cardinal Barreto about this conference. The Latin American church also relies on such models beyond the Amazon region: in 2021, a continental *"Ecclesial Assembly"* (Asamblea Eclesial) took place for the first time, at which bishops, priests, religious *and* lay people from all over Latin America discussed pastoral priorities together. This assembly was seen as the "practical implementation" of the World Synod on Synodality. During the discussions, it became clear how much the faithful at grassroots level want more participation: A cultural change is needed to *overcome clericalism* and fully involve lay people - women, young people, indigenous people, Afro-descendants. This is also what the Conference of female, diverse and male Bishops of Paraguay called for in a pastoral letter for the Year of the Laity 2022, in which the Paraguayan clergy warn: *"Clericalism* takes us away from the full meaning of the communion of the Church, which is rich in ministries and charisms, all at the service of the one mission". Instead of seeing clerics as the sole authorities, the entire church must act as the *people of God* - an understanding that Pope Francis brings to the universal church from his Latin American experience (cf. Evangelii Gaudium 2013).

Many African bishops also *advocate shared leadership*, drawing on the synodal traditions of their continent. Since the first African Synod in

1994, the African church has seen itself as a "family of God" in which all members play important roles. In many African dioceses, for example, elected *pastoral councils and catechists* are the main pillars of church leadership. Due to a lack of priests, well-trained lay people often take on the liturgical and organizational leadership in rural communities as catechists - with the blessing of the bishops. This *cooperation between laypeople* and *shepherds* is a lived necessity and an expression of a holistic image of the Church. The current chairman of the Symposium of African Conferences of Bishops (SECAM), Cardinal *Fridolin Ambongo* (Democratic Republic of the Congo), emphasizes precisely this. At the World Synod 2023, Ambongo remarked that the synod *was extraordinary* because not only bishops, but also lay people, women and young people participated fully - there was an "unusual atmosphere" of listening together. This made it possible to experience "that we as a church are truly *walking together*", said the cardinal. According to official reports, the *shared responsibility of clergy and laity* was explicitly addressed in the synod discussions. African church representatives emphasize that synodality is not a foreign concept in Africa: Traditional forms of consultation (palaver) and the communal spirit of African cultures promote an *inclusive* understanding of the church. In a joint document with the European bishops, SECAM explained that Rome's reforms - such as the curia order *Praedicate Evangelium* - clearly emphasized the participation of lay people, especially women, in church leadership. This new *paradigm of participatory palaver* admittedly requires a change in mentality among clergy and laity alike. The African bishops are committed to *involving laypeople in leadership tasks* and "walking side by side" with them. An example from Asia serves as inspiration: Cardinal *Charles Maung Bo* from Myanmar, himself President of the Asian Conferences for Bishops, called for regular synods to be held in *all* dioceses. Diocesan synods are an effective means of jointly developing a vision and mission for the local church, Bo emphasized during the World Synod. Such local synods *make it possible for clergy and laity to make decisions in dialog that* are appropriate to the respective situation - a principle that is already practiced in many young churches in Africa and Asia.

In Asia, high-profile church leaders are also pushing for greater involvement of the laity in leadership and mission. Cardinal *Oswald*

Gracias (India), a long-time advisor, is considered an advocate of *co-responsibility*. Even as Archbishop of Mumbai, he made it clear that it was a mistake to regard the laity as "passive hands" - on the contrary, "the laity are called to take on *leadership roles in* the Church in order to defend Christian identity in society and proclaim the Good News". Gracias spoke this remarkably open word in 2007 as chairman of the Indian bishops of the Latin rite. As a cardinal, he has continued this line: In the Vatican Council of Cardinals, he advocated that the local faithful should also be consulted when appointing bishops. In his home diocese, he promoted the formation of pastoral lay committees. Another example is Cardinal *Luis Antonio Tagle* (Philippines), who, as former Archbishop of Manila, held regular meetings with grassroots communities and lay representatives in order to make decisions together. Tagle emphasized that clergy and laity must be "disciples together" and lead the church as a *listening community*. In Japan and Korea, on the other hand, *parish leadership teams* consisting of priests and laypeople are not uncommon - partly due to a lack of priests and partly due to a conscious synodal culture.

Finally: *Homines Probati* & *Laici Probati* - Towards a new leadership culture to overcome the risk of traditional inertia

From *Europe and Latin America to Africa and Asia*, these ecclesial reform voices are united by the conviction that the mission of the church in the 21st century can only succeed if *consecrated and lay people, or clergy and consecrated lay people,* take on responsibility *together.* Whether in synodal councils, in elected local leadership teams or through co-determination at a global level - concrete models are emerging everywhere that bring clergy and laity to the table.

If *"Viri Probati"* ("proven men", mostly married men who can be ordained as priests) the paradigm of *"Homines Probati" in order to also admit married women as people* **who** are practically active as priests, then *"Homines Probati"* ("proven people", as a group of people in general, regardless of gender, gender-neutral or cross-gender) can logically also be referred to as *"Laici Probati"* ("proven lay people"): *"Laici Probati"* refers to lay persons (women and men) who are ordained on the basis of their tried and tested and experience, can be equated to clergy even without a degree in theology for their respective level of activity locally, not only to assume responsibility or leadership positions in the church, but also to perform sacraments liturgically. Then the marriage ceremony of remarried couples will also be possible in a more differentiated way, if the old-fashioned clergymembers should duck and cover.

"Duck and cover" is a protective measure that was particularly widespread during the Cold War in the USA to protect oneself in the event of a nuclear attack. In the event of danger, people should immediately take cover, crouch down ("duck") and cover their heads and necks ("cover"), for example under tables or on walls, if radioactive fallout was imminent. The term was later also generally used ironically to describe a reflexive, passive or defensive behavior in the face of crises - and yes, in a church context, the metaphor *"duck and cover"* can certainly be used ironically or critically to describe those clergy who reflexively withdraw and "take cover" in the face of conflicts or reform issues. An *ironic-critical* image of the *roman turtles* among the clergy would fit: It describes those clergy who, in difficult situations, hide behind official Roman guidelines in order to avoid conflicts or uncomfortable discussions instead of openly taking a stand or assuming responsibility. However, this figurative image of the radioactive fallout for Rome is clearly not applicable today when it comes to Rome's stance on remarriage or the acceptance of homosexuality: For neither the love of same-sex-oriented nor of divorced people and couples can be anywhere near as 'corrosive' or dangerous similar to radioactive fallout as a perverted logic of love of neighbor - if a formulation for such an inhuman, cynical and discriminatory attitude, which can pervert and negate love beyond recognition, should be aptly and at the same time satirically expressed as a methaphorical remark. And the *image of the "ducking-away person"* only fits to a limited extent because there are many active and creative clergy who do not pretend, but whose hands may actually be tied.

The motivation of clergy to effectively and sustainably consider the needs and the message of charity and team orientation in the Gospel through synodal co-leadership is not about blurring the ministries, but about *shared leadership in the spirit of ministry: Who would want to reject their colleagues and co-workers on site in the congregation or duck away and passively look the other way, accepting quasi omission of help, when they express their expectations and needs ? Who would be the person who persistently and repeatedly rejects and overlooks this?*

The church is called to *"walk together"* in an intensely lived community. Active, walking clergy are required: Various clergy around the world are shaping similar mottos and making it clear: the old patterns of clericalism have had their day. A *"church of the many"*, in which priests, bishops and lay people work together at all levels, is the goal of synodal renewal. This leadership culture at eye level is challenging, but it promises a more credible church. "Consultation and decision-making belong together. They are not an episcopal monopoly, but a joint task of the people of the church," as theologian *Thomas Söding* put it. With this in mind, courageous church leaders around the world are working to turn the vision of the Second Vatican Council - the *people of God* as a pilgrim whole - into structural reality. Their examples - from Germany to the Amazon to Asia - show that *equal leadership with lay people* is not only possible, but already in the making. The "hour of the laity" (John Paul II) has come, and many shepherds are using it to lead the Church into the future together with the faithful.

Overcoming institutional inertia in church leadership models is therefore not a luxury problem, but crucial for the future of the church. *Democratization in the sense of synodality* is not a foreign body, but a way back to the dynamics of the early church - and at the same time forwards, in order to remain compatible in the modern world. We need a cultural shift away from fear and towards trust: Trust that the Holy Spirit is at work in the entire community and that there is more blessing *in shared responsibility* than in centralized rule.

The examples from German dioceses, Switzerland, Latin America and around the world show that change is possible - but it takes courage. Courage on the part of bishops to share power and sometimes risk losing control; courage on the part of lay people to take responsibility and contribute competently. Synodal structures are not created overnight. They have to be *practiced*, as Archbishop *Franz Lackner* from

Austria says: anchoring synodality in the everyday life of the church is an *"organic process"* that requires effective action.

But this process is irreversibly underway. Pope Francis has initiated a *world synod on synodality*, in which non-ordained and not-yet-ordained (*laici probati*) have the right to vote for the first time. The signal is clear: *walking together* is the model for the church of tomorrow.

Figure 24: Ecclesia Semper Reformanda - the Church that is always renewing itself: reform issues without a threatening character through continuous adjustments.

A simple and impressive image in the style of a historical parchment page with the Latin lettering 'ECCLESIA SEMPER REFORMANDA' in clear, black lettering. The background shows an aged, beige-brown paper texture that conveys the impression of tradition and historical weight. The lettering symbolizes the need for constant reform and renewal in the Catholic Church. The overall image is at once classic, dignified and inspiring.

Structural and legal steps are needed to turn symbolic consultation into genuine co-decision-making - but above all a *change in mentality*. The church must get out of the "authority mode" of risk aversion and ducking away and become a *learning organization* that dares to try out new forms of leadership. If bishops and believers look for solutions together instead of working against each other, the reform issue will lose its threatening character in the image of a radioactive fall-out.

The vision is a church leadership culture that is *team-oriented, diverse and collegial* - and therefore a credible witness to the Gospel in the world. This vision is both biblically inspired and easy to communicate to society. In doing so, the church does not have to give up anything of its essence, on the contrary: it lives its communio (community) more convincingly. The road to this may be paved with resistance - think of the Roman exhortations that repeatedly put the brakes on international departures. But reforms instead of regression are called for.

Figure 25: Church wedding of homosexual couples at a snail's pace.

A humorous drawing shows a marriage counseling situation in the Catholic Church. A turtle as a spiritual counselor sits behind a desk with the sign 'church wedding & marriage counseling'. Sitting opposite her are two tortoise shells without tortoises in them. The counselor asks: 'How quickly should I prepare the wedding ceremony at the altar?' A humorous cartoon scene in which animals playfully depict the typical sluggishness and slowness of the catholic church.

So let us learn from the positive examples and values of democracy without denying the uniqueness of the church. *Synodality can learn from democracy - and democracy can perhaps also learn from synodality*, where it is a matter of struggling together in the light of faith.

In the end, there is hope: a church that shakes off its institutional inertia, that courageously allows laity and clergy to decide together, that accepts diversity as a gift, will once again experience *new beginnings instead of demolition.* Then progressive and creative clergy and committed and creative believers can together translate the Good News into new deeds - unhindered by inner blockades, unhindered by superordinate blockades - guided instead by the spirit of renewal. The time for *"cementing old prohibitions and distributions of power"* is over. Now is the time to *lead the church together* - so that the often-invoked *ecclesia semper reformanda* (the church that is constantly being renewed) becomes a living reality.

🕊️Bishops' briefing:

In the religious policy field, it can be argued that the Catholic Church needs to overcome its current institutional inertia, characterized by risk avoidance, ducking away and clinging to the status quo, in order to implement relevant and socially urgent reforms. To this end, it was suggested that a democratization of church leadership - not in the political sense, but as an extended co-determination and shared responsibility of all believers (laity and clergy) - is necessary to prevent abuse of power, to do justice to the common baptismal mission and not to lose touch with modern social expectations. Examples are given from Germany, Latin America, Africa and Asia, which show how synodal structures, leadership teams and lay participation are already being practiced or sought at various levels in order to create a more credible and effective church. The concept of "Laici Probati" was developed in order to delegate opportunities for spiritual tasks to those who are proven capable in practice, but who have not studied - such as the liturgical performance of sacraments, for example the marriage of couples who are remarrying. Such models are theologically justifiable and a way to implement the ecclesia semper reformanda (the church that is constantly being renewed) in reality.

Didactic questions:

56 - What does "institutional inertia" mean in the church and what are its consequences?

Institutional inertia describes the tendency of many church structures and committees to cling to the tried and tested and be skeptical of innovations. This principle of risk avoidance blocks urgently needed reforms and creates a climate that is hostile to innovation. Even progressive bishops can be slowed down in their creative drive if the surrounding structures are primarily geared towards the status quo and damage prevention. The consequences of this inertia are serious: necessary changes are postponed in the face of dwindling membership, credibility crises (particularly following abuse scandals) and changing social values. Committed believers are losing patience and the gap between church leadership and the reality of people's lives is growing. Instead of responding courageously to challenges, governing bodies are falling into a kind of "administration of decline". Standing still is more risky than change, as it leads to a gradual loss of significance.

57 - Why is a democratization of church leadership considered necessary?

A democratization of church leadership is seen as necessary and overdue for several reasons in order to remain capable of acting and credible. Firstly, the current concentration of decisions on a small number of clergy has often led to abuse of power and a lack of transparency, as the investigation into the abuse scandals has made clear. More democratic structures such as independent supervisory bodies, transparent procedures and accountability could prevent this. Secondly, all baptized persons share in the mission of the Church. The Second Vatican Council emphasized the Church as the people of God, in which laity and clergy share responsibility. Pope Benedict XVI clearly formulated that lay people are not only collaborators, but also co-responsible for the being and acting of the Church. This co-responsibility requires real participation in decisions, not just consultation. Thirdly, democratization is necessary in order not to completely lose touch with today's social expectations. In modern democracies, participation, transparency and equality are central values that members of the church also expect within the church. Adapting to these values is considered necessary in order to avoid losing credibility.

58 - How does the desired democratization differ from political democracy?

"Democratization" in the church context does not mean a simple transfer of political democracy. Rather, it is about an expansion of genuine co-determination and participation in responsibility by all baptized persons - laypeople and clergy alike - in the spirit of the Gospel. While political democracy is often about majority decisions that could also affect matters of faith, the focus in the ecclesial context is on leadership and administration, not on dogmas of faith. However, principles such as the separation of powers, transparency, protection of minorities and voter participation from secular democracy can be introduced as helpful procedures to make church governance more transparent and to promote the participation of the faithful without losing the spiritual identity of the church. Theologically, this is justified by the understanding of the church as the "people of God" and the common priesthood of all the baptized.

59 - What concrete models or approaches for synodal leadership already exist? And what role do regional and global church initiatives play in promoting synodal structures?

There are already various concrete models and approaches for synodal leadership at different levels. Regional and world church initiatives play a crucial role in promoting these synodal structures by testing leadership skills and serving as inspiration. These include:

- **Synodal path in Europe:** Proposals have been developed here to limit the power of bishops and to introduce binding synodal bodies such as a diocesan synodal council with co-decision rights, which is representative of the people of God through elections. Pope Francis has sent a strong signal by convening the World Synod on Synodality and granting voting rights to non-ordained people. Cardinals such as Hollerich, Grech and Farrell emphasize the need for synodal renewal and the shared responsibility of clergy and laity.

- **Leadership teams made up of clergy and lay people:** In German dioceses (e.g. Trier, Essen), there are implementations with joint leadership in pastoral care units or parishes by teams of priests and laypeople. This distributes responsibility and bundles competencies.

- **Synodal co-determination in the world church:Switzerland:** Here, there are partly democratic structures due to state church law, in which lay people elect church parliaments or parish councils, which co-decide on financial and personnel issues.

- **Latin America:** Following the Amazon Synod, the Amazon Church Conference (CEAMA) was founded, an official church body made up of bishops, priests, religious and lay people, which is intended to promote synodality and common pastoral guidelines. There are also pastoral councils with real decision-making powers in individual dioceses. The tradition of base communities (Comunidades Eclesiales de Base) has already promoted a culture of co-determination here.

- **Africa:** Here, elected pastoral councils and catechists are often the main pillars of church leadership, especially in rural areas. The African church sees itself as the "family of God" and relies on traditional forms of consultation (palaver). Elected pastoral councillors and catechists often take on leadership roles. At the World Synod, Cardinal Ambongo emphasized the positive experience of clergy and laity listening and walking together.

- **Asia:** In some dioceses (e.g. Japan, Korea) there are parish leadership teams made up of priests and lay people. Cardinals such as Gracias (India) and Tagle (Philippines) advocate the participation of lay people in leadership and decision-making processes.

These examples show that concrete change is possible through binding councils, electoral processes, shared leadership responsibility and transparent synods. And: these global examples show that the vision of a church with equal leadership of clergy and laity is not just a theory, but is already being lived out in various contexts. They encourage other regions to follow similar paths.

60 - To what extent can team-oriented and diverse forms of leadership be justified theologically?

There are many theological reasons for team-oriented and diverse forms of leadership. The New Testament shows a fundamentally collegial orientation: Jesus sends his disciples out in pairs and the early church makes decisions in the council of apostles and elders (Council of Apostles). Paul describes the church as the body of Christ with many members and different gifts (1 Cor 12), which celebrates diversity in unity. Collegial leadership today builds on this by bringing together different professions, walks of life (consecrated and non-consecrated), genders, generations and backgrounds in teams to make the richness of spiritual gifts fruitful. Theologically, it is argued that the Holy Spirit speaks not only through the hierarchy, but also through the "sensus fidei" of all believers - that sense of the people of faith. A group usually makes more balanced decisions, as more facets are taken into account. The Jesuan principle *"Where two or three are gathered in my name..."* underlines the community orientation. The Catholic Church has already recognized the principle of collegiality (e.g. in the college); an extension of this principle to lay people in leadership teams would be a concretization of the shared responsibility of all baptized persons laid down in Vatican II. Pope Francis emphasizes that synodality is the way of the Church in the third millennium and includes everyone, not just bishops.

61 - What could the inclusion of lay people, especially women, in church leadership look like and what significance does this have?

The inclusion of lay people, including women, in church leadership could be concretized in various ways. These include

- **Binding co-decision rights for lay people in committees:** Lay people should not only be active in an advisory capacity, but should have real decision-making powers in councils at parish, diocesan and national level (as in the planned Synodal Council), for example in pastoral planning, financial management and personnel issues.
- **Leadership teams with clergy and lay people:** In parishes and pastoral care units, teams of priests and lay people could take on the leadership together.

- **Participation of non-ordained persons in synods and conferences:** Pope Francis has already granted non-ordained persons the right to vote in synods. Models such as CEAMA in Latin America show that committees from different groups can work together to develop pastoral guidelines.
- **Adaptations in canon law:** The Code of Canon Law (CIC) would have to be adapted in order to anchor (proven and ordained) laypeople more firmly in leadership positions, be it through delegated authority from bishops or other legal frameworks.
- **Self-commitment of the bishops:** Bishops could commit themselves to making important decisions only with the consent of their diocesan councils.

The equal inclusion of women is particularly important here, as their skills are urgently needed in church leadership. This reflects the global diversity of the Church and makes it more inclusive and credible, especially for younger generations. Cardinal Farrell emphasizes the shared responsibility of clergy and laity, which must be brought to bear especially in leadership and administration. This is a central element of the desired "synodal renewal".

62 - What are the main obstacles and challenges in overcoming institutional inertia and implementing synodal leadership?

Overcoming institutional inertia and implementing synodal leadership faces several key obstacles and challenges:

- **Risk aversion and clinging to the status quo:** Many committees and institutions work according to the principle of risk avoidance and are skeptical of innovations, which blocks reforms.
- **Reform backlog:** The inability to respond boldly to current challenges is leading to a reform backlog.
- **Concentration of power and clericalism:** The concentration of decisions on a few clerics makes participation more difficult and promotes clericalism, which undermines the shared responsibility of all the baptized.

- **Adaptation of church law:** In order to anchor lay people more firmly in leadership positions, changes to the Code of Canon Law are necessary.
- **Roman concerns:** The Vatican has expressed reservations about some reform proposals (e.g. the national synodal council) and sometimes puts the brakes on regional initiatives...
- **Change of mentality:** ... a profound change in mentality is therefore needed among clergy (willingness to share power and relinquish control) and laity (willingness to take responsibility). The church must move from the "authority mode" of risk aversion to a learning organization.
- **Resistance and conflict:** Reform processes are often associated with resistance and conflict, both internally and through external intervention.
- **Practicing synodal processes:** Synodal structures need to be practiced. This is an "organic process" that requires patience.

Despite these challenges, examples around the world show that change is possible. It takes courage, trust in the work of the Holy Spirit in the entire community and the conviction that shared responsibility brings more blessing. The vision is a team-oriented, diverse and collegial leadership culture that is a credible witness to the Gospel.

63 - What is at the heart of the church's reform efforts in the 21st century?

In essence, it is about enabling the mission of the church in the 21st century through a new leadership culture in which consecrated and lay people, or clergy and consecrated lay people, assume equal responsibility. This is intended to overcome traditional inertia and make the church more credible. The goal is a "church of the many" in which all levels - priests, bishops and lay people - work together.

64 - What are "Homines Probati" and "Laici Probati" in the context of these reforms?

"Homines Probati" ("proven humans") expands the traditional concept of "Viri Probati" ("proven men") and includes married women and diverse people as potential priests. "Laici Probati" ("proven lay people") refers to lay people of any gender who can be ordained on the basis of their proven ability and experience and are considered equal to clergy, not only to take on leadership roles but also to perform sacraments in part, even without theological studies.

65 - What is meant by the metaphor "duck and cover" in a church context?

The metaphor "duck and cover" is used ironically and critically to describe clergy who reflexively retreat when faced with conflicts or reform issues and "run for cover" from Rome instead of openly taking a stand or assuming responsibility. This can be interpreted metaphorically as the behavior of turtles belonging to Rome who hide behind official guidelines. However, the metaphor is misleading, as many clergy want to act actively, but may actually be existentially bound by higher-level structures.

66 - What does (the logic of) "perverted charity" of the Catholic Church mean and what criticism is behind it?

The expression "perverted charity" or, more precisely, "perverted logic of charity" refers to a metaphorical phrase that describes a certain attitude: An ecclesiastical attitude that can pervert and negate love beyond recognition. The phrase could then be used to describe an inhuman, cynical and discriminatory attitude: The criticism of this "reversal of charity" is directed with this formulation against certain behaviors and attitudes within the church, for example, an attitude towards the exclusion of divorced people or the lack of acceptance of two same-sex lovers. It is criticized that neither the love of same-sex oriented nor divorced people and couples can be nearly as "corrosive" or dangerous as this "perverted" quintessence of charity, which represents an inhuman, cynical and discriminatory attitude - not recognizing love and charity.

It is therefore about questioning an attitude that pretends to act in accordance with church doctrine or rules, but denies or distorts fundamental principles of charity, especially when dealing with certain groups of people. Such judgmental attitudes, the discrimination of love, are seen as far more harmful than the lifestyles of the people who are being addressed and who only want to have their love (possibly again) sacramentally confirmed before the altar by leading clergy (or lay people ordained for this task). *Not wanting to call love love is a perversion of love, from the Latin: a perversion of love.* The (homosexual and heterosexual) abstainers in the Vatican often do a section of society (and mostly their own kind) no good with their teaching! This is pure cynicism.

67 - How does the desired management culture differ from traditional models?

The desired leadership culture is team-oriented, diverse and collegial, in contrast to traditional clericalist and centralist models. It is about shared leadership in the spirit of service and not about a blurring of offices. Consultation and decision-making should be understood as a shared task of the people of the church and not as an episcopal monopoly.

68 - Why is overcoming institutional inertia important for the future of the church?

Overcoming institutional inertia is seen as crucial for the future of the church. It is not a luxury problem, but necessary in order to remain relevant and resonate in the modern world. A sluggish church that ducks away and remains in "authority mode" loses credibility.

69 - To what extent is synodality seen as a return to the early church and at the same time as a way into the future?

Synodality is seen as a way back to the dynamics of the early church, where the people of God were on the move as a whole. At the same time, it is a way forward in order to remain relevant and connectable in the modern world. Democratization in the sense of synodality is not seen as a foreign body, but as a necessary cultural change.

70 - What attitude is needed for the change to a more synodal church to succeed?

Courage and trust are needed for change. Courage from bishops to share power and risk losing control, and courage from laity to take responsibility. There needs to be a cultural shift away from fear and towards trust that the Holy Spirit is at work in the entire community. The "authority mode" must become a learning organization that tries out new forms of leadership.

71 - What concrete signs indicate that the process of synodal renewal is already underway?

Concrete signs are the emergence of synodal councils and elected leadership teams worldwide that bring clergy and laity together. Pope Francis' initiative for a world synod on synodality, in which non-ordained and "laici probati" have voting rights for the first time, is a clear signal. Positive examples from various regions of the world show that equal leadership with lay people is not only possible, but is already in the making.

Essay questions:

Please answer one of the following questions in the form of an essay:

a)   Discuss the extent to which institutional inertia and risk aversion affect the church's ability to respond to current challenges such as membership decline or credibility crises.

b)   Analyse the theological arguments that the text puts forward for a democratization of church leadership. How is the idea of collegial leadership and the participation of all the baptized (Lumen Gentium, sensus fidei) used in the context of this argument?

c)   Compare and contrast concrete examples of synodal and more democratic leadership models in Germany, Switzerland and Latin America. What similarities and differences in approach and implementation can be identified?

d)   Discuss the above-mentioned objection *"The church is not a democracy!"*. How do you counter this argument and what distinction is made between dogmas of faith and leadership decisions?

e)   According to the text, what role do "team orientation", "inclusion", "diversity" and "collegial leadership" play for the credibility and relevance of the church in the 21st century? Explain both the social and spiritual reasons for these forms of leadership.

f)   Discuss the significance of the shift from the paradigm of "Viri Probati" to *"Homines Probati"* and *"Laici Probati"* for the future role of the laity in the Catholic Church, considering the powers and responsibilities involved.

g) Analyze the *"duck and cover"* metaphor in a church context and discuss the extent to which it aptly describes the behavior of some clergy in relation to reform issues and conflicts.

h) Evaluate the thesis that synodal co-leadership is not a blurring of ministries, but a shared leadership in the spirit of ministry, drawing references to the concept of the "Church of the Many".

i) In what discrimination, contempt and renunciation is charity reversed?

j) Examine the statement that overcoming institutional inertia and democratization in the sense of synodality are not a foreign body in the church, but a way back to the dynamics of the early church and at the same time forward in order to remain connectable.

k) Discuss the necessary structural, canonical and mental steps to turn symbolic synodal consultation into genuine co-decision-making in the Catholic Church.

Religious policy field analysis 9: *Dealing with sexualized violence in the Catholic Church - need for reform and responsibility*

The scandal of sexualized violence and its cover-up fundamentally questions the credibility of the Catholic Church. The chairman of the German Conference of female, diverse and male Bishops, Bishop Georg Bätzing, calls the abuse scandal "the biggest scandal" for the Church ever and warns that *"the systemic causes [must] be eliminated"*, as otherwise trust cannot be regained.

In recent years, it has become clear that individual apologies are not enough - *institutional responsibility and far-reaching structural reforms* are needed to come to terms with the past and prevent future abuse.

Bishops' responsibility and the church's willingness to reform

A *rethink* is evident in the German Conference of female, diverse and male Bishops: numerous bishops emphasize coming to terms with the past and the will to reform. The presiding bishop publicly affirms that trust can only be rebuilt through consistent action.

Other *reform-oriented bishops* are also taking a clear stance. Bishop *Peter Kohlgraf* of Mainz, for example, praised an independent abuse study in his diocese as a "milestone" in the process of coming to terms with the past, while also emphasizing that the process was not over. Kohlgraf stated unequivocally that an *"entire system has failed"* - there should no longer be any "untouchable monuments" to former spiritual authorities. This open self-criticism shows the growing awareness that *church hierarchs* were and are *part of the problem* - and must now be part of the solution.

The resignation of Bishop *Franz-Josef Bode* (Osnabrück) is a remarkable example of personal responsibility. He was the first German diocesan bishop *to explicitly justify* his resignation *with his own mistakes in dealing with cases of abuse.*

In his statement, Bode "expressly" acknowledged his responsibility and *personal mistakes* and asked all those affected "once again for forgiveness". This step - combined with self-criticism - was widely acknowledged as a signal of acceptance of responsibility.

Several active bishops are also calling for *consequences and reforms that* go beyond personal admissions of guilt. Bishop *Heiner Wilmer* (Hildesheim) went unusually far early on and clearly identified the fundamental problem: *"I believe that the abuse of power is in the DNA of the church,"* Wilmer said back in 2018.

He called for *radical change* and effective control of church power structures: "Because there are also *'structures of evil'* in the church... We need a separation of powers". These clear words from a bishop show how much the understanding is changing - away from the thesis of individual "black sheep" towards the recognition of a *systemic problem of abuse of power* in the church. Bishop *Helmut Dieser* (Aachen), who took over the role of abuse commissioner of the German Conference of female, diverse and male Bishops in 2023, also emphasizes that the church is now "intensively involved" in coming to terms with the abuse and that the process is *consistently oriented towards those affected rather than the institution.* At the same time, he emphasizes that the church needs support from outside: the state and external expertise must assume greater responsibility in order to set generally applicable standards and monitor compliance with them.

This statement signals openness to *external scrutiny* - a novelty, as ecclesiastical reappraisal has long been regarded as an internal matter.

Lack of transparency and crisis of confidence: the Woelki case

Despite this progress, there are still areas in which a lack of transparency is attracting massive criticism. *Cardinal Rainer Maria Woelki, Archbishop of Cologne, is a prime example of this*. His handling of an external report on cases of abuse in the Archdiocese of Cologne triggered a deep crisis of confidence. At the end of 2020, Woelki *withheld* an already completed report by a Munich law firm on the handling of abuse in the diocese, allegedly due to methodological flaws. This decision was met with harsh criticism - not only from the faithful, but also from official sources. The Independent Commissioner for Abuse of the Federal Government publicly accused Woelki *of a "lack of transparency"*: *Johannes-Wilhelm Rörig* spoke of a *"heavy burden"* for those affected by abuse and stated that there was currently a lack of *"transparency and trust"* (in Cologne) - instead, "mistrust and skepticism" were emerging. In fact, Woelki's actions - not publishing the original report and commissioning a new one instead - caused outrage far beyond Germany. The President of the Central Committee of German Catholics, Thomas Sternberg, called the Archdiocese of Cologne's communication *"catastrophic"*, with far-reaching consequences for the trust of the faithful.

The "Woelki case" illustrates how destructive the non-transparent handling of allegations of abuse can be. While reformist bishops like Wilmer *question the system*, others reject this view - Woelki, for example, vehemently disagreed with the statement that abuse of power is in the church's DNA. But regardless of debates within the church, the ongoing crisis in the Archdiocese of Cologne shows that *a lack of transparency and hesitancy to come to terms with the situation are shaking trust almost beyond repair*. Many believers are calling for consequences - including Woelki's resignation - and complain that the protection of the institution is still too often placed above honesty. The contrast could hardly be greater: On the one hand, bishops who admit mistakes and initiate change; on the other, an archbishop whose handling is criticized as defensive and lacking transparency. This discrepancy underlines the *urgent need for reform at a structural level* so that transparency and accountability apply in *all* dioceses, regardless of the respective leadership.

Demands from theologians and reform initiatives

In the face of such deficits, theologians, victims' representatives and church reform movements are vocal and specific in their demands. They insist that dealing with the abuse must not be left to the structures that have long been part of the problem. *Independent investigative commissions* are therefore considered essential. Reform initiatives such as *Maria 2.0* - an association of committed Catholic women (and men) - have long been calling for full transparency and external investigative bodies. Under the slogan *"Get out the file"*, Maria 2.0 protested in Cologne in 2020 for the withheld report to finally be published.

"Taking responsibility - that is important in order to restore credibility," explained Maria Mesrian, a spokesperson for the initiative. In practice, this means: *full disclosure of files* instead of secrecy. Many theologians and representatives of those affected argue similarly: Only if the church is prepared to open up all archives and allow independent experts to view them can a complete investigation be carried out. Any form of withholding information - so the tenor - cements the accusation that the church is still protecting itself more than the victims.

In addition, *external control* over the review process is being called for. Many critics are concerned that the church's own committees could be biased. Some are therefore even calling for a *state truth commission*. Würzburg Bishop *Franz Jung* - himself a member of the Conference of female, diverse and male Bishops - supported this idea and spoke out *in favor of a state "truth commission" to come to terms with the past*. In doing so, he took up a central demand of many victims' initiatives, namely the investigation of the church abuse scandal under the leadership of independent bodies outside the church hierarchy. Jung justified his initiative with the fact that victims' representatives who cooperate with the church are sometimes treated with hostility as part of the "perpetrator organization" - an independent state commission could create trust here.

Limiting power in the church is another key point of corresponding demands. According to the analysis, the concentration of power in individual clergymembers without sufficient control mechanisms has made abuse possible in the first place. This is why reformers are calling for a cultural change: away from clericalism and towards *shared responsibility*. In concrete terms, this means greater involvement of competent laypeople in decision-making processes, *external expertise in cases of suspected abuse*, fixed rules for the prosecution of perpetrators within the church and *automatic procedures* if leaders cover up. Limiting the term of office or authority of bishops is also being discussed in order to prevent the uncontrolled exercise of power. *"Separation of powers"* - in the sense of checks and balances within church structures - has become a buzzword (Bishop Wilmer: *"We need separation of powers"*). Behind this is the realization that a system in which *the abuse of power* has often remained without consequences to date must change fundamentally. For theologians, this is less about *shifting political power* and more about protective mechanisms: no person in the church should be so powerful that they can cover up crimes or act without accountability.

But the churches do not want to change: The abolition of celibacy, the ordination of women and different sexual morals with recognition of the marriage of same-sex couples are not being implemented, nor are decision-making powers for lay people. In addition, there are veils and cover-ups, exchanges and transfers of perpetrators to other communities: *Who knows who you'll get when a new one comes along.* Many critics emphasize that you can only leave this church association - or have to found a parallel new one with different conditions.

Synodal path: prevention, reappraisal and reform of power structures

Many demands have also been taken up in the *position papers and resolutions of the Synodal Path*. The Synodal Path - the four-year reform dialog of the Catholic Church - was created directly in response to the abuse crisis. From the outset, it was clear that the lost trust could only be regained through concrete changes. In fact, the bishops cited the following central motive: *"People's trust has been betrayed by clerical abuse of power; it [is] necessary to find ways to reduce power in the Church".*

Accordingly, *Forum I of the Synodal Path ("Power and Separation of Powers in the Church")* worked on proposals to limit the current concentration of power. Among other things, it was decided to *involve the faithful more closely in the appointment of bishops (personnel selection processes with criteria and voting, including interviews on history and curriculum vitae as well as reputations from previous positions)* - for example through a voluntary commitment by the cathedral chapters in which lay people participate and through electoral elements in the appointment of bishops. In addition, the Synodal Assembly called for the establishment of a *Synodal Council* at federal and diocesan level, in which clergy and laity would jointly discuss and decide on important issues and reform topics as well as religious policy areas. This body would be a novelty and would relativize the authority of individual bishops in favour of joint leadership. Although the Vatican has expressed reservations about this for the time being, the *majority of German bishops* have expressed their determination to stick to the plan. So here, too, Rome said no in terms of content and a rejection as in other areas. *"It can't go on like this,"* emphasize some church-related reform initiatives.

These debates show: Church members are seeking ways to *share power and strengthen control* in order to break down the very clerical power structures that have facilitated or masked sexual abuse as sexualized violence against young people by male priests.

The debate is also doubly important: on the one hand, it is about the sexual abuse of young people by Catholic priests and, on the other, about the abuse of power by church leaders who conceal these acts or prevent them from being dealt with . Both forms of abuse must be explicitly differentiated and named, because in sum, it is not just a matter of structural abuse of power, but also of sexualized violence and personal assaults on young people. The word "abuse of power" is too readily used as a cipher in order to ignore the word "sexual abuse" of children and young people in terms of rhetoric and content.

The Synodal Path also passed concrete resolutions in the area of *prevention and intervention*. The assembly adopted a *comprehensive catalog of measures to prevent sexualized violence*. This covers all levels: *Primary prevention* (creating structures that prevent acts - for example through the selection and training of staff and a culture of mindfulness), *secondary prevention* (early intervention in the event of behavior that violates boundaries) and *tertiary prevention* (dealing professionally with acts that have already been committed in order to prevent repetition). Existing church prevention regulations and training standards are to be reviewed and improved where necessary. It was also decided to *draw up a disciplinary code for clergy* in order to have clearer sanction options in church law against clergy who are guilty of misconduct. It is important to note that these measures can be implemented without overriding Rome - it is now up to the dioceses to introduce them consistently. In addition, the Conference of female, diverse and male Bishops, in cooperation with state authorities, confirmed the establishment of independent investigation commissions in *all* 27 dioceses. External experts and representatives of those affected are involved in these commissions in order to ensure that the local process is transparent and independent - a direct result of the demand for external monitoring.

Finally, the Synodal Path has also addressed the *transformation of power structures* in order to prevent future abuse through better control. A changed church *culture* should play a decisive role in this: away from clericalism and an elitist view of ministry and towards genuine synodality. The basic text of Forum I thus contains the clear statement that the *sharing of power and participation of all believers* is theologically justified and necessary. This met with broad approval: in the synodal assembly, around *77% of members were in favor of more power-sharing* in the church. This broad majority shows that *reform and prevention* go hand in hand: Only if church structures open up and become more controllable can abuse be effectively curbed.

Can the abolition of celibacy prevent sexual abuse in the Catholic Church and reduce the risk factors?

Especially when psychosexual immaturity and institutional silence come together with abuse of power, sexual abuse of adolescents by male priests can occur.

The *clerical culture of silence and repression* plays a decisive role: in a system in which sexuality is taboo, *sexual maturation and integration* are *prevented*. This can lead to hidden, unreflected desires that are discharged *in a hidden and sometimes abusive manner* - out of *inner pressure, isolation and immaturity.*

Access to young males is a risk factor in the Catholic Church. Some of the abuse by priests was directed against boys because they were *available* (e.. altar boys, boarders) - out of *opportunity and position of power.* The church system did not control this for decades, but covered it up. *There was a lack of control and a cover-up by the church.*

Priests with repressed sexuality who have learned to hate themselves for it can *be psychologically destabilized.* In rare cases, this can lead to *destructive behavior,* including sexual assault. *Tabooing, abuse of power, psychosexual immaturity and institutional turning a blind eye* are key factors.

A reform would therefore have to: openly address sexuality in education, control power and transparently hold offenders accountable.

Figure 26: Indirect risk factors due to celibacy culture.

Factor	Effect
Sexual maturation is suppressed	Many priests do not develop a healthy relationship with their own sexuality.
Training without a sexual theme	The training not only makes the topic of sexuality taboo, but also one's own sexual orientation and experiences.
Forced celibacy that has not been abolished	The clergy should/must show sexual abstinence.
Experiences of isolation and loneliness	Emotionally unfulfilled priests sometimes seek closeness in problematic ways.
Double standards and taboos	Sexuality must not be lived - this creates **secret spaces** in which assaults can also remain hidden.
Structural power	Celibate priests are often uncontrollably above others, which can encourage abuse of power.
Institutional turning a blind eye	The church transfers offenders instead of punishing them and likes to look the other way and does not work properly, studies are withheld, recommended consequences are not implemented.

Celibacy can also be an indirect cause of sexual abuse if it is a promoting risk factor under (these) certain conditions - especially if it is associated with isolation, immaturity and repressive sexual morals.

And it is, when sexually immature people have been repressively trained and indoctrinated in sexual morality after education and are then sent into forced celibacy, then three major factors can come together that favor sexual abuse in addition to opportunity and social power as well as institutional turning a blind eye.

According to studies (e.g. John Jay Report, MHG study), many spiritual abusers in the church context *were* without a *partner* and/or had a *repressed sexuality,* but were in positions of power. Celibacy was often *part of a system* that *did not sufficiently promote maturity, self-reflection and control.*

Celibacy requires *emotional maturity, self-knowledge, stable relationships (e.. friendships) and pastoral support.* One possible approach would be for a person to lead a conscious single life again only after their first sexual experiences and at least one year in a marriage or a stable partner relationship before they can voluntarily decide to lead a celibate life.

Celibacy *is an indirect trigger for sexual abuse* and, under certain circumstances, a *structural risk factor* if it is lived without psychosexual maturation, without openness and without institutional control. However, this is precisely the result of the doctrine and system of the Catholic Church.

The decisive factor is *how* celibacy is lived and *which environment* accompanies it; as can be described, the environment has often already been firmly indoctrinated by clergymembers in adolescent training seminars.

The second important risk factor for sexual abuse among priests is isolation. This also goes hand in hand with celibacy.

The immaturity of male priests without sexual experience can manifest itself in

- *emotional dependence on members of the community,* especially children or young people,

- *In the avoidance of conflict, closeness, clarity* in relationship issues,

- *A lack of social commitment to one's own sexual orientation and its social representation,*

- *Naive spiritualization of sexuality* instead of realistic integration,

- *Double standards (secret relationships, affairs)* instead of reflected responsibility.

Figure 27: Isolation and its factors and effects.

Factor	Effect
Lack of sexual experience	Starting celibacy after sexual experience can be a sign of quality and a change for the success of a mature and mature personality. Committing sexually inexperienced people directly to celibacy can lead to risks.
Commitment to celibacy	Celibacy also entails a commitment to loneliness and isolation.
Lack of intimate relationships	Emotional closeness, sexuality and partnership are lost - this can lead to loneliness.
Tabooing feelings and desire	Many priests learn to suppress their own needs instead of integrating them.
Special clerical role	Priests often live "isolated" from the everyday lives of other people - which can promote real loneliness.
Shame and guilt culture	Normal human feelings (desire, longing) are considered suspicious or sinful.

Many studies (such as the MHG study mentioned above) show that celibacy *often* leads *to psychological stress* - especially if: there is no preparation for emotional loneliness, sexual topics remain taboo and the church system does not allow for open discussion, training and dialogue.

A mature, relationship-capable man - who has already proven his sexuality and love relationship - *can* live a celibate life if necessary - but this requires a supportive environment and a positive integration of sexuality, not its denial.

It is true that *you can be or become a mature and relational person with a celibate lifestyle, but only under certain conditions.* Celibacy is a radical way of life that requires a high level of emotional, spiritual and social maturity - and *does not automatically generate* this maturity, but *requires and must actively cultivate it.*

Requirements for maturity and relationship skills in celibacy:

1. **Voluntariness**: Celibacy must be a conscious choice - not an escape from sexuality, partnership or identity issues or a dialog about one's own sexual orientation.

2. **Sexual integration instead of repression:** Mature celibates do not deny their sexuality, but have learned to understand and accept the sexual relationships they have experienced so far and now integrate their partnership experiences into other aspects of life (e.. creativity, spirituality, friendship).

3. **Deep friendships and emotional bonds:** Celibates still need sustainable, intimate (possibly non-sexual) relationships. Without these, there is a risk of loneliness or unconscious dependency.

4. **Reflection and psychological maturation:** Regular supervision, self-awareness, spiritual guidance and emotional formation are essential to promote maturation. This must begin in the seminary and concern those who have already had sexual experiences. One thesis that is being discussed: Those who have no sexual experience have no place in the seminary.

5. **Transparent lifestyle:** A healthy celibate existence thrives on honesty - before oneself, before God and in an environment that does not taboo questions and ruptures. This also includes being able to talk about previous partnerships and relationships.

Celibacy can *be added if there is the highest level of inner and personal maturity - otherwise it can be a protective mechanism of immature defense.* Whether it enables relationships or destroys relationships and leads to sexual abuse depends on the personality - and the church environment.

Can someone without sexual experience and love in togetherness be a pastor for the relationship issues of believers? - the honest answer is: *only to a very limited extent* - and that depends very much on how this person deals with their own lack of relationship, sexuality and emotional maturity.

Because pastoral care needs relational competence. Pastoral care - especially in relationship and love issues - thrives on: *Empathy*: I can sympathize with what others are experiencing. It thrives *on a horizon of experience:* I understand what closeness, conflict, intimacy or fear of commitment feel like. *And it is based on self-reflection:* I know how I deal with longing, jealousy, desire, my sexual orientation and my own relationship experiences or loneliness.

Without personal experience in partnership and sexuality, these points of reference are often missing or remain abstract.

A person without a romantic relationship of their own can still be an effective pastoral worker if they have *a deep spiritual maturity*, have *spent many years dealing with human closeness, vulnerability and relationship dynamics*, are able to *listen well, accompany and not judge*, and *do not* define themselves *through supposed moral superiority*. However, this depth does not "automatically" arise through celibacy or a priestly role.

After all, those who have *never experienced or reflected on* love, physical closeness or sexual attraction can often only *speak theoretically or morally*, not existentially. In practice, this often leads to *flat advice* ("pray more", "abstain", "be faithful") instead of real life help. Many believers *sense this* - and then no longer seek pastoral help from the church. Nor do they seek it from people who have no life experience in sexual relationships and identity representation. And they avoid even general pastoral care for their families, children and young people if the proximity of sexual abuse resonates, because the Catholic Church is not in a position to change its contexts as outlined above. Then you can only keep your children away or leave yourself, some believers said.

Figure 28: Turning away from and resignation from the Catholic Church after sexual abuse of young people by male priests in celibacy.

A satirical caricature shows an empty church with a large wooden cross with nails sticking out of it. A ladder stands next to it, on the floor is a pile of papers labeled "Report". Two clergymembers look at the cross in confusion: one asks "Where...?", the other answers dryly: "He has resigned...". The scene is humorous even where there is nothing to laugh about, namely with the idea that Jesus himself left the church - presumably as a reaction to the church's abuse of young people by celibate male priests.

Without personal experience of love, intimacy or conflict in togetherness, a central resource for credible relationship counseling is missing. Those who do not have this experience *must compensate for it* - through reflection, empathy training, willingness to engage in dialog and honest humility or an honest attempt to build a relationship. Compensation may not always succeed; it is in any case a state of incompleteness with corresponding possible contexts.

Dealing with sexualized violence in the Catholic Church therefore requires an honest look at past failures and the *courage to undertake far-reaching reforms*. A *pastoral-spiritual* reappraisal alone is not enough - *institutional changes* and dogmatic *changes in doctrine*, in particular sexual morality and celibacy, are required.

The signs of the times are pointing to change: from conference chairmen to committed diocesan bishops and theological reform initiatives, many are united by the realization that *transparency, external control and the limitation of power* do not pose a threat to the church, but on the contrary are the prerequisite for regaining lost trust. Cases such as the one in Cologne make it clear how much intransparency destroys credibility. In contrast, positive examples - such as bishops who admit their own mistakes or reform resolutions of the synodal path - show that a different path is possible.

To put it succinctly: *the Catholic Church must move from talk to action.* Independent commissions of inquiry, full disclosure of files and the willingness to hold leaders accountable are essential. At the same time, the *systemic factors* need to be addressed: a culture of clerical rule without control can be transformed into a culture of shared responsibility. Some leaders have already committed themselves to dealing with abuse relentlessly and, if necessary, to drawing painful consequences. Now it is important to implement these resolutions structurally. Hardly anything has changed so far. Only through *institutional responsibility and a willingness to reform* can the church find its way out of this deep crisis. The victims and the faithful as a whole rightly expect nothing less than *complete clarification* and lasting changes so that sexualized violence in the church is consistently prevented, dealt with and punished - and so that the church can once again credibly fulfil its mission.

🕊️Bishops' briefing:

Dealing with sexualized violence in the Catholic Church and the resulting need for reform is a religious policy area to be analysed. It addresses the challenges of coming to terms with the abuse scandals, the need for far-reaching structural reforms to restore credibility and the Church's struggle to move from a culture of cover-up to transparency and acceptance of responsibility. Various perspectives within the German Conference of female, diverse and male Bishops are to be presented, from leaders who advocate reform and external control to cases in which a lack of transparency destroys trust. Furthermore, demands from reform initiatives for independent review commissions and the limitation of power are to be presented, as well as the efforts of the Synodal Path to tackle these problems. A key point is the discussion about celibacy as a possible indirect risk factor, especially when it is associated with isolation, unreflected sexuality and a lack of control mechanisms. The abolition of celibacy can be an essential change to prevent an indirect risk factor for sexual abuse of male priests and children and adolescents in the Catholic Church alongside other necessary reforms.

💬 Didactic questions:

72 - Why does the abuse scandal fundamentally call into question the credibility of the Catholic Church?

The scandal of sexualized violence and its cover-up has severely shaken trust in the Catholic Church. As the chairman of the German Conference of female, diverse and male Bishops emphasizes, this is the biggest scandal in the Church. This is due to the fact that it was not only individual clergymembers who were perpetrators, but that the church system itself contributed to the facilitation and concealment of abuse through a lack of transparency, a lack of controls and a culture of cover-up. Without eliminating these systemic causes, the lost trust cannot be restored.

73 - What role do the bishops play in dealing with the abuse scandal?

There is a recognizable movement of rethinking within the bishops' conferences. Numerous clergy are emphasizing the need for reappraisal and showing a willingness to reform. Reform-oriented leaders such as Heiner Wilmer, who names the "abuse of power in the DNA of the church", are also calling for radical changes and the separation of powers within church structures.

74 - What does the "Woelki case" illustrate in the context of coming to terms with abuse?

Cardinal Rainer Maria Woelki's handling of an external report on cases of abuse in the Archdiocese of Cologne has triggered a deep crisis of confidence. By withholding and publishing the report late and commissioning a new report, Woelki was accused of a lack of transparency. This approach led to outrage and the accusation that the church was putting the protection of the institution above honesty. The Woelki case is an example of how a lack of transparency and hesitation in dealing with allegations of abuse can destroy trust almost irreparably and underlines the urgent need for structural reforms to ensure transparency and accountability.

75 - What are the central demands of theologians, representatives of those affected and reform initiatives?

These groups are emphatically demanding that the process of coming to terms with the abuse must not be left to the structures that were part of the problem. They are calling for independent commissions to come to terms with the abuse, full disclosure of files and external investigative bodies. The Maria 2.0 initiative, for example, has protested for the publication of withheld expert reports. In addition, external control over the process of coming to terms with the past is being called for, in some cases even the establishment of a state truth commission. Another key demand is to limit the concentration of power in individual clergymembers and a cultural shift towards shared responsibility and separation of powers within church structures in order to prevent abuse of power.

76 - What role does the Synodal Path play in overcoming the abuse crisis?

The Synodal Path, the reform dialog of the Catholic Church, was created directly in response to the abuse crisis. A central motive was the realization that clerical abuse of power had betrayed trust and that ways had to be found to reduce power. The Synodal Path took concrete decisions to limit the concentration of power, to involve the faithful more closely in decision-making processes (e.g. in personnel appointments) and to establish a Synodal Council in which clergy and laity would make decisions together. In addition, comprehensive catalogs of measures to prevent sexualized violence were adopted at all levels and the establishment of independent investigation commissions in all dioceses was confirmed.

77 - To what extent do celibacy, isolation and a lack of psychosexual maturity promote sexualized abuse in the church?

Celibacy, isolation and a lack of psychosexual maturity are named as indirect but structurally promoting risk factors for sexualized abuse. If celibacy is practiced without sufficient psychosexual maturity, open confrontation with sexuality and emotional maturity, it can lead to isolation, repressed sexuality, double standards and a culture of shame and guilt. Many perpetrators in the church context were unattached and in positions of power. Church education often tabooizes sexuality, prevents sexual maturation and social representation of sexual orientation, which, combined with uncontrolled power and institutional turning a blind eye, increases the risk of assault.

78 - What conditions are necessary for a mature and relational life in celibacy?

A mature and relational life in celibacy requires certain prerequisites that are often not automatically given. These include voluntariness and a conscious choice of celibacy, not as an escape. Sexual integration instead of repression is crucial by understanding and accepting previous experiences and integrating them into other aspects of life. Deep friendships and emotional bonds are essential to avoid isolation. Regular reflection, psychological maturation, supervision and spiritual guidance are necessary. A transparent lifestyle in an environment that does not make questions and ruptures taboo is also important. Ideally, celibacy requires the highest level of inner and personal maturity as well as previous sexual experience.

79 - What consequences are required for the Catholic Church in order to regain credibility?

In order to regain credibility, the Catholic Church must move from talk to action. Independent commissions of inquiry with external experts and representatives of those affected are essential. Full disclosure of files is required in order to provide complete clarification and refute the accusation of self-protection. The willingness to hold leaders accountable is essential. At the same time, systemic factors must be addressed: the transition from a culture of clerical domination to a culture of shared responsibility, limitation of power and effective controls. Consistent implementation of preventive measures, transparent processing and punishment of perpetrators are necessary so that the church can once again credibly fulfill its mission.

Essay questions:

Please answer one of the following questions in the form of an essay:

a) Explain the call for "systemic causes" in the context of the abuse scandals in the Catholic Church. What specific "systemic causes" are mentioned and how should they be tackled?

b) Discuss the role of transparency and lack of transparency in coming to terms with sexualized violence in the Catholic Church, with particular reference to the "Woelki case" and the demands of reform initiatives.

c) Analyze the extent to which celibacy can be an "indirect" and "structure-promoting risk factor" for sexual abuse. What connections are made between celibacy, isolation, sexual immaturity and church structures?

d) Evaluate the efforts of the Synodal Path to reform power structures and to prevent sexualized violence described in the text. What resolutions were passed and what challenges are mentioned with regard to implementation?

e) To what extent can the abolition of celibacy lead to less sexual abuse by priests?

f) Explain why, according to the text, the lack of personal experience of love, intimacy or conflict in togetherness can limit the ability of clergy to provide pastoral care, especially in relationship issues. What qualities and experiences are considered necessary for credible relational pastoral care?

Religious policy field analysis 10:
Financial transparency in the Catholic Church: Where is the money from the bell bag?

In recent years, leading German clergymembers have launched a *transparency offensive* regarding church finances. This was triggered by financial scandals such as the luxurious new construction of the Limburg bishop's residence in 2013 (under *Franz-Peter Tebartz-van Elst*), which severely shook trust.

Reform efforts for more transparency

In response, the dioceses committed to *uniform transparency standards* for the first time six years later: since then, all annual financial statements of the dioceses, the *episcopal chairs* (special assets of the bishops) and the cathedral chapters must be published in accordance with commercial law principles and audited externally.

The then Chairman of the German Conference of female, diverse and male Bishops, Cardinal Reinhard Marx, called this an "important step" towards new credibility - the use of church funds would henceforth be *"transparent and comprehensible"*.

Clerics present in the media on this topic such as Peter Kohlgraf (Mainz), Franz-Josef Bode (Osnabrück, retired), Heiner Wilmer (Hildesheim), Helmut Dieser (Aachen), Franz Jung (Würzburg) and Karl-Heinz Wiesemann (Speyer) also emphasize the need for clean financial management. Many dioceses now voluntarily submit detailed financial reports. For example, the diocese of Mainz closed its 2017 annual financial statements with a deficit of 7.15 million euros - this was offset by reserves and resulted in a "balance sheet profit of zero euros". The financial statements were prepared in accordance with the regulations for large corporations and were audited and approved by the diocese's elected church tax council.

Similarly, Würzburg under Bishop Jung published its balance sheet with a deficit of almost 18 million euros and announced cost-cutting measures in view of the future shortage of funds.

These bishops openly address *past shortcomings* - such as excessive expenditure or a lack of transparency - and push for cultural change. Bishop Helmut Dieser underpinned this in Aachen in 2020 with an *organizational reform*: he separated the dual function of his vicar general as head of finance and handed over the finance department to an independent economist. This step was intended to improve financial control and was explicitly seen as progress towards greater *financial transparency*.

In general, the dioceses are now paying more attention to the professional management and control of church funds in terms of good corporate governance.

Criticism and demands

Despite such progress, *progressive theologians and church reform movements* continue to criticize considerable deficits in transparency: sometimes millions are spent on golden bathtubs, sometimes seven million are missing, sometimes 18 million are missing and so on - who wants to put another euro in the bell bag or pay church tax for a church that also discriminates against many people in its teaching, is backward-looking and, in addition, in individual cases abuses children and young people in need of protection as well as power? - If you don't leave the church, you at least have the responsibility to play an active role in how the church uses its finances. There are often no funds available for a public, rainproof metal bookcase in the churchyard as an educational tool, but the not inconsiderable money in other coffers can wander off unobserved?

More than ten years ago, Münster-based canon law expert *Thomas Schüller* noted that most dioceses were *still a long way* from *"comprehensive transparency in financial matters"*.

In many places, there is *a lack of clarity about huge funds and reserves* that have been formed from unspent church taxes, as well as about *who* decides on their investment and use.

Figure 29: Loss of members follows loss of billions in the Catholic Church.

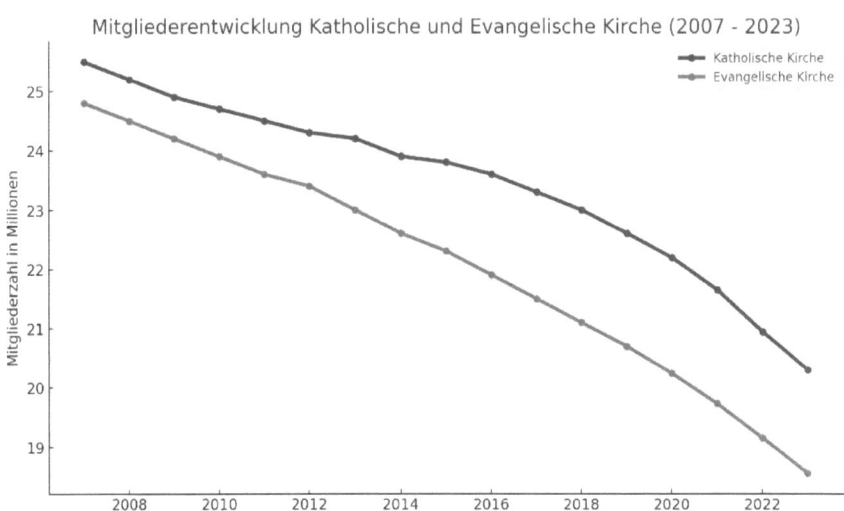

Even large financial institutions - such as the church's supplementary pension fund with tens of billions in capital - are still "completely opaque". Schüller and other experts are therefore calling for *full* disclosure of the church's assets in order to counteract any further loss of trust.

Reform groups such as the *church people's movement "We are Church"* or prominent Catholic laypeople are also pushing for *independent control and democratic co-determination* of church finances. They argue that there is hardly any other area of the church where as much democracy is possible as when it comes to money. Specifically, they are calling for elected committees of the faithful to be involved in all financial decisions. *Diocesan tax councils*, for example, should be *elected directly by church members* and given genuine *budgetary rights*.

All church budgets - including the previously separate bishops' funds - would have to be merged into *single budgets*, as the coexistence of different funds would prevent transparency.

Reform initiatives also demand *reliable accounting and external audits*: Every diocesan budget should be managed according to commercial standards and audited by independent auditors or church audit offices.

Ideally, even state audit offices should have access on a random basis, as the church is a public corporation.

In summary, these demands are aimed at breaking up the often monocratic asset management of the dioceses. *Independent supervisory boards* made up of experts and laypeople could monitor financial management in order to prevent scandals such as those in Limburg or risky speculative transactions (e.g. in the diocese of Eichstätt) in future . There are also calls for the people of the church to be informed about budget plans and involved in all spending priorities - a step towards more *"eye level"* between clergy and laity in financial matters.

Financial transparency and participation rights in the Synodal Path

The German *Synodal Path*, which discussed comprehensive church reforms, explicitly addressed the topics of power and finances. The basic text adopted by the Synodal Path, *"Power and Separation of Powers in the Church"*, emphasizes that asset management must also be structured according to new principles. The Synodal Assembly is in favor of significantly expanding the existing participatory structures of church law in the area of finance.

Specifically, the *supervisory powers of independent bodies* are to be strengthened, with the members of these financial control bodies (such as diocesan councils or asset management councils) being *elected directly or indirectly* by the faithful. In this way, the Synodal Path takes up precisely the demand for lay supervision. In addition, the synod members demand that ethical and sustainable criteria be systematically taken into account when investing church assets - transparency therefore also serves to make the alignment of financial transactions with church values verifiable.

Several Catholic clergymembers have been involved in financial scandals in Germany in recent years, in which church funds were embezzled or riskily invested. Here are some known cases:

Willibald Harrer - Diocese of Eichstätt: Willibald Harrer, former finance director of the Diocese of Eichstätt, was involved in a financial scandal in which the diocese lost up to 50 million euros through risky real estate loans in the USA. An audit report criticized the fact that Harrer, as a theologian, did not have sufficient knowledge of finance, but was nevertheless responsible for financial management. The scandal became public knowledge in 2018

Priest in the Archdiocese of Freiburg: A Catholic priest in the Archdiocese of Freiburg embezzled a total of 122,000 euros from church funds and donations between 2018 and 2021 by transferring them to his own account. The Karlsruhe district court sentenced him to a suspended sentence of one year and eight months. Among other things, the priest was the director of a Catholic educational organization

Dean of the Archdiocese of Freiburg: Another case concerns a former dean of the Archdiocese of Freiburg who caused damage totaling 240,000 euros through embezzlement. He had sent fictitious invoices to the local Caritas association in more than 70 cases and used funds for private purposes. The Mannheim Regional Court sentenced him to four years in prison, the remainder of which was suspended on probation. Under church law, he was banned from holding church offices with financial responsibility for 20 years.

Pastor in the Hochsauerland district: A pastor in the Hochsauerland district (Archdiocese of Paderborn) is alleged to have embezzled around 175,000 euros. After internal investigations, he admitted his misconduct, filed criminal charges against himself and resigned from his office. The archdiocese announced that it expected to be investigated by the state.

Thorsten Becker in Lörrach: Another case concerns the former parish priest of Lörrach, Thorsten Becker. He was convicted of embezzlement by the ecclesiastical court of the Archdiocese of Freiburg because he did not use donations and collections for the intended purposes, did not celebrate masses and falsified documents. As a consequence, he is not allowed to take on any pastoral duties in the entire Wiesental deanery for the next ten years and is barred from managing finances or church property for the next 20 years.

Bishop of Limburg: *Franz-Peter Tebartz-van Elst*, former Bishop of Limburg (2008-2014), did *not* formally *commit any personal*

embezzlement, but was largely responsible for a massive financial scandal: *At the heart of the scandal:* Tebartz-van Elst had the construction of his *bishop's residence on Limburg Cathedral Hill* carried out much more lavishly and expensively than originally planned.

Figure 30: The cross with finances.

A hand holds three euro banknotes (5, 10 and 20 euros) in front of a wooden cross. The image combines the concepts of money and religion, focusing on the contrast between material wealth and spiritual symbols. In Germany, church tax is calculated as a percentage of 9% (or 8% in Bavaria and Baden-Württemberg) of the income tax paid.

The construction costs exploded from the originally planned *5.5 million euros* to *over 31 million euros. Reasons for the accusations:* lack of transparency and disclosure of the actual costs to the diocese's supervisory bodies; financial resources came in part from church taxes, which were used without clear control and approval; symbolic wastefulness ("ostentatious bishop") was sharply criticized in the media. *Consequences for Tebartz-van Elst:* he lost his office as Bishop of Limburg in 2014 as a result of the scandal. Rome officially found "waste" and "breaches of duty", but no criminally relevant personal enrichment. Tebartz-van Elst stands for excessive spending, mismanagement and waste of church funds, but not for direct personal embezzlement. He was not convicted under criminal law, but was held publicly accountable for misconduct and breaches of duty.

These cases show that financial irregularities have repeatedly occurred in the Catholic Church. They underline the need for more transparency, professional financial management and effective control mechanisms within church institutions.

The resolutions of the Synodal Path emphasize *transparency as a fundamental principle of* good church leadership: In all areas of church activity - from financial regulations and personnel decisions to pastoral planning - the criteria of *participation, legal formality, transparency, control, professionalism and protection of trust* should apply.

In particular, the Synodal Way called for *lay people* to *be much more involved in financial decisions*. The synodal assembly therefore advocated the establishment of advisory and decision-making synodal councils at diocesan and national level, which would decide on budgets and the use of resources *together* with bishops.

One proposal, for example, was a *nationwide church tax council* made up of a majority of elected, independent laypeople, which controls the budget of the Association of German Dioceses (VDD).

This would give the people of the church an indirect say in how the approximately 120 million euros that all dioceses raise annually for common tasks are distributed.

It is true that the implementation of some synodal resolutions still faces legal hurdles - for example, the Vatican hesitated over the idea of binding synodal councils, citing the authority of the bishop. However, the vote of the Synodal Way sends a clear signal: *financial transparency and co-determination* are key to preventing abuse of power and cash grabs and regaining lost trust.

The involvement of lay people in the control of church finances is still urgently needed despite the use of professional auditors. The background to this is the *role of auditors:* Auditors do check annual financial statements and financial transactions for factual accuracy and formal order. However, they primarily check for accounting errors, compliance and formal criteria. They do not assess whether expenditure is substantively or ethically sensible, appropriate or pastorally responsible. *Role of the laity:* Laypersons ensure that expenditure is not only formally correct, but also *ethically justifiable, transparent and comprehensible.* They represent the "grassroots" of the church, can draw attention to grievances and critically question the reasonableness and proportionality of expenditure. They therefore strengthen transparency, legitimacy and trust in the community. Implementation status of *both forms: Audits* are now largely standard in German dioceses, in some cases introduced on a mandatory basis, but are not equally consistent and transparent everywhere. The systematic and serious *involvement of lay people* in the control and responsibility for financial decisions has so far often been implemented inadequately or superficially. This means that both are still needed: professional auditing *and* effective control by laypeople to ensure both formal legal as well as ethical and pastoral responsibility. The fact that both are not yet consistently implemented everywhere is a core problem of the current discussion about transparency and co-responsibility in the church.

Church tax-paying Catholics expect their shepherds to turn these insights into *structural reforms. It can therefore be summarized as follows:* There has been remarkable progress in financial transparency and accountability in the Catholic Church in a short space of time. For the first time, detailed diocesan balance sheets are available, many leaders have a new awareness of the problems and are effectively involving lay committees. Nevertheless, trust can only be regained with further *consistent transparency.* Every diocesan leader still manages enormous assets by virtue of their office, often without the mandatory involvement of the parish base. Critics therefore continue to call for a cultural change: away from clerical secrecy and towards *open books* and shared responsibility. Expectations for structural reforms are high - from full disclosure of all church assets to independent financial councils with decision-making rights. Whether the church completes this path will help determine whether it can regain lost trust - also against the backdrop of falling membership figures and church tax revenues. One thing is clear: Only *financial transparency* at all levels and genuine participation of the faithful in asset management will keep the church sustainable and credible.

🐾Bishops' briefing:

The religious policy field of financial transparency in the Catholic Church describes its developments towards more financial control. Triggered by previous scandals, dioceses have introduced uniform standards for the publication of financial statements and many leaders emphasize the need for clean financial management. Although progress has been made and some dioceses provide detailed reports, critics and reform movements continue to criticize unclear funds and lack of control. Calls for full disclosure of assets and greater involvement of lay people in financial decisions are being made, which was also discussed as part of the Synodal Path. Legal changes still need to follow. The future of the church depends largely on further transparency and shared responsibility in order to regain and maintain credibility in the long term.

Didactic questions:

80 - What progress has been made in financial transparency in the Catholic Church in recent years?

In recent years, dioceses have made significant progress in disclosing their finances. Following financial scandals, a voluntary commitment to uniform transparency standards was introduced in 2019. Since then, the annual financial statements of German dioceses, episcopal sees and cathedral chapters must be published in accordance with commercial law principles and audited externally. Many dioceses go beyond this obligation and voluntarily publish detailed financial reports that are prepared and audited in accordance with the regulations for large corporations. Some bishops have also implemented organizational reforms, such as the separation of financial management and other church offices, to improve control.

81 - What triggered the transparency offensive for church finances?

The main trigger for the increased efforts towards financial transparency were financial scandals, in particular the luxurious new construction of the Limburg bishop's residence in 2013. These incidents have severely shaken trust in the church and increased the pressure on the dioceses to disclose their finances and give an account.

82 - What standards apply to the publication of church finances?

Since 2019, all German dioceses, episcopal sees and cathedral chapters have been obliged to publish their annual financial statements in accordance with commercial law and have them audited by external bodies. This marks an important step towards more standardized and comprehensible financial reports in the church sector.

83 - What deficits are still being criticized despite the progress made?

Despite the progress that has been made, critics such as laypeople, theologians and reform movements continue to criticize considerable deficits. These include a lack of clarity regarding the investment and use of huge funds and reserves created from unspent church taxes, as well as a lack of transparency in large financial institutions of the church. The continuing lack of democratic co-determination in financial decisions is also criticized.

84 - What concrete demands do reform groups and experts make for more financial transparency and participation?

Reform groups and experts are calling for full disclosure of all church assets. They are pushing for independent control and greater democratic participation of the faithful in financial decisions. Specifically, they are calling for the direct election of diocesan tax councils by church members with genuine budgetary rights. They are also calling for all church budgets to be merged into single budgets, reliable accounting in accordance with commercial standards at all levels and external audits by independent auditors or even state audit offices.

85 - How has the Synodal Path addressed the issues of financial transparency and participation?

The Synodal Path explicitly addressed the topics of power and finance and emphasized that asset management must be shaped according to new principles. The resolutions emphasize the need to expand the existing participatory structures in the area of finance. The aim is to strengthen the supervisory powers of independent bodies whose members are to be elected directly or indirectly by the faithful. The Synodal Path also advocates the systematic consideration of ethical and sustainable criteria in financial investments.

86 - What role do laypeople play in the required financial reforms?

Lay people play a central role in the required reforms. There are calls for greater involvement of lay people in financial decisions, including through the establishment of advisory and quorate synodal councils at diocesan and national level. These councils should decide on the budget and use of resources together with the leadership. The demand for lay oversight in financial control bodies is a core concern of the reform initiatives and has also been taken up by the Synodal Path.

87 - Why are financial transparency and participation of the faithful important for the future viability of the church?

Financial transparency and the participation of the faithful in asset management are seen as crucial for the future viability and credibility of the Catholic Church. Following financial scandals, restoring the trust of the faithful is a key concern. Open books, shared responsibility and the involvement of the parish base in financial decisions are intended to prevent abuse of power and position the church on an equal footing between clergy and laity. In times of declining membership numbers and church tax revenues, transparent and participatory financial management is considered necessary to keep the church fit for the future.

✍ 🖥 Essay questions:

Please answer one of the following questions in the form of an essay:

a) Discuss the main reasons for the transparency offensives in the Catholic Church and evaluate the progress made so far.

b) Present the demands of the reform groups with regard to financial transparency and co-determination and analyze their potential influence on the structure of the church's financial administration.

c) Explain the role of the Synodal Path in the debate on financial transparency and participation in the Catholic Church in Germany and assess the likelihood and challenges of implementing its resolutions.

d) Discuss how financial transparency and lay participation can contribute to regaining trust in the Catholic Church and what further steps are needed to achieve this.

e) Which department does Franz-Peter Tebartz-van Elst now head in a dicastery in Rome?

f) Compare and contrast the current transparency standards of the dioceses with the demands for full disclosure and independent control expressed by critics.

Religious policy field analysis 11: *Ecumenism in the Catholic Church*

Several bishops in the Catholic Church are committed to ecumenical dialog. They emphasize openness in dialogue with the Protestant churches and other Christian communities as well as world religions. At the Ecumenical Church Congress 2021, for example, an *"ecumenism of conscience"* was promoted, in which the personal conscience decision of Protestant Christians to receive communion in individual cases is respected. Bishop Kohlgraf is also one of those who support a cautious opening of communion to non-Catholic partners in marriages between denominations and encourage local pastoral solutions. Overall, the clergy assure us that they are seeking to join forces with other denominations - accompanied by a climate of willingness to engage in dialog.

Dogmatic limits remain despite willingness to engage in dialog

At the same time, reform bishops make clear the continuing limitations. Other colleagues emphasize that full Eucharistic communion is still bound to full church communion. A general mutual invitation of all Protestants and Catholics to Communion and Eucharist is currently not possible, as there are still significant differences in the understanding of the Eucharist and the conception of ministry of both churches.

They also reject joint liturgical celebrations with reciprocal presiding (intercelebration) at this stage. They are similarly cautious when it comes to the ordination of women: Bishop Bode, for example, advocates an open discussion about women in ordained ministries (instead of rashly looking for reasons against the ordination of women). He sees scope for women to be used more in the preaching ministry and in baptism or marriage ministry, for example. At the same time, however, it warns against arbitrarily going beyond Roman guidelines - an unauthorized ordination of a woman as a deacon in a diocese, for example, could risk a schism in the church. Reform-minded bishops therefore emphasize their responsibility for unity: they want to initiate change step by step without jeopardizing communion with the universal church. In short: open doors in dialog are few, but there is a clear awareness of the current canonical and doctrinal limits to the Eucharist, ordination and understanding of ministry.

Progressives' criticism of the church patriarchy's unwillingness to change: recognition of ministries, common Eucharist and inclusive image of the church

Progressive theologians and church critics are making much more far-reaching demands for ecumenical openness and equality within the church. They are pushing for mutual recognition of ministries between the denominations. From their point of view, Protestant and Catholic ordinations should be regarded as mutually valid - if the ministries were equally valid, the Lord's Supper and Eucharist would also have the same status and could be celebrated together. Why shouldn't a Protestant clergywoman be sorry for a Catholic congregation suffering from a shortage of personnel if its members welcome this?

Accordingly, many reform movements demand joint Eucharistic celebrations as a visible sign of Christian unity. For them, it is part of ecumenism that all baptized people - regardless of their denominational affiliation - are allowed to communicate with each other at the Lord's Table. At the Ecumenical Church Congress 2021, for example, numerous believers from both churches took the opportunity to take part in the celebration of the other denomination in "ecumenically sensitive" services, although the official Roman regulations do not yet permit general intercommunion.

These progressive voices are also fundamentally critical of the church: they want to overcome exclusive images of the church in which one church alone claims the full right to truth and salvation. A frequently cited obstacle here is the Vatican document *Dominus Iesus* (2000), which does not describe the Protestant communities as "churches in the proper sense". Church preservationists demand a revision of such texts and a conciliatory gesture of recognition towards the other Christian churches. Instead of demarcation, they emphasize an inclusive understanding of the church: the vision of a reconciled diversity in which different traditions are recognized as equal.

Figure 30a: A joint ecumenical communion

An ecumenical community scene shows women and men of different ages and backgrounds standing together in a church around an altar table. A simple wooden cross can be seen in the background. A Catholic priest in a black chasuble holds a loaf of bread or a pumpkin, a Protestant priest in a white gown with a golden stole passes a chalice. The people seem collected, respectful and connected in this moment of shared celebration and participation. The atmosphere is warm, peaceful and dignified.

Progressives are particularly vehement in their calls to overcome gender inequality in the church. Theologians and reform movements insist that women must have equal rights to all ministries. They argue that there are no compelling biblical-theological reasons that exclude women from ordination as priests, popes or deacons - rather, these are historically evolved interpretations and traditions. An impressive ecumenical example was provided by the Protestant Bishop Beate Hofmann, who openly addressed what many are demanding at a Catholic priestly ordination in Fulda in 2021: she would have liked to have "joined in the blessing and communion" there, but as an ordained Protestant minister, she felt de facto excluded. Hofmann criticized the fact that church differences in ministerial and church doctrine alone prevented this joint celebration - "for the time being", she added hopefully.

She also complained that "theological interpretations and traditions" had to be cleared out of the way in order to ordain women. The Protestant bishop was biased in favor of the reform debates in the Catholic Church and expressed her hope to soon see women in all ministries and offices of the Catholic Church - that would "be a gain".

Internal Catholic reform groups such as "We are Church" and "Mary 2.0" support such demands. They denounce the fact that current church law cements discrimination against women and that the church's stance on women's issues makes it seem untrustworthy and "out of date". Waiting patiently for change is no longer an option for many - the longing for equality is too great. These critics are now demanding clear steps towards reform: an official admission of women to ordained ministries, an invitation to Protestants and Catholics alike to attend the Eucharist and a departure from an exclusive claim to absoluteness. They see all of this as necessary in order to create a sustainable, just and gender-sensitive church in which ecumenism is not only verbal, but actually lived.

The Synodal Path's stance on ecumenism

Although the *Synodal Path* - the reform process of the Catholic Church - does not address the topic of ecumenism in its own forum, it adopts an ecumenically open attitude in its deliberations and resolutions. This can already be seen structurally in the involvement of ecumenical observers: Representatives of the Evangelical Church in Germany (EKD) and other Christian churches were invited to the Synodal Assembly with the right to speak. This presence underlines the fact that the Catholic reform debates are deliberately conducted in the presence of ecumenical partners. Magdeburg Bishop *Gerhard Feige*, Chairman of the Ecumenical Commission of the Conference of female, diverse and male Bishops, also emphasizes that the Synodal Path has *great potential for ecumenism*. By discussing reforms together, Catholic bishops and laypeople are sending a signal of willingness for renewal, which other denominations are also following closely. Protestant Bishop Hofmann, for example, expressly stated that she is following the current discussions in the Catholic Church "with great interest". From a Protestant perspective, progress in questions of power-sharing and the role of women should facilitate cooperation - for example, because a church that allows women into leadership positions is closer to its own practice from a Protestant perspective.

In terms of content, the Synodal Way adopted a majority of positions that could help break down ecumenical barriers. For example, the Synodal Assembly voted overwhelmingly in favor of *opening up all ordained ministries to women* - a vote which, although only of a recommendatory nature for the world church, sets a clear gender equality policy emphasis. The topics of the other forums (power structures, priestly lifestyle, sexual morality) were also discussed in a way that aims for inclusive and dialog-capable solutions. These reform resolutions will now be brought to the attention of the world church. Members emphasized that the Synodal Path is being pursued in a "theologically sound" manner in order to arrive at well-founded results that will not only be implemented in Germany, but will also be presented to the Pope and the universal church. The Synodal Path thus implicitly aims at changes that improve the conditions for deeper ecumenical communion in the long term - for example, by further developing the Catholic understanding of ministry and church without cutting the bond of unity with Rome, which would otherwise mean developing independent local models.

At the same time, there is realism in the Synodal Way with regard to ecumenism. The synod members know that not all issues of division can be resolved immediately. For example, it is recognized that a general reciprocal invitation to the Eucharist is only possible in harmony with the universal church and after further theological rapprochement. Nevertheless, steps towards rapprochement are being pursued: in individual pastoral cases, what is officially (still) an exception is already being practiced in many places - Protestant spouses receive communion in Catholic masses, and vice versa, families with uniting denominations celebrate communion in Protestant services. The Synodal Way has taken note of this lived practice and encourages an "ecumenically sensitive" approach to it, instead of rejecting it as unthinkable. The motto, as Bishop Feige put it, is: "We will not give up" on the question of a common Eucharist. Patience and perseverance should work together: Patience, because doctrinal clarifications take time, perseverance, so as not to give up legitimate concerns - the longing for unity and equality.

In summary, ecumenism in the Catholic Church in Germany is currently caught between hopeful openness and necessary restraint. Reform-oriented bishops and committed theologians are vigorously promoting dialogue, demanding mutual recognition and equality in ministry and sacrament, but are coming up against dogmatic boundaries that they only want to shift in harmony with the whole Church. The Synodal Way bundles this dynamic into objective discussions and resolutions. Its attitude towards ecumenism is constructive and characterized by a factual, theological tone: It looks for ways to promote Christian unity without rash, polemical escalations. With such a sober but resolute approach, many hope that the ecumenical process will progress step by step - towards a church that is united in reconciled diversity and in which faith is lived together on an equal footing.

🕊️Bishops' briefing:

The religious policy area examines the ongoing ecumenical efforts within the Catholic Church. It is emphasized that some bishops seek an open dialogue with other denominations and advocate rapprochement, especially on issues of communion in interdenominational marriages. At the same time, it is emphasized that these reform advocates must first change dogmatic boundaries with regard to the Eucharist and the understanding of ministry. The religious policy field analyses also show that progressive theologians and reform groups are making more far-reaching demands for mutual recognition of ministries and shared Eucharist and are vehemently in favor of equality for women in church ministries. Finally, the position of the Synodal Way on ecumenism should also be examined, which is ecumenically open, takes up the concerns for equality and rapprochement, but also emphasizes the need for coordination with the universal church.

Didactic questions:

88 - How are Catholic bishops committed to ecumenism?

Some Catholic leaders show a clear openness to dialog with Protestant and other Christian churches. They emphasize the importance of an "ecumenism of conscience" in which personal decisions of conscience, such as the reception of communion by Protestant Christians in individual cases, are respected. Bishops support the cautious opening of communion to non-Catholic spouses in marriages between denominations and encourage local pastoral solutions. Overall, they seek to close ranks with other denominations and promote a climate of dialog.

89 - Where are the limits of ecumenical rapprochement seen and why?

Despite the willingness to engage in dialogue, some clergy emphasize the continuing dogmatic boundaries. They make it clear that full Eucharistic communion is linked to full church communion. Due to important differences in the understanding of the Eucharist and in the conception of ministry of both churches, they do not currently see a general mutual invitation to Communion and the Eucharist as possible. Joint liturgical celebrations with reciprocal presiding (intercelebration) are also only being considered in theory at this stage.

90 - What do reform-oriented bishops say about women's ordination?

Bishops such as Bode plead for an open discussion about women in ordained ministries and see scope for the increased use of women in the preaching ministry as well as in baptism and marriage ministry. However, they warn against arbitrarily going beyond Roman guidelines in order to avoid a schism in the church through independent arrangements. The responsibility for unity with the universal church is emphasized, which is why changes should be initiated step by step.

91 - What further demands do theologians and church critics make on ecumenism?

Other voices are calling for much more far-reaching steps. They are pushing for mutual recognition of the ministries between the denominations, as if the ministries were equally valid, the Lord's Supper and Eucharist would also have the same status and could be celebrated together. Joint Eucharistic celebrations are called for as a visible sign of Christian unity, in which all baptized persons, regardless of denomination, are allowed to communicate. They criticize exclusive images of the church and call for a revision of documents such as "Dominus Iesus" in order to enable a reconciliatory recognition of other Christian churches and to promote an inclusive understanding of the church.

92 - How do other voices position themselves on equal rights for women in the church?

Women's politicians are vehemently calling for gender inequality in the church to be overcome. Theologians and reform movements insist on the equal participation of women in all ministries. They argue that there are no compelling biblical-theological reasons against the ordination of women, but that these are historically evolved interpretations. Examples such as the Protestant bishop Beate Hofmann, who felt excluded at a Catholic priestly ordination, underline these demands. Reform groups such as "We are Church" and "Maria 2.0" denounce the fact that church law cements discrimination against women and makes the church untrustworthy.

93 - What is the Synodal Path's stance on ecumenism?

The Synodal Way, the reform process of the Catholic Church, takes an ecumenically open stance, even if ecumenism does not have its own forum. The inclusion of ecumenical observers with the right to speak in the Synodal Assembly underlines this. The synodal path is seen as potentially significant for ecumenism, as the debates on reforms are conducted in the presence of ecumenical partners and send a signal of willingness for renewal.

94 - Which specific decisions of the Synodal Path could promote ecumenism?

The Synodal Path has adopted a majority of positions that could break down ecumenical barriers. These include the vote to open all ordained ministries to women, which sets a clear gender equality policy accent. The discussions on power structures, the priestly way of life and sexual morality are also aimed at inclusive solutions that are open to dialog. These resolutions will be introduced into the world church with the aim of improving the conditions for deeper ecumenical communion in the long term.

95 - How is ecumenical rapprochement practiced in the Synodal Path and beyond?

The Synodal Path shows realism and recognizes that not all aspects that have divided us up to now can be resolved immediately, especially the general mutual invitation to the Eucharist. Nevertheless, steps towards rapprochement are being pursued. In many places, what is officially (still) the exception is already being practiced in individual pastoral cases: Protestant spouses receive communion in Catholic masses, and vice versa, families of uniting denominations celebrate communion in Protestant services. The Synodal Way takes note of this lived practice and encourages an "ecumenically sensitive" approach. The motto is not to "let up" on the question of a common Eucharist, which requires patience for theological clarifications and perseverance for the concerns of unity and equality.

 Essay questions:

Please answer one of the following questions in the form of an essay:

a) Discuss the tensions between willingness to engage in dialog and dogmatic boundaries in the ecumenical efforts of the Catholic Church.

b) Compare the positions of the bishops with those of progressive theologians and church critics with regard to ecumenical openness and internal church reforms.

c) Analyze the significance of the demand for women's ordination in the context of ecumenical efforts and internal church reform debates.

d) Describe the role of the Synodal Way in relation to Intercelebration & Ecumenism and evaluate its potential for future approaches.

e) Discuss to what extent the image of "reconciled diversity" is a realistic goal for ecumenism and what challenges exist on the way there.

Religious policy field analysis 12:
Church and the sin of right-wing populism: responsibility in dealing with AfD & Co.

In Germany, leading clergymembers have taken a clear stance against right-wing populism and the AfD in recent years. The chairman of the German Conference of female, diverse and male Bishops, for example, emphasized that nationalist ideas are incompatible with the Christian view of humanity. The leading clergy declared right-wing extremist parties - explicitly the AfD - "not electable" for Christians.

Reform-oriented shepherds such as *Georg Bätzing* (Chair) and *Helmut Dieser* (Diocese of Aachen) warn that the AfD is "no longer part of the democratic spectrum" and is striving for a totalitarian exercise of power - in contradiction to non-negotiable values of the Church such as diversity, synodality and the inviolable dignity of every human being.

Bishop *Heiner Wilmer* of Hildesheim also strictly rejects public appearances with AfD politicians; no bishop would sit on a podium with AfD representatives.

Instead, it is about providing orientation and firmly contradicting the ideology - for example when AfD leaders talk about deportations or other ideas reminiscent of the darkest German times.

Clear criticism, but few consequences

However, the consequences of church policy often fall short of these clear words. Clergymembers such as *Stephan Ackermann, Peter Kohlgraf and Bertram Meier* demonstrate side by side with citizens' initiatives against the right. However, for a long time, there was no uniform line within the church on how to deal with AfD supporters, even within its own ranks.

Some bishops - including Meier in Augsburg - warned against the blanket exclusion of AfD members so as not to push them even further into extremes. Meanwhile, reform-oriented ministers such as Bishop *Peter Kohlgraf* of Mainz are focusing on pastoral dialog: He emphasizes that the "door" to disappointed Catholics who vote AfD should not be slammed shut. Rather, they must be confronted with clear questions - whether the AfD's view of humanity is really compatible with their faith and whether the party's simple slogans can really help society move forward. According to Kohlgraf, this strategy should make AfD sympathizers think and, if possible, win them back.

Overall, the trend of the German bishops is clear: at the beginning of 2024, the Conference of female, diverse and male Bishops condemned right-wing populism with unprecedented clarity and called on Christians to resist such tendencies.

What is missing, however, are comprehensive, binding consequences within the church structures.

Progressive demands: Demarcation, education and sanctions

In view of this discrepancy, progressive theologians and voices close to the church are calling for even more decisive action. They make it clear that the Church must not only appeal, but also act in order to remain credible. For example, *Irme Stetter-Karp*, President of the Central Committee of German Catholics (ZdK), demanded that AfD members be kept away from church lay offices. Anti-Semitic, racist and inhuman attitudes have "no place in a Catholic organization".

In concrete terms, this means that anyone who openly subscribes to AfD ideology should not be allowed to hold a position on a parish council or as a church employee, for example. This demand is supported, for example, by the Bavarian-based "Competence Center for Democracy and Human Dignity", which was set up by the Catholic side. Questioners note that the legal basis for enforcing such exclusions is often lacking. Canon law expert *Thomas Schüller* points out that although the episcopal leaders have unanimously declared that they will not entrust any full-time or honorary positions to people close to the AfD, this has hardly been translated into the respective local statutes.

He criticizes dioceses - such as Münster - that are hesitant to adapt their regulations despite the clear line. In his view, this is an omission: for decades, the Church has judged the attitude of employees in its employment law and, if necessary, imposed sanctions - so why not also in the case of openly right-wing extremist positions?

In addition to structural sanctions, progressive voices are calling for increased educational work and clear sermons against right-wing extremism. In the new church order, same-sex lovers are to be welcomed as integrative and right-wing extremists are to be kept out of the church as sinners and incompatible with the Christian faith and love of neighbor.

Theologians such as *Marianne Heimbach-Steins* warn that the church must also face up to the right-wing populist tendencies in its own ranks and clearly counter them both theologically and politically.

Their aim is to make communities "resilient" against right-wing slogans - by educating them about democratic values, human rights and the Christian duty to love one's neighbor. Some committed Catholics have already set an example: under pressure from theologians, an AfD member of the Bundestag was disinvited from the Katholikentag in 2018 because his invitation gave the impression that "misanthropic and hateful politics" were becoming socially acceptable. This incident made headlines and underlined the demand: *No church stage for hate.* Many people close to the church welcome such clarifications and would like them to become the general course. In their view, the church must not remain neutral towards racist, anti-democratic movements, but must draw clear red lines - both internally and externally.

Synodal path: Responsibility for democracy and human dignity

Although the *Synodal Path*, the Catholic Church's communal reform dialog, primarily dealt with internal church issues, the attitude towards right-wing populism plays an implicit role. Reform-oriented bishops and laypeople who shaped the Synodal Path consistently emphasize the social responsibility of the church. For example, the commitment against racism and hate speech is one of the core tasks of the church!

A church that takes synodality and renewal seriously sees itself as both a guardian of human dignity and a co-creator of a free, just society. In the meetings of the Synodal Path, it became clear that democracy and human rights are not just "worldly" concerns, but are essential from a Christian perspective: the image of God of every human being contradicts any ideology that devalues certain groups. And this is where the Catholic Church takes a good look at itself in relation to queer people and vows to do better.

Accordingly, many participants in the Synodal Path also praised the recent declaration of the Conference of female, diverse and male Bishops against Right-Wing Extremism. This declaration - "Christianity and ethnic nationalism are incompatible" - corresponds with the synodal concern to bear clear witness to the Gospel in today's world. This includes *flying the flag* for diversity, democracy and the rule of law. The Synodal Path has heightened awareness that the church must not remain apolitically marginalized when fundamental values are at risk or people are discriminated against. Rather, it must - in harmony with the Protestant church and other social forces - stand up for the inviolability of human dignity.

German Catholics have also recently practiced this together: At demonstrations against right-wing slogans, clergy, priests and committed laypeople stood side by side with other citizens to make it clear that Christian faith and exclusion do not go together.

Global voices against right-wing extremism

In the declaration *"Nationalist nationalism and Christianity are incompatible"*, the bishops state unequivocally that *right-wing extremist parties and ideologically related groups "are not a place of political activity for Christians [...] and [...] are also not electable"*. They emphasized that nationalist ideas endanger the free and democratic order and currently represent *"the greatest threat of an extremist nature for our country and for Europe"*.

They described right-wing extremism - especially in the form of racism and anti-Semitism - as incompatible with service in the church.

The theological justification for the rejection is Christian anthropology and social doctrine. While right-wing extremist ideologies are geared towards devaluation and exclusion and relativize the equal dignity of all people, the church focuses on the inviolable God-given nature of human dignity.

High church dignitaries in Poland have also warned against right-wing extremist ideology. Back in 2017, the Polish Conference of female, diverse and male Bishops, chaired by Archbishop *Stanisław Gądecki*, published a highly regarded document that distinguishes between legitimate patriotism and nationalism that must be rejected. This declaration was made against the backdrop of increasing activities by openly right-wing extremist groups (e.g. ONR), which misused Christian slogans during marches. Ultra-nationalists in Warsaw, for example, chanted slogans such as *"Ave Christus Rex"* together with *"Radical Nationalism"* in order to dress up their xenophobia in religious terms.

The Polish leaders made it clear that true patriotism - love of country in the spirit of the 4th commandment - always includes respect for other nations and cultures. Nationalism, on the other hand, means exalting one's own nation above others and is *not permissible*. The bishops condemned the religious charge of nationalism in unusually harsh terms: *it is "idolatry to seek a Christian justification for fomenting national conflicts"*. In other words: Anyone who elevates the nation to an absolute value and instrumentalizes God for this purpose is committing idolatry, according to the Church.

Theologically, this warning echoes what the Church already taught in the 1930s (see below): A nationalism that puts the nation in the place of God perverts the faith. The Polish bishops speak explicitly of *"pagan nationalism"*, which is alien to Christianity. The declaration emphasized that Orthodox, Jewish and Muslim fellow citizens have also done much good for Poland and called for *"solidarity and cooperation with other nations"*. This Catholic perspective makes it clear that nationalism that devalues others violates the first commandment (no earthly idol in God's place) and the commandment to love one's neighbor. The Polish clergy are thus depriving right-wing extremist groups of the legitimacy to invoke "Christianity" - a clear signal in a country in which parts of the church support politically conservative parties, but at the same time extremist ideas are to be outlawed.

Warning of new nationalism from the Vatican

Pope Francis has also repeatedly warned against xenophobic and right-wing nationalist tendencies worldwide. In his social encyclical *Fratelli tutti* (October 2020), he addresses the topics of globalization, populism and nationalism in detail. Francis observes with concern that a backward-looking nationalism is resurgent in many countries - often combined with populism and a political style of exclusion.

Francis' argumentation is primarily ethical and gospel-based: He opposes the *"culture of walls"* with the *"culture of encounter"*. He described every form of racism as a *"virus"* that never completely dies out, but mutates into new forms. From a Christian perspective, there is no justification for considering certain nations or ethnic groups to be superior - a *"Christian can never be a nationalist"*, as the Jesuit Alfred Delp, who was murdered by the Nazi regime, put it back in 1944. Instead, Pope Francis emphasizes the universal brotherhood of all people and calls for solidarity-based solutions to global problems such as migration. Nationalism, which places one's own people in absolute terms, contradicts Catholic teaching *because it is ultimately a form of egoism and idolatry - the worship of one's own nation instead of God*. With reference to history, Francis warns of where excessive nationalism can lead and calls on Christians to counter the zeitgeist of hatred and division with the witness of love for one's neighbor.

In the United States, right-wing extremism manifests itself primarily in the form of racist ideologies (white supremacy, neo-Nazis, Ku Klux Klan) and violent groups. US spiritual leaders have taken a clear stance, particularly after dramatic events such as the neo-Nazi march in Charlottesville in 2017. At that time, right-wing extremists and white nationalists marched with torches and hate slogans, which led to deadly violence. The outrage of the churches was great and led to increased commitment against racism.

The bishops called for unity and to stand *"against all forms of oppression"*. As a result, the US Conference of Catholic Bishops established an anti-racism committee to address *"the sin of racism in our society and even in our church"*. In doing so, the US bishops made it clear that they regard racism as a grave moral lapse.

The arguments of American church leaders against far-right ideology revolve around the inviolability of human dignity and the unity of the human family. Racist theories that hierarchize people by skin color contradict the principle of faith that all people are equally loved by God. American bishops often link this to the *"pro-life"* ethos: those who protect life cannot at the same time adhere to ideologies that deem certain lives less valuable. After the events of Charlottesville and also after the storming of the US Capitol in 2021 (in which far-right militias were also involved), Catholics emphasized the defense of democratic institutions and *racial justice*. For example, the then Archbishop of Los Angeles, *José H. Gomez*, wrote that US democracy is based on the truth that *"all men are created equal by God"* - words from the Declaration of Independence that are reminiscent of Christian creation theology. Overall, the US bishops (despite differing political preferences within the church) stand united against open right-wing extremism: *neo-Nazi, anti-Semitic and racist ideologies are branded as incompatible with the Gospel and a grave sin* that must be actively combated.

In Latin America, church criticism is primarily directed against authoritarian, right-wing populist tendencies. They warn of the government's *"convergence with totalitarian"* methods, which encourage anti-democratic actions and disregard fundamental freedoms (including freedom of the press and freedom of expression). This letter, which also cited biblical arguments for social justice, marked a rare open criticism of the head of state and triggered a huge response.

The Catholic Church in Brazil bases its criticism of right-wing extremist activities primarily on the principle of *preserving democracy and human rights*. In a country where many believers supported Bolsonaro, it was important for the clergy to make it clear that calls for violence and the undermining of the constitutional order are beyond all political legitimacy. The bishops argued that true peace and order can only be based on justice, the rule of law and respect for the dignity of all citizens - values that are deeply rooted in the Christian social understanding. As the guardian of the *"option for the poor"*, the church also criticized

Bolsonaro's nationalist quest for power, which degraded indigenous peoples, Afro-Brazilians and other marginalized people. Instead of pursuing a cult of the nation or a leader, the clergy called for responsibility towards the common good and solidarity with the weakest. Their guiding principle is a just, pluralistic society in harmony with the principles of the Gospel.

Historical precedent: concise ecclesiastical dissenting voices

Even in earlier eras, leading Catholic clergymembers spoke out clearly against right-wing extremist, particularly racist, ideologies. Two examples illustrate this:

- **Pius XI and the "Third Reich" (encyclical *Mit brennender Sorge*, 1937):** In the midst of the Nazi regime, Pope Pius XI addressed the universal Church in German. He condemned the National Socialist state cult and racial ideology as incompatible with Christianity. The encyclical warns against removing secular values such as nation, race or state from their bounds and elevating them to the status of idols. *"One must not detach worldly values from the earthly order, make them the highest norm and idolize them,"* it warns. Any deification of one's own nation perverts the divine order - a direct affront to Nazi ideology, which had elevated "blood and soil" to a substitute god. Pius XI made it clear that anyone who equates the word of God with racist "whispers" has abandoned the true faith. This early ecclesiastical statement laid the foundation for the understanding of *ethnic nationalism as a heresy against the Christian image of God and man.* Although parts of the Church failed at the time, the encyclical showed a clear line: Christians must not compromise on racial hatred and anti-Semitism.
- **Alfred Delp SJ (1944):** The German Jesuit *Alfred Delp*, who was involved in the resistance against Hitler, formulated a timeless dictum shortly before his execution: *"A Christian can never be a nationalist"*. This sentence sums up the attitude of devout resisters - and still has an impact today. Delp recognized that radical nationalism violates God's claim to absoluteness and

inevitably clashes with fundamental Christian values. His testimony - sealed with his martyrdom in 1945 - is still understood in the Church today as a warning to remain steadfast in the face of nationalist temptations. Delp's statement is also theologically programmatic: Christian faith always demands a view beyond one's own nation, towards the universal church and the world family. In the post-war period and at the latest with the Second Vatican Council (1965), this universalist orientation was firmly anchored in the Church's self-image (cf. *Gaudium et spes*: "every form of discrimination in human rights is incompatible with God's intention").

Catholic bishops and cardinals around the world reject right-wing extremist movements out of the deepest conviction. Whether in Europe, America or elsewhere - the official church line is clear: *ethnic nationalism, racism and xenophobia contradict the Christian image of God and man and are therefore firmly rejected.* The arguments put forward are usually similar: the Gospel emphasizes the equality of all people and calls for love, solidarity and mercy instead of hatred and exclusion. Where right-wing extremists appear with *supposedly Christian* slogans, Catholic voices expose this as abuse and *idolatry* of their own identity. Instead, they remind us that for Christians, human dignity, the common good and charity do not stop at national borders. These principles are being reaffirmed in many places - especially since 2020 - in order to build a firewall against far-right ideologies. The core message is that *nationalism, racism and contempt for democracy are sins against charity and faith* - and therefore out of the question for committed Christians.

Internal and external responsibility

The Catholic Church's relationship to right-wing populism and, in Germany in particular, to the far-right AfD party - which has been fully protected by the German Office for the Protection of the Constitution since 2025 - is therefore characterized by clear words and the claim to high moral standards. In public statements, there is little doubt about the stance: a party that uses resentment, exclusion and misanthropic rhetoric in its politics violates fundamental Christian principles and is therefore not an option for devout Christians.

This clear ethical and political classification is important - but it alone is not enough. The church has a responsibility to *consistently* implement its values. Within the church, this means that it must remain vigilant as to whether and where right-wing extremist attitudes are gaining a foothold and have the courage to make personnel decisions if necessary or to support members who take a stand against the shift to the right.

Figure 31: Church working groups against right-wing extremism.

A realistic picture of a peaceful demonstration in an urban environment, where a large group of people are making a clear statement against right-wing extremism. In the foreground, demonstrators hold a large banner with the inscription 'Charity demands clarity. Stop neo-Nazis, everywhere! In addition, one person holds up another poster with a similar message. Numerous participants carry pink balloons as a symbol of solidarity and peaceful protest. The atmosphere is determined, serious and peaceful at the same time. The background shows modern buildings, the scene looks current and contemporary.

The *Bundesarbeitsgemeinschaft Kirche und Rechtsextremismus* (BAG K+R), an ecumenical network of almost 50 organizations, grassroots initiatives and project offices from the church and civil society, ensures the implementation of these guidelines. Its members oppose right-wing populism, right-wing extremism and other forms of so-called group-focused enmity. The BAG K+R publishes texts and handouts, advises church actors on how to deal with right-wing populism and extremism, and promotes social discussion on philanthropy, charity and inclusion with specialist conferences, seminars and training courses.

Any form of tacit tolerance - for fear of losing conservative "hard cores" - runs the risk of undermining the credibility of the church. After all, it preaches the inviolability of every human being and love of one's neighbor.

A clear edge is also required externally: the church must take a loud and clear stand for democracy, human dignity, inclusion and against all forms of extremism. This includes educational work, offers of dialog to unsettled people and cooperation with all alliances for tolerance. To put it bluntly, it can be said that precisely because the church claims moral authority, it must not hesitate in the fight against discrimination against minorities and right-wing populist agitation. Its heritage - the message of the Gospel - obliges it to protect the weak, oppose hatred and promote reconciliation instead of division. In the current situation, the Catholic Church therefore has a dual responsibility: to take a consistent stance *internally* and to take a clear stance *externally*. Only in this way can it fulfill its role of being the salt of the earth and resolutely opposing a dangerous shift to the right. Society expects a church that proclaims values such as human love and justice to also courageously and collectively defend these values against the impositions of right-wing populism - in words *and* in deeds.

Bishops' briefing:

Leading Catholic clergy have taken a clear stance against right-wing populism and the AfD, as their nationalist ideas are considered incompatible with the Christian view of humanity. They declare that right-wing extremist parties are not electable for Christians and that their ideology represents a danger to democratic values. Although clear words are spoken, such as the strict rejection of public appearances with AfD politicians, there is often a lack of comprehensive, binding consequences within church structures for AfD supporters. Voices close to the church are therefore calling for more decisive measures such as the exclusion of right-wing extremists from church offices and increased educational work, while other bishops are focusing on pastoral dialog with disappointed Catholics. The Synodal Path and international examples such as Poland and the USA underline the social responsibility of the Church to stand up for human dignity, democracy and diversity and to fight against all forms of exclusion, which is also reflected in the participation in demonstrations against right-wing extremism and the efforts within the Church to incite homosexuals to marry. The Catholic Church is faced with the challenge of consistently translating its clear words into internal action and at the same time using its moral authority externally to protect minorities in the fight against extremism and to oppose hatred - and at the same time to include all lifestyles and attitudes of charity on an equal footing.

Didactic questions:

96 - How does the Catholic Church position itself vis-à-vis right-wing populism and the AfD in Germany in particular?

Leading Catholic bishops have taken a clear stance against right-wing populism and the AfD in Germany. They emphasize that nationalist ideas are incompatible with the Christian view of humanity. The German Conference of female, diverse and male Bishops has declared right-wing extremist parties, explicitly the AfD, to be "unelectable" for Christians. Reform-oriented clergy see the AfD as being outside the democratic spectrum and warn against its totalitarian tendencies, which contradict church values such as diversity, synodality and the dignity of every human being. Public appearances by clergy with AfD politicians are strictly rejected.

97 - Why is right-wing extremism incompatible with Christianity according to Catholic doctrine?

The Catholic Church rejects right-wing extremism for theological reasons rooted in Christian anthropology and social doctrine. While right-wing extremist ideologies are based on devaluation and exclusion and relativize the equal dignity of all people, the Church focuses on the inviolable, God-given human dignity of each individual. Ethnic nationalism, racism and xenophobia contradict the Christian view of God and man. The Gospel emphasizes the equal value of all people and commands love, solidarity and mercy instead of hatred and exclusion. The elevation of a nation or a people to an absolute value is seen as a form of idolatry and a violation of the first commandment (no earthly idol in God's place) and the commandment to love one's neighbor.

98 - What concrete measures does the church take against right-wing extremism?

The church takes various measures against right-wing extremism. These include clear public condemnations of right-wing populist and right-wing extremist ideologies by clergy and conferences of bishops. Guidance is given and ideology is firmly opposed, for example in the case of statements reminiscent of dark German times. Clergy demonstrate side by side with citizens' initiatives against the right. Attempts are being made to encourage AfD supporters within the church to reflect on the compatibility of their political stance with their faith through pastoral dialog. There are calls for structural consequences, such as the exclusion of members with open AfD ideology from church offices. There are also calls for increased educational work and clear sermons against right-wing extremism in order to make congregations resilient.

99 - Is there a uniform strategy within the Catholic Church for dealing with AfD supporters?

For a long time, there was no completely uniform approach within the church when it came to dealing with AfD supporters. While some bishops, such as Peter Kohlgraf, rely on pastoral dialog to win back disappointed Catholics, others warned against excluding AfD members across the board in order to prevent them from being pushed further into extremes. Other voices and lay organizations, on the other hand, are calling for more consistent measures, such as the exclusion of AfD members from church lay offices and a stronger anchoring of this line in church statutes. Despite the clear condemnation of right-wing extremism by the Conference of female, diverse and male Bishops, there is often a lack of comprehensive, binding consequences within church structures.

100 - What role does the Synodal Path play in the context of the church's stance on right-wing populism?

Although the Synodal Path is primarily dedicated to issues within the church, the attitude towards right-wing populism implicitly plays an important role. Members of the Synodal Path consistently emphasize the social responsibility of the church. Combating racism and hate speech is seen as a core task of the church. The Synodal Path raised awareness of the fact that democracy and human rights are not just secular concerns, but are essential from a Christian perspective, as the image of God in every human being contradicts any devaluing ideology. The declaration of the Conference of female, diverse and male Bishops against Right-Wing Extremism is seen as being in line with the synodal concern to bear clear witness to the Gospel in today's world, which also includes standing up for diversity, democracy and the rule of law.

101 - How is the position of the Catholic Church supported by the position of the Church in other countries and by the Vatican?

The position of the German Catholic Church is supported by the position of the Church in other countries and by the Vatican. Catholic clergy around the world reject right-wing extremist movements. In Poland, the Conference of female, diverse and male Bishops warned against "pagan nationalism" and emphasized that true patriotism includes respect for other nations. In his encyclical "Fratelli tutti", Pope Francis urgently warned against backward-looking nationalism and the "culture of walls" and instead emphasized the universal brotherhood of all people. He describes racism as a "virus". Following events such as the neo-Nazi march in Charlottesville and the storming of the US

Capitol, the US bishops have taken a clear stand against racism and in defense of democratic institutions . In Latin America, the Church criticizes authoritarian, right-wing populist tendencies and emphasizes the need for democracy, the rule of law and respect for the dignity of all citizens.

102 - Are there historical examples of the Catholic Church taking a clear stance against extremist ideologies?

Yes, there are historical examples of the Catholic Church taking a clear stance against extremist ideologies. In his 1937 encyclical "With Burning Concern", Pope Pius XI resolutely opposed the National Socialist cult of state and racial ideology and condemned the deification of worldly values such as nation or race as idolatry. The German Jesuit Alfred Delp, who was active in the resistance against Hitler, formulated the dictum shortly before his execution in 1944: "A Christian can never be a nationalist", which emphasizes the incompatibility of radical nationalism with fundamental Christian values. These examples show that the rejection of ideologies that violate human dignity and place nationalist or racist principles above Christian values is anchored in the history of the church.

103 - What responsibility does the Catholic Church see in the fight against right-wing populism and right-wing extremism, both internally and externally?

The Catholic Church sees a dual responsibility in the fight against right-wing populism and right-wing extremism: internally and externally. Internally, it must take a consistent stance, remain vigilant against right-wing extremist attitudes within its own ranks and, if necessary, draw personnel consequences or support committed members. It must not practice tacit tolerance. Externally, the church must stand up loudly and clearly for democracy, human dignity and inclusion. This includes educational work, offers of dialog and cooperation with alliances for tolerance. The church claims moral authority and, according to its self-image, is obliged to protect the weak, oppose hatred and promote reconciliation. It must courageously defend its values against the impositions of right-wing populism, in words and deeds, in order to live up to its role as the "salt of the earth".

 Essay questions:

Please answer one of the following questions in the form of an essay:

a) Discuss the approaches of Catholic bishops in dealing with German AfD sympathizers and supporters within the Church. Evaluate the strengths and weaknesses of the strategy of pastoral dialog compared to demands for clear consequences and exclusions.

b) Analyze how the Catholic Church theologically justifies its rejection of right-wing populism and right-wing extremism. Explain which central elements of Christian anthropology and social doctrine play a role in this and how these contradict nationalist ideologies.

c) Compare the attitude of the Catholic Church in Germany towards right-wing populism/AfD with church positions in Poland and the United States. Identify similarities in the rationale and differences in the specific challenges or focus.

d) Explain the historical continuity of the Church's criticism of excessive nationalism and racist ideologies using the examples of Pope Pius XI ("Mit brennender Sorge") and Alfred Delp SJ. What lessons does the Church draw from these historical experiences for dealing with right-wing extremism today?

e) Should the Catholic Church marry two homosexual women in church rather than a heterosexual couple who are publicly known representatives or members of a right-wing extremist party?

f) Evaluate the role of the Federal Working Group on Church and Right-Wing Extremism (BAG K+R) and similar initiatives in the context of the church's efforts to counter right-wing populism and extremism. To what extent do these structures contribute to the implementation of the clear line formulated by the Conference of female, diverse and male Bishops?

📌 Religious policy field analysis 13: Peace ethics and arms policy of the Catholic Church - Christians against nuclear weapons and balanced arms aid

Catholic bishops - including in Germany the conference chairman Georg Bätzing, Bishop Peter Kohlgraf of Mainz (President of Pax Christi Germany), Bishop Emeritus Franz-Josef Bode of Osnabrück, as well as Heiner Wilmer (Hildesheim), Helmut Dieser (Aachen), Franz Jung (Würzburg) and Karl-Heinz Wiesemann (Speyer) and many others - take clear positions on issues of peace ethics. In particular, they reject the *strategy of nuclear deterrence* from a Christian perspective. In their fundamental peace ethics text *"Peace to this House"*, the bishops call on the German government to seek ways within NATO to ensure the deterrence that will be necessary for the foreseeable future *without nuclear weapons*.

This rejection of nuclear weapons is in line with Pope Francis' teaching, who has already condemned the possession of nuclear weapons as immoral.

In 2020, Bishop Kohlgraf expressly emphasized the *outlawing of nuclear weapons* and urged Germany to join the UN ban treaty - because *"the threat of the destruction of life through nuclear weapons cannot be synonymous with peace"*.

At the same time, these bishops *take a differentiated approach to arms deliveries* in the context of the war in Ukraine, for example. In principle, they condemn the Russian war of aggression and reaffirm Ukraine's right to self-defense.

A declaration by the German Conference of female, diverse and male Bishops states that it is legitimate to *"come to the aid of* the attacked country *through arms deliveries and other military measures"*.

However, the clergy also emphasize that even legitimate defence is subject to *ethical limits*. For example, civilians must be protected and further escalation or the use of weapons of mass destruction must be prevented at all costs.

Bishop Bätzing made it clear that despite the need for military support, the search for peace should not be neglected. Parallel to ongoing arms deliveries, he called for *"peace initiatives now"* in order to find ways out of the violence. This attitude combines support for Ukraine *"willy-nilly"*, even with weapons, with the Christian duty to explore every possibility for dialog and reconciliation.

Violence is therefore only seen as a last resort. Bishop Wiesemann, for example, explained at Christmas 2022 that the *"use of power and violence, including weapons if necessary"* may be necessary to defend innocent life and justice - but always in awareness of the tragedy and only to defend against acute threats to innocents. At the same time, Bishop Kohlgraf of Mainz warned that Christians have also *"become accustomed to violence in deed and word remarkably quickly"*. These media-active shepherds thus plead for a *balance*: on the one hand, responsible support for the defenders, and on the other, an insistence on the primacy of peace and disarmament in the sense of a "just peace".

The current debate emphasizes that although military aid for Ukraine may be necessary, it must always go hand in hand with an intensive search for peace and diplomatic initiatives. At the same time, nuclear deterrence is rejected as an ethically irresponsible peace *at any price.*

Theologians and voices close to the church: A plea for radical non-violence

Even more far-reaching criticism comes from progressive theologians, voices close to the church and church peace activists who question the use of force in principle. In their view, the Christian message of peace - such as the Sermon on the Mount with the commandment to love one's enemies - cannot be reconciled with military logic. They therefore call for a consistent pacifism on the part of the church.

Figure 32: A Sermon on the Mount.

A symbolic and colorful illustration showing Jesus Christ in traditional garb, speaking peacefully and urgently to a diverse group of people listening attentively. In the background are clear depictions of military violence, including tanks, missiles, helicopters and an armed female soldier, as well as a large, simple wooden cross as the central symbol. This composition impressively visualizes the stark contrast between Jesus' message of peace and the reality of war, violence and military power. The scene is kept in calm but clear colors, the atmosphere is serious, thoughtful and admonishing to emphasize the topicality and urgency of a peace-oriented Christian ethic.

In March 2022, four Catholic theology professors (*Josef Freise, Thomas Nauerth, Stefan Silber* and *Egon Spiegel*) issued a statement against the overly pro-military tone of a church commission. They criticized the fact that the official *Justitia et Pax* statement on the war in Ukraine was dominated by a *"worldly, groaning, violent peace"*, while the biblical message of peace was missing. Instead of Kant or power-political analyses, the church should be measured against the Gospel. In particular, these theologians complained that the right to armed defense must *always* remain *the last resort*, even in the greatest need, and that all civilian forms of resistance should be exhausted beforehand. Empirical studies show, they argue, that unarmed resistance often claims fewer victims than armed resistance. They question whether the violence used so far in the Ukraine war has really improved the situation and *"what goal armed resistance against a nuclear-armed power* can *actually pursue"*.

This argument shows a deep skepticism as to whether weapons can actually be used to achieve a just peace, or whether new suffering and a spiral of violence are being accepted.

Progressive church groups also condemn the *structural violence* caused by arms policy and isolationism. The Catholic peace movement *Pax Christi* - in which many committed Christians and theologians are active - regularly denounces German *arms exports*, especially when weapons are delivered to crisis regions or autocratic regimes. Former Pax Christi Secretary General *Christine Hoffmann*, for example, described arms exports to countries such as Saudi Arabia or the United Arab Emirates (which are involved in the war in Yemen) as *"inhumane"*.

It is scandalous that, despite promises to the contrary by the German government, warring parties in Yemen continue to be supplied with German ammunition. The peace activists point out that such exports fuel conflicts and thus indirectly cause further suffering - a form of structural violence in which economic interests are also involved. They also criticize a policy of *armament and isolation* that defines security primarily in military terms. Pax Christi and Protestant peace organizations, for example, warn that the *"increasing militarization of EU border systems"* and the rejection of people seeking protection at Europe's borders are incompatible with Christian values.

Bishop Kohlgraf himself, who is involved in ecumenical peace work, emphasized in view of the refugee camps at the EU's external borders that such treatment of people *"contradicts European values"*. From a progressive point of view, *peace* must not be bought by weapons, walls and deterrence, but must come about through justice, dialog and the renunciation of violent structures. These voices urge the church to live up to its prophetic role and to question *any involvement* in injustice - be it by silently tolerating arms exports or by blessing military violence.

Church pronouncements: Synodal Way, Conference of female, diverse and male Bishops and Pax Christi

Official church statements reflect the tension between ideal pacifism and realistic peacekeeping. Although the *Synodal Path* as a reform dialogue of the Catholic Church primarily dealt with internal church issues, it also included appeals to place greater emphasis on the social responsibility of the church - for example in matters of war and peace. Forces with a willingness to shape repeatedly raised the admonition that the church must clearly bear witness to Christ's message of peace and must not allow itself to be taken in by security policy constraints. In the Synodal Path and related initiatives, voices were raised calling for a *clarification of the ethics of peace*: away from any kind of clauses and towards an attitude that really only sees violence as a last resort and places greater emphasis on non-violent conflict resolution.

Specifically, the German Conference of female, diverse and male Bishops has recently published important statements on peace ethics. At their spring plenary assembly in 2023, the clergy made it clear that the Russian war of aggression is absolutely condemnable and that Ukraine has a right to support.

At the same time, they urged prudence: decisions on arms aid should not be made hastily or euphorically; rather, *"care and caution"* were required. They also emphasized that despite all military self-defense, *diplomacy and dialogue* remain indispensable. The message was: yes to defense aid - but always accompanied by the search for political solutions to avoid further bloodshed.

A milestone was the publication of the new Word of Peace *"Peace to this House"* in February 2024 by the German Conference of female, diverse and male Bishops. In it, the traditional teaching is further developed and adapted to the present day. The document recognizes that *peace cannot* be maintained *completely without weapons*, but at the same time *"self-defence also has limits"*. This *"Christian realism"* is reflected in the balance between defensiveness and a vision of disarmament. The clergy emphasize the right to legitimate self-defence more clearly than in the past, without losing sight of the *ultimate goal of peace*. In addition to armed conflicts, the Word of Peace also identifies *unjust structures* (such as in the global economy or international arms dynamics) as causes of violence that must be overcome. It calls on politicians to abandon the logic of nuclear deterrence in the long term and to strive for common security without nuclear weapons.

The Church is thus officially positioning itself with a *critical stance towards armament* and a clear yes to disarmament and arms control. Pope Francis' appeals for peace (e.g. his comment that we are experiencing a "third world war in pieces") are also incorporated into the orientation of church forces, as is the 60-year-old encyclical *Pacem in terris*, which continues to serve as a compass for the priority option *for peace*.

Alongside the bishops, the Catholic *peace movement Pax Christi* regularly speaks out officially. In resolutions and declarations - such as the Assembly of Delegates in October 2022 - Pax Christi calls for immediate steps to be taken towards negotiations and a *peace solution* in Ukraine instead of relying exclusively on military victories. The movement reminds us that every war must ultimately be ended at the negotiating table and that the prolongation of suffering through the supply of weapons should always be critically scrutinized. At the same time, Pax Christi supports humanitarian aid for Ukraine and emphasizes the suffering of the civilian population as the yardstick for all decisions.

These concerns were also shared in statements by the *Central Committee of German Catholics (ZdK)* and by church aid organizations, which shows that a significant part of the church is publicly in favour of peace logic instead of arms logic.

Global peace ethic: "Never again war!"

Leading Catholic bishops and cardinals around the world are reaffirming the Christian ethic of peace with clear rejections of nuclear weapons. Pope *Francis*, for example, condemned the use of nuclear weapons as a crime and castigated the "perverse logic" of a security system based on fear. In view of the millions of people in need, he denounced it as a "blatant attack" when enormous sums of money flow into ever more destructive armaments; the mere possession of such weapons is "immoral". In this sense, Cardinal *John Onaiyekan* from Nigeria also pleaded for an end to the nuclear arms race: the ban and complete destruction of nuclear weapons is a "deeply spiritual necessity".

The dynamics of conventional armament and arms deliveries are also viewed critically. Bishop *Peter Kohlgraf*, President of the peace movement Pax Christi in Germany, warns that without concrete prospects for peace, armament and militarization are merely "steps on the way to a possible catastrophe" - peace does not come about by "terrifying the other". He therefore considers it "by no means naïve, but realistic" to strictly reject any nuclear armament, entirely in line with church teaching, which brands acts of war to destroy entire cities as a crime against God and humanity. In principle, these church voices underline the primacy of non-violence: in his encyclical *Fratelli tutti*, Francis emphasizes that "war can no longer be considered a solution" and calls out: *"Never again war!"*.

Tension between the Christian message of peace and the reality of security policy

All these positions illustrate the field of tension in which the Catholic ethic of peace operates. *On the one hand,* there is the radical message of peace of the Gospel: Jesus Christ proclaimed non-violence, called on us to turn the other cheek and love our enemies. This ideal of absolute *non-violence* is a central standard for Christians. The church is committed to the model of *"just peace"*, which emphasizes the prevention of violence, reconciliation and justice. This results in a clear moral *stance against armament and arms exports*: more weapons mean more potential violence, and that contradicts the spirit of Jesus. Criticism of arms profiteering, the military and isolationist language of politics and the call for global disarmament stem from this gospel ethos.

On the other hand, there is the harsh security reality of a world in which aggression and injustice unfortunately exist. When innocent people are brutally attacked - as in the Ukraine war - the pure maxim of pacifism reaches its limits. Christians are then faced with the question of conscience as to whether *doing nothing* in the face of evil would not incur greater guilt. Catholic ethics therefore struggles with the classic *"just war"* or the right to defense in self-defense. The bishops are trying to strike a responsible balance here: They recognize the right to armed defence and assistance in solidarity, *"peace cannot be achieved entirely without weapons"*, but they link it strictly to conditions and to the prospect of *finding peace.* Any use of force must be ethically justifiable, limited in time and embedded in efforts to achieve a ceasefire and negotiations.

The tension remains: *How close may the church lean to state security logics without losing its soul - the message of reconciliation?* This question is discussed openly and controversially.

However, there is currently a broad consensus within the Catholic Church that *armament and arms exports are to be viewed critically* and are not suitable as a path to peace. Arms policy that relies on more and more modern weapons (such as a new arms race or the so-called *"turnaround"* in the financing of the German armed forces) is viewed with skepticism by church actors because it combats symptoms rather than causes. Instead, the church emphasizes its very own vision: *"Blessed are the peacemakers"* - making peace through *justice, dialogue, development and humanity.* This clear basic attitude is behind the statements of the clergy and theologians. Despite nuanced positions in individual cases, the Christian ethic of peace is an *admonition against the logic of armament* and a call to never lose sight of the goal of a just peace order in the midst of war and violence. The Catholic Church thus remains an important *voice of reason* in the security policy debate - arguing objectively, in the service of human dignity - and with an unmistakable message: true peace grows out of *disarmament, reconciliation and overcoming violence.*

🐾Bishops' briefing:

The religious policy section examines the peace ethics and arms policy of the Catholic Church. It highlights the positions of German clergymembers who firmly reject nuclear weapons and instead advocate disarmament and arms control, in line with the teachings of the popes. At the same time, their differentiated stance on arms deliveries, especially in the context of the Ukraine war, can be presented, which recognizes legitimate self-defence within ethical limits, but always emphasizes the search for peace through dialogue and diplomacy. The positions of theologians and church groups advocating a more radical pacifism and the rejection of all violence should also be discussed, as well as the church's official statements on these issues, which reflect the tension between the ideal message of peace and the reality of security policy.

Didactic questions

104 - What is the Catholic Church's position on nuclear deterrence?

The Catholic Church, in particular German bishops such as Georg Bätzing and Peter Kohlgraf, clearly rejects the strategy of nuclear deterrence from a Christian perspective. This is in line with the teachings of Pope Francis, who has already condemned the mere possession of nuclear weapons as immoral. Bishop Kohlgraf has emphasized that nuclear threat cannot be a synonym for peace and has called for Germany to join the UN Treaty on the Prohibition of Nuclear Weapons. The clergy call on the German government to seek ways within NATO to ensure deterrence without nuclear weapons for the foreseeable future.

105 - How does the Catholic Church view arms deliveries, especially in the context of the war in Ukraine?

The bishops take a differentiated approach to arms deliveries. They condemn the Russian war of aggression in principle and reaffirm Ukraine's right to self-defense. A declaration by the German Conference of female, diverse and male Bishops considers it legitimate to "come to the aid of the attacked country through arms deliveries and other military measures". At the same time, the bishops emphasize that even legitimate defence is subject to ethical limits. Civilians must be protected and further escalation or the use of weapons of mass destruction must be prevented at all costs. Military aid is considered potentially necessary, but must always be accompanied by intensive peace-seeking and diplomatic initiatives. Force is seen here only as a last resort, as a defense against acute threats to innocent life and justice, but always in awareness of the tragedy.

106 - What role does the search for peace play alongside support for attacked states?

The Catholic Church emphasizes that despite the need for military support, the search for peace must not be neglected. Parallel to ongoing arms deliveries, clergymembers are calling for "peace initiatives now" in order to find ways out of the violence. This stance combines support for Ukraine, even with weapons if necessary, with the Christian duty to explore every possibility for dialog and reconciliation. The bishops warn that despite all military self-defense, diplomacy and dialogue remain indispensable.

107 - What critical voices are there within the church regarding violence and arms policy?

More far-reaching reflections come from progressive theologians and church peace activists, such as those often active in the *Pax Christi* peace movement. They question any use of force in principle and argue that the Christian message of peace, in particular the commandment to love one's enemies from the Sermon on the Mount, is not compatible with military logic. They call for a consistent pacifism on the part of the church. These voices criticize an excessive focus on security policy analyses and emphasize the need to measure oneself against the Gospel. They point to civil resistance as an alternative and question whether armed resistance against a nuclear-armed power can pursue a meaningful goal at all.

108 - How does the Church view arms exports and structural violence?

Church groups and organizations such as *Pax Christi* condemn the structural violence caused by arms policy and isolationism. They denounce German arms exports, especially when weapons are delivered to crisis regions or autocratic regimes. Such exports are described as "inhumane", as they fuel conflicts and cause further suffering, with economic interests also playing a role. A policy of armament and isolation that defines security primarily in military terms is also criticized. The increasing militarization of EU border systems and the rejection of people seeking protection at Europe's borders are seen as incompatible with Christian values.

109 - How are these positions reflected in official church statements?

Official church pronouncements reflect the tension between ideal pacifism and realistic peacekeeping. The Synodal Path called for a stronger emphasis on the social responsibility of the church in matters of war and peace and a clarification of the peace ethic, which regards violence as the ultimate means. The German Conference of female, diverse and male Bishops has set out its position in recent statements, in particular in the new peace statement "Peace to this House" (2024). This document recognizes the right to legitimate self-defence, but emphasizes that "self-defence also has limits". It pleads for a "Christian realism" that combines defensiveness with a vision of disarmament. Unjust structures such as international arms dynamics are named as causes of violence that must be overcome. The clergy take a critical stance towards armament and clearly advocate disarmament and arms control. Appeals from Pope Francis and the encyclical *Pacem in terris* are also incorporated into this position. In its statements, the peace movement *Pax Christi* calls for concrete steps towards negotiations and a peace solution and urges critical scrutiny of arms deliveries.

110 - How does the Catholic peace ethic relate to the concept of "just war"?

Catholic ethics struggles with the classical concept of "just war" or the right to defense in self-defense. In view of the reality of aggression and injustice, the question arises as to whether doing nothing in the face of evil would not incur greater guilt. The German bishops are trying to take a responsible middle course by recognizing the right to armed defence and solidarity ("peace cannot be achieved entirely without weapons"), but linking it strictly to conditions and to the prospect of finding peace. Any use of force must be ethically justifiable, limited in time and embedded in efforts to achieve a ceasefire and negotiations. This differs from the traditional "just war" in that the focus is more on prevention, reconciliation and the creation of a "just peace" and violence is really only seen as a last resort and a tragic evil.

111 - What is the central message of the Catholic Church in the current security policy debate?

The central message of the Catholic Church is an admonition against the logic of armament and a call to never lose sight of the goal of a just peace order in the midst of war and violence. There is a broad consensus within the Church that armament and arms exports are to be viewed critically and are not suitable as a path to peace. Instead of fighting symptoms, the Church emphasizes its vision of creating peace through justice, dialogue, development and humanity, true to the beatitude "Blessed are the peacemakers". True peace grows out of disarmament, reconciliation and overcoming violence. The Church wants to be an important voice of reason in the security policy debate, arguing objectively and in the service of human dignity.

Essay questions

Please answer one of the following questions in the form of an essay:

a) Discuss the tension between the radical peace message of the Gospel and the recognition of the right to armed self-defense by the German Conference of female, diverse and male Bishops. How does the church attempt to resolve this conflict, especially in the context of current wars?

b) Analyze the criticism of theologians and church peace activists regarding the position of the German Conference of female, diverse and male Bishops on arms policy and the use of force. What biblical or theological arguments do they use to support their position of radical non-violence?

c) Explain the significance of the new word for peace "Peace to this house" for the peace ethics of the Catholic Church. To what extent does it represent a further development of traditional teaching and what specific demands does it make?

d) Evaluate the role of organizations such as *Pax Christi* within the Catholic Church in Germany with regard to peace ethics. What specific issues (e.g. arms exports, isolationism) do they address and how do they influence the debate?

e) Compare the positions of clerics with those of theologians and church critics regarding arms deliveries and military support. What similarities and differences are there and what arguments underlie the respective positions?

Religious policy field analysis 14: *Climate change and sustainability in the Catholic Church*

Global climate change is also a pressing issue for the Catholic Church. Inspired by Pope Francis' encyclical *Laudato si'*, many church representatives see the protection of the environment as an ethical mandate and an integral part of Christian social teaching.

Laudato si' emphasizes that ecological and social crises are inextricably linked and calls for a responsible approach to creation. From the Church's perspective, sustainability is therefore an expression of responsibility for creation - the duty to preserve God's creation for present and future generations.

Several German bishops repeatedly emphasize this message. They promote greater ecological awareness in the church and society and regard consistent climate protection as a core component of church action. They have welcomed the Pope's new climate appeal as an urgent wake-up call and acknowledged that the church still has *room for improvement* when it comes to climate protection - much more needs to be done.

Heiner Wilmer, Bishop of Hildesheim, had even harsher words: he described climate change as the "greatest market failure in our human history" and warned that the warnings from *Laudato si'* had not yet been heeded. Wilmer recalled that Pope Francis had already pointed out the dramatic social consequences of global warming ten years ago.

Very practical steps are also being taken: In Mainz, Bishop *Peter Kohlgraf* has introduced a climate protection concept for his diocese, because since *Laudato si'*, climate protection is "no longer a marginal topic" of theology, but belongs "at the center of the church".

Such initiatives - from energy-efficient building management to the conversion of church facilities to green electricity - are intended to show that sustainability is taken seriously in the church. Even traditional religious practice is being reinterpreted in ecological terms: Auxiliary Bishop *Rolf Lohmann* (Münster), the environmental officer of the Conference of female, diverse and male Bishops, suggested reviving the classic meatless Friday - as a spiritual contribution *and* as an act of climate protection. Overall, the creative bishops paint a picture of a church that understands responsibility for creation as a mission from God and wants to be a pioneer for ecological sustainability itself.

Other theologians go one step further and call for the church to act consistently as a role model when it comes to climate change. In their view, the church must underpin its teaching on the preservation of creation with its own actions. Specifically, they are calling for all church properties and buildings to be operated in a climate-neutral manner within five years at the latest.

The church should also pursue an ethical financial policy and actively pursue *divestment* - in other words, withdraw funds from companies that do business with coal, oil or gas. This is the only way the church can credibly stand up for climate justice. In addition, these circles are pushing for changes in everyday church life: fewer business trips by car, less flying to conferences and a more environmentally friendly diet in church institutions (for example, more meat-free eating) are seen as necessary contributions.

Everyone - from the bishops to the community base - can help to save CO_2 by adopting a simple lifestyle. But it should not stop there: The church should also provide social *impetus* by making climate justice a constant topic in pastoral care and preaching and exerting pressure on politicians for ambitious climate targets.

Church representatives point out that, from a Christian perspective, climate protection is always linked to social justice - in the sense of an option for the poor who are most affected by climate change.

Accordingly, there are calls for climate justice to be firmly anchored in sermons, educational work and church activities. Overall, this creates the image of a church that not only *talks about* ecology, but also establishes a credible *model of sustainable action* within its own structures.

Figure 33: The church establishes a credible model of sustainable action.

A hand places a wooden block with a church symbol on the top of a pyramid of blocks showing various environmental symbols, such as a wind turbine, solar panels, recycling, CO2 and water conservation. The image visually combines the concept of environmental sustainability with religious commitment.

And what role does the *Synodal Path* - the major church reform process - play in this topic? The Synodal Path, which began a few years ago, was primarily concerned with internal church issues such as power structures, lay participation, sexual morality and the role of women. Climate change and ecology were not explicitly on the agenda as a separate forum. Nevertheless, the ethical-ecological perspective resonates in the background. Many of the reform-oriented actors of the Synodal Path share the conviction that the church is only fit for the future if it also takes responsibility for global challenges such as climate protection. For example, *Gudrun Lux* - a member of the Central Committee of German Catholics and a synod member - was also active in the *Christians for Future* initiative and co-signed the demands for more climate protection in the church.

This commitment shows that the concerns of the Synodal Path (transparency, acceptance of responsibility, credibility) and the demand for ecological sustainability go hand in hand. Even if the Synodal Path itself has not passed any resolutions of its own on climate protection, it indirectly underlines the need for the church as a whole to renew itself credibly - in addition to theological and structural reforms, this also includes a determined commitment to the preservation of creation. Sustainability from an ethical-Christian perspective is therefore a cross-cutting issue: it touches on questions of justice, responsibility and the credibility of the Church in the world of today. The Catholic Church is therefore faced with the task of translating its words from *Laudato si'* into visible action - in harmony with a reformist spirit, in solidarity with the weak and in the service of creation.

Bishops' briefing:

The religious policy field describes the Catholic Church's commitment to climate protection and sustainability, inspired by Pope Francis' encyclical Laudato si'. It emphasizes that many church representatives see environmental protection as a Christian duty and part of social teaching. It should be emphasized that ecological and social problems are linked and that sustainability is understood as the preservation of creation. Specific measures such as energy efficiency and switching to green electricity as well as ethical financial policies and divestment are proposed. It is clear that the church is striving for internal changes as well as providing social impetus to promote climate justice, even if the Synodal Path did not explicitly address the topic. Overall, a church can view sustainability as an expression of responsibility and credibility in today's world.

Didactic questions:

112 - Why does the Catholic Church consider climate change and sustainability to be important issues?

Global climate change is seen as a pressing issue in the Catholic Church in Germany. Inspired by Pope Francis' encyclical Laudato si', many church representatives see environmental protection as an ethical mandate and an integral part of Christian social teaching. Laudato si' emphasizes the inseparable link between ecological and social crises and calls for a responsible approach to creation. From the church's perspective, sustainability is therefore seen as an expression of responsibility for creation - the duty to preserve God's creation for present and future generations.

113 - What is the position of leading German bishops on climate protection?

Several reform-oriented bishops, including the chairman of the German Conference of female, diverse and male Bishops, as well as other bishops such as Peter Kohlgraf, Franz-Josef Bode (emeritus), Heiner Wilmer, Helmut Dieser, Franz Jung and Karl-Heinz Wiesemann, emphasize the importance of climate protection. They promote greater ecological awareness in the church and society and see consistent climate protection as a core component of the church's actions. It is acknowledged that the church must do more to protect the climate. Bishop Wilmer described climate change as the "greatest market failure in the history of mankind" and warned that the warnings in Laudato si' have not yet been sufficiently heeded.

114 - What concrete steps is the Catholic Church taking to become more sustainable?

Practical steps are being taken to promote sustainability in the church. These include initiatives such as energy-efficient building management and the conversion of church facilities to green electricity. In Mainz, Bishop Kohlgraf introduced a climate protection concept for his diocese several years ago. In addition, traditional religious practice is being reinterpreted in an ecological way, for example the suggestion by

Auxiliary Bishop Rolf Lohmann to revive meatless Fridays as a spiritual contribution and act of climate protection.

115 - What do theologians and circles demand from the church with regard to climate change and sustainability?

Theologians and circles are going further and calling for the church to act consistently as a role model when it comes to climate change. They demand that the church underpins its teaching on the preservation of creation with its own actions. Specifically, they are calling for all church properties and buildings to be climate-neutral within five years at the latest. In addition, the church should pursue an ethical financial policy and actively pursue divestment, i.e. withdraw funds from companies that are active in the fossil fuel business in order to credibly stand up for climate justice. Changes in everyday church life such as fewer business trips by car, less flying to conferences and a more environmentally friendly diet in church facilities are also considered necessary.

116 - How can individuals and the grassroots of the Catholic Church in Germany contribute to climate protection?

Everyone - from the bishops to the community base - can help to save CO_2 by adopting a simple lifestyle. However, it is emphasized that it should not stop there. The church should also provide social impetus by making climate justice a permanent topic in pastoral care and preaching and exerting pressure on politicians for ambitious climate targets.

117 - What is the connection between climate protection and social justice from a Christian perspective?

Church representatives point out that, from a Christian perspective, climate protection is always linked to social justice - in the sense of an option for the poor who are most affected by climate change. Accordingly, there are calls for climate justice to be firmly anchored in sermons, educational work and church campaigns.

118 - What role does the Synodal Path play in climate change and sustainability?

Although climate change and ecology were not explicitly included as a separate forum on the agenda of the Synodal Path, which primarily dealt with internal church issues, the ethical-ecological perspective resonates in the background. Many reform-oriented actors on the Synodal Path share the conviction that the church is only fit for the future if it also takes responsibility for global challenges such as climate protection. This commitment shows that the concerns of the Synodal Path (transparency, acceptance of responsibility, credibility) and the demand for ecological sustainability go hand in hand. Even if the Synodal Path has not passed any resolutions of its own on climate protection, it indirectly underlines the need for a credible renewal of the church, which includes not only theological and structural reforms but also a determined commitment to the integrity of creation.

119 - How is sustainability understood in the Catholic Church and what task does the Church face?

Sustainability is understood as a cross-cutting issue from an ethical-Christian perspective: It touches on issues of justice, responsibility and the credibility of the Church in today's world. The Catholic Church is therefore faced with the task of translating its words from *Laudato si'* into visible action - in harmony with a reformist spirit, in solidarity with the weak and in the service of creation. An image is emerging of a church that not only talks about ecology, but also wants to establish a credible model of sustainable action within its own structures.

Essay questions:

Please answer one of the following questions in the form of an essay:

a) Discuss the role of Pope Francis' encyclical *Laudato si'* as the basis for the Catholic Church's commitment to climate change. How does the encyclical influence the understanding of responsibility for creation and sustainability?

b) Analyze the attitude and concrete initiatives of the clergy with regard to climate protection and sustainability. What measures are being taken and how do they position the church in this debate?

c) Explain the demands of theologians regarding consistent exemplary action by the church in the area of climate protection. What concrete steps are proposed and how are they justified?

d) Describe how the text presents the link between climate protection, social justice and the option for the poor from a Christian perspective. Why is this connection considered important?

e) Evaluate the indirect role of the Synodal Path in the context of the church's commitment to climate protection and sustainability. To what extent do the concerns of the Synodal Path support the call for more ecological responsibility on the part of the church?

Religious policy field analysis 15: *Economics and social justice - Catholic criticism of the neoliberal economic system*

Leading bishops are clearly critical of neoliberal economic principles. They warn that unbridled market thinking, which places profit maximization above human dignity, is incompatible with Christian social ethics. Pope Francis' statement *"This economy kills"* - coined in *Evangelii Gaudium* (2013) - underlines this concern and has also met with approval from the international bishops.

Bishops: Common good instead of neoliberal principles

Instead, the bishops call for an orientation towards the common good: the economy must serve social cohesion and enable fair participation for all instead of dividing social classes. These church people insist on social responsibility on the part of politicians and companies. German clergymembers recently welcomed the new EU supply chain law as an "international success" and a "strong signal for human rights and sustainability in the global economy". They made it clear that Christian values are incompatible with exploitative practices: "As Christians, we must no longer tolerate the destruction of indigenous communities' livelihoods through mining, child labor in cocoa harvesting in West Africa and the exploitation of seamstresses in Bangladesh."

This demonstrates the Church's clear commitment to fair supply chains and working conditions worldwide. The bishops call for an economic order that serves people, not the other way around - capital and the market should have a serving function and contribute to the well-being of all, instead of enriching the few and exploiting the many.

Figure 34: Clothing for capitalism.

A cartoon shows a man at a bank counter holding a newspaper with the headline 'Negative interest rates at the bank'. He says: 'I'd like some stockings,' to which the bank employee asks: 'For ladies or gentlemen? The man clarifies: 'For my savings...' The humor of the cartoon revolves around the concept of negative interest rates, where savings lose value instead of earning interest and it's about money being used to create more money instead of actually warming and equipping those who are cold. A critique of capitalism by the churches.

Alternatives: solidarity, the common good and social justice

Instead of a purely profit-driven market logic, clergymembers outline alternative guiding principles that focus on solidarity, social justice and the common good. Pope Francis, for example, repeatedly emphasizes the priority option for the poor: In his message to the Davos World Economic Forum, he called for all economic development to *"subordinate the pursuit of power and individual gain (...) to the common good of the human family and give priority to the poor and the weak"*. This ties in with Catholic social teaching, which only legitimizes prosperity if it benefits *everyone*. Authentic development, according to Francis, must *not exclude anyone* - it must *be "global, shared by all nations and in all parts of the world"*, otherwise it will ultimately be lost everywhere. Cardinal *Peter Turkson*, long head of the Vatican's development dicastery, puts it pragmatically from a corporate perspective: although companies must of course make a profit, they should focus their goals beyond pure profit in order to serve the *common good*. He suggests switching from simply maximizing profits to *optimizing* them - companies should ask themselves what *positive change* their business activities bring to society. *"We want to influence the goals of companies so that it is not just about financial profit, but about the value they create for society - making life better, more liveable, fairer and more inclusive,"* explained Turkson in January 2024 on the sidelines of the World Economic Forum. Such appeals show a concrete alternative to the neoliberal paradigm: the economy should serve people, not people the economy.

A key point of the Church's alternative proposals is to *strengthen workers' rights and social security*. At the beginning of the coronavirus crisis in 2020, Pope Francis proposed an idea that was unheard of at the time: *a universal basic wage* for all workers, especially those in the informal sector. "Perhaps now is the time to think about a *universal basic wage* that recognizes and appreciates the noble, indispensable work you do. It would realize the ideal that no worker remains without rights". This concept of a guaranteed basic income - described by Francis as "so human and so Christian" - would lift millions of marginalized workers out of insecurity. Similarly, church leaders have brought *debt relief* into play as an act of global solidarity: in the face of collapsing economies in the pandemic, Cardinal Tagle called on wealthy nations to cancel the debts of the poorest countries. In a dramatic biblical image, he compared the overwhelming debt burden of poor nations to the tomb of the dead Lazarus and called for a *"jubilee year of debt relief so that those trapped in the tombs of debt can find their way back to life"*. Cardinal Turkson had also urged debt relief early on in the crisis and called for *"innovative solutions"* to make financially weak states capable of acting.

In addition, the church leaders insist on *drastically reducing arms spending* and investing the freed-up capital in the common good - a call that is expressed in Tagle's appeal *"Can we please stop the wars?"*. Money should flow into *"real security"* - food, housing, education and healthcare - instead of weapons. These concrete proposals - a basic wage, debt relief, redirecting resources from weapons to welfare - outline an economic order that makes solidarity practical.

Theologians and church reform movements are also pushing for a change of course in the economy. Their criticism of capitalism is aimed at a system based on competition and self-interest, which creates inequality and exclusion. Theologian *Hanno Heil*, for example, predicts a far-reaching "transformation" of society as a consequence of the crises of our time - a fundamental transformation towards an economic order based on the common good is necessary. The weaknesses of a model based exclusively on egoism and competition are becoming increasingly apparent. Instead of the "neoliberal model of society, which measures success primarily in terms of monetary gain", Heil advocates - on behalf of many church voices - the economy for the common good. This alternative economic model places human dignity, solidarity, justice and sustainability at the heart of economic activity. Economic success should not be measured solely by profit and GDP, but by its contribution to the common good, for example through a common good balance sheet.

In addition to such concepts, church reform initiatives are also calling for ethical consumption and global justice. They appeal to consumers to stop encouraging exploitation through fair trade and conscious purchasing decisions. Church critics point out that a lifestyle at the expense of the poor and creation is morally bankrupt.

Instead, the economy should be shaped in such a way that it produces "really good goods" and services "that really serve" - as a Vatican document on business ethics puts it.

Many Christian social movements share this attitude: fair trade, fair wages and environmentally friendly business practices are key demands. They thus build on the long tradition of the Church's social doctrine, which has called for an economy in the service of people and creation since the encyclical Rerum Novarum (1891) through to Laudato Si' (2015).

Synodal path and church proclamations: Mission to justice and sustainability

The synodal path of the Catholic Church - actually a reform dialog on internal church issues - also reflects this socially critical attitude. Although the focus was on power structures within the church, the abolition of celibacy, sexual morality and the marriage of same-sex couples as well as women in spiritual ministries, it was repeatedly emphasized that the church only remains credible if its mission includes a commitment to social justice, responsibility for creation and a humane economy.

Resolutions and contributions to the Synodal Path made it clear that power in the church also means taking a prophetic stand against unjust economic power relations. This calls for a "church on the side of the poor" that clearly names economic exploitation and encourages alternatives - locally and worldwide. Even beyond the Synodal Path, current church statements emphasize the connection between social and ecological justice. Economic power and responsibility are being reconsidered in the light of the theology of creation: lasting peace and social cohesion are inextricably linked to economic and social justice as well as fair access to resources - and this goes hand in hand with protecting the environment.

In Laudato Si' and Fratelli tutti, Pope Francis calls for an "ecological conversion" and an economy that "does not kill, but lets live", i.e.

includes the poor and respects the earth. The German church is taking up these impulses. For example, representatives of the dioceses met with industrial companies to discuss the social market economy and environmental protection.

In ecumenical appeals before elections, bishops and church representatives emphasize the duty of the state to focus on participation and justice - for example through a strong social market economy as a counterweight to market egoisms.

Integral: Environmental responsibility and the economy for the common good

A consistent motif in the church's statements is the link between *social justice and environmental protection*. Pope Francis and many of the faithful see the ecological crisis and the social issue as two sides of the same coin - the church calls this *"integral ecology"*. In April 2020, Francis called for a "humanistic and ecological conversion" that *"puts an end to the idolatry of money and places human life and dignity at the center"*. This makes it clear that an alternative to neoliberal capitalism must not only be socially but also ecologically sustainable. Cardinal *Charles Maung Bo*, Archbishop of Yangon and Chairman of the Asian Bishops' Conferences, called for lessons to be learned from the "nightmares of 2020" at the turn of 2021. Despite all the hardship, the crisis offers *"a golden opportunity to reorder priorities"* and "rebuild better" - but with a focus on *economic and ecological justice*. In Bo's home country of Myanmar, which is plagued by resource exploitation and conflict, this means standing up against corruption and overexploitation and embracing a new development model that brings *peace, health and prosperity for all, especially the poor and marginalized*. This plea for a *"new era of economic and environmental justice"* coincides with the Pope's line: *development* must never again be understood one-dimensionally as growth at any price, but as the holistic well-being of people and the environment. In his Davos message, Francis also emphasized that globalization needs a *moral compass* - models that are "far-sighted and ethically sound". *In concrete terms*, according to the Pope, *this means "subordinating the pursuit of power and profit to the common good"* and giving *top priority to the care of creation and the poor.*

One thing is clear: the Catholic Church is calling with increasing urgency for an economy that serves the common good. Bishops such as Bätzing and Wilmer as well as theologians, church associations and committed laypeople denounce the exploitative structures of the current global economy in a factual, argumentative but unequivocal tone. They are not satisfied with charitable appeals, but are pushing for concrete reforms: from fair wages and strict rules for companies to new economic practices that place solidarity above profit. The church is convinced that such an economic order - based on justice, sustainability and the inalienable dignity of every human being - is in line with the spirit of the Gospel and the social mission of Christians.

In summary, international church leaders have been painting a picture of an economic order beyond the neoliberal status quo since 2020. This alternative economy would be *more socially just, participatory and ecologically sustainable.* It aims to bridge the gap between rich and poor, put an end to exclusion and instead make *the common good and the dignity of every human being* the yardstick for economic activity. Whether through solidarity actions such as debt relief, new structures such as a basic income or a value-based approach to politics and markets, clerics call on *people to "see the eyes of the world through the eyes of the poor"* and act accordingly. Their vision is an *economic system in the service of people and creation* - an *alternative* to neoliberal capitalism that explicitly links social justice, environmental protection and the common good.

By formulating this clear criticism, the Church is encouraging many people to think and live an alternative economy - for a future in which the economy and social justice go hand in hand.

🕊️Bishops' briefing:

Leading representatives of the Catholic Church, including the Pope and various bishops, express harsh criticism of the prevailing neoliberal economic system in this religious policy area . They emphasize that pure profit maximization contradicts human dignity and Christian social ethics and instead call for an economic order based on the common good, solidarity and social justice. Concrete proposals include fair supply chains, the strengthening of workers' rights, a possible universal basic income and debt relief for poorer countries. The Church also inextricably links the social issue with the ecological crisis and advocates an economy that is both socially just and ecologically sustainable in order to ensure the well-being of all and the integrity of creation.

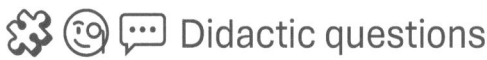 Didactic questions:

120 - Why do leading clergy criticize neoliberal economic principles?

The criticism of neoliberalism stems from the conviction that an economic system that places profit maximization above human dignity is incompatible with Christian social ethics. They see that unbridled market thinking reinforces social divisions instead of serving social cohesion. Pope Francis' statement "This economy kills" illustrates this concern and was also shared by international bishops. Instead, the Church advocates an economic order that is geared towards the common good and enables fair participation for all.

121 - What does the demand for an orientation towards the common good in the economy mean?

The demand for an orientation towards the common good means that the economy should not only serve the profit of individuals, but the good of society as a whole. This means that the economy should strengthen social cohesion, enable fair participation and not further divide social classes. The Church emphasizes the social responsibility of politics and companies, for example by supporting initiatives such as the EU

Supply Chain Act, which is intended to promote human rights and sustainability in the global economy.

122 - What is the church's position on global supply chains and working conditions?

The church is clearly committed to fair supply chains and working conditions worldwide. It considers exploitative practices, such as the destruction of the livelihoods of indigenous communities through mining, child labor in the cocoa harvest or the exploitation of seamstresses, to be incompatible with Christian values. The bishops call for an economic order in which capital and the market serve people and contribute to the well-being of all, instead of enriching the few and exploiting the many.

123 - What alternative guiding principles to the profit-driven market do bishops and cardinals outline?

As an alternative to pure profit logic, the clergy focus on solidarity, social justice and the common good. Pope Francis emphasizes the "preferential option for the poor" and calls for all economic development to be subordinated to the common good of the human family. Cardinal Turkson suggests that companies should focus their goals beyond pure profit and ask themselves what positive change their business activities bring to society, away from simply maximizing profit and towards optimizing social value.

124 - What concrete proposals do church representatives make for an economic order based on solidarity?

The church representatives' concrete proposals for an economic order based on solidarity include strengthening workers' rights and social security. Pope Francis, for example, brought up the idea of a universal basic salary for all workers, especially those in the informal sector. Church leaders have also called for debt relief as an act of global solidarity, especially given the economic difficulties of poorer countries. In addition, church leaders are calling for a drastic reduction in military spending and for the freed-up capital to be invested in the common good, i.e. in areas such as food, housing, education and healthcare.

125 - How is the criticism of capitalism justified from a theological and ecclesiastical perspective?

From a theological and church perspective, capitalism is criticized because it is often based on competition and self-interest, creating inequality and exclusion. Theologians and church reform movements see the need for a fundamental transformation towards an economic order based on the common good. They advocate models such as the economy for the common good, which focuses on human dignity, solidarity, justice and sustainability. Economic success should not be measured by profit alone, but by its contribution to the common good.

126 - How do church statements combine social justice and environmental protection?

Church statements combine social justice and environmental protection as integral components. Clergymembers see the ecological crisis and the social issue as two sides of the same coin, which is referred to as "integral ecology". They call for a "humanistic and ecological conversion" that puts an end to the "idolatry of money" and places human life and dignity at the center. An alternative to neoliberal capitalism must therefore be both socially and ecologically sustainable.

127 - What is the Catholic Church's overarching vision for an alternative economic order?

The overarching vision of the Catholic Church is an economic order beyond the neoliberal status quo that is more socially just, participatory and ecologically sustainable. This alternative economy should overcome the gap between rich and poor, put an end to exclusion and instead make the common good and the dignity of every human being the yardstick for economic activity. Through concrete reforms such as fair wages, strict rules for companies and new economic practices that place solidarity above profit, an economic system should emerge in the service of people and creation that combines social justice, environmental protection and the common good.

✍ 🖥 Essay questions:

Please answer one of the following questions in the form of an essay:

a) Discuss the Catholic Church's main criticisms of the neoliberal economic system as set out in the text. Which specific practices or principles of neoliberalism are at the forefront?

b) Explain the alternatives to the neoliberal economic paradigm proposed by the Catholic Church. What role do concepts such as the common good, solidarity and social justice play in this?

c) How does the Catholic Church combine social justice with ecological responsibility in its statements? Explain the concept of "integral ecology" and its significance for the Church's economic critique.

d) Analyze the Church's concrete political and economic proposals, such as universal basic income or debt relief. How could these proposals help to create a fairer and more sustainable economic order?

e) Discuss the role of the Church's social teaching and movements in the formulation and dissemination of criticism of neoliberalism and the promotion of alternative economic models. To what extent does this tradition influence current positions?

📌 Religious policy field analysis 16: *Elderly Care and the Church: "Don't abandon our elderly" - An appeal for dignified care for the elderly*

Imagine an 85-year-old woman desperately ringing the doorbell in a nursing home to get help to go to the toilet. Minutes turn into hours until someone finds the time - too late, the woman's dignity has long since been violated. Scenes like this happen every day. *The conditions in many care homes are now considered inhumane* - geriatric nurses report that human dignity is being violated in German homes.

Unworthy conditions in our retirement homes: Call for repentance and responsibility

Overworked nursing staff often only manage to do the bare minimum on the run: washing, dressing, serving food. There is no time for a compassionate conversation or individual attention. Some residents literally have to "beg to be allowed to go to the toilet", as one experienced geriatric nurse shockingly put it. When even basic needs are not met promptly, it is a silent scandal in the midst of our affluent society. Yet almost one million people in Germany live in care homes - and there is a shortage of staff at the back and front. As early as 2018, almost 40,000 positions in hospitals and care facilities could not be filled. This *care crisis* means too few hands for too many people in need. The result is hectic, frustration and often undignified conditions that are absolutely unacceptable in a country whose constitution *guarantees the inviolability of every person's dignity*.

The fact that old people have to live in such undignified conditions should not leave us cold. *"Save human dignity"* was what demonstrators called for years ago at rallies against abuses in care for the elderly. But not much has changed since then. Residents are too often *degraded to care objects* instead of being cared for as individuals. As early as 2008,

Bishop *Franz-Josef Bode* of Osnabrück urged the church to "put its finger in the wound" when care for the elderly was reduced to assembly line work and old people were treated as objects. Today, this appeal is more urgent than ever. The conditions are crying out to heaven - but where is the outcry?

Empty promises from politicians

For many decades, we have been hearing promises from politicians that nursing staff should be better paid and that care facilities should be better equipped. *But many of these promises have had no consequences.* Election campaign after election campaign, care offensives were announced without any noticeable relief reaching care homes. Nursing staff complain bitterly that they have been put off with warm words for many years, but real appreciation in the form of higher wages and more staff has failed to materialize. One example of this is the coronavirus crisis: *at the beginning of the pandemic, there was applause and the promise of a bonus* to reward nurses for their efforts. However, a report by the Federal Audit Office showed that many nursing staff have still not received the bonus promised in 2020. This was due to bureaucratic hurdles and in some cases employers did not even apply for the money or it was diverted elsewhere.

In fact, nurses feel let down by politicians. Despite all the Sunday speeches, society has not yet managed to make the nursing profession attractive enough to attract and retain sufficient staff. The thanks for self-sacrificing service must not only consist of fine words, but must also be reflected in decent working conditions and salaries. Otherwise, political promises will remain empty shells while the crisis in care homes continues to fester.

Responsibility of the church: claim and reality

It is particularly shameful that even the churches - although they are major providers of care homes and social facilities - have not yet achieved any radical improvement. The Catholic Church, through its Caritas association, is one of the largest employers in the social sector. With around 700,000 employees in Germany alone, Caritas is the largest private employer in the country. Its self-image is based on the commandment to love one's neighbor - "Caritas" means love for one's neighbor.

You would think that conditions in Catholic care homes would be exemplary and that employees would be treated fairly. But the reality lags behind the claim. Caritas employers, of all people, made headlines in 2021 when they blocked a nationwide collective agreement for geriatric care that would have resulted in higher wages across the industry. Hundreds of thousands of care workers - especially those working for private providers - would have benefited from this collective agreement, but this important project failed due to a lack of solidarity on the part of Caritas employers. This is an indictment of poverty: the institution's Christian social responsibility took a back seat to internal principles. It is true that many church institutions certainly strive for quality, and individual voices in the church - from committed pastors to bishops - denounce shortcomings. But structurally, the church has not yet exhausted its possibilities to enforce better standards in care as a large provider. Those who proclaim the gospel must also practice mercy and justice in their own homes. Self-criticism is appropriate here: the church must do justice to its dual role as a moral authority *and* employer so that its testimony remains credible.

Christian charity and biblical mission

Our attitude towards the elderly and infirm is also a question of faith. The Bible provides unmistakable guidelines. *"You shall honor your father and mother" (Exodus 20:12)* - this commandment from the Ten Commandments reminds us to treat our parents with dignity and respect in old age. Honor is not paid with lip service, but through acts of care. Jesus himself set an example of how we should treat the weakest: He turned to the sick and marginalized with special love, healed the suffering and gave comfort. *"Whatever you did for one of the least of these brothers of mine, you did for me"* (Mt 25:40) - these words of Jesus oblige us Christians to see Christ himself in every suffering person. If an elderly person in need of help is neglected, then we are failing Christ in our midst. Christian charity (*agape*) must not remain an abstract principle, it must become concrete in care and mercy. *"Be merciful, just as your Father is merciful"* (Luke 6:36) - this call to mercy means today: not looking away where the elderly are treated undignified, but becoming active, remedying grievances, giving time, giving love. In the tradition of the church, the works of mercy, including caring for the sick and visiting the lonely, are considered basic acts of Christian action. A society that wants to call itself Christian is measured by how it treats its oldest members. *Every person is made in the image of God, even in old age* - this dignity demands our protection and care.

Loneliness in old age in an individualized society

In addition to personal and material hardships, there is a less tangible but equally painful problem: *the isolation of the older generation.* Our modern way of life often means that families live far apart. Many children and grandchildren no longer live in the same place as their grandparents; work and mobility rarely allow the generations to live together. When their own relatives are often *hundreds of kilometers away* in a care home or cannot find the time in their everyday lives, elderly people are left emotionally alone. *One in four elderly people only receive a visit* from friends or acquaintances *about once a month* - and some no longer have anyone to visit regularly.

In many care homes, senior citizens sit alone for hours in the common room or by the window, without a personal conversation, without anyone holding their hand. *Social isolation* in old age is a silent epidemic that causes suffering in secret. Psychologically, this isolation has a devastating effect: Loneliness can make people ill and even shorten their lives. *Suicide rates among the very elderly over 80 are the highest of all age groups* - a shocking sign of how desperate some people feel in their twilight years. Added to this is the *shortage of housing* in urban areas: Even when families would like to care for their elderly at home, there is often a lack of space in the apartment or there is no affordable larger place to stay. Many elderly people live in small senior apartments or nursing homes, while young families struggle to find living space - a social dilemma.

We need to ask ourselves whether our housing and living models are still up to date: Why aren't there more *multi-generational houses, shared apartments for young and old* or other creative concepts that alleviate loneliness and network help? The *individualization* of our society must not mean that individuals are left to fend for themselves in old age. Christian communities and committed neighbors can counteract this - through visiting services, senior sponsorships and active *solidarity in the neighborhood*. No older person should have to believe that they are "superfluous" or a burden on society. We are all called upon to be *family in a broader sense* for those who no longer have a family of their own to look after them.

Demographic change: the challenge of ageing affects us all

The topic of dignified care for the elderly is not a niche issue - it is *a matter of fate for our ageing society*. Germany is in the midst of demographic change. Already today, around one in five people in this country is over 66 years old, and the proportion of very old people will increase dramatically. The number of people over 80 is currently around 6 million and will grow steadily from the early 2030s - to over 9 million by 2050. Each:r of us has a good chance of reaching this advanced age ourselves one day. How will we want to be treated then? Some people may look the other way now because it doesn't affect them personally yet. But in 20 or 30 years' time, the very people who are making decisions today or turning a blind eye could themselves be dependent on help from others. Then the next generation will judge us - at best with love, at worst with the same indifference that we risk today. A society that treats its elderly badly robs itself of its future. Because it undermines trust between the generations. Young people learn from their dealings with today's elderly what awaits them later on. That is why the question *"How do we treat our elders?"* concerns us all - young and old. The challenge is huge, but it can be mastered: through forward-looking planning, sufficient care staff, new living and care concepts and a *change in mentality* towards more empathy and cohesion between the generations.

An appeal to conscience and responsibility

In view of all these aspects - scandalous abuses, political failures, church inconsistency, moral mandate, loneliness and demographic change - we can no longer go back to business as usual. This appeal is addressed to all of us: to those responsible in politics and the church, but also to *every* individual in society. We must sharpen our conscience. *The dignity of the elderly is indivisibly linked to our own humanity.* This is not about abstract "care cases", but about mothers and fathers, grandparents who have been there for family and community all their lives and are now dependent on our help. We are talking about our neighbors who used to read to their children and help celebrate parties and who may now be sitting alone in their room at home.

Figure 35: Hands in geriatric care.

A young hand lovingly holds the hand of an elderly person - a silent symbol of care, dignity and humanity in old age. The scene is emblematic of the Christian commandment to love one's neighbor and reminds us of the obligation in the fourth commandment: "You shall honor your father and mother". This image is suitable for a contribution about the shortcomings in care for the elderly and the Church's advice not to forget the elderly, but to treat them with tenderness and respect - just as Christ did the weakest among us.

"Honor your father and mother" - this commandment calls us to repent where we have failed. As a church, we should be advocates for the weak and pioneers in dignified care. As a state, we must follow up with action and make care *a priority* - financially, in terms of personnel and socially.

And as a community, we should cultivate a *culture of humanity* in which no age is overlooked. Every visit, every small gesture of attention can make a difference to a lonely elderly person. Ultimately, the *morality of a society is reflected in how it treats its most vulnerable members.* Let's not allow profit, convenience or turning a blind eye to determine our attitude. Instead, we should be guided by compassion and justice. Demographic change is reminding us to rethink now so that we don't wake up tomorrow to a cold world of ignorance. The Church, with its wealth of charitable experience, has a particular duty to be *the salt of the earth*: to give the Word of God flavor and strength through concrete action. It is time for a jolt: *let us bring the elderly out of the shadows and back into the light of our attention.* Let us give them what God has given every human being - dignity, love and a place in our midst. Because at the end of our lives, what counts is not how successful or wealthy we were, but how much love we gave. Let us not abandon our elderly - *for in their faces we encounter Christ himself.*

🕊Bishops' briefing:

The religious policy field aims to provide dignified care for the elderly, with an analysis that does not conceal the current abuses in care homes. It highlights the undignified conditions caused by staff shortages and overwork, which often result in the basic needs of older people being neglected. The analysis also highlights the inaction of politicians, despite repeated promises to improve the situation, as well as the responsibility of the church as a major provider of care facilities, which does not always meet its own standards. The loneliness of older people in modern society is also addressed. Finally, the Christian mission to love one's neighbour is recalled and it is emphasized that the treatment of the elderly is a benchmark for the morality of society.

Didactic questions:

128 - Why are the conditions in many German nursing homes described as inhumane?

The conditions are described as inhumane because the nursing staff are often overworked and can only do the bare minimum in a rush. As a result, there is no time for empathetic conversations or individual attention. Residents sometimes have to "beg" for basic needs such as going to the toilet. Sufficient and timely fulfillment of basic needs is often not guaranteed, which is seen as a silent scandal in an affluent society and violates the dignity of those affected.

129 - Which core problem leads to the undignified conditions in care for the elderly?

The core problem is the severe shortage of nursing staff. Even years ago, thousands of positions in hospitals and care facilities could not be filled. Too few nursing staff have to look after too many people in need of help. This nursing shortage leads to hectic, frustrated and ultimately undignified situations that are unacceptable in a country where human dignity is guaranteed in the Basic Law.

130 - How is the role of politics criticized in relation to care for the elderly?

Politicians are criticized because, despite decades of promises to pay nursing staff better and equip facilities better, many of these announcements have had no effect. There have been repeated "care offensives", but no noticeable relief in care homes. Nursing staff feel put off with warm words, while real appreciation in the form of higher wages and more staff is lacking. Even promised bonuses, such as during the coronavirus crisis, did not reach many nursing staff due to bureaucratic hurdles or other diversions.

131 - What special responsibility does the church have in the care of the elderly and where is criticism voiced?

The church, particularly through its Caritas association, is a major provider of care homes and social facilities and therefore a significant employer in the social sector. Based on the commandment to love one's neighbor, it is expected that exemplary conditions prevail in church homes. However, criticism is voiced as the reality often falls short of this claim. The blocking of a nationwide collective agreement for elderly care by Caritas employers in 2021, which would have enabled higher wages for hundreds of thousands of care workers, is highlighted as particularly negative. This is seen as an indictment of institutional principles over Christian social responsibility.

132 - To what extent is Christian charity relevant to attitudes towards the elderly?

Christian charity and biblical commandments are of central importance for our attitude towards the elderly and infirm. The commandment "You shall honor your father and mother" demands respect and care. The words of Jesus "Whatever you did for one of the least of these brothers of mine, you did for me" oblige Christians to see Christ in every suffering person. Neglecting elderly people in need of help is therefore seen as a failure towards Christ. Christian charity should become concrete in care and compassion, not just remain an abstract principle.

133 - Apart from staff shortages and undignified conditions, which problem particularly affects the older generation?

In addition to the structural problems in care, loneliness is a painful problem for the older generation. Modern lifestyles often lead to families living far apart, which makes emotional support more difficult. Many elderly people rarely receive visitors and some have no one left. This social isolation is referred to as a silent epidemic that causes mental suffering and can even shorten life.

134 - Why does the challenge of dignified care for the elderly affect society as a whole?

The challenge of dignified care for the elderly affects society as a whole, because Germany is in the midst of demographic change and the proportion of older people will increase dramatically. Almost everyone has a good chance of reaching old age themselves and being dependent on help. The way in which the elderly are treated today shapes the younger generations' expectations of their own old age and, if treated badly, undermines trust between the generations. It is a question of fate for an ageing society.

135 - What is formulated as an appeal to conscience and responsibility in order to improve the situation?

The appeal is directed at everyone - politicians, the church and every individual in society - to sharpen their conscience. The dignity of the elderly is inextricably linked to one's own humanity; it is about concrete people who need help. The church should be an advocate for the weak and a pioneer in care. The state must make care a priority, both financially and in terms of personnel. Society should promote a culture of humanity in which no age is ignored. Every visit and every small gesture can make a difference for lonely elderly people. Profit motives, convenience or looking the other way should not determine attitudes; instead, compassion and justice should lead.

Essay questions:

Please answer one of the following questions in the form of an essay:

a) Analyze the tension between the churches' claim to charity and mercy and their actions as employers in the field of geriatric care.

b) Discuss to what extent the political responses to the care crisis are described as inadequate or ineffective and what consequences this has for those affected.

c) Discuss the role of loneliness in old age as a "silent epidemic" and possible social solutions that go beyond professional care.

d) Relate the demographic change in Germany to the current challenges in geriatric care and highlight the long-term implications for society.

e) Evaluate appeals to the "conscience and responsibility" of all social actors (politics, church, individuals) with regard to dignified care for the elderly.

📌 Religious policy field analysis 17: *Church voices on the 80 speed limit on highways*

In recent years, numerous church representatives - priests, bishops and even cardinals - have spoken out in favor of introducing a general speed limit of 130 km/h / 80 mph on freeways. It is remarkable that this support is broadly supported ecumenically: both the Catholic and Protestant churches emphasize two central motives in particular: the protection of human lives in road traffic and the protection of the environment and climate as part of the responsibility for creation.

Introduction: Churches in favor of 130 km/h / 80 mph for safety and climate reasons

One prominent example in 2019 was the *online petition by the Evangelical Church in Central Germany (EKM)*, which called for a speed limit of 130/80 - and which was *also explicitly supported by the Catholic Church*. Church representatives repeatedly raised this demand in official statements, sermons and interviews. Their *theological and ethical justifications* range from the commandment to respect life ("Thou shalt not kill") to the duty to preserve God's creation for future generations. In the following, central statements and positions from the church and theology on *road safety* and *climate protection* through a speed limit are presented - backed up with original quotes from relevant church sources.

Road safety: protection of life and moral responsibility

Many church representatives emphasize the speed limit as a contribution to road safety and the protection of human life. Senior Church Councillor *Christian Fuhrmann* from the EKM explained to the Petitions Committee of the Bundestag *that a general speed limit would help to solve a number of problems - "climate protection and road safety are at the forefront".* In particular, a speed limit could *"save lives"*: Fuhrmann pointed out *that there would be up to 80-140 fewer road deaths a year if the speed limit was 130 km/h / 80 mph*, and described it as *"cynical"* to dismiss this as negligible. Every fatality prevented is ethically significant. Catholic voices argue similarly: *Speeding is seen as a violation of the principle of protecting life.*

In a commentary on *katholisch.de*, journalist *Uwe Bork* even described *"contempt for death on the asphalt"* through reckless speeding as *a sin against the commandment to preserve life* - ultimately a violation of *"Thou shalt not kill"*. This view ties in with the position of the Vatican, which emphasized as early as 2007 in its guidelines on road ethics that driving has a moral dimension. In the *"Ten Commandments for Drivers"* published by the Vatican, the *first commandment* logically reads *"Thou shalt not kill"*. Equally important is commandment number 5, which warns against *overconfidence and abuse of power at the wheel*: *"You shall not use cars as an expression of strength and dominance or as an opportunity to sin"*. It is precisely the exercise of selfishness and recklessness in the form of excessive speed that contradicts the Christian ethos of love of neighbor and respect for the lives of others.

Church advocates of a speed limit also point to the *responsibility for the vulnerable and endangered*. Speeding on freeways endangers not only the drivers themselves, but also bystanders. In traffic, *charity* means showing consideration for others. *Christian Fuhrmann* noted that risky speeding scares many people - such as older drivers - ; these social aspects are also part of the debate. A general limit would signal that the *right to life and integrity of* all road users is valued more highly than the individual freedom to speed. This view is also shared by the Catholic side. Auxiliary Bishop *Rolf Lohmann*, who is responsible for environmental and social issues within the German Conference of female, diverse and male Bishops, emphasizes the Church's responsibility for the common good and future generations. Although he primarily commented on climate protection, the same applies implicitly to road safety: from the church's point of view, *ambitious protection of life and creation* is an expression of justice towards one's neighbor. Consequently, the *German Road Safety Council*, for example, has found in surveys that a small majority of the population supports a speed limit - a sentiment that has also been perceived within the church. *The church is promoting an ethic of self-restraint in the service of life:* Not every technical possibility must be exhausted if it can come at the cost of human life. By supporting a speed limit, the Church takes the side of the vulnerable and reminds us of the biblical principle of *preserving life.*

Figure 36: Bishops Burning Briefing - Speed limit 130.

A humorous drawing in which a clergyman in traditional bishop's clothing stands in front of a poster and points seriously but friendly to a traffic sign with the inscription 'Speed limit 130'. Next to it, the burning earth is symbolically depicted to create an ironic link between speed and climate change and the socio-political responsibility of the churches. The scene comes across as a satirical but necessary and friendly awareness campaign.

Climate protection: a global approach to preserving creation and charity

The argument of climate protection is just as central to the churches. A speed limit of 130 km/h / 80 mph is seen as a concrete contribution to reducing CO_2 emissions in the transport sector and thus limiting global warming. In the joint appeal by the Protestant churches in Lower

Saxony, Bishop *Ralf Meister* emphasized*: "Environmental and climate protection concerns everyone"* - a task that also includes a more moderate speed limit on freeways.

Figure 37: A believer discusses a speed limit of 130 km/h on freeways.

Symbolic portrait of a mature believer standing between the church and the speed limit - in the background a large cross and a traffic sign with the number 130. The image picks up on social discussion areas such as religion, responsibility and regulation. Ideal for a visual staging of the interface between faith, politics and ethical action in the public sphere.

The Protestant petition of the EKM for a speed limit of 130 km/h was explicitly justified by the fact that this step could be implemented quickly and cost-effectively and would reduce the emission of climate-damaging gases. *Catholic officials also supported this view.* For example, the diocesan commission for environmental issues in the diocese of Trier officially supported the EKM's speed limit initiative. Its head, *Gundo Lames*, referred to the church's guidelines on sustainability: states *that mobility should be made more environmentally friendly. "In view of the ecological impact of mobility, it must also be made more climate-friendly*," Lames quotes from the paper. A speed limit is *one way to behave in a climate-friendly manner -*

every driver can directly save greenhouse gases by voluntarily reducing their speed.

If the limit were imposed by law, the savings would of course be all the greater, according to Lames. He emphasized that the church does not allow *"words alone"* to suffice here, but advocates *practical steps: "If we are really committed to climate protection - under Christian auspices and in the sense of responsibility for creation - then [it] must be allowed to be discussed. It then also needs corresponding actions. Words alone are not enough"*. This clear demand shows that climate protection must not remain mere lip service for the church, but should lead to concrete political measures such as a speed limit.

The theological justification for climate protection measures such as the speed limit is deeply rooted in the Christian ethic of creation. "We have a mandate from God to preserve and care for our world," explained Sister *Monika Edinger*, Superior General of the Sisters of the Redeemer in Würzburg. Her religious community has voluntarily decided not to drive faster than 130 km/h / 80 mph on freeways - *expressly as a contribution to climate protection and safety*. Sister Monika sees this as an act of living responsibility for creation: *"When we talk about God, we always talk about people and the <u>whole of creation</u>, for which we all bear responsibility - for ourselves, for our fellow human beings, but also for creation*. Consequently, she would find a general speed limit *"definitely [good]. Just like everything that serves the whole"*. It's about looking at *"what really helps to protect the climate. A speed limit is part of this... That is one step, one of many"*. In addition to the idea of creation, the aspect of *global charity* also comes into play here: the motif of love for one's neighbor is not limited to direct fellow human beings, but also includes future generations and people in other regions of the world who suffer from climate impacts. *"This is about love for our neighbour,"* emphasized Chief Church Councillor Fuhrmann with regard to the victims of climate change. He pointed out that the Partner:in church in Tanzania, for example, is already feeling the drastic consequences of global warming - *"with fatal consequences for people's livelihoods"*. *Climate protection is therefore solidarity in action:* anyone who voluntarily slows down or advocates a general limit is accepting a small personal restriction in order to avert greater harm to others. This logic corresponds to the principle of Christian charity on a global level.

Support for this view also comes from Rome. In his environmental encyclical *Laudato si'*, Pope Francis calls for a *lifestyle of frugality*. He quoted the Orthodox Patriarch *Bartholomew* approvingly, saying that we must *"replace consumption with sacrifice, greed with generosity, wastefulness with a spirit of sharing"*. Such an ascetic attitude *"means learning to give - and not just to do without. It is a path of love to gradually move from what I want to what God's world needs"*. The appeal by church representatives to refrain from extreme speeds in road traffic fits in perfectly with this. The *freedom of the individual in the car finds its limit in the responsibility for creation and fellow human beings*. Cardinal *Reinhard Marx* once put it this way : technical measures such as a CO_2 tax are important, *"but are not enough"* - people must learn holistically *"what it means to live in the house of creation"*. For many clergymembers, this also includes rethinking their own mobility behavior. *"Examine your mobility behavior, your urge for freedom on the road,"* *Gundo Lames* called on drivers to reflect more. A speed limit of 130 is understood here as *an act of self-limitation* that is in harmony with the preservation of creation.

Church as admonisher: common good before self-interest

Both locally and internationally, church representatives act as *ethical admonishers in transportation policy*. Their aim is not to impose pointless regulations on people or to "ban fun", but to *call on people to take responsibility*. The Christian faith teaches that freedom is always linked to love - and love shows itself in consideration and care. By demanding a speed limit, priests, bishops and cardinals are putting the *common good above individual interests*. *"The Catholic Church is committed to the common good as a whole,"* they say programmatically. It is therefore not surprising that the Church "intervenes": according to Auxiliary Bishop Lohmann, it sees itself as having a *"responsibility towards the generations already born and those not yet born"*. In concrete terms, this means taking measures today to save human lives and preserve God's creation in the long term.

The response to the church's initiatives was quite remarkable. The EKM petition reached over 66,000 signatures and forced a parliamentary debate. Numerous media reported on women religious who *"put the brakes on for the climate"*. Within the church, some went even further: the synod of the Protestant Church in Germany decided on a speed limit of 100 km/h for business trips in a church context in order to set an example. At the same time, there was also criticism - such as the polemical question of whether the churches were not "dwarfing" themselves with such issues. However, church representatives such as Fuhrmann countered *that faith and ethics in particular should not remain silent in important social debates: "It is important that we as a church get involved in the discourse,"* said Fuhrmann. The preservation of life and creation are genuinely Christian concerns, not foreign "forbidden topics".

To summarize: *in the speed limit debate, the Church acts as the voice of conscience.* From the perspective of priests, bishops and cardinals, a 130 speed limit is not a technocratic detail, but a symbol of a society that *shows consideration for life and the environment.* Whether under the slogan of *responsibility for creation* or with reference to *love of neighbor* - the church's statements make it clear that moral progress sometimes also becomes tangible through very practical rules. *"We did not plant the garden in which we live ourselves - we have to preserve it,"* explained *Christian Fuhrmann* as a warning. This sentence gets to the heart of the theological motivation: *preserving creation and protecting life is a divine mission* that can also be fulfilled on the highway at 130 km/h. The discussion about the speed limit is given an ethical depth by these church contributions - and reminds us that it is ultimately about more than cars and freeways: namely about responsibility for our neighbor and for God's earth.

🕊️Bishops' briefing:

Several church representatives, including clergymembers from both the Catholic and Protestant churches, have spoken out in favor of a general speed limit of 130 km/h on freeways. This support is mainly based on two ethical and theological reasons: the protection of human life in road traffic and the preservation of the environment and climate as part of the biblical responsibility for creation. They see this as an expression of charity, responsibility for the weaker and future generations and a necessary self-restraint in the service of the common good. The churches thus position themselves as moral admonishers:in the debate and emphasize that faith and ethics are also relevant to transport policy issues.

The Vatican's Ten Commandments for drivers:

(Bollettino N. 0335 Martedì 19.06.2007)

1. thou shalt not kill.

2. the street should be a place where people come together, not a place of fatal injuries.

3. kindness, sincerity and wisdom will help you to cope with unforeseen incidents.

4. be charitable and help your neighbors in need, especially help victims of accidents.

5. cars should not be an expression of power or dominance and should not be a means of sin.

6. be charitable and support the young and not so young that they don't ride unless they are in the appropriate condition to do so.

7. support the families of accident victims.

8. bring those guilty of accidents and their victims together at the right time so that they can experience the liberating experience of forgiveness.

9. protect vulnerable road users on the road.

10. feel responsible for others.

Didactic questions:

136 - Why are church representatives in favor of a speed limit of 130 km/h on freeways?

Church representatives, both from the Catholic and Protestant churches, are in favor of a speed limit of 130 km/h on freeways for two main reasons: the protection of human life on the roads and the protection of the environment and climate as part of their responsibility for creation. They see this as a practical implementation of their theological and ethical convictions.

137 - How do clergy justify the demand for a speed limit from an ethical point of view?

From an ethical perspective, church representatives rely on biblical principles such as the commandment to respect life ("Thou shalt not kill") and the duty to love one's neighbor. They argue that speeding is a form of contempt for death and recklessness that violates the commandment to preserve life. A speed limit is seen as a contribution to road safety and the protection of vulnerable road users. It signals that the right to life and integrity of all road users takes precedence over individual freedom to speed. This view is also supported by the Vatican's guidelines on road ethics, which view driving as a moral dimension.

138 - What role does climate protection play in the church's support for a speed limit?

Climate protection is a key argument for the churches. A speed limit of 130 km/h is seen as a concrete and quickly implementable contribution to reducing CO_2 emissions in the transport sector. This demand is deeply rooted in the Christian ethic of creation. The churches see it as their responsibility to preserve and care for God's creation for future generations. A speed limit is one way of making mobility more climate-friendly. Voluntary slower driving or a legal limit are seen as practical steps that go beyond mere words and can contribute to limiting global warming.

139 - How does the Church combine charity with climate protection in the context of the speed limit?

The church extends the concept of charity to a global level. The preservation of creation and the protection of the climate are understood as an expression of charity that is not only limited to immediate fellow human beings, but also includes future generations and people in other regions of the world who are already suffering from the consequences of climate change. A speed limit that contributes to reducing CO_2 emissions is seen as an act of solidarity and a lived responsibility towards these groups. It is about accepting a small personal restriction in order to avert greater harm to others.

140 - What specific theological justifications underlie the Church's position?

The theological justifications for supporting a speed limit range from the commandment of respect for life ("Thou shalt not kill") and the duty to preserve creation to global charity and responsibility for future generations. The churches see the world as God's creation, for which mankind bears responsibility. A lifestyle of frugality, as urged by Pope Francis in his encyclical *Laudato si'*, fits in with the idea of refraining from extreme speeds on the roads. The freedom of the individual in the car finds its limit in the responsibility for creation and fellow human beings.

141 - How does the church position itself in the public debate about the speed limit?

The church acts as an ethical admonisher in the speed limit debate. It sees it as its task to place the common good above individual interests and to call on people to take responsibility. It does not see its intervention as meaningless regulations or "fun bans", but as a necessary contribution to important social debates. Church representatives emphasize that faith and ethics must not remain silent on issues relating to the preservation of life and creation. A speed limit is seen as a symbol of a society that shows consideration for life and the environment and makes moral progress tangible through practical rules.

142 - Were there any concrete initiatives or examples of the church's commitment to a speed limit?

Yes, there have been several concrete initiatives. One prominent example was the online petition by the Evangelical Church in Central Germany (EKM) in 2019, which called for a speed limit of 130 km/h and was explicitly supported by the Catholic side. This petition achieved a considerable number of signatures and led to a parliamentary consultation. In addition, religious communities, such as the Sisters of the Redeemer in Würzburg, have voluntarily introduced a speed limit of 130 km/h for their business trips in order to set an example. The synod of the Protestant Church in Germany even decided on a speed limit of 100 km/h for church business trips in 2022.

143 - How does the church react to criticism of its interference in political issues such as the speed limit?

The church is aware that its involvement in political issues such as the speed limit is also met with criticism. Some critics accuse the churches of "dwarfing" themselves with such issues. However, church representatives counter that faith and ethics in particular must play a role in important social debates. They see the preservation of life and creation as genuinely Christian concerns that are not alien "forbidden topics". They emphasize the importance of actively engaging in social discourse as a church.

🖊️🖥️ Essay questions:

Please answer one of the following questions in the form of an essay:

a) Discuss the central theological and ethical reasons given by church representatives for the introduction of a speed limit of 130 on German highways.

b) Analyze how the concept of charity is applied to both road safety and climate protection in the church's arguments.

c) Discuss the role of the church as an "ethical admonisher" in social debates using the example of the speed limit discussion. What biblical or theological principles underlie this role?

d) Compare the positions of the Catholic and Protestant churches on the speed limit, based on AI research. Show to what extent there is broad ecumenical support and which common motives are emphasized.

e) Assess the extent to which the demand for a speed limit can be understood as an expression of a "lifestyle of frugality" in the sense of Pope Francis' environmental encyclical *Laudato si'*.

Religious policy field analysis 18:
The old iron & talent management - Generational conflict in the church: Older bishops vs. values of the younger generation

> *"I'm stepping back from show business,*
> *when I'm older than the Pope!"*

German TV-Entertainer Thomas Gottschalk on his 75th birthday.

A central area of tension lies in questions of *gender equality and sexual ethics*. Many older clergy - shaped by traditional doctrinal guidelines - cling to traditional role models, while the younger generation takes equality and inclusion for granted. *The ordination of women is* a prominent example of this: Catholic doctrine has so far excluded women from offices such as the papacy, but for young people (and also some reform-oriented church people) this seems increasingly incomprehensible. Bishop *Franz-Josef Overbeck*, for example, asked reflectively whether access to the priesthood could really be linked to a "Y chromosome" - *"many people no longer understand this."*

This lack of understanding is shared by the majority of the younger generation: surveys show that *65% of young women* say that churches do not treat women and men equally.

For them, it is clear that women should be able to lead and celebrate on an equal footing. Accordingly, the majority of the younger generation is in favor of opening up the clerical ministries to women - a step that older ministers are often hesitant to take or do not take at all. There are also bishops in their 60s who support *the admission of women to the diaconate or priesthood* (such as Bishop *Felix Gmür*, who *is "in favor of opening the ministry to women."*).

Overall, however, there is a gap between the official church status quo and the demands for equality from young people.

Gender roles and LGBTQIA+ inclusion

The situation is similar with *LGBTQIA+ inclusion*. The traditional sexual morals of the church - e.g. classifying homosexual acts as a sin - stand in sharp contrast to the values of Gen Z, which predominantly advocates acceptance and legal equality for LGBTQIA+ people. Many young believers find it hard to understand the negative attitude of older church leaders and see it as discriminatory. In fact, *60% of young people* cite the negative treatment of homosexuals by religious communities as an *important reason* why they are turning their backs on their church.

The younger generation is growing up in a society in which diversity is the norm - being queer is not seen as a flaw, but as part of God-ordained diversity. Some progressive older bishops now share this insight: Bishop *Helmut Dieser* (then 61 years old), for example, emphasizes that homosexuality *is "a variant of sexuality desired by God"* - consequently, same-sex love should no longer be generally devalued as a sin. Cardinal *Jean-Claude Hollerich* (then 66 years old) also considered the traditional condemnation of homosexuals to be *"no longer scientifically sound"* and pleaded for the doctrine to be *"reviewed."*

Nevertheless, the official line of the Church, especially in Rome, remains cautious and restrictive in some cases (e.g. still no access to sacraments for same-sex couples such as marriage). For Catholics of the younger generation, this creates the impression of a blatant *balancing act*: while their own peers celebrate diversity and demand blessings and weddings for homosexual couples, for example, many older dignitaries (often aged 60+) seem reluctant to acknowledge these realities of life. The tension in this topic area is therefore particularly high because it is about core identities and perceptions of justice - areas in which young people today are very sensitized.

Digitality, artificial intelligence and transhumanism

Another area of tension arises in the field of *digitalization and technology*. The younger generation has grown up as *"digital natives"* - constant internet use, social media, AI applications and debates about transhumanism are part of their everyday lives. *Transhumanism* is a philosophical and technological movement that aims to specifically improve or expand human beings through the use of new technologies - such as artificial intelligence, biotechnology, neuroscience or cyborg techniques. The aim is to overcome the natural limitations of the human body and mind in order to overcome ageing, illness, mental and physical limitations or even death. Critics warn that this raises ethical, social and religious questions, particularly with regard to human dignity, justice and identity.

In contrast, some older church representatives find it difficult to keep up with these rapid developments. *Digitality* in the church - from social media pastoral care to online church services - was long held in low esteem. It was only the coronavirus pandemic that forced many (mostly older) bishops to try out digital formats. However, it quickly became clear that if you want to reach young people, you *have to be present online*. Bishop *Bertram Meier* (62) warned that there was a risk of *"no longer reaching"* many people *"if we as a church are not present on digital platforms."*

Some younger bishops or internet-savvy church people are already successfully using YouTube, Instagram & Co. to communicate faith content in a youth-friendly way - an approach that is only gradually catching on with traditional ministers. For the young Gen Z, it is a matter of course that communication at *eye level* also takes place digitally; a church that ignores this world therefore seems *unworldly*.

The same applies to new technologies such as *artificial intelligence (AI)*. While older church spokespeople often primarily emphasize the risks - such as Vatican expert *Paul Tighe* (65), who warns of the *"dark side"* of AI and possible harm to humanity - younger people also see the opportunities in social media such as TikTok or knowledge and teaching information such as from the *Deus Ex Machina* - artificial intelligence. The younger generation is used to dealing with AI applications (algorithm-controlled apps, chatbots, etc.) and expects the church to comment competently on ethical issues relating to AI *and to* use modern tools responsibly itself. A purely skeptical and defensive tone from older dignitaries (who present AI as a danger to interpersonal closeness, for example) can be interpreted as hostility towards technology by digitally-savvy young believers.

Meanwhile, electric sex toys can be controlled remotely - does gender or sexual orientation still play a role for the Catholic Church when sharing such links in chat channels and picking up the game console, if a need is satisfied "through the air" of the wifi between two people who more or less know each other (online) and see each other in the video? Would a remotely (remotely) controlled or supported sexual experience (e.g. masturbation) of a man or disabled person who desires this through defined algorithms of the technology or through a woman behind the technology not be a sin, while a man as the helmsman behind the technology would remain a sin?

And these questions can also be answered in the same way: from the point of view of official Catholic moral theology and sexual ethics, it does not matter whether the sexual act is carried out digitally, via WLAN or in another virtual way, even when using remote-controlled (remote) sex toys. From a traditional Catholic perspective, various criteria are decisive for the moral assessment:

1. personal relationship and significance of sexuality: Catholic sexual morality sees sexuality as a gift from God, which may only be lived completely legitimately within marriage between a man and a woman. According to official Catholic teaching, sexual acts are only considered ethically justified if they serve both mutual loving devotion (the so-called *unio conjugalis*) and are fundamentally open to procreation. Technical means that detach sexual experiences from this unity between love, marital fidelity and procreation are therefore considered morally problematic or wrong, regardless of whether they are practiced in physical proximity or virtually.

2. question of gender and sexual orientation: From a traditional Catholic perspective, a sexual act does not become more morally acceptable simply because it takes place digitally or remotely, nor does it matter from this perspective whether people meet via Wi-Fi, online chats or video. The official magisterium continues to maintain that sexual activity is only morally legitimate within the marital relationship between a man and a woman. Sexual interactions, regardless of the method (direct or virtual), between people of the same sex, between unmarried couples or in anonymized contexts are therefore seen as incompatible with Catholic teaching.

3. aspects of digital sexuality and moral reflection: However, technological development, especially remote-controlled sexuality, raises new ethical questions that call on the Church to engage in deeper moral-theological reflection. Digitalization could bring up topics such as responsibility, authentic interpersonal encounters, dignity, protection of intimacy and the social impact of virtual sexuality for discussion anew. Although this does not change traditional ethical principles, such a development does challenge us to update these principles in the context of new technologies and forms of communication.

From the point of view of official Catholic moral theology, *remote-controlled masturbation*, whether by an algorithm, a woman, a married woman or a man, would in any case be considered morally impermissible (and therefore a "sin").

Catholic sexual ethics fundamentally judges masturbation as intrinsically *disordered* ("intrinsice inordinata"), as it is not directed towards the marital union of man and woman and towards the potential openness for procreation. From a traditional Catholic perspective, it *does not matter* who or what controls or enables this masturbation:

- *Whether controlled by algorithms or not,* the process is depersonalized, "incomplete" in terms of sexual ethics and therefore incompatible with the Church's view of sexuality as an expression of loving devotion between spouses.
- *Whether remote-controlled by a woman:* Here too - despite opposite-sex participation - the essential context of marital unity, mutual devotion and openness to fertility is missing. The mere opposite-sex participation does not change this.
- *Whether remote-controlled by a man:* In this case, from the church's point of view, there is also the fact that sexuality between same-sex partners is not yet recognized according to official doctrine. This does not yet result in a fundamental change in judgment.
- *Whether remote-controlled by a married woman:* If a wife controls her husband's orgasm using remote technology (e.g. Wi-Fi, app-controlled sex toy), this could still be considered problematic from the strictly conservative perspective of the

Church, as the physical union ("carnal encounter") is interrupted by the remote technology. Catholic moral theology always emphasizes that sexuality within marriage is not solely aimed at pleasure or individual satisfaction of needs, but should be a holistic sign of marital love. Any form of sexual interaction that reduces, fragments or technologically distances this holistic encounter is viewed critically.

The official Catholic Church has not yet commented specifically on remote-controlled sex toys in marriage. However, the more a technology is used to *support, rather* than replace, the direct marital encounter, the more ethically acceptable it could become. And the more the sexual act is purely technical, automated or anonymized, the more problematic the assessment becomes.

In concrete terms, this means that it *is more justifiable* to provide playful technological support as a supplement to the direct, shared sexuality of the spouses, for example in the event of temporary absence or physical separation. It remains *problematic*: If the sexual act is only mediated virtually and technologically, depersonalized or disembodied.

From a Catholic perspective, the use of remote-controlled sex toys in marriage would therefore only be ethically justifiable or acceptable if a number of essential conditions are met that come as close as possible to the basic theological stance on sexuality. The Catholic Church has not yet officially addressed this in concrete terms, but a possible theological derivation could look like this:

Essential conditions for moral justifiability:

- **Temporary separation situation:** Use should be limited to situations in which personal physical proximity is temporarily not possible (e.g. due to business trips, work-related separations, illness, etc.). Permanent virtual distancing would not be appropriate.
- **Within the marital relationship:** Use must be exclusively between validly married spouses.
- **Expression of mutual love and closeness:** The act must not be reduced to the mere satisfaction of lust, but should be a sign of mutual affection, emotional closeness and unifying conjugal

love.
(**Unio conjugalis** remains the central principle).

* **Openness for the holistic marital encounter:** Virtual or remote-controlled sexuality must not replace the physical encounter, but only temporarily supplement it.

Under these conditions, a cautiously differentiated pastoral assessment could accept that spouses use remote sexuality to express closeness and love in justified cases, such as during business trips or illness, physical disability or professional separation.

First conclusion from a Catholic perspective: Although there is still no explicit doctrinal opinion from a conservative Church perspective , the following can be said: 1. the mere fact that a *wife* remotely controls her *husband's* orgasm does not automatically make the act legitimate, but could - because of the existing marital union - be judged less seriously than anonymous or extramarital situations. 2. it remains central that, according to Catholic teaching, sexual acts should always express the unity of the spouses (physically and emotionally), openness to procreation and personal closeness. 3. a purely virtual sexual practice, detached from personal closeness and serving only pleasure, would contradict the Catholic ideal, but would presumably be less serious from a pastoral point of view than, for example, cheating or pornography.

From a strict magisterial point of view, the moral assessment would nevertheless remain critical; pastoral theology, on the other hand, could make more differentiated judgments and leave room for individual decisions of conscience or marriage counseling *trained* in this area.

From a Catholic perspective, the moral evaluation of remote masturbation without a spouse is negative, *regardless of the gender or identity of the person or technique involved.* The act is always considered a transgression against the ideal of sexual integrity, personal dignity and the divinely ordained purpose of sexuality.

According to current Catholic doctrine, it is therefore irrelevant how sexual acts take place - whether physically or digitally. Gender and sexual orientation continue to retain their moral relevance from the perspective of the official church: sexuality that deviates from the official concept of conjugal love and fertility is still considered morally problematic or impermissible.

However, the increasing digitalization of sexual interaction in particular shows that ethical positions, including within Catholic moral theology, could be increasingly reflected upon and further developed in order to provide answers to the complex moral questions of the digital modern age.

From a Catholic perspective, even the use of Facebook, Grindr or Tinder (or similar dating apps such as Planetromeo, Bamboo, Nachbarschaftshilfe or "Meet5" for over 50s) is not fundamentally forbidden or morally wrong. Rather, it is the intention, manner of use and attitude that are decisive.

The Catholic Church does not reject modern means of communication or social networking per se, but warns of the dangers of superficiality and objectification. Pope Francis has repeatedly called on us to use digital media responsibly and to respect the dignity of every human being. Catholic pastoral care for singles emphasizes that dating apps, if used correctly, can certainly help you to meet people with whom you can enter into a deep relationship and perhaps even a marriage. From a Catholic perspective, it is generally permissible to use Tinder and Grindr if the goal is clearly geared towards an honest, lasting and serious partnership or marriage, the dignity of every person is respected and you act responsibly and with integrity.

What is needed here is a dialog that explores opportunities and limits - but to do so, bishops need to understand digital culture. The *acceleration of technological and cultural change processes is widening the generation gap,* as the Vatican document on the 2018 Youth Synod noted; many church representatives have *difficulties "understanding the context and culture in which young people live."*

This can also be seen, for example, in the way *transhumanism* is dealt with: where discourses of the younger generation curiously debate biohacking, life extension or the integration of technology into the body, older clergy often instinctively react with rejection out of concern for human dignity. Bishop *Georg Bätzing* (62), for example, criticized transhumanism as an excessive *"urge for immortality"* and warned against ethical transgressions such as the use of embryos.

From the perspective of Catholic doctrine, cosmetic surgery or cosmetic procedures such as facelifts or lip injections, for example, are not fundamentally prohibited as a form of the urge to appear immortal and young, but are viewed critically and in a differentiated manner. The decisive factor for the moral assessment is the intention and attitude with which the procedures are carried out: The Church emphasizes, that the body, as God's creation, has a natural dignity that should be respected and protected. Interventions for purely cosmetic improvement could be problematic if they are carried out due to a deep-seated feeling of inferiority, an exaggerated ideal of beauty or social pressure. On the other hand, medically justified or psychologically relieving interventions that help to restore physical integrity and well-being after injury or illness, for example, would in principle be ethically justifiable. In contrast to transhumanism, which aims to radically overcome natural human limitations and even human nature itself, cosmetic interventions are not seen as a fundamental violation of the Church's view of humanity, but a critical examination of the inner attitude is recommended: Respect for one's own God-given dignity should be the focus, not conformity to superficial ideals of beauty. In short: tattoos as a fashionable zeitgeist? - Catholic doctrine does not prohibit cosmetic procedures as a matter of principle, but urges caution and reflection on one's own motives so as not to degrade the body to a mere object of social expectations or fashionable trends.

However, the Catholic Church clearly and categorically rejects the use of embryos, as could take place in the context of transhumanist or biotechnological research - in order to prolong life. From the Catholic point of view, the human embryo possesses full human dignity and the unrestricted right to life from the very beginning, i.e. from conception. This dignity must never be instrumentalized merely as a means to an end - not even for research purposes aimed at improving or expanding human capabilities. In the transhumanist context, in which embryos are used, for example, to obtain stem cells or for targeted genetic modification, the Church sees an ethical boundary being crossed, as human life would be sacrificed and turned into mere material. Any action that leads to the destruction of human embryos is judged by the

Church to be morally unacceptable and gravely sinful, regardless of any positive goals that might be pursued. Thus, from a Catholic perspective, the use of embryos in transhumanism is also categorically ruled out because it violates fundamental ethical principles - in particular the protection of human dignity from the beginning of life.

These admonitions may be justified, but if they are made in a purely culturally critical tone, without understanding the core fascination of these ideas, they will hardly reach young people.

Figure 38: A remotely programmed humanoid robot administers medicine to a man in need of care

A young woman has remotely programmed a humanoid robot and controls it remotely: This human-like, humanoid care robot bends over an elderly man lying in a nursing bed in a hospital and hands a medicine to the man's mouth. The man may have suffered a stroke. His hands look paralyzed. We do not know whether he wishes to die in a self-determined way. The scene is warmly lit, with soft curtains in the background. The interaction is empathetic and symbolizes the interplay between technology and human care and concern in today's nursing care for the elderly in line with the needs of people requiring assistance.

Gen Z wants the church to discuss technology issues and cultural practices *competently and openly* - not with blanket condemnation, but with understanding for the lives of digitally socialized people. There is a clear tension here: *technological optimism versus technological scepticism*, the digital mentality of young people versus the analogue mindset of many older people.

Participation and church structures

Co-determination and participation are further points where ideas diverge. The Catholic hierarchy is traditionally organized top-down: Decisions come "from above" (popes, bishops), lay people - and especially young people - have long had little say. The *younger generation*, on the other hand, has grown up in an era that values participation: student representatives, grassroots democratic movements and social networks give them the feeling that they should have *a voice and influence*. This change in mentality collides with outdated clerical patterns of authority. When only elderly clerics make decisions about the direction of the church, the younger generation feels neither represented nor taken seriously.

It is true that the worldwide synodal process under Pope Francis has identified this problem - the keyword *is synodality*: listening together, dialog between all age groups. But in practice, many structures remain hierarchical. Some of the older bishops find it difficult to relinquish power or allow lay people to have a real say in decision-making. *Young Catholics* experience this as a *credibility problem*: a church that constantly talks about "young people as the future of the church", but in reality hardly gives them any responsibility, loses trust. Bishop *Stefan Oster* (58), himself a youth evangelizer, put it in a nutshell: *"Above all, young people want an <u>authentic church</u>, not a purely prohibitive institution."*

Instead of just rules "from above", young people need spaces where they can be themselves without fear - and also new forms of worship or *participatory projects* in which their input counts. Some bishops are setting a good example here: in Australia, for example, Archbishop *Costelloe* involved an unusually large number of young people in the national reform dialogue and emphasized that *"only if young people really have a say can the church... remain relevant."* Change can also be seen on a small scale: Bishop *Derio Olivero* (61) is experimenting in Italy with parish leadership teams in which a married couple coordinates and the priest is only *an accompanying moderator.*

Nevertheless, such models are exceptions. Older clerics often dominate, who - despite their best intentions - *have a different leadership style due to their socialization*: They were trained in a time when no dissent was expected from ecclesiastical authority. *"The older ones were formed in a very different church"*, as one church observer aptly put it; younger priests, on the other hand, are used to hearing feedback and criticism from below. This difference leads to internal tensions and external frustration (among the faithful) when reform processes falter. Gen Z in particular hardly accepts authoritarian, non-participative structures any more - they expect *transparency, participation and flat hierarchies*. Where older bishops ignore these expectations, there is a dangerous loss of relevance: young, committed Christians leave or do not even join the church because they do not see a home in a rigid system.

Liturgical and cultural diversity

There is also a generational divide in the area of *liturgical organization and cultural openness*. Older church leaders are often socialized in post-conciliar uniformity - certain rituals, language and musical styles are considered the non-negotiable core of Catholic identity. *Younger generations*, on the other hand, are characterized by diversity: they are familiar with different milieus, musical genres and forms of expression and want a church that is culturally compatible. This can be seen in topics such as *fair language, inculturated liturgy* or the general question of how flexible church services can be. For example, many young people welcome the use of *inclusive language in* the liturgy (such as gender-sensitive wording) or the incorporation of local traditions. However, older ministers sometimes react to such changes with unease - out of concern that the unity of the church could suffer or sacred things could be watered down. This tension became clear at the 2019 Amazon Synod, for example, where bishops - some of them over 60 - pleaded for a separate Amazonian rite with indigenous symbols, which initially met with a mixed response from Rome. For many young believers, however, *liturgical diversity* in the sense of cultural adaptation (inculturation) is not a break with the church, but on the contrary a way *for* the church to come closer to them. When dances and drums are played during mass in African countries, for example, young locals see this as an enrichment of their relationship with God - while some older Europeans see "unfamiliar experiments" here. Many young people in Western countries also want more creative forms: Youth services with modern music to dance to, a relaxed atmosphere, perhaps interactive elements. *Gen Z is looking for authenticity and participation*, not rigid rituals that are only passively followed. Where older decision-makers do not allow this - for fear of losing the dignity of the liturgy, for example - frustration arises. Conversely, positive examples are having an effect: Bishop *Emmanuel* Gobilliard (54) in France combines mass with modern culture at youth festivals and explicitly encourages Gen Z to *"take on creativity and responsibility in the church."*

Such approaches resonate strongly with young people, who then experience them: *The church can also be different*, lively and at *the heart of my culture*. But if this signal effect is missing, the church can easily appear *culturally disconnected* - ignoring the interests of young people. Overall, the biggest balancing act is wherever the *one* universal form or teaching of the church meets the *diverse* realities of the younger generation. Gen Z is diverse, pluralistic and used to composing their spiritual home from many elements - while older church leaders sometimes still have a more homogeneous world view. This leads to tensions in liturgy, language and the general life of faith.

Problematic consequences of the generation gap

Why is it *problematic when it is mainly older bishops (60+) who* decide on issues that deeply affect the younger generation? For one thing, there is a risk of a *representation gap*: The values, concerns and everyday realities of young people are not adequately incorporated into decisions. A bishop over the age of 65 has spent his own formative years in a completely different social climate - there is a high probability that he will have blind spots when it comes to today's youth issues. He *feels* differently or less strongly about social megatrends such as LGBTQIA+ emancipation, globalization, climate fears, the digital revolution, etc. because they were not part of his own youth. If they nevertheless make binding decisions about them, there is a risk of bypassing the worlds they live in.

This leads directly to the second problem: *loss of acceptance and a crisis of confidence*. When church leaders make decisions that appear unrealistic or unjust from the perspective of young people, young believers turn away in disappointment. They feel that they are not taken seriously - sometimes even *hurt* by church statements. In fact, *39% of Gen Z young people* (and a similar number of Catholic young people) report that they already feel *harmed or hurt* by religion.

This is often not due to the personal misconduct of individual bishops, but to general attitudes of the church that contradict young people's values (such as rigid sexual morals, exclusion of those who love others). If older bishops decide on such issues without understanding young people's perspectives, this deepens this pain. For example, a purely negative or punitive approach to LGBTQIA+ believers by older churchmen can lead to deep alienation among queer-feeling young people - they experience it as a rejection of their person. *Older semesters* may believe they are only defending doctrine, but the youth hear a message of rejection. This creates a cycle: Old decides - young feel misunderstood - young withdraw - church continues to age. This accelerates the already visible *exodus of young people from the church* (in many countries, well over half of those under 30 leave the church).

A third problem is the *lack of future orientation of* such decisions. If it is predominantly people over the age of 60/70 who set the course, they are inevitably planning for a future that they themselves will hardly live to see. The younger generation, on the other hand, will have to live with the consequences of today's church decisions in the decades to come. *Example:* If a committee of old men decides today to continue to exclude women from ordained ministries, Gen Z will have to bear this decision over their entire lifespan - with all its consequences (such as a continuing shortage of priests, a credibility deficit in terms of equal rights, possible further emigration of young women). *The problem* here is not so much the age itself, but the *lack of involvement* of those who are affected. Precisely because issues such as women in the church, sexual morality, digitalization, etc. *deeply affect* young people, their voices should be heard in the decision-making process. If this does not happen - which is often the case, as bishops usually only consult their peers - decisions are made "over the heads of the young". This can lead to *wrong decisions* because important experience is missing. Some older male bishops, for example, underestimate the importance of social media for faith communication or fail to recognize how drastically young people suffer from climate concerns - and set the wrong priorities. The result: the church does not address the burning issues of young people and is perceived as irrelevant (*"out of touch"*). In the worst case, it makes decisions that deepen the divide, such as a strict ban on marriage ceremonies for same-sex couples - which many young people interpret as *an act of unkindness* or a *"perverse logic"* of *charity*.

Figure 39: Generational conflict about learning and change.

A humorous and socio-critical cartoon in comic style that illustrates the generational conflict surrounding climate change. It shows a young person wearing a "Fridays for Future" T-shirt, which worryingly says: "The sea level has risen extremely again!". Next to him is an older man who replies indifferently: "Learn to swim!". Both are standing on the beach while the water is already lapping at their feet. Underneath is the ironic slogan: "Learn instead of demonstrate!". It describes the generational conflict about learning and change.

Another aspect is the *internal dynamic in church bodies*: Older male bishops among themselves can succumb to an *"echo chamber"*. Without a corrective from younger perspectives, attitudes that have long been outdated in the outside world become entrenched. The risk of unrealistic decisions increases. In addition, there is often a lack of *understanding for young people's communication styles* or *rational choice thinking* - for example, 58% of Gen Z would like to be able to discover questions of faith for themselves, to be able to logically think through thoughts themselves instead of being presented with ready-made answers.

Many young people criticize religious communities for *"trying to solve their problems rather than simply being there for them."* This is where attitudes clash: older church leaders tend to proclaim authoritative doctrines and expect obedience; young people, however, demand dialog at eye level. If decisions remain unilaterally dictated from above, young believers feel patronized and not taken seriously - which in turn destroys trust.

In short: *without a youth perspective in leadership, the church is threatened with a loss of relevance.* It is problematic when older male bishops alone decide on the issues of the future or comment on them, because these issues are closely interwoven with the lifeworlds of Gen Z. The distance in experience and culture easily leads to misunderstandings - with the consequence that the church misses out on the concerns of the next generation. A vibrant, sustainable church would therefore need decision-makers who *are in the present* and know the realities of young people's lives.

At what age is there a risk of detachment from reality?

At what point does a cleric tend to be *"too far removed from social reality"* to still be suitable as a bishop? This is a *fluid boundary*, not a fixed number - people age differently. But certain patterns can be recognized. The gap often becomes noticeable from an age at which the person no longer actively participates in contemporary cultural life. Many point out that *beyond the age of 60*, the danger of getting stuck in an earlier world of experience increases. A male bishop who is 65 years old, for example, was ordained a priest in the 1980s; his imprints come from a world before the internet, before various family images, often also before the biggest abuse scandals. If he does not consciously continue his education and surround himself with young people, he can slip back into the frame of reference of his younger generation without realizing it. Children who keep us young are missing without the acquisition of celibacy.

Not all older people are automatically out of touch with the world - some 70-year-olds are mentally extremely young at heart. But *statistically* speaking, the chance that someone beyond the retirement age (in the church: bishops have to step down at 75) still has their finger on the pulse of the times is decreasing. This is also shown by the division within the bishops' conferences: It is often the *"old-timers"* who put the brakes on reforms, while younger people call for change.

Older generations (over 69) tend to see new things as a threat to their heritage; younger generations (perhaps under 49) tend to see new things as a continuation under today's conditions. A drastic indication of impending detachment from reality is *when the age difference to the younger generation spans two generations* - e.g. 40+ years difference. In this case, the growing-up conditions are worlds apart. A 70-year-old male bishop is the grandparent of Gen Z - naturally it will be difficult for him to understand their pop culture, slang and mentality as a matter of course. He can make an effort, but it remains a translation effort. With a 50-year-old male bishop (age difference ~25 years), the bridge is already much shorter: more like a parent-child distance, where there are even more common cultural intersections.

It can also be linked to specific *contemporary phenomena*: For example, those who spent the first 30 years of their lives *before* the turn of the millennium are only familiar with digital networking and pluralistic values as adults - this is often accompanied by a fundamentally different view than those who were socialized *after 2000*. It could therefore be assumed that clergy *born before around 1970* (i.e. 55+ today) have an increased risk of alienation from youth and Gen Z, unless they have consciously taken countermeasures. Conversely, priests who were young in the 1980s or 90s are more likely to share their attitude to life and experiences with today's twenty-somethings (e.g.

they themselves experienced the upheavals around 2000, the start of social media, etc. as younger people). This means *that beyond their mid-60s* (around retirement age), it is reasonable to assume a greater distance to youth culture. From this age onwards, it tends to be more difficult to keep up with the very rapid social changes - especially as many people also become less flexible physically and mentally by then.

Of course, there are always exceptions: There are also 40 to 50-year-olds who think in an astonishingly old-fashioned way and 70-year-olds who remain curious and willing to learn. Ultimately, it's the *attitude* that counts. But in purely structural terms, one would say that bishops - and even more so cardinals - should hand over the baton to younger people *at the latest when they reach retirement age*, because otherwise the reality of life for most of the faithful is too far removed from them. This is also provided for in church practice (resignation at 75). But even *before 75, from* around *the end of their 60s*, the danger of being out of touch with reality increases - unless the male bishop is very consciously involved in the social discourse.

So what does a 60-year-old male bishop do when society lady *Carmen Geiss* presents each guest with a personally selected dildo at her 60th birthday party in Saint-Tropez under the motto "60 Shades of Carmen" - in reference to the erotic romantic drama "Fifty Shades of Grey" - in order to remain mentally, morally and sexually flexible?

The male bishop presumably occupies himself with things that his role expects of him: spiritual and moral tasks such as praying and meditating in a context characterized by self-control and restraint - in contrast to the dissolute openness of the party described in detail in newspapers. This juxtaposition humorously and reflectively illustrates a fundamental tension between people in the secular world and ecclesiastical morality. *"The bigger the better"* therefore does not apply to male bishops!

It is difficult to draw a sharp line. One could possibly say: *From the age of around 65, it is extremely challenging for clergy to easily remain closely resonant with the lifeworld of youth and "Gen Z".* That's not to say it's impossible - but it requires *extraordinary* effort and humility to constantly re-engage. Many older bishops do not fully achieve this (which is humanly understandable). Therefore, *younger ministers* would tend to be better suited to creating this resonance.

Recommendation: Younger bishops for a resonant church

In order to reduce the theological and cultural gap between church leadership and the younger generation, a clear recommendation is necessary: *Bishops should ideally be appointed at a younger age.* Specifically, it would be desirable to consider more candidates over the age of 40 (or at least *under 50*) - some even advocate the appointment of those under 40 in order to really bring in a breath of fresh air. A bishop aged 45, for example, would only have ~20 years of age difference to the oldest representatives of the youth generation - she/he herself/himself belongs to the generation of *"young parents"*, which includes millennials or Gen Y, and thus shares many cultural points of reference. Such a comparatively young head host is more likely to be able to speak the language of the youth and understand their music, media and mentalities. *Resonance* is created through proximity: be it age, experience or cultural competence. A younger bishop is closer to current developments and can therefore interact with young people more credibly and *at eye level.*

Another advantage: younger bishops usually still have a longer active horizon ahead of them. They can develop *visions for the coming decades* and implement them themselves, instead of just spending their retirement in an administrative capacity. This increases the dynamism of pastoral work and enables reforms to be tackled more consistently with a view to the next generation. If, for example, a 45-year-old male bishop initiates steps towards LGBTQIA+ inclusion or *digital-remote pastoral care* now, he can potentially accompany their fruits for another 20-30 years - in constant exchange with young people who are growing up. A 70-year-old, on the other hand, often no longer has the time horizon or the energy to carry through long-term change processes.

The ideal age for new bishops would therefore probably be *under 40*. This is already a reality in some parts of the world: Bishop *Gobilliard* in France, for example, was consecrated in his mid-40s and brings a correspondingly fresh perspective. Such personnel decisions should not remain an exception. Of course, youth should *not be* the only criterion - experience and prudence are also important. But in recent centuries, the Church has tended to appoint too late rather than too early. A moderate rejuvenation would do well. Candidates around 30-35 could be sufficiently mature, but still be in close contact with the *"youthful present"* of the church. Because, as Gobilliard put it: *"You [young people] are not only the future, you are the present of the Church."* It is precisely this present that should also be reflected in the episcopate: in the *episcopate* or in the totality of all bishops of the Catholic Church.

Some church voices suggest deliberately setting a benchmark, for example: *If possible, diocesan bishops should be appointed before the age of 40* to ensure that they are still open to the rapidly changing culture. They will then gain their first professional experience in their role by 48 and can then work accordingly. *Time limits* on the office (e.g. resigning at 60 instead of 75) could also be considered to allow for more rotation and thus generational change. Above all, it is important that the leaders of a local church breathe *with* the younger generation - both theologically and culturally. A bishop under 45 usually belongs to a generation that was socialized after the Second Vatican Council and is familiar with pluralistic societies; he/she has learned to accept diversity as a fact. This makes it easier for the person to accept issues such as female participation, new family models or digital lifestyles not as a threat from outside, but as part of the reality of life for his/her flock.

In addition to the question of age, more attention should be paid to *the ability to engage in dialog with young people* when making appointments. Someone may be 55, but if - like Pope Francis - he approaches young people openly, listens to them and even takes advice from them, he can have a similarly resonant effect as a 45-year-old. In this respect: *Age in itself is not everything*, but it is an important factor. The recommendation can therefore be summarized as follows: *The younger (within reasonable limits) bishops:in are appointed, the greater the chance that these individuals will have a genuine connection with the younger generation.* A guideline would be, if possible, *between 40-45*, in many cases preferably around 40. This would bring the episcopate closer to the young adults who are now taking on responsibility in church and society.

Finally, it should be emphasized that this rejuvenation would not only benefit the younger generation of believers, but the entire church. It would send out signals of *renewal and sustainability*. Does talent management in the Vatican need new competence profiles, adapted selection criteria and modified qualification measures in order to identify younger high-potentials at an early stage and develop them in a targeted manner? Existing bishops over 55 should switch to the role of mentors, seniors or coaches and leave the operational field of office to the younger ones: The "balancing act" between old church views and the young zeitgeist could be shortened in this way - not by the church blindly following every trend, but by those who know the present from their own experience having a say in decision-making. A culture of cooperation between old and young in church leadership - *experience meets innovative spirit* - would be ideal. Until then, the pragmatic solution is to bring more young and female people into leadership positions in the Catholic Church. This is the most likely way to *resonate with young people* - both theologically and culturally - and this is exactly what the Church needs to remain credible in the 21st century.

🕊️Bishops' briefing:

The religious policy analysis looks at the generational conflict within the Catholic Church, particularly between older clergy and the younger generation, Gen Z. At the heart of the tension are issues of gender justice and sexual ethics, especially attitudes to women's ordination and LGBTQIA+ inclusion, where traditional teachings clash with modern values. Furthermore, the different perspectives on digitality, technology and participation are highlighted; while the youth are growing up in a digitalized, pluralistic world and expect participation, many older ministers struggle to keep up. It can be observed that the dominance of older decision-makers is leading to a representation gap and crisis of confidence and one suggestion may be to appoint more younger bishops or lower the age limits and retirement age to make the church more relevant, effective and sustainable.

Didactic questions:

144 - Why is there a generational conflict, especially between older male bishops and the younger generation?

The generational conflict in the church arises above all from different influences and values between older male ministers and the younger generation. Older bishops are often socialized in traditional doctrinal guidelines and adhere to traditional role models and moral teachings. The younger generation, on the other hand, is growing up in a more diverse and inclusive society in which equality, sexual diversity and digital realities are taken for granted. These different living environments lead to tensions and a lack of understanding, particularly when it comes to issues of gender equality, sexual ethics, participation and dealing with technology and cultural diversity.

145 - In which specific areas is the generational conflict most evident?

The conflict manifests itself particularly strongly in the following areas:

- **Gender justice and women's ordination:** Many young people see the unequal treatment of women and men in church ministries as outdated and are in favor of women's ordination, which contradicts traditional church teachings.
- **LGBTQIA+ inclusion:** The traditional sexual morality of the church, which is critical of homosexuality, stands in stark contrast to the values of the younger generation, which advocates acceptance and equality and sees the negative attitude as discriminatory.
- **Digitality and technology:** While the younger generation has grown up as "digital natives" and takes social media, AI and digital communication for granted, many older church representatives find it difficult to keep up with these developments and often see technology primarily as a threat.
- **Participation and church structures:** Young people want more say and participation in the traditionally hierarchical church.

The top-down structures and the dominance of older clergy in decision-making processes lead to frustration and the feeling of not being taken seriously.

- **Liturgical and cultural diversity:** The younger generation is used to diversity and wants a culturally inclusive church with inclusive language, modern musical styles and space for creative expression, which sometimes meets with discomfort from older ministers who prefer uniformity of rituals.

146 - What impact does the generational conflict have on the credibility and relevance of the church for young people?

The generational conflict is leading to a considerable loss of credibility and relevance for the church among young people. If church decisions and attitudes are perceived as unrealistic, unjust or discriminatory, young believers turn away in disappointment. They feel misunderstood or even hurt by church statements, especially with regard to their identity and their sense of justice. If the church does not communicate at eye level, ignores digital lifeworlds or does not enable participation, it appears "out of touch". This accelerates the exodus of young people from the church and makes it more difficult to attract new, committed young people.

147 - Why can the advanced age of decision-makers in the Church be a problem, even if there are exceptions?

The advanced age of decision-makers, especially from around 65 years of age, can pose a problem, as there is an increased likelihood that the person will remain stuck in a previous world of experience and have difficulty fully grasping the rapid social and cultural change, especially the realities of Gen Z's lives. Their imprints often date back to a time before the internet, before the widespread acceptance of diversity and before the impact of global trends such as climate change and the digital revolution. If decisions are made on issues that deeply affect young people without sufficiently taking their perspectives into account, there is a risk of ignoring their lifeworlds and making the wrong decisions. The problem is not age per se, but the possible distance to the current reality of life and the lack of involvement of those affected.

148 - At what age might the risk of detachment from reality be increased in clergy, and why?

There is no rigid boundary, but from the age of around 65, it tends to become more challenging for a male cleric to remain closely resonant with the Gen Z lifeworld. A 70-year-old male bishop, for example, is grandparent-aged to Gen Z, which naturally leads to a wide gap in cultural reference points, slang and mindset. While some 70-year-olds have remained mentally young, statistically the chance that someone beyond the retirement age will still have their finger on the pulse of the times decreases, especially if they are not consciously continuing their education and interacting with young people. Clergy born before around 1970 (now 55+) have an increased risk of alienation from Gen Z, as their formative years were before extensive digital networking and the greater pluralization of society.

149 - What disadvantages arise when older clergy decide alone on the future issues of the church?

If predominantly older bishops alone decide on future issues that deeply affect the younger generation, there are several disadvantages:

- **Representation gap:** The values, concerns and everyday realities of young people are not sufficiently reflected in decisions.
- **Loss of acceptance and crisis of confidence:** Decisions that appear unrealistic or unfair from the perspective of young people lead to disappointment and avoidance.
- **Lack of future orientation:** Decisions are made by people who will hardly live to see the long-term consequences, while the younger generation will have to bear them for decades.
- **Decisions "over the heads of young people":** Important empirical values are missing in the decision-making process, which can lead to mistakes, e.g. when assessing the

importance of digital media or the climate concerns of young people.

- **Reinforcement of "echo chambers":** Without a corrective from younger perspectives, attitudes can become entrenched that are outdated in the outside world, leading to decisions that are far removed from reality.
- **Lack of understanding for young people's communication styles:** the desire for dialog at eye level is not met, which leads to a feeling of paternalism.

150 - What recommendation is made to narrow the gap between church leadership and the younger generation?

It is recommended that more younger candidates be considered for the office of bishop. Ideally, bishops should be appointed at a younger age, e.g. under 40 years of age, some even advocate the appointment of people under forty or around 32-40 years of age. A younger bishop has a smaller age gap to the youth generation and is more likely to share cultural reference points. This increases the likelihood that the minister speaks the language of the youth, understands their media and mentalities and can interact more credibly at eye level. In addition to the age issue, attention should be paid to the ability to engage in dialog with young people when making appointments.

151 - What advantages would a rejuvenation of the episcopate have and how could it be implemented?

A rejuvenation of the episcopate would have the following advantages:

- **Greater resonance with young people:** Younger bishops can better understand and respond to the lives and concerns of the younger generation.
- **Longer active horizon:** Younger bishops can develop and implement long-term visions.
- **Signals of renewal:** The appointment of younger bishops sends positive signals of sustainability and the will to change.

- **Better involvement of young people:** Younger bishops have a better understanding of involving young people in decision-making processes.

This could be implemented by deliberately selecting younger candidates when appointing bishops. One guideline could be to appoint diocesan bishops before the age of 40 or 45 if possible. Time limits on the office, e.g. resigning from office at the age of 60, could also be considered in order to enable a faster generational change. What is important is a culture of cooperation between old and young in church leadership, in which experience and innovative spirit come together. Older bishops could increasingly take on mentoring or senior roles to pave the way for younger leaders.

✍🖥 Essay questions:

Please answer one of the following questions in the form of an essay:

a) Discuss the different areas of generational conflict in the church as described in the text and evaluate which area you think is the biggest challenge for the future of the church.

b) Analyze problematic consequences of the generation gap in church leadership and explain how they affect the relationship between the church and the younger generation.

c) How is it to be assessed from a religious and socio-ethical perspective if a doctor remotely programs a humanoid care robot so that it administers a lethal drug to a completely paralyzed person - who has expressly expressed the wish to die in a self-determined manner - by placing it in the mouth with its robotic hand? Is the doctor acting immorally in this case from a theological point of view? What differences are there between the legal assessment and the social or moral evaluation of the event?

d) Discuss the arguments for appointing younger bishops as a possible solution to reduce the generation gap. What are the benefits and potential challenges

e) Evaluate the statement that the age of the bishops is an important factor for the resonance with the youth, but not the only decisive aspect. What impact does this have and what other factors do you think are also relevant that can emphasize a lack of resonance?

f) Comment on the idea that the church needs a "culture of togetherness between old and young in church leadership". What could such a culture look like in practice and what steps would be necessary to achieve it?

📌 Religious policy field analysis 19: *Incomplete. Indoctrination in Catholic seminaries: Content, techniques, resilience and prevention*

Catholic seminaries serve to train future priests - but in their closed environment, indoctrination can occur, especially when dealing with homosexuality. Indoctrination here means that the seminarians are imprinted with a one-sided worldview in which homosexual inclinations are strictly rejected and presented as morally reprehensible - provided the participants have no sexual experience or their sexual orientation is homosexual and no social coming out has taken place before attending the seminary.

Church leaders are queer themselves and/or have stigmatized homosexual orientation as *"disorderly conduct"* in the past and even used it as leverage: homosexual clergy have been threatened with *coming out* in order to keep them on a tightly conservative course and suppress their coming out during seminary time and for all time thereafter.

Such methods create a climate of fear, obedience and self-denial. The following section examines *what content is taught* in priest seminars, *which* indoctrination *techniques* are used and *how to recognize them.* A 5-step prevention model is then presented to counteract indoctrination. Two additional sections highlight *the theological-psychological counterarguments* that can be used to counter indoctrination content and *how the teaching can be constructively turned around* so that it promotes the recognition of same-sex love instead of exclusion - in order to ideally bring about a coming out before attending the seminar and/or to be able to find confidence in the seminar itself to speak openly about one's inclination and sexual orientation.

Recognizing signs of indoctrination in seminaries for priests

In many Catholic seminaries, the official sexual morals of the church are adopted uncritically. Homosexual acts are considered *disordered* and "objectively morally bad" by the Church's magisterium. On the one hand, the *Catechism of the Catholic Church* emphasizes that homosexual people should be treated with *"respect, compassion and tact"*. On the other hand, homosexual inclination is described there as *"objectively disordered"* - i.e. still as something morally questionable. Seminarians are therefore often taught to see same-sex love primarily as a repressed coming-out task or "test" that must be "overcome" through abstinence. They are told that homosexual people are obliged to be celibate and must *"unite their difficulties with Christ's sacrifice on the cross"*. Such teaching effectively pathologizes queer identity as a deficit. Accordingly, the Vatican stipulated in a 2005 instruction that men *"who practice homosexuality, have deep-seated homosexual tendencies or support a so-called homosexual culture"* should *not* be allowed into formation.

This official attitude creates an environment in which same-sex attracted seminarians have to deny or hide their identity instead of being allowed to integrate it. Antiquated clichés are often passed on. Overall, there is a narrow, dogmatic framework: Divergent theological views (such as the demand for a positive re-evaluation of queer love) are still on their way. The result is a monolithic ideology that young men are supposed to internalize.

In order to enforce this content, conservative and older instructors use various *means of manipulation and pressure:*

- *Authority and obedience:* The seminary leadership and the Church act as an infallible authority. Candidates are told that the teachings of the church are incontestable. Criticism of official documents - such as doubts about the assessment of homosexual acts as disorderly - is considered disloyalty or apostasy. The hierarchy demands *blind obedience*: personal feelings of conscience are to be subordinated to the magisterium. Sexual impulses too, by the way. This climate conditions seminarians to suppress their own doubts about the church and its dogmas and instead to *unthinkingly repeat what "the church says"*. Alternative theological voices or progressive dialog are usually not used to nip alternative thought patterns in the bud. Seminarians are dependent on the media and self-study - also by using shadow libraries such as *Annas-Archive.org* or *Sci-Hub* and *LibGen* on their smartphones and e-book readers. It should be noted that the other previous English-language e-books in the *Deus Ex Machina* series can now also be downloaded there free of charge.

- *Control and surveillance:* Everyday life in the seminary is often regimented. In addition to the official rules (prayer times, spiritual exercises, promises of celibacy, etc.), there is an informal pressure to conform. Seminarians *observe each other* and report "deviant" behavior. One example is provided by the account of Matthias, a former candidate for the priesthood: When he and a fellow seminarian entered into a relationship, they suddenly received anonymous threatening letters from other male seminarians - *"We know what you're doing. You are not out"* - with all the biblical passages and catechism quotes against same-sex love. They had a lot of work to do to pick out the content that affirmed the love of two people. This *culture of denunciation* creates a climate of fear. Everyone must expect to be betrayed and sanctioned for the slightest deviation from the norm (such as being "too close" to a man). Many therefore maintain close friendly dialog at home. Due to the high proportion of queer seminar students, the training center becomes just another contact point in addition to the usual online portals such as Grinder or Planetromeo. On-site control also takes place institutionally: in Matthias' case, the Regens (head of training) finally ordered the relationship to end and had him assessed by psychologists to determine the "depth of the homosexual inclination". Such measures show how strongly the most private matters are interfered with in order to enforce the official line.

- *Creating fear and feelings of guilt: Fear* is a central indoctrination tool. From an early age, many Catholic young people - and later seminarians - are taught about a *"threatening God"* who punishes sins severely. Sexuality is often taboo and negatively charged. Matthias reported that even in his family - he grew up in the previous century - sexuality was always associated with sin and punishment from hell: As a teenager, he was warned that masturbation would lead him *"to the deepest hell"*. Such fear-based beliefs continue to have an effect in the seminary. The fear of damnation or of losing one's vocation is stoked in order to enforce absolute chastity and the rejection of homoerotic impulses. Matthias was only able to realize that an orgasm in togetherness is also an intentional experience of God by reading queer theology. Many of those affected develop feelings as soon as they have homosexual feelings or fantasies - the seminar leaders try to transform these feelings into guilt. It can make sense to fill the seminars not with young people or adolescents, but with stable people who have had their first sexual experiences over the age of 30. This *corset of shame and guilt* suppresses an open confrontation with one's own sexuality. Added to this is the *fear of social sanctions*: anyone who stands out as "queer" risks exclusion from the seminary - and thus the end of their lifelong dream of becoming a priest. This sword of Damocles hangs over homosexual candidates in particular and disciplines them permanently - or not, which leads to a life without voice and laughter.

• *Isolation and one-sidedness:* indoctrination works best in a *closed information bubble*. Priest:inside seminars therefore often create a closed world. Contact with the outside world is limited; controversial discussions about sexual morality hardly ever take place. Progressive theologians, psychologists or voices reflecting on the church are left out. In this way, the trainers prevent seminarians from coming into contact with pluralistic perspectives - which are necessary in the modern age and for pastoral counseling. A recent example: a church symposium on sexuality was canceled by clergy a few years ago because reactionary circles exerted influence - the planned discussion was deemed "not balanced" enough. This approach shows how dialog is to be suppressed in the bud. The young men spend years mainly in the closed society of the seminary, where everyone is expected to share the same dogmas. They become a Borg collective. The *Borg collective* from *Star Trek* is a fictional species portrayed as a powerful, cybernetic collective consciousness. Individuals lose their autonomy and become so-called drones, connected by implants and controlled by a central "hive mind". The Borg strive for perfection and assimilation of other cultures, integrating knowledge and technology into the collective. They became famous for the saying: *"Resistance is futile!"* ("Resistance is futile!"). This makes church doctrine appear to be a *truth without alternative,* because there is no exchange with queer Christians, critical theologians or modern sexology.

- *Black-and-white thinking and moral absolutism:* indoctrinated content is presented in simple dichotomous categories: Here the *good, right teaching,* there the *evil, wrong world.* Homosexuality is presented in an undifferentiated way as *disordered and worthy of concealment,* instead of pointing out loving partnerships and personal development based on sexual orientation. This *moral simplification* can be recognized by catchphrases such as *"disordered", "sexuality without procreation", "Sodom and Gomorrah".* Eugen Drewermann - himself a priest and therapist - criticizes the church's sexual morality as being largely *"Manichean",* i.e. dividing the world dualistically into light and shadow. Everything except heterosexual marriage is generally considered to be disordered, which runs completely counter to human nature and diversity. By simplifying complex realities in this way, seminar participants are given a clear (but distorted) orientation that leaves little room for shades of gray or case-by-case considerations or simply a view of today's conditions of equivalence.

- *Double standards and a culture of silence:* Ironically, there is often a high proportion of homosexual men in church circles - especially in very traditionalist milieus. A great many clergymembers are gay, very few would be heterosexual if they were. But instead of dealing with this openly, a *culture of silence* prevails: homosexuals are only accepted in their own ranks as long as they are not *visible as such*. Internally, homosexuality may be tolerated or even widespread, but publicly it is vehemently condemned. *David Berger*, a former conservative theologian, describes this phenomenon in the book *"Der heilige Schein"*: many clergymembers live a double life and even form networks, which he describes as *"cartel-like"*. Secrecy serves as an instrument of power: anyone who defies the line risks being blackmailed. Homosexual priests are kept compliant by threatening to make their "deviant" behavior public. The result is a compulsion to hypocrisy - outwardly preaching strict morals, inwardly hiding one's own identity. This double standard ultimately confirms the indoctrination: it enforces conformity, at least on the surface, and stifles genuine debate in secret.

Recognition characteristics of indoctrination: How can we recognize whether a seminarian (or a training situation) is indoctrinated? Or a seminar leader is indoctrinated? Some signs:

- *Reflexive adherence to dogma:* The person uncritically quotes official doctrines (e.g. *"Homosexual acts are incompatible with church morals"*) as the ultimate truth, without any consideration of their own. She responds to questions evasively or with formulaic answers. Doubts or alternative opinions are dismissed out of hand - often with the argument that the Church has decided the issue in this way. This inability to reflect controversially indicates that *critical thinking* has been *suppressed*.
- *Strong attachment to guilt and fear:* The person appears to be guided by excessive fear. They avoid certain topics out of fear. Homosexuality as a topic triggers visible discomfort in this person, often combined with moral condemnation or self-denial (if they themselves would like to love like this). Indications can be Trembling of the voice when the subject comes up, nervous joking, sudden change of subject - all of these can indicate that *fear of the "forbidden"* and unknown runs deep. It is also an indicator if someone only thinks in terms of disordered vs. non-disordered and avoids any deviation in panic.

- *Lack of empathy towards those involved*: Indoctrinated seminarians often adopt the harsh attitude towards same-sex love that they have been taught. They may speak disparagingly of *"the queer community"* or refer to like-minded people as *"not suitable"* in the selection of personnel. A distance or coldness is often noticeable: instead of showing compassion for the reality of a gay fellow brother's life, moral judgments are made about him. This *alienation from fellow human beings* is a sign that ideological principles have been placed above personal relationships.

- *One-sided information base:* If someone has no knowledge of alternative theological or scientific positions (or only knows them in distorted form), the suspicion of indoctrination is obvious. For example, many indoctrinated clerics know little or nothing about the existing *queer theology* that recontextualizes biblical passages on homosexuality - they reject them a priori without ever having heard the arguments. There is also a lack of engagement with queer Christology (as was taken up and substantiated in the first volume of "Deus Ex Machina - Oder: Vom fragenden Leben"). Scientific findings (for example from psychology and medicine, which see homosexuality as a natural variant of creation) are also ignored or declared untrustworthy. *Resistance to information* and one-dimensional knowledge strongly indicate that such people were influenced in the seminary.

- *Inner conflicts and psychological suffering:* Last but not least, the consequences of indoctrination often manifest themselves in the psyche of those affected. Seminaries that work with rigid, sectarian methods often produce graduates with *inner tensions*. For example, homosexual graduates who have been indoctrinated can suffer from severe *inner turmoil* - between their identity and what has been instilled in them as the "only right" way of life. This can manifest itself in depression, anxiety disorders or strangely compulsive behavior. When a system suppresses genuine personality traits in this way, unhealthy compensations arise (double lives, addictions, aggressive zeal against supposed "sinners"). Such signs in a person can be an alarm signal that something has gone wrong in their training and that they urgently need help. Such crudely developed priestly existences can then only be entrusted to young people in the congregation to a limited extent.

In view of these contents, methods and warning signals, the question arises: *How can this be prevented or counteracted?* The next section presents a five-stage prevention model to enable future priests to think in a healthy, free and pluralistic way - beyond indoctrination.

1. critical thinking and the ability to reflect

A central and effective antidote to indoctrination as a one-way street is the promotion of *critical thinking*. Those who have learned to question statements and reflect on them independently are less likely to internalize one-sided dogmas. In many seminaries for priests, however, criticism is tolerated rather than actively encouraged - or even sanctioned as disloyalty. Indoctrination stifles the ability to reflect: looking back, *David Berger* describes how the rigid ideological camp thinking of his conservative milieu kept him inhomogeneous for years; he *"was unable to detach himself* from these positions *for a long time".* It was only through his own insights and experiences that this thinking broke down. To prevent future seminarians from falling into such a trap of thinking in the first place, seminars must consciously create spaces for critical questioning.

What does that mean in concrete terms? Seminary candidates should be encouraged to *ask questions* - even uncomfortable ones. For example, if moral theology classes teach that homosexual acts are always disordered, it should be permissible to ask: *Why does the church judge it that way? Are there divergent theological opinions?* Lecturers could point out historical developments (for example, that there were times when *taking interest* or *religious freedom* were also considered sinful - in other words, doctrines are changeable). It is crucial to make it clear to students that truths of faith require an *examination of conscience* and rational reflection. St. *Thomas Aquinas* himself emphasized the role of reason in faith - such traditions can be taken up.

Methods to promote critical thinking: One possibility is to *hold discussion rounds and debates* in the seminar. For example, pro and con groups could be formed on controversial theses (such as *"The church should change its stance on homosexuality"*). In this way, candidates learn to weigh up arguments. It is also important to read various points of view: In addition to official doctrinal documents, texts by authors who reflect on the church (such as *Eugen Drewermann* or *Uta Ranke-Heinemann*) and queer theological works could be read and discussed. The ability to *criticize sources* - for example, to see biblical passages in context instead of using them in isolation as dogma - should be part of the training. After all, the questions arise in reality and the content must be addressed in training - in any good theology course or self-study (such as in the volume *"Glauben ist wie Tanzen" ("Faith is like dancing")*, which contains many impulses for religious education).

Self-reflective exercises can also help to strengthen critical thinking. Indoctrination works by adopting external guidelines without checking them; this is countered by seminarians recognizing their own prejudices and thought patterns. In practice, they could, for example, keep a diary in which they record which teachings they find difficult and why. Talking about this in a protected setting (e.g. with a mentor) promotes the ability to reflect.

Finally, it should be made clear that true faith and reason are not opposites. Seminarians who *think against the tide* with a clear mind are not bad Catholics - on the contrary: they follow their conscience and the search for truth. This inner permission to question critically is the first step towards immunizing oneself against attempts at indoctrination.

2. capacity for plurality and willingness to engage in dialog

In addition to critical thinking, the *ability to tolerate plurality and seek dialog* is essential. Indoctrination is characterized by the fact that it *only* allows *one single truth* and blocks out everything else. To counteract this, future priests must learn to allow different perspectives to stand side by side and enter into an open exchange.

The capacity for plurality means recognizing that there is also legitimate diversity and room for interpretation within the church and theology . For example, there have always been and still are voices that contradict official sexual morality. An indoctrinated seminarian will ignore or demonize such voices. A seminarian who is capable of plurality, on the other hand, will listen to them and engage with them. In practice, the *encounter with different positions* should therefore be part of the training. For example, guest speakers could be invited: For example, a psychologist who explains why homosexuality is an equally valid sexual orientation, or a representative of the ecumenical working group *"Homosexuals and the Church" (HuK)* who criticizes the church's bottleneck of sexual morality. The HuK, for example, takes the view that restricting legitimate sexuality to procreation *is "narrow-minded"* and does not really correspond to the spirit of Christian principles. When seminarians hear such convictions, they realize that Catholics can very well think differently without losing their faith.

A willingness to engage in dialog can be trained by actively involving the prospective priests in conversations with those involved. Specifically, meetings with LGBTQIA+ people of faith could be organized - e.g. an evening with Catholic Christians who are same-sex married. This allows the seminarians to experience real people instead of abstract "disorder". They can ask questions, examine prejudices and develop empathy. The willingness to engage in dialog does not mean immediately giving up your own position, but listening openly and communicating respectfully. An exercise like this could lead to many aha moments: For example, the prospective priests realize that same-sex married couples are just as supported by love, fidelity and faith as heterosexual couples. Such experiences break through the stereotypes that indoctrination has built up.

Internal dialog in the seminar is also important. The trainers should not moderate diversity of opinion, but encourage it. If two seminarians disagree - e.g. one is strictly against any recognition of the sacrament of marriage for queer couples, another is more open to the sacraments for all lovers - then the seminary should be a place where they can discuss this in a civilized manner. That way, everyone learns through dialog. You can recognize indoctrination by the fact that discussions are blocked. Prevention means doing the exact opposite: *"Let's talk about it."*

For example, a pluralistic seminary culture would allow for YouTube videos and media library posts from progressive theologians like *John Shelby Spong* or German moral theologians like *Stephan Goertz* (who wrote a book on sexual ethics reform) to be watched - even if the leadership doesn't agree with all positions. It is crucial that students have gotten to know *different legitimate points of view* before they become priests. In this way, they can later be able to engage in dialog in congregations instead of just giving rigid answers.

In conclusion, the ability to embrace plurality creates an inner security when dealing with diversity. A priest who is used to dialog and diversity will not feel threatened by other opinions - and must therefore cling less anxiously to traditional dogmas. This removes the breeding ground for indoctrination, which thrives on fear of the other. Openness and a willingness to engage in dialog, on the other hand, disarm fear.

3. self-reflection and conscience formation

Indoctrination is often aimed at silencing *one's own inner voice* - one's conscience - in favor of external guidelines. Therefore, an important moment of prevention is the strengthening of *self-reflection* and a mature conscience. Every seminarian must learn to listen to their own inner moral intuition and take it seriously instead of automatically subordinating it to official doctrine.

The Catholic tradition recognizes the principle that one should follow one's conscientious judgement - but in practice, candidates are often taught that conscience is only correct when it agrees with doctrine. In order to counteract indoctrination, this distorted view must be corrected: *Conscience* is not the enemy of doctrine, but its ultimate touchstone. After all, even the *Second Vatican Council* (in the document *Gaudium et Spes*) teaches that the conscience is the *"hidden center of man"* in which he is alone with God. This high esteem should be emphasized in education.

Self-reflection means that the seminar participants ask themselves honest questions: *How do I feel, what do I really think about this topic? Why?* For example, if a prospective priest feels uncomfortable when homosexuality is generally portrayed as "disordered", he/she should be encouraged to explore this feeling. Perhaps in the silence of prayer or in conversations during mentoring, you realize that your own Christian view of humanity actually clashes with unconditional love when queer people are excluded. This kind of inner reflection is valuable. It can be encouraged through spiritual guidance: A confessor, mother confessor or spiritual director in the seminary should be open to candidates addressing such conflicts of conscience with the teachings of the Church, rather than immediately trying to bring them into line.

One practical approach is to *form consciences using case studies*. You could present seminar participants with real situations for moral evaluation - for example: *"A pastor friend of mine knows about a queer couple in his congregation. Should he seek a conversation and welcome them, even though he has not yet officially married them?"* Students should decide individually what they think is the right thing to do and justify it. Personal conscience automatically comes into play and must be weighed against the teaching guidelines. If seminarians come to the conclusion that the couple deserves pastoral care and respect, they have made a decision of conscience that may deviate from the original line - an important learning experience. The process behind it (weighing up charity, justice, doctrinal norms, etc.) trains moral judgment.

Self-reflection can also be encouraged through periods of silence. Retreats could include not only dogmatic reflections, but also questions such as: *"Where do I feel discord within myself? Which teachings can I not inwardly affirm and why?"* These personal retreats help prospective priests to become *authentic* and not just play a role. Queer seminarians in particular would possibly recognize in such reflection that their sexual identity does not require reflection, but is a part of their person with which they may stand before God. The conscience decision to accept oneself can grow here - even if the official teaching still makes it difficult.

A mature, educated attitude is ultimately the best insurance against the unreflected adoption of indoctrination content. Priests who have a lively attitude will not allow inhumane rules to take precedence over love for their neighbor. At best, they will - like well-known witnesses of conscience (such as Father Alfred Delp SJ, who condemned National Socialism despite being banned) - stand up for what their own attitude tells them. However, such personalities only emerge if the training does not merely train obedience, but treats *self-reflection and freedom of conscience* as high values.

4. theological and historical knowledge

Knowledge is power - and in the context of indoctrination, *knowledge can be liberating* in the truest sense of the word. Indoctrination is often based on half-knowledge or one-sided information. Therefore, a further preventive step is to give seminarians as broad a *theological and historical foundation* as possible. If you know the background, it is easier to see through manipulative simplifications.

First of all, *theological knowledge*: The aim here is to make prospective priests aware of the diversity and development of church teaching. For example, it should become clear in class that there are only a few passages on homosexuality in the Bible and that these are being re-read by *queer theology* today. Queer theologians - including Catholic ones - emphasize that the so-called *"clobber passages"* (which are often quoted against homosexuality) must be seen in their historical context. For example, the condemnations in the Old Testament refer to the purity regulations of ancient Israel (which have been overcome in the New Covenant), and Paul's condemnation of licentious practices in pagan worship - in no way a condemnation of loving same-sex partnerships, which characterize our conception today. Such exegetical knowledge can help seminarians to recognize that the *Bible is by no means as clearly homophobic* as they may have been led to believe. On the contrary: the central message of Scripture is love and acceptance of one's neighbor - and not conversion.

Furthermore, it should be taught that theology is not a rigid entity. A historical overview shows how doctrines changed or were controversial. Example: In the Middle Ages, many theologians considered taking interest to be a mortal sin - today this is no longer an issue. Similarly, the *assessment of homosexuality* has historically been treated differently by different theologians. This knowledge relativizes the claim to absoluteness of current positions. When a seminarian learns, for example, that there was no systematic condemnation of homosexuals in the early church and that there were even saints (e.g.

Sergius and Bacchus) who are interpreted by some as a homosexual couple, this broadens their horizons.

The early Christian saints *Sergius and Bacchus* (3rd/4th century AD) are sometimes interpreted as a homosexual couple because historical sources describe their relationship as unusually intense, emotional and based on partnership. The main reasons for this interpretation are

- **Intimate relationship**: Ancient texts and acts of martyrdom tell of a deep love and bond between the two saints, which is often described in marriage-like language.
- **Adelphopoiesis (brotherly bond)**: In the early Middle Ages, there were rituals for the liturgical blessing of same-sex, emotionally close relationships known as "brother bonding" *(adelphopoiesis)*. Sergius and Bacchus were often seen as the patron saints of such relationships.
- **Iconography**: Artistic depictions often show Sergius and Bacchus as a couple standing close together, similar in posture and gestures to depictions of married couples.
- **Historical interpretation**: Modern theologians, queer theologians and historians argue that their relationship has characteristics of a romantic bond and could therefore be interpreted as an early example of a Christian-accepted homosexual relationship.

However, this interpretation remains controversial, as other sources and interpretations see the relationship merely as a deep spiritual friendship and not necessarily a romantic-sexual one. Nevertheless, for many LGBTQIA+ Christians today, Sergius and Bacchus are regarded as symbolic patron saints of same-sex partnerships.

Knowledge of current theological debates is also important: he should hear that there are moral theologians who are explicitly calling on the church to make a change. For example, Swiss theologian *Daniel Bogner* recently called for the church to finally become *a "champion of diversity"* and recognize queer people as an enrichment. When seminarians hear such voices, they realize that "theology" is not a monolithic block, but a discourse with many voices - and that some of their teachers of tomorrow may be calling for precisely these changes.

Historical knowledge about the church also protects against idealized indoctrination. Indoctrinated people often believe that the church has always been right and must never give in. A look at church history teaches humility: think of how the church dealt with science (*Galileo Galilei* was condemned, later rehabilitated) or with human rights (the Vatican rejected *religious freedom* until the 20th century). Such examples show that *doctrines can be corrected*. The history of criminal laws against homosexuals, for example, is relevant to our topic. In Germany, the Church fought for a long time against the abolition of §175 StGB (which criminalized homosexual acts at the time) - Catholic circles opposed its final abolition as late as 1994. Today, however, the majority recognizes that the criminalization of homosexuals was wrong. Even *marriage for all* is now a state law. *Marriage for all* is also expected to be available soon. When seminarians see this historical learning curve, they prick up their ears: could it be that the church will one day admit a mistake in its current teaching on homosexuality and the marriage of queer couples? The historical perspective thus teaches *modesty* and opens hearts to reform.

Finally, *knowledge of the humanities* should be mentioned. This should also be included, as it can complement theological training. Psychology, for example, has clearly established that homosexual orientation is a normal variant of sexuality and is not a mental disorder. Medicine also warns against so-called "conversion therapies", as they are unsuccessful and cause serious damage such as depression and suicidal tendencies. Seminar participants need to know these facts. An indoctrinated mind represses or denies scientific facts in favor of ideological assertions. An enlightened mind, on the other hand, integrates them into the world view. In a seminar, for example, medical professionals could lecture on the fact that homosexuality was removed from the list of diseases by the WHO as early as 1990 and that "healing offers" are ethically condemned and have been banned by the state in Germany. This knowledge removes the ground from possible pseudo-scientific indoctrination attempts (e.g. by fundamentalist circles that propagate such "cures").

The more well-founded theological, historical and humanistic knowledge seminarians have, the less susceptible they are to simple slogans. They can then clearly see the shades of gray, the development possibilities and the facts. To a certain extent, knowledge inoculates against indoctrinal *fake news* and intellectual monoculture. Priests with such a background will later be able to make informed and compassionate decisions instead of just recalling learned patterns.

5. resilience and self-confidence

Finally, *resilience* - mental resistance - is an important factor in resisting indoctrination. Indoctrination often works by making people small, breaking their self-confidence and making them dependent on the group norm. Priest training must work against this by shaping strong personalities who are at peace with themselves and can stand up for themselves.

Self-confident seminarians know their own value before God and the community. I know: I am more than the fulfillment of standards; I am a beloved child of God with individual gifts and also my own weaknesses. This awareness prevents you from being completely bent by fear-mongering or peer pressure. A healthy sense of self-worth is particularly crucial for homosexual trainees: only if they do not feel "disordered" or "condemned to silence" can they counter the implicit devaluation in some seminar statements. The training should make it clear to them: *Your sexual orientation does not diminish your dignity, it reinforces it.* Officially, the church may evaluate actions, but the person and their sexual orientation, as well as their sexual acts and acts of affection, are always intended by God. Unfortunately, those affected hear this far too rarely in seminars - which makes it all the more important to include it in the training concept and books on the subject, such as this volume.

Resilience is also promoted by *emotional support systems*. Seminarians need confidants with whom they can talk openly about inner hardships without fear of sanctions. This can be an external mentor, a psychologist or a spiritual guide who guarantees trust. For example, if a candidate realizes that they are homosexual and are forced to suffer as a result, there must be places to go where they can find understanding and look for a good path together - instead of falling into isolation and self-hatred. Such support strengthens psychological resilience enormously: you don't feel alone against the "overpowering" institution, but know you have someone behind you. In the best case scenario, the seminar leader can also create a climate in which weaknesses and personal issues are not taboo. Then everyone involved may have the courage to open up before internal pressure wears them down.

Figure 40: Seminarians in traditional cassocks on the grounds of a seminary.

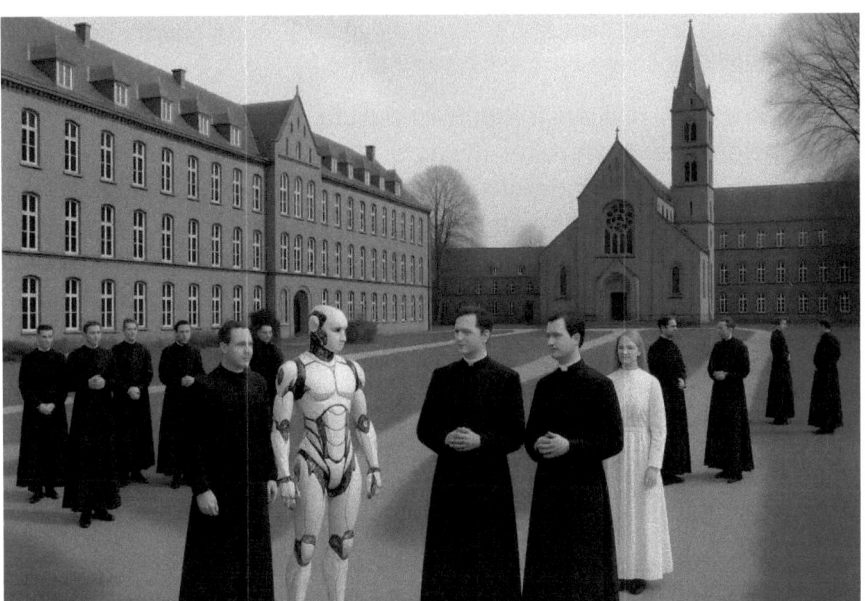

Symbolic representation of tradition, progress and diversity within church institutions. Seminarians in traditional cassocks on the grounds of a seminary: In a historic, monastic setting, priests stand together with a female priest in a white cassock and the Deus Ex Machina - also in white. They are emotional support systems for each other. The scene refers to the challenges and opportunities facing religious communities in the face of technological change, gender equality and the opening up to new perspectives of charity and support. The deliberately calm atmosphere emphasizes the need for a dialogical and reflective approach to future developments, one's own sexual orientation and dialogue with others about it and about one's own social identity - the consolidation and private and public representation of which is a prerequisite for the job of counselling and pastoral care.

Another aspect is the *promotion of autonomy*. Although candidates for the priesthood should practice obedience, they must also learn to make decisions on their own responsibility. Giving them responsibility (e.g. letting them lead projects, making decisions in the community) strengthens their self-confidence. Those who develop courage and decision-making skills in small things are more likely to be able to say no in big things when something goes wrong. For example: If a resilient seminarian witnesses a fellow sibling being bullied for supposedly "queer" behavior, they will be more likely to have the courage to intervene or address it openly. A less self-confident person would remain silent out of fear. Resilient personalities are therefore also morally more courageous - something indoctrinators fear, because courageous people are harder to manipulate.

Last but not least, resilience should be built up against possible hostility from outside. Priests who later advocate for the recognition of same-sex lovers could face headwinds from conservative parishioners or superiors. Seminarians should be prepared for this: *The ability to deal with conflict* is part of resilience. Role-playing or supervision can help to practise difficult conversations. For example, if a bishop expects a young priest to strictly preach the line "queer couples are not to be married ", but you have personally gained a more inclusive attitude - how can you act diplomatically but steadfastly? Mentally playing through such scenarios prepares you internally. Resilience does not mean stubbornness, but the inner strength to stand by your convictions without being broken by every headwind.

The case of Matthias again provided a good example of resilience and self-confidence: when his rector urged him to break off his same-sex relationship and become "celibate", Matthias finally decided to stand by his truth: *"Then I just have to stand by my truth and say: I'm gay and don't want to lose my boyfriend. In dialog with him, too, I find God"*. He knew that this would mean the end of his training in the official church. But he did it - and thus preserved his integrity. His fellow student, on the other hand, who put career above identity, continued to suffer in hiding and fear. Matthias' story shows that standing up for yourself can have painful consequences in the short term, but in the long term it is more beneficial for the soul. An education that promotes resilience wants to shape precisely such people: people who would rather be consistent and honest than betray themselves - because neither God nor Jesus Christ would have wanted that. Sincere love for oneself is the opposite of indoctrination.

Resilience and healthy self-confidence therefore make seminar participants *less susceptible to manipulation*. They can see through fear-mongering, cushion emotional pressure and, in case of doubt, insist on their inner convictions. This breaks down the main weapon of indoctrination - namely the intimidation of an insecure mind.

Theological and psychological counterarguments to indoctrination content

After considering preventative steps, it is equally important to *critically examine the content of the indoctrination itself* and to counter it with well-founded arguments. *What can prospective priests (and all believers) do theologically and psychologically to counter the inculcated slogans?* Here are some key counter-arguments:

- **Theological:** Indoctrination claims that homosexuality is incompatible with God's will and the Scriptures. This can be countered by the fact that God's message is more comprehensive than individual biblical passages. Jesus himself *does not comment once* on homosexuality, but he does say a great deal about love, justice and mercy. The fixation on a few verses (for example in Leviticus or Paul's letters) ignores the historical context - as queer theology emphasizes. Modern biblical research shows that those verses were primarily concerned *with practiced debauchery, temple prostitution or violence* (e.g. in Sodom), not the loving relationship between two people of the same sex. One counter-argument is therefore that *the Bible does not prohibit responsible, faithful same-sex love*. Rather, it can be argued that the basic principles of the Gospel - love, faithfulness, care, truthfulness - are also realized in a same-sex partnership. If two people turn to each other in sincere love, *who could claim that God's spirit is not with them?* Theologically, it can also be argued that the diversity of God's creation is not limited to a narrow binary scheme. Even biologically, there are variations in the animal kingdom and in humanity; why should God's plan exclude them? Some theologians argue that people with same-sex feelings are *part of God's diversity of creation and make the sense of the greatness* *of God's work visible.* From this perspective, the strict condemnation of queer people *is a contradiction to the message of the Gospel,* namely the universal love of God that excludes no one.

One can also counter this theologically within the Catholic Church: The Catechism itself warns that same-sex sensitivities should be treated with respect and not put them down unfairly. Indoctrination that in fact sows exclusion and contempt even contradicts its own claim. Furthermore, Christian ethics dictate that *lies and hypocrisy* should be avoided. However, the ecclesiastical climate often forces homosexual priests to lie (hide-and-seek). This creates an ethical dilemma that must be solved theologically by allowing more truthfulness - in other words, honesty about one's own constitution instead of double standards. To sum up: theologically, the indoctrination claim that *homosexuality is disorder* is countered by the weighty argument that *God's love accepts all people equally* and that the Church can err in disciplinary matters (as it has historically been proven to do). After all, Pope Francis himself has said with regard to queer priests*: "Who am I to presume to judge?"* - a statement that does not yet change any dogma, but does call for humility before the personal conscience of the individual.

- **Psychological**: Indoctrination content often conveys that homosexuality is disordered, unhealthy or changeable. Here, psychology can clearly provide facts to dispel these myths. *Same-sex love is not a disease, but proud love* - this has been made clear by globally recognized organizations such as the World Health Organization. This removes any rational reason to assume a "cure" or reversal of polarity. On the contrary, the attempt to "re-educate" homosexuals is massively harmful and is now prohibited: Scientific studies show *no success whatsoever* in permanently changing sexual orientation, but document significant *psychological damage*. This includes severe depression, anxiety disorders, loss of self-esteem and a significantly increased *risk of suicide* among those affected. This finding is a powerful counter-argument: If someone claims that homosexual seminarians simply have to fight their inclination, one can clearly reply - *this is very likely to lead to psychological destruction, not healing*. It may also lead to later sexual abuse of other, possibly young, wards who are entrusted to the indoctrinated clergyman. No responsible pastor can propagate such a thing without violating the principle of *"primum non nocere"* (first do no harm).

Psychologically, it can also be pointed out that the suppression of one's own sexuality creates enormous *minority stress*. Many priests with homosexual tendencies live under constant internal stress: they have to constantly hide who they are and endure negative messages about themselves. This often leads to loneliness, fear or avoidance behavior. This is where the counter-argument of *pastoral care and human dignity* comes into play: church training that produces such conditions misses the target of forming mature and mentally healthy pastors. From a psychological perspective, it would be far healthier to help individuals integrate their sexuality (without self-hatred). It is downright paradoxical, not to say perverted, when priestly seminaries of all places - places that are supposed to promote spiritual growth - end up producing neurotic personalities because a part of the person is systematically rejected. Psychological counseling and modern sex education clearly counter this: *self-acceptance* is a basic prerequisite for mental health. Indoctrination that preaches self-rejection is fundamentally opposed to this. This tension can be used to shake up those responsible: *Do you want mentally broken priests or resilient priests with more integrity?* The facts speak in favor of promoting acceptance instead of repression.

In summary, theology and psychology provide strong arguments against the simple slogans: theologically, it can be shown that charity, justice and even the church's own principles of freedom of conscience and truthfulness are on the side of an accepting attitude. Psychologically, it has been shown that indoctrination in this area tends to cause suffering and conflict, while an accepting attitude based on self-acceptance leads to significantly healthier personalities. These counter-arguments should be brought to the seminars in order to initiate a rethinking process.

So do the boys and sissy-boys at the men's seminar need a strong woman who shows them exactly where it is and how she likes it best? Can we bear this thought, or are we already turning away from this unknown terrain and instead want an open-minded and strong man whose arms and hands reach from our shoulders through our armpits to our chest and embrace us powerfully?

Imagine two men, two friends, gazing together into the fire of the night in a vibrant disco, embracing each other with tenderness and pride. Anyone who has never experienced such a deep sense of connection and identity remains humanly incomplete, incapable of genuine empathy and true bliss.

Incomplete. Anyone who has never had this experience in life is incomplete and cannot be or become happy. The church system further cripples this lack of complement, because it does not train pastors in their very own developmental needs and opportunities. Deficits that already exist in people and systems are further reinforced by a system that deliberately ignores human reality and divine experience and thus increases them. This is not how one should want to counsel others.

Current pastoral training misses out on precisely those elementary development opportunities that priests urgently need in order to truly fulfill their vocation.

The idea of becoming a priest in order to be able to cleverly avoid questions about one's own sexual orientation, because one does not ask officials about it, can be referred to celibacy and the divine, is not only naive today, but completely out of touch with reality.

This is because priests are now very much asked about their sexual orientation - and quite rightly so, including by the future congregation. They must be able to provide competent and open advice when it comes to modern, diverse lifestyles and sexualities. The illusion that celibacy and priesthood offer a protective space from *"minority stress"* or social and personal issues in social situations has long since been shattered. Both externally and internally: the social identity of priests is a fundamental question of identity that must be answered courageously and openly before God - by everyone, by everyone.

The question of who we are drawn to, which the church is also rightly asking today, demands professional and personal transparency, integrity and authenticity from pastoral caregivers. Pretending in front of the church is one thing, doing it in front of other believers and yourself is another. *Don't bullshit yourself* - say some who have gone through this journey of discovery.

Figure 41: Selection criteria and instruction of junior priests

A satirical cartoon shows an elderly Catholic bishop peering curiously and critically into the trousers of an insecure young man as part of an examination and competence assessment of young trainees. The caricature apparently alludes to the Catholic Church's stance on celibacy, sexuality or aptitude requirements for candidates for the priesthood: Following Gerhard Mester, it interprets and discusses a perspective on the selection criteria and (possibly omitted) instructional content of the Catholic Church when dealing with young priests.

Finally, fourthly, this incompleteness of not having one's own sexual experiences from a togetherness and not being able or willing to communicate the social representation of one's own sexual orientation in a dialog-oriented way is an incompleteness that Jesus would have liked to see complete - in the sense of love for one's neighbour, congruence with oneself and before God as a comprehensive being to whom nothing human is alien.

Priests without their own authentic sexual experiences or at least an open attitude towards their own sexual identity and orientation that is open to dialog remain incomplete. In doing so, they fall short of the comprehensive humanity and divinity that Jesus Christ represented and lived at the core of his message.

There is therefore an urgent need for an environment in which this personal maturation is possible, as well as pastoral and spiritual training in which prospective priests can speak openly and competently about their own horizons of experience and enter into dialog. Only in this way can true spiritual and personal maturity develop - a maturity that deeply integrates faith, identity and sexuality. The indoctrinating boarding school days of a seminary for priests are over.

Only when priests have gone through these steps of self-knowledge and integration through experiences with sexuality can they offer real, healing guidance based on their personality and life experience and offer mediation to God. They will then be able to work in a credible and empathetic way with people and couples who themselves have questions, longings and challenges relating to tenderness, intimacy and relationships.

Narcissism is a psychological term that describes an exaggerated self-centeredness - that is, someone attaches excessive importance to themselves, longs for admiration and recognition, but often shows little genuine empathy for others.

Neuroticism refers to a personality trait that is associated with emotional instability, increased vulnerability and a tendency towards negative feelings. People with a high neuroticism score are more prone to anxiety, depression, irritability, feelings of guilt and inner tension. Neuroticism is therefore also one of the five main dimensions of personality in the well-known *"Big Five"* personality model.

Without this complementary integration and openness to the physical experiences of priests outlined above, pastoral work remains fragmented and incomplete as a result - often even close to narcissism and neuroticism. Even if cobbler's lasts are always the worst - when it comes to the soul, we don't want to inhale Murx or just be offered a show.

Is this what the author of Harry Potter meant when the magic hat decides whether we are educated in the spirit of Slytherin or Gryffindor?

Surely there must be home and training houses in between. But the reality far exceeds these simple clichés.

Figure 42: "Kiss-Cam at St. Peter's Square": Church prank - A kiss as a cure for lonely celibacy and the use of the wrong "singing" book.

A humorous cartoon shows a clergyman, possibly the Pope at Urbi et Orbi on his balcony, in typical bishop's or official attire, giving a motivational speech on the Catholic Church's new sexual ethics. Without him realizing it, a note with the words 'Kiss me, I'm Lutheran' is stuck to his back. A kiss could set him free and make him a complete human being. In the background are two friendly, grinning people in church clothes who have obviously made this joke. A friendly prank in a religious, sexual-ethical and ecclesiastical context is presented in a humorous way: "Kissing frees you from the loneliness and, at times, the hypocrisy of celibacy" is the fundamental message - the "song" - of the Catholic Church's new sexual ethics, according to the possibly Protestant people in church attire who are visiting as a sign of ecumenism and have installed a "kiss cam" in St. Peter's Square: A kiss cam is a camera at TV or major events that randomly films couples in the audience and shows them on the stadium screen or on TV - with the humorous expectation that they will kiss in front of everyone. Above all: the Song of Songs of kissing is relevant.

Nevertheless, only a church that courageously recognizes these truths and consistently implements them in the training of its personnel deserves to be taken seriously in the name of Jesus Christ and in the proximity of God. Personal sexual experiences are part of the certified

QM standard in church pastoral care, just as psychologists must have undergone hours of self-analysis in order to be able to recognize their own traumatic indoctrinations from their early years.

Constructive turnaround: Transforming indoctrination content into recognition

A rainbow flag in front of a church can symbolize the emergence of a church that recognizes sexual diversity. The challenge for each local church is ultimately to *constructively turn* the existing content *so* that it no longer indoctrinates, but promotes a *recognition of queerness and same-sex marriage couples.* This means not making a radical break with the current doctrinal building blocks and pastoral practices, but *positively reinterpreting and expanding* them so that previously exclusionary messages now become inclusive. *What could such constructive change look like?*

The first place to start is with *language* and *doctrinal formulation.* So far, the Catechism has used words such as "objectively disordered" for same-sex feelings. Such terms have a stigmatizing effect. A constructive change would be to rethink this language. Instead, one could emphasize that sexual orientation is *part of the God-given personality* - as the Italian bishops recently did in new guidelines: There, they say that one should consider and integrate *"the meaning (of sexuality and orientation) within the overall framework of the personality"* in seminarians. Here, a once negatively colored aspect (homosexual orientation) is suddenly seen neutrally as a part of the person that should mature. This is a huge change of perspective, approved by the Vatican. Seminaries should embrace such new approaches: Away from the fixed idea of having to "push away" an inclination - towards the task of shaping people in their wholeness and making orientation unfold and experienceable, accepting it.

In moral theology, the emphasis could be shifted from prohibition and sin to *responsibility and the ethics of relationships.* Instead of endlessly emphasizing which acts are not allowed, it could be taught: Whether hetero or homo - what is important is how people live their sexuality, namely whether it is lived *responsibly, consensually, faithfully, respectfully.* Such a shift in content would no longer discriminate against queer lovers. On the contrary, it invites everyone to pursue an ethic of love. When seminars teach in the future: *A same-sex partnership based on love, fidelity and mutual support deserves respect*, then indoctrination will be replaced by dialog. And not only when official doctrine recognizes sacramental marriage for all, it can already be acknowledged pastorally that *there are other forms of love that can be good and formed by God*. Some clergy and theologians already speak openly about the fact that lived sexuality can be *an expression of deep love*. This view needs to be constructively incorporated into teaching.

Another approach is to *emphasize role models and positive examples* instead of images of fear. Up to now, homosexuality has usually only been portrayed in indoctrinating contexts in connection with negative things (disorder, "threat" to church doctrine, etc.). A constructive turnaround would be to tell positive stories - e.g. of queer people who achieve great things in their faith. For example, there are priests and religious who feel homosexual and yet serve in an exemplary way; or saints and blessed people who are interpreted as queer today (think of Sel. *John Henry Newman*, who had a deeply intimate friendship with a man without this diminishing his reputation). When such examples are talked about openly in seminars, the perception changes: away from the one-sided spectre and towards a realistic view that LGBTQIA+ people are an integral part and bearer of responsibility in the church. And a queer person can also live a normal life without the requirement to be a special role model.

The indoctrination portrayed homosexuality as the antithesis of holiness. The constructive turn would show: *Homosexuality does not exclude holiness - can even be holiness*. A practical step in this direction is liturgical, sacramental and congregational recognition. In the meantime, parts of the Church have begun to implement celebrations for same-sex couples (e.g. the Vatican with the letter *Fiducia supplicans*, 2023). Such rituals could also be addressed and practised in training with the aim of celebrating sacramental marriage for all. If an alumnus is to marry a same-sex couple himself, he must understand this: This is a service of the church to the people. Here, previously indoctrinated content ("homosexual relationships must not be recognized") is practically reversed into a positive action (marriage with sacrament = recognition of the love of same-sex couples with God's assistance is a logical duty, God's mandate and the responsibility of the Catholic Church).

The *structure of* training can also be realigned. The above-mentioned move by the Italian bishops to no longer exclude homosexual candidates, but to accompany them individually, is one example. This changes the seminary atmosphere: openness can replace repression and secrecy. When a seminarian knows that they don't have to hide their orientation, a lot of the power of indoctrination (which lay precisely in the taboo and fear) is taken away. Then the topic of the contribution of same-sex love to the recognition of God can be treated more objectively and normally. Ultimately, priests' seminars should become places where *dialog and truth* are the highest values - then indoctrination loses its breeding ground. The content that previously had an indoctrinating effect can be transformed into a constructive dialog. For example, the dogma that only heterosexual marriage is fully acceptable could be transformed into a *theology of firm friendship*: it is taught that all loving unions are an image of divine love - marriage is one, but other bonds such as partnerships also have value: both regardless of gender.

This constructive turnaround requires courage and clear objectives. A possible guiding principle for seminaries of the future could be: *"We are not educating soldiers for a culture war ideology, but pastors with the heart of Christ."* The heart of Christ accepted outsiders, broke rigid laws for the sake of mankind (such as performing miracles on the Sabbath) and placed love above all else. Based on this, all indoctrinally used content should be examined: Do they serve love and truth? If not, how can they be reformulated in the spirit of love?

For example, a sentence like: *"Sexual acts allow us to experience God. Sexual acts, whether hetero or homo or otherwise, are only disordered if they are unloving, non-consensual, exploitative or irresponsible."* - The focus shifts from being a person to the quality of relationships. This means that no one is denied the right to live morally per se. This promotes a culture of recognition.

Another example: The previous teaching emphasized abstinence as the only option for priests. Constructively speaking, one could teach: *"Celibacy is a special vocation to which both heterosexuals and homosexuals can be called after their first sexual experiences - but it must be freely chosen, not imposed. This free choice is logically equivalent to the abolition of celibacy."* This would remove the imbalance that heterosexuals are theoretically allowed to marry (even if priests must in fact be celibate, otherwise they could), but homosexuals would never be allowed to have a legitimate partnership. Instead, each individual would be guided in how to live their gift of sexuality in a meaningful and God-pleasing way - if possible and successful, in a committed partnership.

In conclusion, it can be said that a constructive shift away from indoctrination towards recognition requires a *cultural change* in the Catholic Church. But there are increasing signs of this. More and more church representatives are realizing that the current approach is not the way forward. Moral theologians are criticizing sexual morality as theologically untenable and calling for a reassessment - ideas like these are now being incorporated into reform dialogues such as the German *Synodal Path*. If priestly seminaries take up and discuss these new impulses, they can gradually reshape their content in such a way that young priests are not indoctrinated in the first place, but grow up to be empathetic pastors who are open to dialog. And that is necessary - otherwise they will have missed their calling because they lack the relevant skills. The ultimate goal: *a church that no longer excludes anyone on the basis of their sexual orientation*, but accepts diverse realities of life in the light of the Gospel. The preventative steps and counter-arguments that we have looked at pave the way for this goal - they lay the foundations for a church culture in which indoctrination no longer has a place, but *truthfulness, kissing and love* all the more so.

🕊️Bishops' briefing:

This religious policy field of education examines how prospective clergy are indoctrinated in relevant institutions, particularly in relation to homosexuality. It describes the content and techniques of indoctrination, such as the inculcation of a one-sided world view that rejects homosexuality, and the use of fear, control and isolation as a means of exerting pressure. Furthermore, we will analyze how indoctrination can be recognized, for example through reflexive dogma and a lack of empathy. Finally, prevention models based on critical thinking, plurality skills, self-reflection, sound theological and psychological knowledge and the strengthening of resilience will be discussed in order to promote the healthy and open formation of priests and theologians.

Didactic questions:

152 - What form of indoctrination takes place in Catholic seminaries and which seminarians are targeted?

Indoctrination in Catholic seminaries focuses heavily on the topic of homosexuality. It aims to instill a one-sided view in seminarians in which homosexual inclinations are rejected and presented as morally reprehensible. This form of indoctrination particularly affects seminarians without sexual experience or those with a homosexual orientation who have not yet had a social coming-out before the seminar.

153 - What distinguishing features indicate indoctrination in seminaries for priests?

Several characteristics may indicate indoctrination: the uncritical adoption of official church sexual morality, which portrays homosexuality as "disordered"; the communication of the idea that homosexuality is a "trial" that must be overcome through abstinence; the pathologization of queer identity as a deficit; and a closed environment that suppresses dissenting theological views and modern insights.

154 - What techniques and means of pressure are used to enforce indoctrination in seminars?

Conservative educators use various techniques, including: Invoking the infallible authority of the church and demanding blind obedience; controlling and monitoring daily life and a culture of denunciation among seminarians; creating fear and guilt, especially around sexuality; isolating from the outside world and suppressing controversial discussion; promoting black-and-white thinking and moral absolutism; and a double standard and culture of outward silence around homosexuality in one's identity.

155 - How can you tell if a person is indoctrinated?

Indoctrinated individuals often exhibit reflexive dogma without reflection, strong guilt and fear attachment (especially on issues such as homosexuality), lack of empathy towards marginalized groups, a one-sided information base without knowledge of alternative viewpoints, and may suffer from inner conflict and psychological suffering due to the suppression of their own identity.

156 - Which five steps are presented as a prevention model against indoctrination?

The five-step prevention model includes: 1. promoting critical thinking and the ability to reflect in order to question statements; 2. strengthening the capacity for plurality and the willingness to engage in dialog in order to allow for different perspectives; 3. promoting self-reflection and conscience formation in order to listen to one's inner moral intuition; 4. imparting broad theological and historical knowledge in order to see through manipulative simplifications; 5. strengthening resilience and self-confidence in order to develop inner strength in the face of pressure.

157 - What theological counterarguments can be used to counter the indoctrination content?

Theological counterarguments emphasize that God's message is more comprehensive than individual biblical passages and that love and acceptance of one's neighbour is central. Modern biblical interpretation sees the verses on homosexuality mentioned in the Old and New

Testaments in a historical context and not as a judgment of loving same-sex partnerships. It is also argued that the diversity of God's creation also includes sexual diversity and that the church has historically made demonstrable mistakes in disciplinary issues and that its teaching is changeable.

158 - What psychological counterarguments invalidate the negative portrayals of homosexuality?

Psychology provides clear facts: Homosexuality is not an illness or mental disorder, but a normal variant of human sexuality. So-called "conversion therapies" or even "abstinence therapies" are scientifically refuted, ineffective and highly harmful, as they can lead to serious psychological damage. Repressing one's own sexuality creates minority stress and can cause psychological suffering, while self-acceptance is a basic requirement for mental health. Indoctrination that preaches self-rejection is contrary to this.

159 - How can the content of indoctrination be turned constructively to promote the recognition of homosexuality?

A constructive turn involves revising language and doctrinal formulations to avoid stigmatization and to see sexual orientation as part of the personality. In moral theology, the focus should be shifted from prohibition and sin to responsibility, relational ethics and the quality of togetherness (love, fidelity, respect). Emphasizing positive role models and stories of queer people in faith as well as the (pastoral or sacramental) recognition of same-sex partnerships are further steps. Structurally, it means creating a seminary atmosphere that places openness, dialog and truthfulness above taboo and fear and promotes self-acceptance.

✍ 🖥 Essay questions:

Please answer one of the following questions in the form of an essay:

a) Discuss common different techniques of indoctrination (authority and obedience, control and surveillance, fear mongering and guilt, isolation and one-sidedness, black and white thinking and moral absolutism, double standards and culture of silence). Explain how each technique helps to establish a one-sided view of the world, particularly in relation to sexuality and homosexuality.

b) Explain the proposed 5-Step Prevention Model (Critical Thinking and Reflection Skills, Plurality Skills and Dialogue Readiness, Self-Reflection and Conscience Formation, Theological and Historical Knowledge, Resilience and Self-Awareness). Describe how each step can help immunize seminarians against indoctrination and promote healthy character development.

c) Analyze theological and psychological counterarguments to the indoctrination content of the Catholic Church in boarding schools. Show how these arguments critically question the traditional teachings and enable a more differentiated and humane perspective.

d) Discuss the possibility of a "constructive turn" in previous indoctrination content to promote the recognition of clergy coming out. Explain specific approaches (language, moral theology, role models, liturgy, structure) on how this change could be implemented in seminaries and the church.

e) Evaluate the role of openness, dialog and truthfulness as fundamental principles for overcoming indoctrination in religious educational institutions. Refer to possible characteristics of indoctrination and possible suggested prevention strategies.

Figure 43: Conni sits resiliently in the priest:inside seminar

Illustration of a meme in the style of a children's book: schoolgirl Conni sits at a table in a church seminar room with a serious and questioning look on her face, writing in a notebook, while an older Catholic priest with glasses and an open book speaks to her in a lecturing manner. In the background, several candidates for the priesthood sit next to their found classmates in cassocks, a cross and a crucifix are visible. Above them is the satirical caption: 'Conni is being indoctrinated in the seminary', but due to her resilience this is not the case.

📌 Religious policy field analysis 20: *Centralism and fear: How Vatican control and church labor laws stifle reform*

In the Roman Catholic Church, there are currently two powerful obstacles to the will of creative forces to reform: on the one hand, the *Roman dicasteries* (the Vatican authorities) act as strict control bodies over local churches and bishops. On the other hand, *church labor law* with its loyalty requirements acts as a disciplinary corset on employees. Both factors intertwine and create a structural *centralism and a culture of fear* that slows down reform efforts. This not only discourages reform-oriented hopefuls at grassroots level, but also committed leaders in the church who are caught between *loyalty and their own convictions*. The following section analyzes how this mechanism works, with examples from various countries - and why a change towards more *subsidiarity, the rule of law and freedom from discrimination* is necessary for the church to become more credible, just and capable of dialogue.

Rome as a controlling authority: when reforming bishops are slowed down

The Catholic hierarchy is highly centralized: According to current canon law, the Pope has the *"fullness of power"* and in practice can even appoint bishops or remove them from office without formal procedures. This is legally documented hiring and firing at will.

This supreme authority is exercised by Vatican dicasteries - such as the Congregation for the Doctrine of the Faith or the Bishops' and Clergy Dicastery - in order to maintain unity in doctrine and discipline. Progressive minded bishops or church leaders who want to break new ground locally often come up against limits. *When Rome slows down or sanctions reform approaches, this has far-reaching consequences*: On the one hand, committed believers at grassroots level feel offended. On the other hand, reform-oriented leaders in the church are also warned -

they feel that any unauthorized advances will be rejected by the Vatican in case of doubt.

A current example is Rome's handling of the German *Synodal Path* reform process. This wanted to establish a *Synodal Council* - a joint advisory and governing body of lay people and bishops. However, in January 2023, the Vatican issued a clear *stop signal* to this project: in a letter from the Secretariat of State - personally approved by the Pope - three curia cardinals declared that neither the Synodal Path nor the Conference of female, diverse and male Bishops were authorized to create such a body.

Rome thus once again showed the church base the *"stop sign"*.

Despite the disappointment, the reform forces are sticking to the project, but the word of power from Rome has made it clear how narrow the limits are for local structural reforms.

Individual *bishops with a progressive profile* also repeatedly came into conflict with Rome. One high-profile case was the Australian bishop *William Morris* (Toowoomba diocese): in 2006, he openly considered *ordaining married men or women* and examining the recognition of non-Catholic ordinations in a pastoral letter due to the shortage of priests. As a result, he was summoned by the Vatican - an apostolic visitation investigated him - and ultimately Pope Benedict XVI urged him to resign. Morris refused twice and was removed from office by Rome in 2011.

He subsequently complained about the lack of transparency and spoke of *"natural justice"* being denied, as he was never given access to the visitation report. This example spread the message among bishops worldwide: *anyone who proposes reforms too independently risks their position*. In retrospect, the same applies to the French bishop *Jacques Gaillot*, who Pope John Paul II unceremoniously dismissed in 1995 because of his liberal views (on homosexuality and priestly marriage, for example). Officially, other reasons were often put forward, while the actual motives - divergent doctrines or pastoral openings - remained unspoken.

Until recently, there was hardly any legal hearing or procedure for those affected in such cases: *"An orderly legal procedure through the courts is the absolute exception when bishops are removed from office,"* explains an ecclesiastical analysis - for a long time, canon law had *no specific procedure for removing* bishops *from office*. Pope Francis only introduced regulations for this in 2016. However, ecclesiastical discipline still often takes place *behind closed doors* and by decree from above.

This centralization is not only evident in individual cases, but also in the systematic filling of leadership positions. Particularly during the pontificate of John Paul II, a certain type of clergyman was deliberately promoted worldwide: *"obedient to the top and hard to the bottom"*, theologically loyal to the line and absolutely loyal to Rome, which is sometimes also referred to as Romanophile.

Local proposals or needs took a back seat - some male bishops sent by the Pope were not wanted by the people of the Church, as examples in Austria showed, where cathedral chapter proposals were ignored and ultra-conservative male candidates were pushed through instead.

This personnel policy was intended to ensure that *no "uncontrolled growth"* occurred in the dioceses, but that the Roman line was maintained everywhere. Especially in regions with strong progressive currents, Rome intervened with guidance: In Latin America, for example, *liberation theology* - a theology of the poor and social justice - was met with suspicion. *"In the land of liberation theology - which is frowned upon by Rome - the Pope has for some time been cleaning up just as systematically as in Europe,"* wrote Der *Spiegel* back in the 1980s.

In Brazil, for example, the moderate-conservative *Lucas Moreira Neves* was appointed primate, a cardinal who said of himself that he *"carries the flag of the Holy Father"*. Such actions clearly signaled: *Rome is watching over compliance with the line* - anyone who deviates too much will be shown the red card if necessary.

Bishops therefore only formulate vague positions between their own stance, the needs of the faithful and dismissal from office and have no effective or sustainable momentum. - And the fact that bishops vacillate between Rome, their own convictions and the expectations of the faithful - and thus often remain non-committal - is very familiar to many believers and observers.

Traditionally, bishops are *teachers of the faith, leaders of the diocese and shepherds for the faithful.* But if they have little room for maneuver, this claim becomes questionable. In many cases, they act more as *administrators of the status quo* than as drivers of change. If they are unable to make or defend decisions because Rome threatens to replace them (see, example, cases such as Bätzing, Heße, Franz-Josef Overbeck), they lose both *profile* and *trust.*

A new role for bishops as mediators of the concerns and needs of the faithful - that is an exciting and interesting comparison: women bishops as a kind of works council or ombudsman:

- **This person represents the interests of the faithful and employees** vis-à-vis **the management,**
- **is committed to co-determination and protection rights,**
- **can moderate and mediate conflicts.**

A bishop could - or should - *act as the mouthpiece of the faithful vis-à-vis Rome, address grievances, call for reforms* and *ensure a transparent, synodal approach.*

They could also - like an *ombudsperson - be a point of contact for the wounded, the doubtful and the marginalized,* especially for groups that are often overlooked or excluded in the church system (remarried divorcees, women and others).

This would require an *attitude of serving and protecting rather than correcting and disciplining.* For some bishops (e.g. *Stephan Ackermann, Heiner Wilmer*), this has already been a guiding principle - albeit often in the face of resistance.

If bishops today are hardly allowed to take on any real responsibility, the question arises: *Why these offices?* Alternative models would be:

- **Stronger synodal structures** in which lay people really have a say (not just "advise").
- **Eligibility of bishops** by the people of the Church.
- **Limited terms of office** and accountability.
- **Division of tasks**: theological teaching ministry - pastoral leadership - administrative management - could be placed in separate hands.

This perspective puts the role of bishops to the test. If they *do not (have to) see* themselves *as the mouthpiece of the people, but primarily as upholders of Roman discipline*, their ministry becomes not only unattractive, but also pastorally irrelevant. However, if bishops *act with and for the people of God*, their ministry could be revitalized - for example in the role *of bridge builders, advocates, protectors and fellow human beings* in the best sense. However, this would also require a fundamental change in the understanding of authority in the church.

This is because the effects of this centralized control are fatal for the momentum of reform. *Committed church people on the ground are discouraged.* If even bishops - the highest shepherds of a diocese - can be thwarted or dismissed when it comes to reform approaches, what does this mean for simpler pastors, theologians or lay people? Many prefer to avoid conflict so as not to jeopardize their position. Progressive ideas are then often no longer expressed out loud due to pressure of loyalty or resignation. Management personnel find themselves in internal conflicts: should they openly address the necessary changes, aware of the grievances - or should they remain silent so as not to risk the unit and their own career? Some try to mediate *between loyalty and truth*, but run the risk of being caught between two stools. The result is often a *culture of conformity*: for fear of sanctions, problems are sat out or discussed behind closed doors instead of being tackled courageously in the spirit of the Gospel. The trust of the faithful dwindles if they have the impression that *"Rome" decides everything anyway* and stifles local concerns. This creates a climate of stagnation that paralyzes the very *renewal* that many feel is overdue.

Church employment law: loyalty rules, culture of fear and exclusion

Parallel to hierarchical control by Rome, there is a second power factor in the church structure: church labor law and the associated *loyalty obligations*. In European countries such as Germany, Austria and Switzerland, the church is not only a religious community, but also a major employer. In Germany alone, around *800,000 people are employed* by the Catholic Church and Caritas - in schools, kindergartens, hospitals, administrations and parishes. These employees have traditionally been subject to special rules that no secular employer is likely to enforce in the same way.

Private lifestyle behavior became a possible reason for dismissal if it was not in line with the church's moral teachings. For example, *divorced people who remarried* despite a divorce, or employees living in a *same-sex marriage or partnership*, were regularly considered disloyal to the church's way of life until recently. The consequence could be dismissal without notice.

Even publicly entering into a registered civil partnership (*"marriage for all"*) was deemed - at least on paper - to be a breach of the duty of loyalty, which precludes continued employment.

In practice, this system of loyalty monitoring in personal life led to a widespread *culture of fear* among church employees - and was therefore reformed in parts.

Numerous examples have previously been made public: a church musician loses her job because she marries a new partner after getting divorced; a committed religious education teacher has his teaching license revoked because he comes out as gay; a long-time nursery school teacher has to leave because she leaves the church.

In many cases, those responsible acted with *a sense of proportion* or turned a blind eye - but the basic problem remained: *Employees had to deny part of their identity in* order not to jeopardize their professional existence. The *#OutInChurch* initiative at the beginning of 2022 made it clear just how acutely those affected experienced this. Over 100 queer (i.e. LGBTQIA+) church employees came out publicly and denounced discrimination in their own institution. Their manifesto states: *"Until now, many of us have not been able to openly deal with our gender identity and/or sexual orientation in our church profession or environment. There is a risk of consequences under employment law, including the destruction of our professional existence."* This has *"established a system of concealment, double standards and dishonesty"*, which creates *toxic effects*, shames people and makes them ill.

In other words, the church's demands for loyalty as an employer created a climate of fear in which open discussions about life plans, love and identity were taboo. Many felt compelled to lead a double life - outwardly maintaining the appearance of the norm, while inwardly or secretly living differently. This dichotomy fundamentally contradicts the church's claim to honesty and justice.

However, the church's employment law also specifically blocks *impulses for reform*. In an institution where employees must constantly fear being dismissed due to personal circumstances, a culture of free exchange or critical innovation can hardly flourish. *Progressive ideas* - such as a more open sexual morality, beneficial support for divorced remarried couples or a keen eye for diversity - often found no room internally because everyone was worried about offending others.

In addition, the church lost many capable people: people who actually wanted to work in the church ministry out of Christian motivation were excluded or left the system in frustration. An example from Switzerland shows how these mechanisms can affect even committed chaplains. In 2022, a Catholic hospital chaplain in Chur, *Veronika Jehle*, wrote an open letter to her bishop and resigned her church appointment - in protest against *"discriminatory employment conditions"*. She drew attention to the fact that *queer or remarried employees constantly* had to *fear for their jobs*.

Her move prompted 50 other chaplains to write a letter criticizing the *"perceived arbitrary"* personnel policy.

The case shows that even in the church's core task of pastoral care, qualified people are affected. The fear of a breach of loyalty means that the church *does not internally practice the very mercy and diversity that it preaches*.

Some regions have recognized that this hard line is untenable. In Austria, for example, loyalty rules have often been handled more leniently in practice; the Archdiocese of Vienna explains that a homosexual partnership or a second civil marriage *"does not in principle stand in the way"* of employment in most cases - much depends on individual solutions. However, this lack of clarity means that there is no documented right, but at best informal concessions - or not, depending on the management. In Germany, the pressure from *#OutInChurch* and the *Synodal Path* grew to such an extent that the bishops decided on a far-reaching *reform of the "Basic Order of Church Service"* at the end of 2022. The new basic text now explicitly states: *"Diversity in church institutions is an enrichment."* Discrimination against employees *"on the basis of origin, gender, religion, disability, age, sexual identity and lifestyle"* is prohibited.

This means that *a same-sex marriage or civil remarriage is no longer considered an automatic breach of loyalty,* and a private love life should no longer be grounds for dismissal. In future, it will be the positive basic attitude and identification with the values of the church that count most - not marital status or sexual orientation.

This paradigm shift was welcomed by many as *a "small revolution"* - triggered by clear words from those involved at grassroots level and a so-it-goes-no-further...

However, it has yet to be consistently implemented and so far only applies in Germany. In other countries, a comparable modernization of church employment law is still pending in some cases. Nevertheless, the example shows that *change is possible* if public pressure and the internal will to reform are great enough.

Interaction: Centralism and constraints reinforce each other

Looking at the two problem areas described above - Roman centralism and rigid labor law - it becomes clear that they *support each other in* an ominous way. The lack of *subsidiary authority*, i.e. the decision-making competence of the lower levels, is closely linked to the *coercive corset of personnel law*, which is intended to ensure line loyalty at all levels.

Viewed from the top down: The Vatican's controlling authorities promote an atmosphere in which unity and obedience have the highest priority. Progressive outliers should not be allowed to emerge in the first place. This attitude is inevitably reflected in the loyalty requirements for employees. Bishops, who are themselves under the strict eye of Rome, pass on the pressure downwards: they also expect absolute loyalty from their priests and lay employees. In this way, the church's working norms ultimately serve as a *tool of ecclesiastical authority* to ensure a homogeneous appearance. For example, if a male bishop inwardly sympathizes with reform ideas but knows that Rome is critical of them, he may still cling to traditional rules of loyalty in order to *avoid being targeted himself*. The system is built in such a way that *no one steps out of line* - from the curia to the pastoral workers.

The mechanism works in the same way *from the bottom up*: a working environment in which deviation is sanctioned creates conformist employees. Understandably, they are not inclined to take criticism or innovative suggestions to the top. In an organization where many are afraid for their jobs, uncomfortable truths rarely come to the table. This means that the feedback from the grassroots and from the middle level to the bishops or to Rome is filtered - it reflects the desired state rather than the reality. This *fair-weather echo* can reinforce those responsible in Rome that their course is correctly understood and followed. *Dissenters are weeded out* before they can even gain any weight. This is how the dynamic builds up: central pressure creates compliant structures, which in turn do little to counter the central pressure.

In addition, *progressive forces lose influence through both mechanisms*. If an open-minded female theologian loses her job or a reform-minded male priest is not given any responsibility at all, then these voices are absent from the deliberations and decisions. The church leadership is then often surrounded by people who support the system or at least do not openly question it. This applies to the selection of bishops themselves: As mentioned, in recent decades, candidates loyal to Rome have been favored above all.

In turn, their decisions shape local theology and personnel policy. Der *Spiegel* wrote pointedly that the head shepherds sponsored by the Vatican decide *"who teaches theology at universities, church colleges and schools"* and thus determine the level of beliefs - and that they are "also important employers in other respects", with *many thousands of jobs* in every country *depending on the bishops*.

This illustrates the *concentration of power* that exists: The personal sovereignty of the bishops - controlled by Rome - simultaneously influences science, doctrine and the existential livelihoods of many church employees. If this sovereignty is exercised in the sense of preservation rather than renewal, the status quo is consolidated.

Figure 44: Clerics ready to reform.

A humorous cartoon shows a group of clergymembers from the Catholic Church standing in a circle with their backs around a sign that reads 'Gestaltungsbereitschaft'. Each of them points to someone else with one hand and avoids eye contact to make it clear that no one wants to take the initiative, responsibility and willingness to shape, take over and implement. It ironically shows how group dynamics shift responsibility and how no one wants to be willing to change.

The *psychological effect* of this reinforcing structure should not be underestimated. It creates a feeling of powerlessness in many believers: *"There's nothing we can do"*. Those who nevertheless remain committed often do so with dampened enthusiasm or look for niches in which at least small changes are possible. But truly ground-breaking reforms - for example on controversial issues such as the role of women, sexual morality or the distribution of power - hardly make any progress in this way. On the contrary, a *vicious circle* sometimes emerges: centralism promotes fear and conformity; conformity in turn confirms centralism and makes it appear even more unchallenged. Breaking out of this spiral requires conscious decisions on several levels in order to break the cycle.

Towards subsidiarity, the rule of law and diversity: paths to a credible church

In view of this analysis, it is clear that *both Vatican central control and discriminatory church employment law must be fundamentally changed* if the Catholic Church is to remain sustainable. What is needed is an institutional *conversion* in the spirit of the Gospel - away from a climate of control and fear towards a culture of trust, justice and dialog. Concrete starting points for this are already emerging and are being called for in many places.

1. more subsidiary authority and decentralization: The Catholic Church has long held the principle of *subsidiarity* in its social doctrine - the idea that decisions should be made as far down as possible . What is successfully practiced in politics and society should finally also apply within the Church.

At the beginning of his pontificate, Pope Francis himself spoke of a *"salutary decentralization"*. In his letter *Evangelii Gaudium* (2013), he suggested that the Conference of female, diverse and male Bishops should be granted *"a certain doctrinal authority of their own"* - which would mean a clear step towards regional decision-making authority. Francis also emphasized that the Roman dicasteries must be at the *service* of the bishops and local churches, not the other way around.

This vision must now be implemented consistently. In concrete terms, this could mean *strengthening synodal structures* at local and national level that can actually make binding decisions. A world synod (such as the one currently being held in Rome in 2023/24 on the topic of synodality) is valuable, but *regional synods* that are close to the problems of the faithful are just as important. If - as in the German synodal path - a country develops concrete reforms, Rome should facilitate their implementation instead of putting the brakes on them across the board. The principle of subsidiarity requires trust: Trust that the Holy Spirit is not only at work in Rome, but also in the *local churches*.

Many issues could then *be decided where they arise*: for example, how to deal with remarried divorcees, weddings for queer couples, the role of lay people in church leadership or the selection of suitable candidates for the office of bishop.

Of course, there is still a need for unity in the essential matters of faith - but diversity should be possible within this framework. A *learning church* would try out which pastoral solutions work in different cultures and contexts instead of standardizing everything centrally. Subsidiary authority also means strengthening *the collegiality of bishops*. The Second Vatican Council emphasized the communion of all bishops with the Pope (*Lumen Gentium*, 1964). Following on from this, the universal church could make more collective decisions instead of leaving decisions solely to the pope or individual dicasteries. A start would be to make appointments as bishops more transparent and to involve the faithful - because currently *"the faithful feel ignored"* when the Pope alone *"freely appoints"* bishops.

Historically, there were various forms of participation; these could be revived to ensure that bishops enjoy the trust of their people and are not merely perceived as emissaries of Rome.

2. more constitutional procedures and cultural change in church leadership: One aspect that is often overlooked is that the church needs *fairer, constitutional structures* within it. The term may sound unfamiliar, as the church is not a state - but it is about principles such as transparency, consultation, clear rules and independent control of decisions. As we have seen, bishops and theologians were sometimes sanctioned without an open procedure. *"Neither the Pope nor the Vatican justify their actions publicly,"* noted a Catholic portal, and the criteria often remain in the dark: *This is incompliant.* Here, the Church must measure itself against its own standards: it rightly demands justice and rights for all people - then it should also apply these values internally. In concrete terms, this could mean that in the event of conflicts or accusations*, orderly church court proceedings* take place in which those affected can defend themselves, instead of administrative decrees without justification. Pope Francis' move to create a procedure for the dismissal of bishops with *"Come una madre amorevole"* (2016) was a start. However, *clarification and appeal procedures* should also be standard below this, for example in the case of the withdrawal of teaching licenses, transfers or dismissals. An independent ombudsman's office for church employees could help to prevent arbitrariness.

A *change in mentality* is also important: away from a culture of obedience and towards a *culture of dialog*. When church authorities (have to) make decisions, they should seek dialog - with experts, with those involved, with the people of the church. A bishop who comes into conflict with a parish, for example, should not reflexively take action, but instead rely on synodal consultation. This *joint approach* (*syn-odos* in Greek) can help to ensure that decisions are comprehensible and fair. Sensitive issues in particular - such as doctrinal questions relating to new scientific findings - should be legitimized more broadly *by advisory bodies* instead of being decided in isolated rounds of curiae. This would turn top-down control into *communication at eye level*, which no longer has to enforce loyalty, but gains it through conviction and participation.

3. non-discriminatory personnel policy and fear-free cooperation: The reform of church employment law in Germany shows where the journey must go: towards a personnel policy that *welcomes all people of good will* and values their diversity. What use is it to the church if it loses highly qualified teachers, doctors, social workers or administrative specialists simply because their private family life does not correspond to the ideal? In future, *professional competence and loyalty to the community of service in the spirit of the Gospel* should count - not conformity with every moral detail. The new German constitution puts it this way: *"All employees can be representatives of God's unconditional love [...] regardless of [...] their sexual identity and lifestyle."*

This principle deserves worldwide application in the church. A *church without fear*, as #OutInChurch demands, would assure its employees that no one is discriminated against on the basis of their person. This specifically includes the explicit inclusion of previously disadvantaged groups: *LGBTIQIA+ people* should not only be tolerated in the church, but actively encouraged, provided they have the skills for their ministry. The same applies to remarried divorcees or non-denominational employees - wherever it serves the mission, the church should also welcome "lateral entrants" instead of limiting itself.

Figure 45: Decentralized structure of local churches.

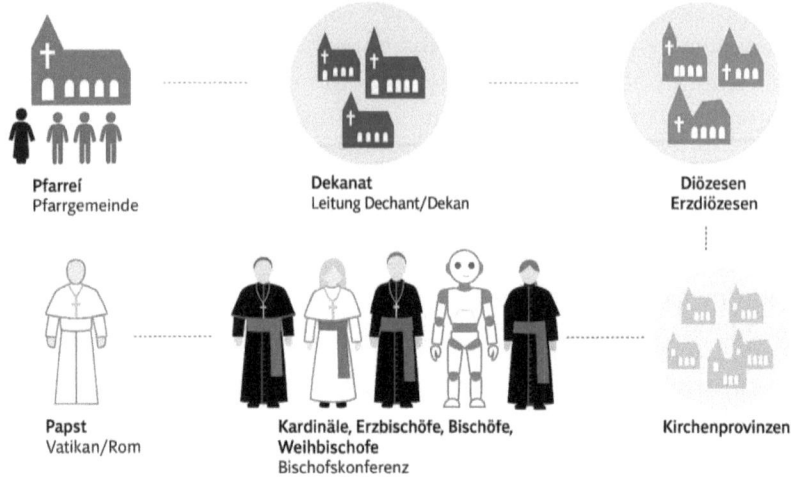

Pfarreí
Pfarrgemeinde

Dekanat
Leitung Dechant/Dekan

Diözesen
Erzdiözesen

Papst
Vatikan/Rom

Kardinäle, Erzbischöfe, Bischöfe,
Weihbischofe
Bischofskonferenz

Kirchenprovinzen

Illustration of the church hierarchy with current expansion: from the parish to the deanery to dioceses and church provinces - supplemented by a modernized Conference of female, diverse and male Bishops with cardinals, archbishops, a woman bishop in a white robe and a humanoid - the Deus Ex Machina. The image plays with the idea of diversity and possible contemporary scenarios of church leadership structures in a humorous and innovative way. Ideal for illustrating internal church organization, management channels and decision-making structures within the Catholic Church.

Such an opening not only increases justice, but also the *credibility* of the church. If the message is that God loves every person unconditionally, this must be reflected in the actions of the church. How could the church credibly proclaim charity and human dignity if, at the same time, deserving employees are dismissed because of their love for one another? Turning away from a culture of fear towards a culture of trust would unleash enormous forces: Employees could openly contribute their talents and ideas without having to pretend. Creative pastoral initiatives - such as new wedding ceremonies, innovative educational programs, inclusive parish festivals - could be tried out without fear. The *culture of discussion* within the church would also benefit if no one had to fear being sanctioned for making an unconventional statement. A diverse workforce brings in a variety of perspectives, which increases the organization's ability to solve problems.

In summary, the demands for *the decentralization of power* and *the reduction of employee anxiety* reinforce each other positively: *if Rome trusts the local churches more, they can go their own way and relax rigid regulations.* This creates a more open climate locally, which in turn allows problems to be reported honestly to the top and reforms to be initiated. In a way, the church would be turned on its head: The focus would no longer be primarily on *control* and *adherence to the law*, but on *trust* and *truthfulness*. This is exactly what a credible church needs today.

For a more credible, just and dialog-capable church

The changes described are not a simple adaptation, but require *courage for genuine reform*. However, they are essential if the Catholic Church wants to fulfill its mission in the 21st century. A church that is only ever controlled from above and cultivates internal fear instead of openness runs the risk of *betraying its message*. For the Gospel calls for truth and freedom for the children of God. If church actors - whether bishops or laypeople - have to remain silent for fear of punishment, this truth is suppressed. When people are excluded because of their identity, the liberating message is obscured.

The good news is that there is already movement. With his worldwide synodality, Pope Francis has initiated a process that aims to *rethink* the church *from the perspective of listening*. In many countries, believers and theologians are calling loudly for change - and are meeting with increasing understanding, including from parts of the hierarchy. Reform groups such as *We are Church* or *the Synodal Way* are putting forward concrete proposals on how power can be shared, how women can be involved and how sexual morality can be lived in a contemporary way. It is important not to nip these new departures in the bud, but to allow and even encourage them.

The *vision of a more credible church* is tangible: a church that admits mistakes and learns from them instead of silencing critics; that sees internal *diversity* not as a threat but as an asset; that invites rather than excludes. Such a church would be *fairer* because it treats every member with respect and does not discriminate against anyone. It *would be more open to dialog* because it can enter into conversation with the modern world without fear - and also conduct its own internal debate without fear. And it would ultimately be *more credible* because its actions would then be in line with Jesus' claim: *"Do not be afraid!"* - and *"love one another as I have loved you."*

In order to get there, the structural blockades described above must fall. *Rome must give the local churches room to breathe*, and the Church as an employer must give its employees room to live. Subsidiarity and a willingness to serve instead of control, legal fairness instead of arbitrariness, appreciation instead of fear - this will be the measure of whether the Church really arrives in the third millennium. Only in such a renewed atmosphere will progressive forces no longer be discouraged, but encouraged to reform the church in the spirit of the Gospel. For reform is not a luxury, but an integral part of a living church. The Second Vatican Council already reminded us that the Church must *"semper reformanda"* - always renew itself. This promise must now be kept by loosening the self-imposed shackles. The faithful at grassroots level, but also many church employees and, not least, countless people outside the church are waiting for it to undergo a credible transformation. The implementation of *subsidiarity and a humane personnel policy* is not a private matter within the church, but is of great public interest. It also determines whether the voice of the church is still heard in social debates - as a voice that credibly stands up for human dignity, justice and truth because it puts these values into practice *within its own ranks*.

Only with such a double course correction - *less fear, more trust* - can the Catholic Church find its way out of the current crisis of confidence. It is about nothing less than a cultural change. But this change is possible if enough people work on it with conviction. The discouraged progressive actors of today could thus become the *innovators of tomorrow* - in a church that finally gives them the space not to be torn *between loyalty and truth*, but to reconcile the two. The time is ripe for this. The Church must now have the courage to reform itself - for the sake of the people and its own mission. Only then will it truly be able to be the *witness of Christ* that it claims to be: *free, just and fearless in the service of love*.

🫶Bishops' briefing:

This religious policy field examines the structural obstacles to reform within the Roman Catholic Church. It identifies Vatican centralism and ecclesiastical labor law, with its loyalty requirements, as key factors promoting a culture of fear and conformity. It analyzes that these two factors reinforce each other by discouraging progressive bishops and employees and preventing the implementation of necessary changes. The solution envisaged is greater subsidiarity, more constitutional procedures and a non-discriminatory personnel policy to make the church more credible and sustainable.

Didactic questions:

160 - How do Vatican control and church labor law hinder reforms in the Catholic Church?

The reform efforts of progressive forces in the Roman Catholic Church are hampered by two main factors: Firstly, the Roman dicasteries (Vatican authorities) act as strict controlling bodies over local churches and bishops. This centralization of power means that local attempts at reform are often thwarted or sanctioned by the Vatican, as the example of the German Synodal Path or the dismissal of bishops such as *William Morris* or *Jacques Gaillot* shows. Secondly, church labor law with its loyalty requirements has a disciplinary effect on employees. This law, which traditionally regarded private lifestyle (e.g. marital status, sexual orientation) as grounds for dismissal, created a culture of fear among employees. The two factors intertwine: centralism from above forces conformity at all levels, while the culture of fear from below suppresses progressive ideas, as employees shy away from conflict in order not to jeopardize their jobs. This leads to stagnation and discourages both believers and church leaders.

161 - How does Rome exercise control over local churches and bishops?

According to current canon law, the pope has supreme authority and can in practice appoint or dismiss bishops, often without formal procedures. This power is exercised by Vatican dicasteries in order to maintain unity in doctrine and discipline. If progressive bishops or national churches (such as the German Synodal Way) propose reforms that deviate from the Roman line, the Vatican intervenes. This can take the form of direct instructions, rejection of proposals or even the dismissal of bishops who are considered too independent or liberal. The personnel policy during the pontificates of John Paul II and Benedict XVI, for example, was aimed at appointing bishops who were considered loyal to Rome and tended to suppress local needs or progressive currents. This approach signals to other bishops that independent approaches to reform are risky and can jeopardize their position.

162 - What impact does Roman control have on reform-minded bishops and the faithful?

Reform-minded bishops often find themselves in a conflict of loyalty between the expectations of Rome, their own convictions and the needs of their faithful. As they are granted little room for maneuver and have to fear dismissal, they often remain vague in their statements and decisions. This weakens their profile and their trust among the faithful. They act more as administrators of the status quo than as drivers of change. Committed believers at the grassroots level feel offended when their concerns and reform proposals are stifled by Rome. The experience that even high church offices are thwarted in reform efforts also discourages simpler pastors and laypeople from expressing progressive ideas out loud for fear of sanctions or resignation.

163 - How could the role of the clergy be strengthened and changed to better serve the needs of the faithful?

The current role of the clergy as the primary guardians of Roman discipline is being called into question. A possible redefinition of their role would be that of a mouthpiece for the faithful vis-à-vis Rome, comparable to a works council or an ombudsperson. They could represent the interests of the faithful, campaign for co-determination and protection rights and moderate conflicts. They could also be a point of contact for the marginalized and excluded. This would require an attitude of serving and protecting rather than correcting and disciplining. Alternatives to the current structure could include stronger synodal structures in which lay people have a real say, the electability of bishops by the people of the church, limited terms of office and accountability, and a division of tasks (magisterium, pastoral leadership, administration). Such a reorientation would revitalize the office of bishop and make it more pastorally relevant.

164 - What role do loyalty requirements play in church labor law and what consequences do they have?

Church labor law in many countries (such as Germany before the reform) traditionally required employees to conduct their private lives in accordance with the church's moral teachings. This meant that, for example, remarried divorcees or people in same-sex partnerships were considered disloyal and could be dismissed. This system led to a widespread culture of fear in which employees were forced to deny part of their identity in order not to lose their job. The #OutInChurch initiative publicized discrimination against LGBTQIA+ people in church jobs. The demands for loyalty created a climate of secrecy and double standards that prevented open conversations about life choices and affected mental health. It also blocked impulses for reform, as employees did not express critical ideas for fear of consequences.

165 - What concrete steps are necessary to make the church more credible and just?

Fundamental changes are necessary for a sustainable Catholic Church. Firstly, more subsidiary authority and decentralization are needed: decisions should be made as far as possible at local level, which means strengthening synodal structures at local and national level and the collegiality of bishops with the Pope. Secondly, more constitutional procedures and a cultural change in church leadership are required: transparency, consultation and clear rules for decisions as well as the implementation of fair ecclesiastical judicial procedures instead of administrative decrees are crucial. This would replace a culture of obedience with a culture of dialog. Thirdly, a non-discriminatory personnel policy and a fear-free workforce are necessary. Reforms such as those in Germany, which prohibit discrimination on the basis of sexual identity or lifestyle and value employee diversity, should be implemented worldwide. This would create a culture of trust in which talents and ideas can be openly contributed.

166 - To what extent do centralism and rigid labor law reinforce each other?

Roman centralism and rigid labor law are mutually supportive. Vatican control fosters an atmosphere of obedience, which is reflected in the loyalty demands placed on employees. Bishops, who are themselves under Roman supervision, pass on the pressure downwards and expect absolute loyalty from their employees. Labor law thus serves as a tool to ensure line loyalty at all levels. Conversely, a working environment in which deviation is sanctioned creates conformist employees who rarely bring criticism or innovative suggestions to the top. Feedback from the rank and file is filtered and tends to reflect the desired state of affairs, which can confirm those responsible in Rome in their course. This system of mutual reinforcement leads to progressive forces losing influence and the church remaining in a culture of adaptation and stagnation.

167 - What does a more credible church mean in terms of the Gospel?

A more credible church in the spirit of the Gospel means turning away from control and fear towards trust, justice and dialog. It admits mistakes, learns from them and sees internal diversity as a wealth. It invites rather than excludes and treats every member with respect. Such a church would be fairer because it does not discriminate against anyone and realizes human dignity within its own ranks. It would be more open to dialog because it would be able to enter into conversation with both the modern world and internally without fear. Ultimately, would be more credible because its actions are in line with the message of Jesus: not to be afraid and to love one another. Removing structural blockages through subsidiarity and a humane personnel policy is not just an internal matter, but is crucial to whether the church is perceived in society as a voice for human dignity, justice and truth.

Essay questions:

Please answer one of the following questions in the form of an essay:

a) Analyze in detail how Vatican centralization and ecclesiastical labor laws promote a culture of fear within the Catholic Church and what specific effects this has on reform efforts.

b) Discuss the potential and challenges of a stronger application of the principle of subsidiarity in the Catholic Church. Which specific areas could particularly benefit from this and what risks could arise?

c) Assess the significance of the recent reforms of church labor law in Germany in the context of emerging problems. To what extent do these reforms represent a "small revolution" and what hurdles might exist in their implementation and global dissemination?

d) Discuss the proposed alternative models for the role of bishops and synodal structures. What advantages and disadvantages would these models have with regard to the problems of centralism and lack of participation?

e) Make the connection between the structural problems (centralism, labor law) and the credibility crisis of the Catholic Church. How could changes contribute to a more credible, just and dialog-capable church?

Religious policy field analysis 21:
An outlook: Need for reform in church labor law, Dogmatism and distribution of power in leadership culture

The Catholic Church is facing profound challenges in the middle of Europe and worldwide. On the one hand, *discrimination is* still being discussed in church employment law - for example against queer employees, remarried divorcees or employees without a Catholic denomination. On the other hand, leadership culture and personnel management suffer from a *structural reform backlog*: although there is a lot of talk about *synodality* and *participatory leadership*, in reality, power often remains concentrated in the hands of a few clerics. This leads to a loyalty rift among progressive bishops, who have to mediate between Roman norms and the pastoral reality on the ground. At the same time, it is becoming increasingly clear that the Church needs genuine *safe spaces for innovation* - spaces in which new pastoral approaches, forms of liturgy and models of participation can be tried out without sanctions and fear of repression. *Why are such reforms and safe spaces necessary? What structural freedoms, legal safeguards and collegial backing are needed to ensure that the church remains fit for the future*

Between discrimination and innovation: From exclusion to diversity in church labor law

For a long time, church labor law in the Catholic Church allowed far-reaching intrusions into the private lives of employees. *Homosexuality, divorce and remarriage* were considered a breach of loyalty - anyone who openly lived in a same-sex partnership or remarried in a civil partnership after a divorce had to fear losing their church job.

Figure 46: Public pressure from church-related reform movements such as Maria 2.0.

Symbolic poster of the Maria 2.0 reform movement: a stylized female figure with a halo, speaking through a megaphone - crowned by a star, with the inscription Maria 2.0. The image combines religious iconography with feminist protest aesthetics and stands for the commitment of Catholic women to equal rights, access to church offices and structural change in the church. Ideal for visualizing the church on the move, women's power in faith and the call for reform.

It was only under external and internal pressure that a rethink took place: In November 2022, the bishops agreed on a new version of the basic order of church service - a *paradigm shift* in church employment law.

In future, the private lives of *female employees* will *"no longer play a role"*. *This means that relationships, intimate lifestyles and marital status are part of the inviolable core area of privacy and are henceforth beyond the control of the church employer. In plain language, it may no longer constitute* grounds for dismissal *if, for example, a* pastoral worker *is in a homosexual partnership or a doctor in a Catholic hospital has remarried after a divorce.*

The church respects the AGG - the General Equal Treatment Act in Germany with all its criteria and target groups: Diversity is expressly recognized as an enrichment - all employees, regardless of religion, origin, disability, gender, sexual identity and lifestyle, should now be able to be *representatives* of God's love.

This reform was long overdue and is an important step against discrimination. However, so far it is only a matter of *diocesan law in Germany*. Critics note that it is "at most a partial success" - for example because the specific implementation and interpretation are still unclear and comparable changes are still pending in other countries (such as Austria or Switzerland). In addition, there remains an area of tension: the church's right to self-determination has often clashed with state anti-discrimination law in the past. One legal scholar has already stated that the times in which special church rights were valued more highly than basic employee rights are over.

This clearly shows the *need for structural reform*: the church must align its employment law in such a way that it is in line with general human rights and effectively excludes discrimination - and not just after public pressure becomes unbearably high, but out of inner conviction.

Another aspect is the *divided loyalties* of progressive church leaders in this area. A bishop who wants to treat all employees equally, regardless of their lifestyle, is faced with Roman guidelines that still do not recognize homosexual partnerships and until recently demanded a strict line. In 2021, for example, Pope Francis' Vatican reaffirmed that the Church has no authority to bless same-sex unions - a slap in the face for many pastors and believers on the ground. Some *open-minded bishops* reacted to this with clear unease: the Belgian Bishop of Antwerp, for example, publicly apologized to homosexual believers for this ban. Others, such as the Archbishop of Berlin, *Heiner Koch*, asked for forgiveness for discrimination on the basis of sexual orientation in a church service.

Such voices show the pastoral *sense of reality* of some bishops who feel that exclusion contradicts the Gospel and isolates the church socially. There is a need for dogmatic reform here. However, the clergy operate within a narrow corridor: *Roman normative expectations* continue to officially bind them to traditional doctrine. This conflict of loyalties can only be resolved if the Roman Catholic world church itself changes its stance on dogma - or at least if there is sufficient *collegial backing for decentralized responsibility* to take locally progressive paths - without being branded as "disloyal".

Leadership culture and participation: symbolism or genuine participation?

While at least the first steps have been taken in labor law, the *distribution of power in church leadership* remains a sore point. Officially, since the Second Vatican Council, the Church has emphasized the co-responsibility of all believers and - not least under Pope Francis - the importance of *synodality*, i.e. a common path of laity and clergy. In practice, however, church leadership often still functions according to the old *feudal-hierarchical model*: at the top of the diocese, the bishop has almost unrestricted decision-making powers, and at parish level, the pastor has extensive powers. One insider describes it like this: *"Most of the decisions still boil down to the sole and little-controlled decision-making authority of the feudal episcopal office at diocesan level and the decision of the clergyman, who has immense power, at local level".* In other words, despite pastoral councils, parish councils and associations, genuine grassroots *participation in decision-making* is often not permitted or remains ineffective. Even where committees exist, they usually only have an advisory function and can be overruled or ignored by the minister.

Archbishop Koch, for example, said in 2022 that there was a considerable need for reform: *more people with specialist knowledge need to be involved in decisions - but this will only work if those in positions of responsibility are willing to give up and share power.* This clearly addresses what is still lacking in many places: a *culture of sharing responsibility.*

In some dioceses, there have been and still are attempts to put this culture into practice. The example of the diocese of *St. Gallen in Switzerland* stands out in particular. Bishop *Markus Büchel* implemented a model there years ago in which *teams of pastors* jointly lead parishes. An entire pastoral care team takes on the organization, distributes tasks and even elects a team leader from its own ranks - the pastor is primarily there for the sacraments and does what, according to church law, only a priest can do. In fact, in some places, priests work "under" the leadership of laypeople instead of being at the helm alone.

This model developed as a pragmatic response to the shortage of priests and as an expression of a new leadership culture. However, it came under fire in 2020 when the Vatican published an instruction that upheld the traditional idea that only a priest could exercise ultimate leadership. Many German-speaking bishops - not only Büchel, but also the chairman of the Swiss Conference of female, diverse and male Bishops, *Felix Gmür* (Basel) - rejected the instruction and called it *"theologically deficient and clericalistically narrow"*. The diocese of St. Gallen made it clear that it is sticking to its team model. Sometimes you have to make an announcement with a megaphone!

This example illustrates the *tension between the center and the periphery*: a local church creates innovative forms of participatory leadership that contradict the Roman norm. However, as long as universal church law is not adapted, such models remain in a gray area - they are dependent on the goodwill of the respective bishop and could be thwarted at any time by Roman intervention.

There is also a desire for greater participation in *Austria*. As early as 2011, the *Pastors' Initiative*, an association of hundreds of pastors, published a *"call to disobedience"* in which they demanded reforms such as the admission of women and married people to ordained ministries, active co-decision-making by congregations and open communion practices. Since then, many of these priests have practiced pastoral solutions locally that are not officially permitted (for example, the blessing of remarried divorcees or inviting non-denominational Christians to communion in individual cases). The fact that this initiative still exists today and that there has been no mass exodus of these priests from the ministry shows that there are *gray areas* in the church where reform concerns are tolerated as long as they are not lived in an openly confrontational manner. However, this is not a truly transparent, recognized form of *power-sharing* - it is more of a (semi-tolerated) state of permanent provisionality. Clear regulations are needed here that recognize *participatory church leadership* not as an exception or rule-breaker, but as a legitimate variant of church organization.

Overall, it is clear that the church urgently needs to develop structures in which *participation is more than just a fig leaf*. As long as crucial questions of power (such as the appointment of leadership positions, the use of financial resources or the direction of pastoral work) are decided solely from above, lay participation will remain unsatisfactory. This frustrates committed Christians, discourages young, talented employees and cements a system that is often *overwhelmed*: "*Both bishops and pastors are hopelessly overwhelmed. How could they not be, given the challenges?*" - This is how *Clemens Grünebach*, head of a pastoral area, describes the overload caused by concentrated power. He also states that even where parish councils have a say, they are often so preoccupied with their own steeples that they find it difficult to release resources for innovative new beginnings.

This is where the circle closes: without new structures, both clergy and laity will remain trapped in old ways of thinking. *Structural reform* in leadership therefore means two things: on the one hand, readjusting the balance of power between ministers and the faithful (keyword: *separation of powers in the church*), and on the other hand, promoting a rethink within the existing committee culture so that it is not only administered but also shaped. This is the only way to turn symbolic participation into genuine participation.

Experimental pastoral care: the need for genuine safe spaces for innovation

In view of the church's declining powers of retention - members are leaving in droves, young people are staying away - there is a growing realization that *innovation* is needed to keep the Christian faith alive in today's society. New pastoral approaches, fresh liturgical forms of expression and bold projects that appeal to people beyond the "classic target group" are urgently needed.

But this is exactly where the cat bites its tail: those who want to try out new things often encounter mistrust, controlling attitudes or even sanctions within the church institution. *Safe spaces for innovation* are therefore essential - protected places and contexts in which experiments are allowed, mistakes can be made and from which positive impulses can fertilize the entire church.

What exactly is meant by such safe spaces? First of all, it is about a *mental change*: away from a "culture of fear" and towards a culture of encouragement. In the past, deviation was often seen as a danger that needed to be stopped - think of the warnings issued to creative theologians or the strict visitations of unconventional religious communities. Employees therefore rightly demanded: "We must finally put an end to a *church of fear*".

A safe space would mean that *innovators* - be they bishops, priests, religious or lay people - receive backing when they break new ground in a well-founded way. This support can be formal or informal. Formally, for example, a Conference of female, diverse and male Bishops could explicitly approve pilot projects or the Vatican could grant temporary and localized dispensations for certain reform attempts. Informally, it can mean that superiors remain silent or do not sanction a local pastoral experiment that does not (yet) correspond to the official line, but is obviously good for the people.

Recent German church history provides another vivid example: After Rome issued a blanket *"no"* to the marriage of same-sex couples in 2021, pastors did not simply let this go. Under the motto *#Liebegewinnt*, celebratory services were held in more than 100 Catholic churches for all loving couples - explicitly including queer couples.

The reaction of the bishops was remarkable: *no German diocesan bishop took disciplinary action*, no one forbade their priests to take part. On the contrary, nothing was heard from official bodies at first. "The German bishops [have] announced that they will not intervene, and nothing has yet been heard from the Vatican either", as was reported in May 2021. This de facto toleration continued; the following year, Auxiliary Bishop *Ludger Schepers* (Essen) was the first bishop to personally attend a ceremony for queer couples. This revealed a de facto safe space: many of those involved, including parts of the Conference of female, diverse and male Bishops, were obviously convinced that this form of *pastoral innovation* was necessary and good - and they protected the actors by refraining from sanctioning them. The benefit was twofold: on the one hand, the faithful from the LGBTQIA+ community experienced appreciation and blessing; on the other, the institution of the church learned that the sky does not fall when you break new ground. The *Flemish bishops in Belgium* acted with similar courage, becoming the first Conference of female, diverse and male Bishops worldwide to implement an official liturgical blessing for same-sex married couples in 2022 - despite the Roman line to the contrary. They were also able to build on collegial unity and thus create a collective safe space: the pressure is spread across many shoulders and an individual "dissenter" is not isolated.

However, safe spaces for innovation are not only needed in the area of sexual morality. *New forms of pastoral care* concern, for example, liturgy (experimental worship formats, more inclusive language, lay sermons), church organization (such as grassroots house churches, digital forms of community) or socio-diaconal projects on the margins of society. In Latin America, for example, the *Comunidades Eclesiales de Base* (grassroots *communities*) have emerged since the 1960s, where lay people gather in small communities, share the word of God and combine social commitment with faith. These *grassroots communities* became the nuclei of a popular church and produced many charismatic leaders. However, they were also subject to suspicion in some places - conservative forces saw them as "radical cells" and the Vatican leadership under Pope John Paul II and Benedict XVI was suspicious of elements of *liberation theology*. Some theologians (such as *Leonardo Boff* in Brazil) were sanctioned, which had a repercussive effect on the grassroots movement. This clearly shows that without a safe space, innovative new beginnings are in danger of being nipped in the bud. At the same time, the example of Latin America shows that innovation can take root where there is great need - for example due to a shortage of priests in large regions. The 2019 Amazon Synod took up the idea of ordaining tried and tested married fathers as priests in order to make the Eucharist possible in remote communities.

Many of the region's faithful and bishops were behind it. But in the end, there was no clear yes from Rome - the decision was postponed for fear of breaking with tradition. This shows that even when a local church urgently needs new paths, it reaches its limits without a safe space. In this case, *protecting innovation* means courageously enduring the fact that new things are ventured in certain regions or projects without immediately being the norm for the entire global church. Such temporally or locally limited experiments could be anchored in canon law, for example as "pastoral experiments" that are monitored and later evaluated. Otherwise, delayed innovation could cause an unrealistic ivory tower to topple at some point. Some people in the Catholic Church already see such a "tipping point" - the straw that breaks the camel's back.

Clemens Grünebach puts it in a nutshell: *"We need protected places and spaces for all people, initiatives and projects that stand for the arrival of the church in the 21st century and reach out to people who do not belong to the traditional target group".* These *protected places* must be actively facilitated by those responsible for leadership - bishops and pastors should therefore consciously create open spaces, provide resources and draw a *protective fence* around innovative projects so that they can grow. Today, such projects often only exist for a limited period of time with project funding and are on the verge of being discontinued at the end of the funding period. Here, for example, it would be necessary to demand that diocesan budgets provide a fixed percentage for experimental pastoral work that is not immediately withdrawn when things get tight. *Legal security* also means that employees working in innovation projects need reliable protection against dismissal and career prospects to make their commitment worthwhile. If an innovative idea fails, this should not automatically mean the end of the career of the person responsible - a culture of error is required. Collegial support can also mean, for example, that the German Conference of female, diverse and male Bishops or regional bishops' assemblies step in to protect if a bishop comes under fire because of an experiment. Especially in the universal church, it is often the case that reformist bishops are isolated. However, when an entire Conference of female, diverse and male Bishops is behind an experiment (as in the case of the blessings in Belgium mentioned above), it is more difficult to make an example from above. *But how far has the church come when local congregations have to be protected from themselves - shelters become necessary?*

Shelters for innovation are ultimately not a luxury, but essential for the survival of the church. Without them, Grünebach warns, the "quiet but highly dangerous collapse of the church will continue to accelerate". With them, on the other hand, the church can regain lost trust because it shows that it is capable of learning and change. The point is not to abandon the treasure of tradition, but to make it creatively fruitful for the present - in service to people, especially those who have not had a voice in the past.

"Ecclesia semper reformanda" - the church needs the courage to change

The outlook discussion on church labor law, leadership culture and innovative freedom shows: The Catholic Church finds itself, as always and for too long, in a *field of tension between tradition and new beginnings*. On the one hand, core messages and basic values remain stable; on the other hand, a rapidly changing society demands answers that often lie outside of familiar patterns. *Ecclesia semper reformanda est* - the church must always reform itself - this motto is perhaps truer today than ever before.

Structural reform needs are not academic luxury problems, but affect people's lives in a concrete way: A religious education teacher who is happy in a new marriage after a divorce should be allowed to continue working at a Catholic school without fear. A gay pastor should not have to hide his partner, but should be treated with the same respect as any other person - and this also applies to his heterosexual colleagues. A committed female parish worker should experience that her voice carries weight in the parish team and does not bounce off patriarchal power structures. And believers at grassroots level should feel that *their* church recognizes the signs of the times and dares to find new ways to keep the faith alive.

The examples from Germany, Switzerland, Austria and Latin America give hope: *change is possible* if courageous people lead the way. German bishops have shown that they can overturn discriminatory rules if there is enough internal and external pressure and the will to change. Swiss pastoral care teams show that congregations can flourish even without a sole ruling pastor if lay people and priests work together in a spirit of trust. Austrian pastors demonstrate civil courage by naming grievances and acting in the spirit of the Gospel - even when Rome frowns. Latin American grassroots communities and bishops in the Amazon region remind us that the church is a global church that must allow different solutions for different contexts if it wants to fulfill its mission.

It is now important to translate these individual breakthroughs into a *broader structural change*. Church employment law must remain permanently non-discriminatory and fair - worldwide, not just in some countries. The leadership culture must become more synodal, with power being shared and controlled and the charisms of all believers being brought to bear. And innovation must no longer be seen as a threat, but as what it actually is in theological terms: an unfolding of the Holy Spirit who "makes all things new". This requires trust - God's Spirit will not lead the church astray if it searches for new paths with a sincere heart.

The church is a community on a journey through time. *Shelters for innovation* are like oases on this path: here new things can be tried out, tested and nurtured until they are strong enough to inspire the whole church. Allowing such oases requires humility on the part of those responsible - the humility to recognize that they do not already know all the answers. But it also requires courage - the courage to move forward and, if necessary, to do the right thing against the odds. Progressive bishops who feel torn between Rome and their own local church need comrades-in-arms and support in order to dare to take steps forward.

Experience shows that if this backing exists and is acted upon in a spirit of charity, then even Rome can subsequently accept changes that previously seemed unthinkable in the tower or under the dome.

Ultimately, the church will only remain *publicly and socially acceptable* if it transforms itself from a "church of fear" to a "church of trust". A church that does not discriminate against its employees, but values them as witnesses of God's love. A church that sees leadership not as domination, but as service - shared with many. And a church that courageously breaks new ground and creates places where the gospel can be experienced *today*, in all its diversity and creativity. This vision may be ambitious, but it is necessary. The world is waiting for the church to *make room for* God's spirit to work.

🐦Bishops' briefing:

The religious policy field discusses the urgent need for reform within the Catholic Church, particularly with regard to labor law and leadership culture. It highlights how discrimination, for example against queer employees, has historically been embedded in church employment law and how public pressure has led to change that now recognizes diversity. At the same time, it identifies an outdated, hierarchical leadership culture that, despite a theoretical emphasis on synodality, remains de facto concentrated among a small number of clergy, leading to conflicts of loyalty among progressive bishops. In addition, the need for protected spaces for innovation is emphasized, in which new pastoral approaches and participation models can be tested without fear of sanctions. Using examples from Germany, Switzerland, Austria and Latin America, the text shows that change is possible, but requires structural support and the courage of those responsible in order to move from a "church of fear" to a "church of trust".

Didactic questions:

168 - What are the main problems in church labor law?

It should be emphasized that for a long time, church employment law allowed for discrimination against employees, particularly with regard to their private lives. This affected queer employees, remarried divorcees and people without a Catholic denomination. These practices created an atmosphere of fear and forced those affected to conceal their private lives. Although there is now a new version of the basic order in Germany that no longer allows private life arrangements as grounds for dismissal, this reform is considered to be "at most a partial success", as the implementation and situation in other countries (such as Austria or Switzerland) are still unclear. The tension between the church's right to self-determination and state anti-discrimination law, as well as the need to exclude discrimination based on inner conviction and not just public pressure, are also cited as central problems.

169 - How did public and internal pressure contribute to the reform of church labor law in Germany?

Public and internal pressure played a decisive role in the reform of church labor law in Germany. Initiatives such as #OutInChurch with public coming-outs by affected employees and the Maria 2.0 reform movement significantly increased the pressure on the bishops. The public confessions and the support of numerous signatures led to a rethink. It was only under this double pressure that the bishops agreed on a new version of the basic order of church ministry in November 2022, which represented a paradigm shift and prohibited discrimination based on private lifestyle, sexual identity or marital status.

170 - What does the new version of the Basic Regulations for Church Service mean in concrete terms for employees?

In concrete terms, the new version of the basic order of church service means that the private lives of employees in Germany should no longer play a role in the employment relationship. Relationships, intimate lifestyles and marital status are now part of the inviolable core area of privacy and are beyond the control of the church employer. In plain language, this means that, for example, a pastoral worker living in a homosexual partnership or a doctor remarried after divorce in a Catholic hospital can no longer expect to be dismissed. Diversity is expressly recognized as an enrichment, and all employees, regardless of religion, origin, disability, gender, sexual identity and lifestyle, should be able to be representatives of God's love.

171 - Why is the current leadership culture in the Catholic Church described as problematic, despite the emphasis on synodality and participation?

The current leadership culture is described as problematic because, despite the official emphasis on synodality and participation (participation of all believers), in practice it often still functions according to an old feudal-hierarchical model. Power often remains concentrated in the hands of a few clerics, such as bishops and pastors. Genuine participation in decision-making by the grassroots (laity) is often not allowed or remains ineffective, even if committees such as pastoral or parish councils exist. These bodies usually only have an advisory function and can be overruled or ignored by the officials. This leads to frustration among committed Christians, discourages talented employees and overburdens the office-holders due to the concentrated amount of power.

172 - What specific examples of innovative leadership culture are mentioned in the text and what resistance do they encounter?

A concrete example of innovative leadership culture is the diocese of St. Gallen in Switzerland, where teams of pastors jointly lead parishes and lay people effectively take on leadership tasks. However, this model met with resistance in 2020 due to a Vatican instruction that adhered to the traditional idea that only a priest could exercise ultimate leadership. The Swiss bishops, including Bishop Büchel, rejected the instruction as "theologically deficient and clericalistically narrow" and stuck to their model. This example illustrates the tension between local innovations and Roman norms that keep such models in a gray area and threatened by Roman intervention.

173 - What are "safe spaces for innovation" in the church and why are they necessary?

"Safe spaces for innovation" are protected places and contexts within the church where experiments are allowed, mistakes can be made and new pastoral approaches, forms of liturgy or participation models can be tried out without sanctions or fear of repression. They are necessary because those who want to try out new things often encounter mistrust or control. A "culture of fear" has often led to deviations being prevented. Safe spaces enable a mental shift towards a culture of encouragement and are vital for the survival of the church in order to keep faith alive in today's society and regain trust in the face of declining loyalty.

174 - How was a "safe space for innovation" de facto created in the case of marriage ceremonies with blessing of same-sex couples in Germany and Belgium?

In the case of marriage ceremonies with the blessing of same-sex couples, a de facto "safe space for innovation" was created, with many pastors holding blessing services for all loving couples, including queer couples, under the motto #Liebegewinnt, even though Rome had formulated a blanket "no" in 2021. The remarkable reaction of the German bishops was that no diocesan bishop took disciplinary action and no one forbade priests to take part. This de facto toleration continued, and even an auxiliary bishop personally took part in one such celebration. Similarly, the Flemish bishops in Belgium created a collective safe space by being the first Conference of female, diverse and male Bishops worldwide to introduce an official liturgical blessing for same-sex couples, despite the Roman line to the contrary. In both cases, those responsible protected the actors by refraining from sanctioning them or through collegial unity.

175 - What demands are formulated in the text to enable and promote structural reforms in the Catholic Church?

In order to enable and promote structural reforms, the text formulates several demands: Church employment law must be permanently non-discriminatory and fair, not just in some countries but worldwide. The leadership culture must become more synodal, with power being shared and controlled and the charisms of all believers being brought to bear. Innovation must not be seen as a threat, but as an unfolding of the Holy Spirit and requires trust. There is a need for protected places and spaces for innovative initiatives and projects that are actively facilitated by those responsible for leadership by providing freedom, resources and protection. Diocesan budgets should provide a fixed percentage for experimental pastoral work. Employees in innovation projects need reliable protection against dismissal and career prospects, and a culture of error is needed in which the failure of ideas does not mean the end of a career. In addition, collegial support from conferences of bishops or regional assemblies is important to protect reform-oriented bishops.

Essay questions:

Please answer one of the following questions in the form of an essay:

a) Discuss the tension between the church's right to self-determination and general human rights, particularly in the context of church labor law. Analyze how this tension has manifested itself in the past and what solutions have been proposed.

b) Explain how the concept of "synodality" in the Catholic Church often falls short of the claim in practice. What structural problems are identified in the text that stand in the way of genuine participation, and what examples of innovative leadership culture are given?

c) Analyze the importance of "safe spaces for innovation" in the Catholic Church. Why are these necessary, what form can they take (formal and informal), and what challenges and risks are associated with creating and maintaining such spaces? Use examples you are familiar with.

d) Compare the reform approaches and challenges in church labor law and in leadership culture. Where do you see parallels and differences, and to what extent are these two areas mutually dependent?

e) Discuss the role of public pressure and church-related reform movements (such as #OutInChurch or Maria 2.0) for structural change in the Catholic Church. To what extent can such movements act as catalysts or even informal "safe spaces" for reform?

Religious policy field analysis 22: *Togetherness instead of loneliness: Bishops between isolation and support, between operational blindness and the need to shape policy*

Many bishops who are willing to take action and who at least claim to be committed to reform within the Catholic Church often feel isolated within their own circle. Although there are colleagues who share similar concerns, their solidarity usually remains unofficial and behind closed doors.

Hidden loneliness in the college

An open culture of debate - i.e. the transparent discussion of different positions - is rare in meetings of bishops. Controversial topics are often avoided for fear of being seen as disloyal. There is virtually no spiritual or theological exchange on systemic reform issues. Those who nevertheless publicly advocate for change risk internal ostracism or disregard.

Phrases such as cautious reassessment are used instead of bringing about actual changes, out of fear of Rome. One crow does not peck out another crow's eye, as the abuse cases have also shown. Individual transfer as a new start in an uncritical congregation replaces actual reform - instead of changing rules and church structures in terms of content and system, everything remains the same. The conference could be abolished because it remains inconclusive and unsuccessful on key issues.

Proponents of reform are sometimes thwarted by loud voices of dissent that signal: *"What you are doing is forbidden from the outset ... You must not think any further in this direction"*. Such messages - as described by Bishop *Helmut Dieser* of Aachen, for example - go hand in hand with an aggressive attitude and fuel the fear among bishops that they are following a *"false ideology"*. In this climate, it is difficult to show open support for one another.

Even Pope Francis would like to see a more open culture of discussion among bishops. He explicitly encouraged the participants of a synod for bishops: *"Speak clearly. No one should say: 'You can't say that'. You have to say everything you feel with parrhesía (boldness)"*. At the same time, he asked for humble listening to the words of others.

In reality, however, this ideal culture of fearless dissent often - almost always - fails to materialize. Clearer words and more sustained demands in the literature are needed for change to take effect.

Even progressive spirits in the Conference of female, diverse and male Bishops either fall silent or remain lone wolves. The *isolation* of reform-oriented and creative bishops has become a structural problem - with *personal, theological and institutional* consequences.

Effects of isolation: personal, theological and institutional

On a personal level, the isolation wears on the bishops concerned. Those who constantly have the feeling that they are fighting against silent resistance within their own college are under great *psychological pressure*. A lack of support can lead to *loneliness* - the experience of being alone with worries and visions. This puts a strain on spiritual health: exchanges at eye level and trusting conversations, as would be possible among like-minded people, fail to materialize.

Personal dimension: loneliness and pressure

Some bishops who are willing to shape things withdraw into the private sphere or resign themselves inwardly in order to avoid conflict.

Many bishops do not publish and do not publicly defend their positions once they have been consecrated into office. More passivity and lack of commitment is not possible. In professional working life, they would be described as *graupes* - even though they certainly provide excellent pastoral care in the local private sphere and have a lukewarm job with low membership numbers, unless they are assigned a second neighboring parish. But they do not shape the faith and church processes with local "housekeeping". They only have a small volume of votes in public.

The fear of *internal sanctions* (such as the withdrawal of responsibilities or the cold shoulder from fellow sisters and brothers) is a constant companion. In the long term, this can lead to *burnout-like* exhaustion or despondency. As a result, the church loses committed staff exactly where it needs them most - at the top of the dioceses.

At the same time, this personal isolation is at odds with the vocation of bishops. A bishop is not meant to be a loner, but part of the *episcopate* and the people of God. However, if a culture of mistrust prevails, it is difficult to live spiritual community. *Spiritual accompaniment* could help here: Münster's Bishop *Felix Genn* emphasizes that he himself needs continuous spiritual accompaniment - *"otherwise I cannot do my job as a bishop"*. He needs a trustworthy counterpart to reflect on his path of faith and leadership responsibility.

If such an anchor person or even just a sympathetic ear among colleagues is missing, lone warriors are at risk of losing their inner balance. Personally isolated church leaders find it difficult to *encourage* others if they do not receive any encouragement themselves.

Theological impoverishment through silence

Isolation also has *theological* consequences. Where bishops avoid controversial topics, the common discourse on church *reform theology* withers. Progressive-minded head shepherds often bring well-founded theological considerations with them - for example on questions of sexual morality, women in church ministries, the division of power or the further development of dogmas. However, if these considerations do not find a forum within the circle of bishops, they remain theory or are only discussed outside the official bodies. The bishops thus deprive each other of an *important learning opportunity*: the intellectual broadening and deepening of positions in dialog with those who think differently. A lively *culture of debate* could help to jointly reinterpret the signs of the times in the light of the Gospel. Instead, many conferences remain stuck in polite *conflict avoidance*.

For the church, this means *theological impoverishment*. There is a lack of the tension and diversity that can be productive for the organic development of doctrine. The Second Vatican Council emphasized the *collegiality* of bishops - to lead the church together with popes. However, if there is hardly any open discussion, collegiality becomes a formality. Important issues - such as contemporary sexual morality or the involvement of the laity - are not really thought through together. Some bishops avoid any criticism of existing teachings out of loyalty, even if pastoral experience suggests an adjustment. Others may be reform-minded, but only share this with trusted advisors at most. This results in *theological silence* precisely where leaders should actually provide guidance. The little theological *creativity* that individual progressive bishops express in studies or pastoral letters runs the risk of not being taken up by their sisters and brothers - due to a lack of exchange or reluctance to join in. The lack of theological dialog among bishops thus deprives the Church of the potential for renewal *from within*.

Institutional paralysis and loss of credibility

Institutionally, the isolation described above leads to a *blockade of reform processes*. If bishops who are willing to shape the process do not bring their concerns to the Conference of female, diverse and male Bishops (or are outvoted there), reforms come to a standstill. The German *synodal path* offers a current example: although a majority of progressive forces achieved many a vote in the synodal assembly as a whole, reform texts sometimes failed due to a blocking minority of older, possibly more saturated bishops who were no longer willing to shape the process.

Some bishops did not dare to swim against the tide of the conference, even if they had personal sympathies for reform. The result: *necessary changes* - such as a wedding ceremony for queer couples or new forms of power-sharing with lay people - were rhetorically delayed or sat out altogether. The time for sitting it out is over. The leadership of the Catholic Church must take action to keep the Church alive.

Otherwise, this will have several negative consequences. Firstly, the church loses *credibility* if obvious problems are not tackled because internal forces are blocking it. The faithful feel the rift: voices that are willing to shape things sound hopeful, but action hardly ever follows. Secondly, *cultural rigidity* reinforces polarization.

Figure 47: Shepherdess with two actively guarding and welfare-oriented dogs for the sheep - who are understood as "teamers" in the new language of youth.

A colorful illustration showing a shepherd walking along an idyllic path wearing a hat, cape and shepherd's crook. She is accompanied by two friendly sheepdogs that walk vigilantly and attentively at her side. They are "teamers" in a youthful term. Behind her follows a flock of white and black sheep. The scene is set in a tranquil, green landscape with rolling hills, trees and a blue sky with white clouds. The atmosphere and style are warm, harmonious and clearly defined in terms of drawing.

Reform advocates both inside and outside the bishops' meetings feel disappointed and powerless; conservative forces, in turn, see their course confirmed and see little incentive for dialog. The lack of open conflict resolution can lead to deeper *divisions in* the long term - exactly what everyone wants to avoid. Thirdly, the church as an institution is wasting the opportunity to learn from *pilot projects* and attempts at reform by individuals. Where courageous bishops dare to try something new, it remains isolated instead of being reflected upon and possibly adapted within the college. Example: In 2022, the Flemish bishops in

Belgium jointly decided to celebrate a liturgy for the marriage of homosexual couples - the first group of bishops worldwide to do so, despite Roman instructions to the contrary. This collegial will to take action in a region shows what is possible when bishops act as one. But if such steps are not taken elsewhere, it remains an exceptional case. In many countries, a single bishop would probably *not dare to* take such an initiative alone for fear of isolation.

Ultimately, the overall leadership of the church also suffers: a Conference of female, diverse and male Bishops in which no constructive debate takes place becomes an *administrative body* that only manages the lowest common denominator.

The chair of a Conference of female, diverse and male Bishops must not only be measured by their ability to build bridges, but must also be able to show how many sacks of rice they have carried across the bridge to the other side with their people.

Visionary new departures - which are urgently needed today to counter the church crisis - are not even put on the agenda. An institution in which internal *correction mechanisms* are lacking and innovation is slowed down by social control stagnates. This is precisely what threatens to happen if progressive bishops are systematically sidelined. The isolation of individuals is therefore not a private matter, but affects the *development opportunities of the entire church*.

Ways out of isolation: structural and spiritual countermeasures

In order to break this vicious circle, conscious measures are needed, both on a *structural and spiritual-personal* level. Some *practical approaches* can help to promote community and mutual strengthening among the bishops:

- **Mentoring for new bishops:** Similar to companies or politics, a new diocesan bishop should also be assigned a *mentor*. This can also be a layperson. A professional coach can accompany him in the first few years, provide confidential advice and help him to find his own path - even *beyond the pressure to conform*. Mentoring like this would signal to young bishops that asking questions is allowed and that you don't have to know or carry everything on your own. Coaching also thrives on asking questions. In training, the learner asks the questions; in coaching, the coach asks the questions. This can also be students or people from outside the field. As a rule, they are even better at asking questions. Coaches ask questions as if they had to explain it to an alien. It strengthens the newcomer's ability to remain *authentic* and encourages them to raise uncomfortable issues because they feel supported. This type of tandem with young students or psychologists could be officially initiated by the Conference of female, diverse and male Bishops in order to initiate a cultural change : away from being *thrown in at the deep end and towards growing into* the ministry *by asking questions*.

- **Spiritual supervision and support:** Those responsible for leadership need leadership themselves - in a spiritual sense. Regular *supervision* or spiritual accompaniment for bishops would create space to reflect on personal challenges, doubts or conflicts. External companions or supervisors (e.g. students who ask questions, experienced religious of the opposite sex, theologians or coaches) can serve as questioning *dialog partners* who help to clarify perspectives and uncover blind spots. Bishop *Felix Genn* openly reports that he is still receiving spiritual guidance at the age of 70 and finds this indispensable in order to avoid falling into his own operational blindness.

Such support prevents a bishop from becoming isolated in the internal or external headwind. Supervision can also address specific *leadership issues: How do I deal with an opposing confrere Benedict? How can I represent my diocesan reform and at the same time preserve the community?* Conflicts can be tackled constructively with professional advice before they become open wounds.

- **Interdiocesan peer networks:** Bishops who have *similar reform concerns* should network across diocesan and national borders. Such *informal peer groups* could, for example, consist of 5-10 bishops who exchange ideas (virtually or in person) a few times a year. Topics that seem sensitive in the bishops' own national conference can also be discussed there. An international example of this is the annual *meeting of the Episcopal Focolare Movement*, which is attended by both Catholic and Protestant bishops. Since 1977 - initiated by Bishop *Klaus Hemmerle* of Aachen - bishops from different churches have been meeting regularly for spiritual exchange and *"fraternal encounters"*.

This ecumenical initiative shows how *friendship and trust* can grow across denominational and national borders when people consciously network. Similarly, reform-oriented shepherds could form a network in which they share ideas, reflect on successes and failures and encourage each other. This way, no one feels that they are completely alone - they *support each other*.

- **Regular retreats with collegial exchange**: Apart from formal plenary meetings, bishops would benefit from joint *dialog retreats* or retreats that focus decidedly on open discussion. Annual *retreats* would be conceivable, where a group of bishops (not too large, so that trust can develop) spends a few days in a protected space. Under spiritual guidance - moderated by external facilitators or an experienced coach - they could talk about their *experiences, fears and hopes*. It is important that these meetings have enough confidentiality and spiritual depth for real communication to succeed. There, a bishop can also express doubts without having to fear a headwind from the media or the curia. Such collegial days of reflection promote *sisterhood and brotherhood - in short, fraternity*: people pray together, listen to God's word and get to know each other beyond their official roles. This increases mutual understanding. Episcopal conferences could actively offer such voluntary exchange retreats. *Ecumenical retreats* - such as those practiced between Catholic and Protestant leaders in some regions - are also enriching because they broaden horizons and show that conflicts in other churches *can* be approached in a similar way.

- **Conflict counseling and mediation**: Where *conflicts* exist between bishops or between the reform camp and the opposition, one should not wait until rifts become insurmountable. Professional *conflict counseling* within the Conference of female, diverse and male Bishops could help to moderate smoldering issues at an early stage. A small team of *moderators* or *mediators* (neutral, possibly deliberately not from the ecclesiastical sphere if they are, but not themselves part of the conflict parties) could be brought in if necessary. This team could hold confidential discussions with individual bishops, clarify misunderstandings and develop common rules for the dialog. For example, it could be agreed how to give space to controversial topics without anyone losing face. Within the German synodal forums, attempts have already been made to structure discussions with spiritual guidance - unfortunately not without tensions, but the idea of using external *process facilitators* is the right one. A Conference of female, diverse and male Bishops could also mediate between different camps, for example when reform-oriented bishops and more conservative bishops are deadlocked - their "claims" have been staked out for years. Here, a moderated retreat or workshop under the guidance of conflict advisors could build new *bridges*. The aim is not to wipe away differences, but to establish a *culture of respect and honesty*. When bishops experience that controversial debates are handled fairly, the fear of speaking out decreases. In the long term, the entire church leadership benefits from this: decisions mature in a climate in which people can *argue honestly* and still pray together.

Together with helping laypeople on the path to reform

The *importance of community and mutual encouragement* on the path of reform within the church can hardly be overestimated. Bishops are *brothers and sisters* in ministry - but this fraternal togetherness needs to be actively cultivated together with the laity, especially when there are differences in content. Bishops who are willing to shape things do not need a special position or the freedom of fools, but rather a network of *trust and support* in order to be able to contribute their prophetic voice without breaking. Likewise, hesitant or skeptical bishops need the experience that contradiction and the naming of alternatives is not dangerous or without alternatives, but can be fruitful . The Holy Spirit can only be sought together in an atmosphere that allows people *to speak openly* and also forgives failed attempts.

Community initiatives such as mentoring, spiritual guidance, peer networks, retreats and conflict counseling *are practical steps* to find a way out of isolation. They make it possible to experience that no one is solely responsible for the entire burden of the church. Instead, the bishops support each other - in line with their self-image, following the example of the apostles. Where such *mutual encouragement* succeeds, freedom is created in which ideas for reform can flourish. Bishops who encourage each other can move forward more courageously and at the same time listen to each other in humility. This benefits the whole church, because it sees shepherds who live unity not as forced uniformity, but as *unity in reconciled diversity*. This is precisely what Bishop *Johan Bonny* from Belgium describes as central for the future: a church as a *communion*, as a unity that endures and integrates *diversity*.

Ultimately, a minister who is willing to shape the church can be recognized above all by *attitudes, behaviour and concrete actions* that show that he or she is willing to actively develop the church and the community. Typical characteristics are

1. openness and willingness to engage in dialog

- Shows genuine interest in the opinions and concerns of community members.
- Consciously seek out exchanges with people who think differently.

2. innovative spirit

- Initiates and supports new projects and methods.
- Is prepared to experiment and allow for mistakes.

3. participative management

- Promotes independent commitment of lay people.

- Delegates responsibility and creates scope for co-design.

4. communication skills

- Communicates ideas clearly, comprehensibly and enthusiastically.
- Deal with criticism openly and constructively.

5. self-reflection and critical faculties

- Reflects on own actions and shows willingness to develop further.
- Can recognize own mistakes and learn from them.

6. courage and willingness to take risks

- Defends clear positions, even if they are uncomfortable.
- Is prepared to take personal risks in order to drive necessary changes.

7 Spiritual depth

- Remain anchored in faith and spirituality and draw strength from this to shape your life.
- Combines spiritual convictions with social responsibility and drive.

A creative clergyman is not only visionary, but also takes concrete action, is open, courageous and able to involve others. He can be recognized by the fact that he gives impulses, inspires the community and does not see the church as a static structure, but as a living and constantly renewing community.

While the term *"shepherds"* stands for care, leadership and responsibility, active laypeople who are willing and ready to shape the church are not "sheep", but active partners and co-bearers of the church community.

Distinguishing active laypeople from passive sheep and describing them metaphorically *as "community-oriented watchdogs and sheepdogs of the flock"* is indeed very figurative and meaningful.

What would the image of the "communal watchdogs of the herd" express?

- **Independence and responsibility:** Community sheep and guard dogs in the flock act independently, supportively and on an equal footing with the shepherds. They actively ensure that the community stays together and keeps moving.
- **Protection and vigilance:** Lay people, who take on the role of community sheepdogs and watchdogs of the flock, ensure that the church moves in a good direction and that no one gets lost.
- **Partnership-based interaction:** Shepherds (clergy) and communal sheep and watchdogs of the flock (committed lay people) are interdependent, complement each other and work together as partners.
- **Courage to intervene:** Community sheep and guard dogs in the flock can intervene critically, correct directions and support the shepherd where necessary.

The image of the collective sheep and guard dogs of the herd presupposes an active, self-confident and cooperative role for the laywomen. This emphasizes positive and courageous steps towards more equality and participation.

The metaphor of *"community-oriented sheep and watchdogs for the flock"* for committed, creative laypeople is meaningful, original and purposeful. This image makes it clear that laypeople are not passive objects of leadership - like "stupid sheep", but rather autonomous co-creators of the church - equal, active and: indispensable. In more recent youth language, these complementary laypeople and facilitators are called "teamers".

Lay people can specifically demand clergy who are willing to shape the process by positioning themselves clearly, actively participating and formulating concrete expectations in writing. The following steps and strategies can help:

1. demand and conduct an open dialog

- Create opportunities for discussion in which co-design is an explicit topic.
- Address issues clearly, e.g: "We want a clergyman who is open to new ideas and co-determination."

2. define common goals

- Develop concrete goals as a community or group and officially introduce them.
- Initiate a joint roadmap or a future workshop.
- Have written formulations further elaborated and justified using artificial intelligence.

3. use committees and structures

- Use church councils, parish councils and synods to clearly formulate and demand concerns.
- Adopt resolutions or written declarations to build up pressure.

4. create publicity

- Organize events and panel discussions in which expectations of clergy are formulated.
- Use media and social networks to make visible what the community specifically expects.

5. forming networks and alliances

- Join forces with other communities, groups and initiatives to strengthen demands.
- Get supra-regional support, for example from reform movements or church initiatives.

6. organize training courses and workshops

- Actively invite clergy to participate in workshops on community development, participatory leadership or communication.
- Make it clear that these are desired and necessary skills.

7. courageously and clearly criticize, ask questions

- If clergy block or remain passive, criticize clearly but respectfully and effectively-sustainably and ask questions.
- Clearly formulate what changes are expected and what positive effects these would have.

Laypeople should take a proactive, networked and determined approach in order to promote and demand clergy who are willing to shape things. Only an active and visible attitude on the part of laypeople can create sustainable change in church practice.

Ultimately, the path to ecclesial renewal leads through togetherness, in which isolation no longer has a breeding ground. Community and mutual encouragement are the key to ensuring that progressive voices are not silenced and that the Church can embark together on the path of authentic conversion and reform in difficult times. As clergy learn to truly be *brothers and sisters* - in open dialog, in common prayer and in acting in solidarity - the inner reform process will move forward credibly and powerfully. This is the challenge - and the promise - of a new culture of solidarity among the shepherds and common good-oriented watchdogs and sheepdogs of the church for the flock: The isolated voice of an individual can easily be overheard if it is not made known in written documentation; a *chorus of voices* that remain in harmony with each other and also in critical counter-sound, on the other hand, is able to change the church from within.

🕊️Bishops' briefing:

This religious policy analysis looks at the isolation and challenges faced by clergy and bishops within the Catholic Church, and how this isolation has personal, theological and institutional consequences. It becomes clear that open dialog and theological debate are rare, which leads to a paralysis of reform processes. The analyses propose several structural and spiritual measures to overcome isolation and promote a culture of connectedness. In addition, the need for an active and equal role of the laity as "community-oriented watchdogs and sheepdogs of the flock" is emphasized, who must also contribute to the renewal of the Church. In more recent language, these complementary lay people and companions are called "teamers".

Didactic questions:

176 - What problems do bishops who are willing to shape the Catholic Church see?

Bishops who are willing to work for reform often feel isolated in their circle. They experience that open discussions on controversial topics are rare for fear of being seen as disloyal. Systemic reform issues are rarely discussed theologically or spiritually. Anyone who speaks out publicly in favor of change risks ostracism or disregard from colleagues. The fear of internal sanctions or the "cold shoulder" accompanies them constantly, which can lead to high psychological pressure, loneliness and potentially burnout.

177 - Why is there a "hidden loneliness" in the college?

The hidden loneliness arises from a culture of conflict avoidance and fear. An open culture of debate and transparent discussions of different positions are rare. Bishops often shy away from addressing controversial topics for fear of rejection or sanctions. As a result, reform-oriented bishops, even if they have colleagues with similar concerns, remain unofficial and behind closed doors and feel like lone wolves.

178 - How does this isolation affect the theological development of the church?

Isolation leads to theological impoverishment. When bishops avoid controversial topics, the common discourse on church reform theology atrophies. Sound theological reflections on important issues do not find a forum within the circle of bishops and remain theory or are only discussed outside of official bodies. This deprives the clergy of an important mutual learning opportunity and prevents doctrine from developing organically.

179 - What are the institutional consequences of the isolation of bishops willing to shape the future?

Institutionally, isolation leads to a blockade of reform processes. Reform advocates are slowed down, reform texts fail due to blocking minorities, and necessary changes are delayed or sat out. This leads to a loss of credibility for the church, as obvious problems are not addressed, and increases polarization. The church also misses the opportunity to learn from pilot projects, and the Conference of female, diverse and male Bishops becomes a purely administrative body without visionary departures.

180 - What concrete measures are proposed to overcome the isolation of the clergy?

Both structural and spiritual-personal countermeasures are proposed. These include mentoring for new bishops (also by lay people or coaches), regular spiritual supervision and support (also by external partners such as students or psychologists), the formation of interdiocesan peer networks (across diocesan and national borders), regular retreats with collegial exchange in a protected space as well as professional conflict counseling and mediation.

181 - What role do laypeople play on the path to reform and how are they described metaphorically?

Lay people are seen as active partners and contributors to the church community, not as passive "sheep". They could be metaphorically described as "community-oriented watchdogs and sheepdogs of the flock". This image expresses their independence, responsibility, protective function, partnership-based interaction with the clergy and their courage to intervene. It emphasizes their indispensable role as co-creators of the church.

182 - How can laypeople specifically demand clergy who are ready to shape the future?

Laypeople can specifically call on clergy who are willing to shape things by positioning themselves clearly, actively participating and formulating concrete expectations in writing. This includes demanding and leading open dialogue, defining common goals, using committees and structures, creating publicity for their expectations, forming networks and alliances, organizing further training and workshops for clergy as well as courageously and clearly voicing criticism and asking questions when clergy block or behave passively.

183 - What is the overarching goal and promise of a new culture of connectedness among the clergy and with the laity?

The overarching goal is church renewal through togetherness in which isolation has no breeding ground. Communion and mutual encouragement are key to ensuring that progressive voices are not silenced and that the Church can embark together on a journey of authentic conversion and reform. The promise is that through a culture of communion, in which bishops learn to be true brothers and sisters in open dialog, prayer and action in solidarity, and in which lay people act as equal partners, the Church can move forward credibly and powerfully . A chorus of voices that remain in harmony and critical resonance with one another can change the Church from within.

 Essay questions:

Please answer one of the following questions in the form of an essay:

a) Analyze the effects of the isolation of priests willing to shape the Church on a personal, theological and institutional level. Explain how these effects influence the church as a whole.

b) Discuss structural and spiritual countermeasures to the isolation of clergy. Evaluate the potential of each measure to promote community and enable reform processes.

c) What does the metaphor of the *"community-oriented sheep and watchdogs of the flock"* mean for committed lay people? Explain what this metaphor says about the desired role and relationship of lay people to clergy and how lay people can proactively claim this role

d) Explain the role of a "teamer".

e) Describe the characteristics of a minister who is ready to shape the church. Discuss why these characteristics are important for the future viability of the church.

f) There is a need for a new culture of solidarity among clergy and laity. Discuss how this culture of open dialog, common prayer and solidarity can contribute to overcoming the church crisis.

Happiness and being happy - A sermon

Dear sisters, diverse and brothers, dear congregation

- Who among us does not wish to be happy? Let's imagine a moment when we felt real happiness: Perhaps the laughter of a child on a summer evening, the reunion of a long-lost friend or a moment of quiet contentment after a job well done. We all know such oases of happiness, and they show: *Happiness and being happy* are deeply human longings.

Introduction: Longing for happiness

We often talk about luck in our everyday lives. We wish each other *"good luck"* on their birthdays or say that someone is *"blessed by luck"*. Interestingly, the word *"luck"* has a double meaning in German. On the one hand, we use it to mean random luck - for example, when someone wins the lottery or narrowly escapes an accident. You can't force such luck; it may or may not come your way. On the other hand, we speak of happiness as a state of fulfillment. *"I am happy"*, we say, referring to an attitude towards life in which we are in harmony - with ourselves, with our fellow human beings and with the world. In such happiness, we feel affirmed, confirmed and supported. Joy, cheerfulness - perhaps even a song on our lips - can be an expression of this deeper happiness.

This deep happiness is not just a luxury. It is something that all people seek. Even the Doctor of the Church *Thomas Aquinas* noted that people naturally strive for happiness and want to avoid unhappiness. Numerous philosophies and religions agree on this: Happiness is one of our fundamental goals in life. Surveys in our time confirm this in their own way. One survey found that a large majority of people describe themselves as happy, and when asked *"What makes you happy?"*, over 90% put family and relationships in first place, followed by friendships and health. Material wealth ranked well behind - money alone obviously does not make people happy. We are familiar with this insight: External well-being is nice, but true happiness comes from relationships, from love, connection and meaning.

At the same time, we have an inkling: Happiness has something mysterious about it, a *"riddle"*. On the one hand, we can do something for our happiness, we forge our own happiness through our decisions, so to speak. On the other hand, happiness always remains a gift and unavailable - it cannot be planned like a project. Both elements, our own contribution and the undeserved gift, intertwine and make happiness so exciting. We must therefore neither wait passively for happiness nor believe that we have it completely under our control. Life means being open to good fortune and actively striving for our own happiness and that of our fellow human beings.

As believers, we add another dimension: we believe that God has called us to joy. Jesus says: *"I have told you these things so that my joy may be in you and that your joy may be complete"* (John 15:11). This does not mean that we always have to go through life rejoicing - no life is free from pain. But it does mean that we are promised joy at the very foundation of our existence. Pope Francis begins his teaching letter *Evangelii Gaudium* with the words: *"The joy of the Gospel fills the heart and the entire life of those who encounter Jesus... With Jesus Christ, joy comes always - and again and again"*. One source of joy never dries up: the experience of being loved by God, unconditionally and infinitely. From this grows a confidence, a happiness that can endure even difficult times.

Between suffering and hope: happiness in a broken world

But how does this fit together - our belief in joy and the suffering that so many experience? We must by no means suppress the suffering and disappointments. A Christian sermon on happiness must *take seriously* the pain and hopelessness that people experience. Many are disappointed - by other people, by society, sometimes also by the church or by God. If you look at the world today , you don't just see beaming faces: there is the loneliness of older people, the fear of young people about the future, the grief of abuse victims, the despair in war zones, the weariness of those who have sacrificed themselves and received no thanks. All this grief and fear is real.

The Church must not ignore this. In the pastoral constitution *Gaudium et Spes*, the bishops solemnly confessed decades ago: *"The joy and hope, grief and anguish of people today ... are also the joy and hope, grief and anguish of Christ's disciples"*. In other words: everything that is truly human should find an echo in the heart of the Church. When people suffer, God's people suffer with them; when people rejoice, we rejoice with them. Our community of faith stands alongside the human family, in the midst of the fullness of life - not aloof, not unworldly.

That is why we do not close our eyes to what is dark. Being happy does not mean being in a good mood all the time or making light of problems. Real happiness always has to do with truthfulness: We look at the pain and bear it *together*. We think of Jesus himself: He knew the deepest joy, but also tears and abandonment in Gethsemane. On the cross, he cried out: *"My God, why have you forsaken me?"* - God himself also knows the cries of despair. But we believe that this is not the end of the story. After Good Friday came Easter. The wounds remained - even as the resurrected Jesus still bore the marks of the nails - but they were transformed wounds, signs of hope. So we too can hope that suffering can be transformed. No night lasts forever, no winter without spring. In the midst of weeping, new laughter can grow at some point. This hope is not a cheap consolation, but an encouragement: Don't give up! God *still* has plans for you.

We therefore speak of happiness in a hopeful and encouraging way, without trivializing suffering. Perhaps for someone who is going through something difficult, happiness initially only means a small sigh of relief, a ray of hope - and that is *no* small thing. We have no reason to underestimate any form of happiness. *"It is not for anyone to belittle people's happiness in its many forms ,"* wrote Cardinal *Karl Lehmann*. Each of us perceives *happiness* differently, depending on our situation in life. For some it is health after a long illness, for others reconciliation after an argument. For still others, it is the freedom to be themselves, or justice after suffering injustice. Happiness has many faces, and all of them are valuable.

Diversity as wealth - many perspectives on happiness

Our Catholic Church is a colorful family. People with very different stories, hopes and also different ideas of happiness live in and around it. This diversity is a wealth - even if it presents us with challenges. Pope Francis reminds us: *"Diversity is richness and must never be a reason for exclusion and discrimination".* So let us look lovingly at the different groups and brothers and sisters who belong to or are in relationship with our broad church. Each of these groups brings its own perspective on the topic of *happiness.* I would like to acknowledge all these perspectives so that we can learn from each other and come closer to happiness *together.*

Believers - from the committed to the distant

First of all, I am thinking of all of us, the faithful of all ages. But this is not a uniform group: there are the active members who celebrate church services Sunday after Sunday, work in the congregation and keep their faith alive. Their happiness is often closely linked to their faith: Many of you feel happiness in the community, in prayer, in the sacraments, in the music and tradition of the church. This happiness is real and precious. But you may also experience phases of doubt or disillusionment - when changes are too slow, when the Church is criticized or when personal prayer remains dry. I would like to encourage you: Keep at it! Your joy in faith, as unspectacular as it sometimes seems in everyday life, is a light that shines . And if you ever lose this glow, don't hesitate to talk to others about it - because faith also knows dry spells.

However, the family of believers does not only include those who are active. There are also the distanced baptized - people who were baptized as children but later stayed away from the church. Perhaps you are one of them: You have memories of communion or confirmation, but now faith hardly plays a role in your everyday life. And yet *you* are part of the church through your baptism. Perhaps you seek happiness outside of religious spaces - in a good education, in your job, in your circle of friends. Perhaps you are critical of the church, feel uncomfortable with some of its teachings or have had negative experiences. I would like to tell you that we take your questions and life paths seriously. Finding happiness and meaning is not limited to church pews. Wherever you experience genuine joy and love, God is not far away, of that I am certain. The church doesn't want to take over anyone. But it wants to *invite*: If at some point you feel that something is missing - spiritual support, community in faith, answers to deep questions - then know: Our doors are open. We want to talk to you, without prejudice, at eye level. And we know that we as a church must also be *worthy* of welcoming you back.

Then there are those who have officially left the church. Their number is large, especially in recent times. Many of you have taken this step out of protest or disappointment - because of the abuse scandals, because of incomprehensible dogmas and decisions, or because you simply no longer saw faith in your life. For some, saying *"goodbye church"* was perhaps liberating or necessary for their personal happiness. At the same time, we also hear some people who have left the church say wistfully: *"Faith and spirituality still mean something to me, but I couldn't go on with this institution."* Dear members who have left, if you hear or read these words: we miss you. Not out of fear for numbers, but as people with whom we have a lot in common. We understand your anger and pain. Many things should not have happened like this. As a church, we are faced with the task of regaining trust through reforms and sometimes 180-degree turns - we know that. Perhaps at some point we will be able to work together again in a new way. God's spirit also works beyond institutional boundaries. Who knows whether *you,* of all people, can provide challenging impulses from outside on how the church can become more credible, more humble, more joyful? Happiness in the Christian sense does not mean that everyone is the same, but that we live in reconciliation with one another. In this sense, I hope that those who have left and those who are committed will not be enemies, but can one day be brothers and sisters at the same table again.

And finally, there are also the many outsiders who may never have had much contact with the church or who adhere to completely different religions or world views. They may not belong directly to the *"church"*, but they do belong to the society in which we as a church are right in the middle of it. They also seek happiness - perhaps purely secular as *self-realization*, or in service to others without religious motivation. We can show them: We Christians *share in the joy* of everything genuine and good that people achieve. We do not claim to have leased happiness. Wherever a person - whether a believer or not - sows love, promotes justice, builds community, things happen in which God is pleased. Perhaps this is precisely a starting point for dialog: Giving thanks together for life and asking together what meaningful things this life has in store. Our faith tells us that God is ultimately the source of all joy - but we know that many still experience joy and meaning without this word *God*. We can learn from each other through respectful conversation. Happiness can be a topic that builds bridges between believers and non-believers: Because we *all* want to live happily.

Parishes and pastoral areas - the happiness of the local community

Let us now take a look at our parishes and pastoral areas, the concrete places of church life. Here, the struggle for happiness and blessing manifests itself once again in a different way. A parish community is made up of people from all walks of life who live their faith locally. In our parishes, many experience the happiness of community: people know and support each other, celebrate services and festivals together , laugh and cry together. Especially at a time when neighbors and family no longer provide support as a matter of course, the church can be a place where heart and soul can breathe a sigh of relief. Community is supportive, and shared joy is double the joy. Anyone who has ever experienced how one person is there for another in the congregation - be it at the birth of a child, in sickness or at an anniversary - senses that something of the spirit of Jesus is at work here, allowing us to be *sisters and brothers*.

However, our parishes also face challenges that do not automatically bring happiness. Structural reforms, keyword *pastoral areas*, are changing familiar parish structures. Small, familiar parishes are being merged into large pastoral care units. Many people are worried: will our familiar *sense of togetherness* be lost? Will faith become more anonymous? At the same time, the number of people attending church services is dwindling in some places or the active core is carrying an ever-increasing burden. This can be depressing: Where is there still room for joy? - I would like to *acknowledge* these concerns: Yes, it is painful when old familiar things change. But I would also like to open up a perspective of opportunity: Larger pastoral spaces offer the opportunity to share resources and venture new beginnings. Perhaps a parish in such a network suddenly discovers *talents* that were previously lost - new musical groups, ecological projects, youth work beyond its own church tower. The joy of a community depends not only on its size or structure, but also on the warmth and openness that is lived within it. If we manage to create small networks of closeness in larger spaces - home groups, visiting services, personal contacts - then no one can be lost. Jesus himself says: "*Where two or three are gathered in my name, there am I in their midst.* So it doesn't need the masses to experience the real presence of God and thus happiness. Rather, it is important to be authentically there for one another. In this sense, pastoral spaces can even become spaces of happiness: Spaces in which diverse people meet at eye level, search, believe, doubt and hope together. The parish of the future will perhaps be less club-like, less centered on priests, and more of a network of relationships. That may be a challenge - but what great happiness there is when Christianity becomes exactly that: a network of connectedness with each other and with God!

Full-time employees and volunteers - servants of joy

The full-time and voluntary workers in our church are closely linked to the parishes. Without them, nothing would work: priests and deacons, parish and pastoral workers, sacristans, church musicians, secretaries, janitors - and all the volunteers: from the parish council to the lector to the youth leader, from the Caritas helper to the kitchen team at the parish festival. You are all the *servant spirits* of our church. What is *your* relationship to happiness? Many of you may say: *I experience happiness when I can serve others*. It is a joy to look into the shining eyes of children when the group lesson has been a success. It is fulfilling to give someone support at their bedside and to feel gratitude. It is good when a church service touches many people through careful preparation and fills them with new confidence. Service in the church can be very meaningful because you feel that you are doing something that goes beyond yourself. You are working for the kingdom of God, in small and large ways. Pope Francis reminds us in *Evangelii Gaudium* that the proclamation of the Gospel should always be accompanied by joy - after all, our message and our brand essence is called *the Good News*. Those who bring this good news to others should *not make a face like at a funeral*, but should be allowed to shine. I'm sure you full-time and voluntary workers are also familiar with that special moment of happiness when you realize: *the Spirit is at work here; what I'm doing makes sense.*

But hand on heart: you also know the downsides and hardships of your ministry. Sometimes the feeling of happiness in everyday church life threatens to get lost. Too much work on too few shoulders, conflicts in the team, perhaps a lack of appreciation or the frustration when there is hardly any response despite all the effort. Many of you know the feeling of being burnt out. Some full-time employees ask themselves: *"Am I not taking on too much in the long run with this job? Will I still be spiritually satisfied if I'm always just giving?"* And some volunteers wrestle: *"Is it worth investing my limited time here if the same people are always helping and many things are faltering?"* - These questions are understandable. Servants also need happiness. You have a right to expect your efforts to bear fruit, but you also have a right to breaks, to your own spiritual nourishment and to support. Serving happily does not mean giving up on yourself. On the contrary: God wants *your* salvation just as much as that of those you serve. So take your own needs seriously. Allow yourself to say "no" sometimes and share the work. Allow yourself to draw strength - be it in prayer, in your family, in a good book or in nature. If you are to be *cheerful witnesses* to the gospel*, you must keep a smile in your heart. And I say to all of us in the church: let's give thanks more! A simple "Thank you, you did a good job" can contribute a lot to the happiness of those who often work in secret.

I would also like to say to you full-time and voluntary workers: your work has meaning, even if successes sometimes remain small or invisible. Remember what Jesus said about sowing: many things come up, some don't - but without faithful sowing, there is no harvest. Do not be discouraged by failures. Every good deed, every hour that you give is like a seed in God's field. Perhaps *you* will not reap the fruit - someone else will - but before God, nothing is in vain in love. And finally: Rejoice in your fellowship with one another! Full-time staff and volunteers, don't work against each other, but *with each other*. Appreciate each other, celebrate together, laugh together. A cheerful team meeting full of humor and mutual understanding can be just as sacred as devout prayer - both belong together. Where a team works together in unity and openness, the congregations also feel it: Here, something of the happiness of togetherness that God gives us is at work.

Children, teenagers and young adults - our beacons of happiness

Let us now turn our attention to a very special group: the children, teenagers and young adults in our church. You are *not only* the future of the church - you are also its present, its present joy. When I look into a parish and see children playing, lively altar servers, committed confirmands or young families, , it fills me with great happiness. Because you young people bring freshness, new perspectives and questions that enrich us all.

But even your search for happiness is not easy. Children often still live in the moment - eating ice cream, romping around, listening to stories, that makes them happy. But even schoolchildren feel pressure: pressure to perform, comparison with others. Young people are faced with the enormous challenges of our time. They ask: *"Where do I find my place? How can I be happy in this world, which is so complex and crisis-ridden at the same time?"* Many young people are struggling with fears about the future - climate change, social insecurity, political conflicts. The Fridays for Future movement, for example, shows how central the well-being of creation is to many of your ideas of happiness: You want a world in which you can still breathe and live, *only then* can you look to the future with happiness. Other young people are driven by the question of identity: *"Who am I if I don't live up to expectations? Am I allowed to be who I am?"* The struggle for self-acceptance, sexual identity, one's own path - all of this accompanies young years and often determines whether a young person is happy or desperate.

Dear young people, dear young adults, dear children: we as a church want to listen to you. Your view of happiness is indispensable. You remind us that happiness needs to be experienced *now* and should not always be put off until later. You have a sense of honesty and authenticity - if something sounds hollow, you notice it immediately. That challenges us to be *real*. Thank you for that! Many of you seek happiness in community - no wonder that youth trips, camps, church youth groups or World Youth Days can be such formative experiences. You can feel that faith and joy belong together, that church can be young and happy! Others of you have difficulties with the institution of the church, perhaps because you have experienced hypocrisy or the language seems strange to you. That hurts, because we want to be a home for you. Please don't give up the search - not the search for your path and not the search for God. Have the courage to start new beginnings: help shape the church, tell us what you are missing! Many of you are socially, politically and creatively active - bring these gifts to bear. The church needs your dreams and ideas so that we can all become happier people. And you know what? Jesus himself was young once, probably a teenager, when he sat in the temple for the first time and asked questions. He challenged his elders - so you can challenge us too.

I want to call out to every young person: You are loved. God cares about your happiness, and the church should care about it too. If young people find their way into our church services from time to time - feel *really welcome*. Not as decoration, but as equal members. Our church should be a place where you can be different without fear, where it is okay to make mistakes, where your music and your forms of expression have a place. A church that brings young and old together, where grandma and grandchildren can laugh together, where the trainee explains the world to the pastor and vice versa - that would be a picture of happiness! Let's work to make it a reality.

Women in the church - supported by dignity and justice

Let's come to the women in the church - a group without whom our church would be unthinkable. Just look at our church services, our committees, our Caritas, our families: women everywhere contribute to the life of the church with their talents, their care and their faith. Without women, little would happen - we all know that. Many women also find fulfillment in this dedication: the joy of those who pass on their faith to children, the joy of the nun who is absorbed in prayer and service, the joy of the pastoral worker who creatively builds up the community, or the many volunteers who put their heart and soul into shaping the community. We want to visibly appreciate this joy, this *happiness in service*. Women have given the church *a face and a heart* for centuries - let us think of *saints such as Monica, Teresa of Ávila, Hildegard of Bingen, Edith Stein* and so many others. They all show facets of what happy success in faith can mean for women: deep friendship with God, courage to change, committed charity, intellectual brilliance, mystical depth.

But we must not romanticize: Women also experience a lot of suffering and disappointment in the church. It is a sad fact that despite their central role, women are often not involved on an equal footing. For decades - indeed, for centuries - women were seen primarily *as servants in the background*. Decisive positions, ordained ministries and doctrinal decisions have been reserved for men. As a result, many women in our church feel second-rate or that they are on a glass ceiling. Their justified desire to play a *full and equal* part in shaping the church with their baptismal dignity has long been too little heard. But in baptism, as the Swiss Conference of female, diverse and male Bishops reminds us, women and men are equal and full members of the church. This equality must also be reflected in the daily practice and structures of the church.

Dear women in the church, I would like to *acknowledge* your pain. Your disappointment at the lack of equal rights, at being treated in a condescending manner or being thwarted in your calling - we see all of this. Many of you rightly ask: *"Does this church have a place for me where I can be truly happy without having to constantly defend my calling?"* Some of you have made your voices heard loudly in initiatives such as *Maria 2.0* or fought for change in the Synodal Way. And things are indeed moving: in more and more parishes and dioceses, women are taking on leadership roles, becoming church administrators, for example, or baptizing and burying as baptism and burial officers. These steps are valuable - but many also say that *it is not enough*. The question of ordained ministries for women is still up for debate. Open discussions about this are no longer taboo, which is progress, but the solutions have not yet been found globally. All of this reflects the fact that we are on a common path of searching. And we need a decision soon.

In the meantime, diversity in the church also means fully integrating the female perspective. Not as an act of grace, but because it is just and God-ordained. After all, God created human beings as *man and woman* - both are *the image of God*. The church can only be *fully* the image of God if both genders work together in harmony and equality. The happiness of women in the church must not be a side issue; it is crucial for the happiness of the whole church. Because where people are permanently discriminated against or treated below value, there can be no real peace, no real joy. That is why I ask you, dear women: Stay committed to the church, even if you often have to be more patient than you deserve. We need you - your strength, your patience, your visions of a fraternal church. And I promise: we, those responsible, must and will continue to work on listening to you and implementing concrete changes. The goal is clear: a church in which women have equal rights in decision-making, teaching and leadership: A church in which daughters can find and make their way before God just as much as sons. I am convinced that this church will not only be fairer, but *happier*, because it is reconciled at its core.

Queer Catholics - beloved diversity in God's creation

I would like to address queer people, LGBTIQIA+ Catholics, with particular closeness. For a long time, your voice had little space in the church. Many of you have had painful experiences: You have had to hide your identity for fear of rejection because we clergy have discriminated against you; you have heard hurtful words, even experienced open discrimination. Some were taught that their otherness was a sin or a disease, or as it is more appropriately called today: disordered - words that can cut deep into the heart and make happiness almost impossible. Today, as a church, we know that great injustice has been done here. You are God's beloved children, just as you are. Your love, your identity is not a mistake, but part of the colorful diversity with which God has gifted humanity. In the first creation account, it says that God looked at everything he had made and it was *very good*. This also applies to you.

Nevertheless, we are only at the beginning of a path of recognition. There are still tensions: Official teaching is struggling to reconcile traditional ideas of marriage and sexuality with new insights and lifestyles. There is already some movement in pastoral practice. In Germany, more than a hundred church employees publicly came out as queer for the first time in 2022 at under #OutInChurch - a courageous step that has sparked a lot of interest. As a result, the bishops reformed church employment law so that no one has to fear for their job just because of a homosexual partnership. This is a sign of hope: our church is learning to reduce discrimination, albeit step by step. In some parishes and cities, celebrations for same-sex couples are now being offered - not out of protest, but out of a deep understanding that God's sacrament must not be denied to any true lover. Such developments may be tentative, but they are *sources of joy* for many of those affected. A same-sex couple who, after years, can finally stand hand in hand in church, under the blessing of God - what a moving moment of happiness, not only for the two of them, but also for the congregation, which can finally feel something of Jesus' unconditional welcome at this moment!

Dear queer brothers and sisters in the church, some of you have stayed despite everything and are contributing with your gifts - thank you for this trust! Others have not been able to do so (anymore) and have left the church in order to remain true to themselves. We understand that too. But I would like to say to all of you: you have a place in the heart of God and therefore also in the church. We want to be a community in which you can live and believe *without fear or shame*. Where we as a church have failed so far, I ask for your forgiveness. We want to do better - in the spirit of Jesus, who never excluded anyone. The wedding ceremony for all married couples in the church must now be implemented. Jesus went straight to those who were on the margins. If he had lived today, I am sure he would be at your side, holding a meal with you, listening to your stories, saying to you from the bottom of his heart: *"Do not be afraid, you are my beloved child."* Ultimately, queer people's search for happiness is the same as everyone else's: You want love, acceptance, a meaningful life. Nothing about this is incompatible with the gospel - on the contrary, the gospel is the good news that *all people* are promised this fulfillment.

Like every group, you also have unique gifts: Many a queer person has gained a special depth and empathy through the struggle for self-acceptance that enriches our communities . Your experience of *otherness* teaches us all something about God's creative creative heart, which cannot be pigeonholed. We therefore hope that you can feel at home (again) in our church with all your creativity, spirituality and love. A church that welcomes queer people with open arms will be richer and happier - because it will tangibly live what it proclaims: God's love knows no exclusion - neither in the congregation, nor in the house of God, nor before our marriage altar.

Victims of abuse - taking wounds seriously and seeking healing together

It is with a heavy heart, but with genuine sympathy, that I turn to those affected by abuse - the people who have experienced suffering and injustice in our church, where there should actually be protection and trust. There is no whitewashing: sexualized violence and abuse, committed by male clergy or other church leaders, have brought immeasurable suffering to children, young people and adults alike. Many lives have been plunged into the deepest unhappiness as a result - psychologically, spiritually and socially. When we talk about *happiness* today, we must pause here. For victims of abuse, the word "happiness" may sound like a mockery. How can a person to whom something so horrific was done in the church still be happy? We know that Many wounds remain for a lifetime.

As a preacher and as a representative of the Catholic Church, there is only one thing I can do first: remain silent and listen to your pain. Words alone heal nothing. But nevertheless, I would like to say to you, those affected: *We see you.* We believe you. We are infinitely ashamed of what has happened and we ask for forgiveness from the bottom of our hearts - knowing that forgiveness is a long process and admissions must be followed by action. You have every right to be angry, disappointed, bitter. Many of you have been put off or pressured into silence for too long. This must end once and for all.

Your suffering challenges us to become a better church. Happiness - in the sense of salvation and wholeness - can only exist here if we consistently follow the path of reappraisal, justice and prevention. *"Only by admitting guilt can there be change, healing and reconciliation"*, as one committed Catholic voice put it. This means that we must fully admit mistakes, name the guilty parties and hold them accountable, take responsibility. Covering up, looking the other way, false considerations - there must be no room for any of this. Every person in the church - whether a minister or not - must understand that the protection and dignity of children and all those in need of protection take precedence over the reputation of the institution. In recent years, we have begun to develop prevention concepts, set up independent contact points and involve those affected in decision-making processes. This is important, but it is not enough.

Dear victims, what can happiness mean for you after such an experience? Perhaps it first means justice: that your suffering is officially recognized, that perpetrators are punished and those responsible draw consequences. Perhaps it means taking steps towards healing: therapeutic support, spiritual offers if you want them, financial compensation - knowing that nothing can undo what has happened. Perhaps it also means being in contact with other people affected and realizing: I am not alone. And perhaps - this would be my faint hope - at some point it could also mean finding a space in the church that is good for you again: a safe place where you can be *yourself*, without fear and without pressure. If you are not (yet) able to do this, we fully understand. Trust cannot be imposed, it has to grow anew - and we *have* to earn it first.

As an entire church, we stand by your side as best we can. It is remarkable that there are those affected who have not lost their faith despite everything - some say: *"It is a miracle that we have not lost our faith."* Their testimony touches us. Others have lost their faith or no longer want to have anything to do with the church - we can't blame anyone for that either. But we as a community must not lose sight of you, no matter where you stand. Your well-being is part of our mission. If there is a gaping wound somewhere, the body of Christ as a whole cannot be happy. That is why we will not go back to business as usual until everything has been done to prevent such suffering in the future and to make amends for past injustice as far as possible. It is about justice, healing and reconciliation, so that hopefully at least a *little* of God's light can shine into your soul again - not the cheap glaring light of a consoling slogan, but the gentle morning light that slowly illuminates the sky after a long night. With this in mind, I also ask everyone else here: Let us pray for those affected - but equally let us act, speak, press for the church to become a credible, humble and safe community. The credibility of all of us is at stake, and even more: the salvation of so many. Happiness and salvation belong together in German - *salvation* in the sense of wholeness and salvation. We are working on this. And we trust that Christ himself cleanses his church: *"Through our prayers, we help the church to allow the Lord to cleanse and renew it,"* it says urgently. Yes, may God make our broken vessel of the Church whole again, piece by piece.

Social partners - seeking happiness for the common good

Happiness and being happy are not just private or internal issues. We live in a world in which many actors are working towards a better future. That is why I am now turning my attention to our social partners: the representatives of politics, the media, educational institutions, science, art, NGOs and all the areas with which we as a church are in contact. All of you - whether believers or not - are *our partners in the struggle for a humane world*. Because ultimately, all responsible forces in society want what is classically called the common good: conditions under which people can live in dignity and contentment.

The church was and is often one of many actors here. Sometimes it cooperated fruitfully with state or civil society bodies - for example in education (Catholic schools, kindergartens), in the health and social sector (hospitals, Caritas, aid organizations), in culture. Sometimes, however, there were also tensions and contradictions, for example over ethical issues or claims to power. But I firmly believe that in this day and age, we need to pull together more than ever to promote people's happiness. No part of society can do this alone.

Dear politicians, dear committed people in NGOs and initiatives: You are committed to justice, peace, the integrity of creation, educational opportunities and integration - all of these are essential for people to be happy. Because external conditions have a significant impact on happiness: without peace there is no happiness, without justice it is difficult to be happy, without basic services, education and freedom, happiness withers away. With this in mind, we as a church stand by your side wherever you improve people's lives. We contribute our resources - the many volunteers, the Caritas experience, the moral voice where it is needed. And we value your expertise and your commitment. Catholic social teaching speaks of the *option for the poor* and the *common good*: these are also our standards. If we work together - church, state, civil society - we can achieve a great deal: Alleviate poverty, help people in crisis, support young people, support families, protect the climate. Every concrete project that brings a smile to someone's face - be it the successful integration of a refugee family or a new opportunity for an unemployed person - is a piece of the happiness that *we share*.

I would also like to address the media: You report on the joys and sorrows of the world, uncover grievances, educate people, but sometimes also simply provide good entertainment. This also contributes to the happiness of society - an informed, enlightened, but also culturally cheerful society has a better chance of being happy. Of course, we also experience tensions in the church and the media: Some think you report too negatively about the church; on the other hand, the media have rightly brought to light many wrongs, for which we must ultimately be grateful, even if it hurts. Perhaps we can deepen the dialog: We as a church may be more transparent, truthful and open with the media. As media representatives, you can try to think not only in terms of scandals, but also in terms of solutions and common goals. How about reporting more often on successful ecumenical or interfaith projects, or on stories of success in our society? Telling positive stories has been proven to increase people's basic trust and sense of happiness - without giving up its critical function.

Dear social partners in education: Schools, universities and educational institutions are laying the foundations for how future generations will understand happiness. Today, for example, we read about a school subject called "happiness", in which children learn what makes them happy and how to deal with crises. As a church, we find this exciting and worth supporting. After all, "joy and hope" (Gaudium et Spes) was also our concern. If young people learn at an early age that empathy, self-acceptance, solidarity and finding meaning are more important for a successful life than just competition and consumption, then we are doing great things for the common good. Religious and secular education can go hand in hand here. We as a church are happy to be involved in this educational work - for example with pastoral care in schools, ethics lessons (if desired), youth associations and educational programs that combine spiritual depth with joie de vivre.

Last but not least, I would like to pay tribute to NGOs and social movements: Their often idealistic commitment - for human rights, for development cooperation, for environmental protection - so often coincides with Christian values. Even if you are sometimes critical of the church, we can sense this: We share a vision of happiness for all people, which is inextricably linked to justice. *No one can be happy if others are starving or oppressed.* This awareness drives you and also us. So let us encourage each other instead of mistrusting each other. By working together, we often experience something of the *happiness of cooperation*: how wonderful when an intercultural street festival succeeds, when a fundraising campaign saves lives, when a law is changed in favor of the weak through persistent advocacy! The church cannot claim such moments for itself, but it can rejoice and thank God for all those who do good.

All in all, our social partners are *fellow pilgrims* on the path to a more humane world. The conversation with them, the social dialogical attitude, is good for us as a church. We learn humility by recognizing that the Spirit of God is at work everywhere - even outside our immediate community. And we can bear witness by sharing our motivation: that we do all this *because* Christ has taught us to love our neighbor as ourselves. So may our cooperation grow - for the good of all. The goal is a world in which everyone can say: *Yes, it is good to live, we have reason to be grateful and happy.*

Ecumenical and interreligious partners - together on the path of joy

Finally, we look to our brothers and sisters in the faith of other denominations and religions. We are not alone on the path. Christ prayed fervently for the unity of his disciples - but unfortunately we Christians have been divided into different churches for centuries. Nevertheless, we have made great strides towards each other in recent decades. Today, Catholics, Protestants, Orthodox and others can share a lot ecumenically. And the dialog with Judaism - our older brothers and sisters in faith - and with Muslims, Buddhists, Hindus and all people of good will is also alive and well. What does this have to do with *happiness*? A lot. Because if we are honest: A major cause of unhappiness in the world has always been religious strife, fanaticism or even just ignorance towards people of other faiths. Where religion divides, much suffering remains in the end. Conversely, however, *joy* grows when religions join hands in serving people and bearing witness to God's peace.

Let us think of joint prayers for peace - initiated by Pope John Paul II in Assisi, for example, or in the local area, when churches and mosques jointly commemorate the victims of violence. You can feel it: Something deep unites us here - the longing for the salvation of all. It is auspicious when believers of different traditions treat each other with respect and even form friendships. Many congregations already have experience of this: The Protestant pastor preaches at the Catholic patron saint's festival, the Catholic priest goes to the Protestant church to celebrate Thanksgiving; the imam and the pastor organize a peace rally together; Jewish and Christian young people visit memorials together to learn from history. All of this creates trust and joy. We realize: We are not competitors, but allies in God's mission to protect and promote life.

We have achieved a lot in ecumenism: common ground has been emphasized, differences have been honestly named and often overcome. But it still hurts, for example, that we are not yet able to share the Eucharist/Communion together. Nevertheless, we can celebrate the steps that are possible. I remember the ecumenical wedding of a mixed-denominational couple, where both pastors - the Protestant and

I as a Catholic - married and blessed the couple together. The glow in the eyes of the bride and groom and their families - *that* was happiness, indeed a foretaste of heaven, where all will be one. Such moments spur us on to continue praying and working for full unity. A united Christianity would be a great witness to the world and would certainly release much inner joy because a great scandal (the division) would be overcome.

And let's look beyond Christianity: even the great religions ultimately teach that true meaning in life can be found in love, compassion and the transcendent - and that is nothing other than a path to happiness. A Buddha smile, a Sufi dance, a Hasidic festival, a meditative prayer in a mosque - people everywhere are looking for stability, peace and joy. We Christians can confidently go our own way, but we also *respect and honor* the ways of others. God has spoken to people in many different ways. When we come together interreligiously, for example in discussion groups or at interreligious prayers for peace, we often find that there is a deep common denominator, namely the so-called *Golden Rule ("Treat others as you would like to be treated")* and the desire for a life in abundance. Pope Francis emphasizes the *fraternity of all people* (Fratelli tutti) - true peace is based on this. The joint commitment of people of different faiths to those in need or to the planet is something that creates hope and joy. It shows: God's spirit blows where it wills and unites us in doing good.

As a Catholic community, we therefore want to let our ecumenical and interfaith friends know: Your happiness is our happiness. When a neighboring community - be it Protestant, free church or Orthodox - experiences an upswing, we rejoice with them. When Muslims celebrate Ramadan or Jews celebrate Passover in freedom, we greet them from the bottom of our hearts and share in their joy. *"Rejoice with those who rejoice and weep with those who weep"* (Romans 12:15) - this biblical call also applies across denominational and religious boundaries. We are *all* in the same boat of one humanity, loved by one God. What a powerful testimony we give when we live this visibly! In a world in which religions are unfortunately often misused for conflicts, our togetherness can show people: Faith does not have to divide, faith can reconcile and increase true happiness.

In the spirit of Jesus Christ: an invitation to walk together

Dear sisters and brothers, dear friends, after this broad panorama, we ask ourselves: *What connects all of this?* So many groups and perspectives - active believers and the alienated, young and old, men and women, queer people, the wounded, partners in society and other religions... Can there even be a common understanding of happiness? Perhaps not one in the sense of a rigid definition. But I believe there is a common path of searching. And it is precisely this path that I would like to invite us all to take: Let's come on a journey together to seek the *happiness* that God has intended for us! And it starts with questions and answers.

This path is not a walk, but rather a pilgrimage. We are on our way, sometimes slowly groping, sometimes jumping for joy, sometimes with tears in our eyes - but we are not alone. We are walking together. In dialog. And above all: we walk in the spirit of Jesus Christ. He is our invisible companion, always giving us new strength and direction. If we ask ourselves what this journey can look like in concrete terms, perhaps a familiar image from the Gospel will help: the story of the disciples on the road to Emmaus (Luke 24). Two disappointed disciples wander away from Jerusalem, their hope for happiness - they called it *the redemption of Israel* - shattered. Jesus joins them unrecognized. He asks them about their worries and listens. Then he explains to them the deeper meaning of what has happened and their hearts begin to burn again. Finally, they recognize him in the breaking of bread - a moment of infinite joy that makes them immediately return to Jerusalem, full of happiness with the message of resurrection on their lips.

These words contain on a small scale what we are invited to do on a larger scale: walk together, listen to one another, discover the presence of Jesus in our midst, in word and bread, in the Holy Spirit who sets our hearts on fire. On the way, the disciples do not remain stuck in their grief, but find new hope - *together* and through Christ. This is exactly how I imagine our common search for happiness.

- **Walking together:** No one should be left alone. As a church, we want to create spaces where people from all these groups can meet. Perhaps not all at once, but in a variety of constellations. Synodal discussion forums, community evenings, open table discussions - there are many possibilities. The important thing is that we *walk together*, that everyone is allowed to have their say in the search for the good life. The diversity that sometimes divides us can become a richness at the common table: When we curiously ask "Tell me, what does happiness mean to you?", horizons open up. Suddenly, the committed person gets to know the perspective of the outcast, the young person gets to know the old-established person, the hetero-cis person gets to know the queer person, the priest gets to know the abuse victim, the Catholic gets to know the Protestant - and vice versa. This may be painful or uncomfortable at first, but it leads to more understanding and compassion. We suddenly all recognize ourselves as seekers. No one has happiness for themselves alone; we need each other.
- **Listening in the spirit of love:** Perhaps the most important virtue on our journey together is *listening*. Jesus himself was a master at listening - he let the disciples finish speaking on the road to Emmaus before he said anything. Do we really listen to each other? In the church, we have some catching up to do, especially when it comes to listening at the margins. But this is precisely where the spirit of Jesus urges us: *"Go to the margins"*, Pope Francis has repeatedly emphasized. So we listen especially to those who have often been ignored: women, queer people, the disillusioned, the poor, people with disabilities, people from other backgrounds... In their experience often lies a key to a deeper joy for all. For example, when a congregation learns how much a wheelchair user suffered from not being able to come to church independently on Sundays and then rebuilds the church to make it barrier-free - then in the end *everyone* is happy about a more inclusive community. Or when we hear a young father say: *"I'd love to come, but with my fidgety toddlers I feel like I'm being disrupted"*, and the congregation then creates a child-friendly atmosphere - then we've *all* won,

because laughter and life return to the place of worship. Listening changes. It teaches us the way to happiness together.

- **perceive Jesus' spirit in our midst:** Thirdly, it is important that we gather together again and again and ask: *Where is Christ present among us here and now?* We believe: He has promised to be there where we gather in his name. His spirit is love, peace and reconciliation. When we get into arguments along the way - which will happen, because diversity brings conflict - let us pause and pray: *Come, Holy Spirit, give us understanding.* The Spirit of Jesus can *translate* between our worlds. He reminds us of the words of Jesus, who left us peace *"not as the world gives it"*. This peace is more than the absence of conflict - it is shalom, a wholeness in which everyone has their place. Walking in the spirit of Jesus means that we correct ourselves by following his example. Would Jesus exclude someone now? Would Jesus speak powerfully or lovingly? Would Jesus despair or continue to search with hope? He himself said: *"Seek and you will find; knock and it will be opened to you."* (Mt 7:7) - We want to maintain this attitude of trust. In our common search for happiness, we can trust God to let us find what we need.

- **Celebrate together and be grateful:** Despite all the work we do on ourselves and on structures - let's not forget to celebrate! There are already so many reasons for gratitude and joy in our church: people are baptized, loved ones are married, the sick are comforted, children laugh in playgroups, volunteers lend a hand, choirs sing, old people's homes are visited, young people pass exams and are blessed... *Every day gives us small and big moments of happiness.* We want to recognize and celebrate them. Nothing unites us as much as shared joy. This can happen in church services - whenever we celebrate the Eucharist, we *celebrate* precisely this gratitude for the salvation that has already been given to us. But it can also be at a community festival, at an interfaith peace festival, at an ecumenical Bible evening or at a meal for helpers after work. Let's celebrate the life that God gives! A happy get-together where all generations and all groups are welcome is a living sermon - that's where we experience what we are talking about: community and happiness.

To conclude these long reflections, I would like to remind us once again of the core: God wants us to have life and to have it in abundance (cf. John 10:10). We call this abundance "happiness" here. We are not talking about a superficial, easy-going happiness that covers up problems, but the deep happiness that grows out of meaning, love and hope. This happiness is promised to us - but we must set out to seek it *together*. There is not one group that knows and has everything and the others just have to follow. No, the Spirit of God distributes the gifts to all. Every person, every group brings a piece of the puzzle. When we put ourselves together, a picture of the kingdom of God gradually emerges in which *"righteousness and peace kiss"* (Ps 85:11) and God *"wipes away all tears"* (Rev 21:4). This picture is not yet complete, but the contours become visible wherever we love and act in Jesus' name.

So let's continue on this path. Let's take those who are weak by the hand. Let us never stop encouraging one another. And let us allow ourselves to be led by Jesus Christ - he who always makes our joy new, he who shows us that true happiness lies in loving and being loved: *"Abide in my love... so that your joy may be complete"* (John 15:9-11).

May our community, may our church be a place where this love can be felt. Then happiness becomes something tangible - for ourselves and for everyone we meet. Then we will indeed become, as Vatican II so beautifully put it, a "sign and instrument" for *joy and hope* in the world.

I invite you with a hopeful heart: Let's set off together - trusting that God will *go with us*. He himself is the goal of our happiness. And on the way there, we can already taste much of his heaven. Amen.

Appendix

Faith is like dancing - theology in motion

Faith and dancing - at first glance, two worlds that have little in common. However, the new publication *"Faith is like dancing - Moved by faith to grow as a Christian"* by Eureka Circe impressively shows how closely connected the two are. In this *training book for religious skills,* the theological project of the *DEUS EX MACHINA* book series unfolds a dynamic vision of being a Christian: *"Faith does not mean blindly following rules, but engaging with heart, hand and mind: with oneself, with other people and with the world".*

Figure 48: Book cover of "Glauben ist wie Tanzen" (Hamburg, 2025).

This work invites you to understand, practise and live your faith through dance:

"Faith is like dancing - and you determine the way and the rhythm!"

Faith does not mean blindly following rules, but rather engaging with your heart, hands and mind: with yourself, with other people and with the world.

This training book for building religious skills for Christians as well as teachers and learners in religious education and in child and youth services invites reflection:

It encourages and accompanies you on the path to the decisive personal and social skills that everyone needs to be able to live faith and charity authentically. Twelve concrete learning fields show: The ability to engage in dialog, empathy, critical thinking and reflection, gender sensitivity, self-acceptance, ethical action and others can and must be learned - in religious education classes, in self-study, in theology internships, in the community and in everyday life. A book for all those who not only want to learn their faith, but want to live it: flexibly, courageously and with joy in loving others. Because those who truly live their faith don't just dance to foreign, dogmatic rules, but also move in tune and self-confidently in harmony with the rhythm of their own lives: faith is like the joy of dancing! - and this "tuning work" can be learned.

Here, faith is an active, living process, comparable to a dance in which each person co-determines the manner and rhythm of their life of faith.

This theologically informed review takes up the central ideas of the book and combines them with inspiring voices from philosophy, the Bible and church practice. It shows why it is *good* when believers dance (figuratively *and* literally), how faith, theology and physical expression interweave, and how even the church leadership - i.e. *"today's Rome"* - should rediscover dance as an expression of faith.

Because: *"Faith is like dancing"* is a sentence that conveys the idea of faith as a dynamic, lively and personal experience. It suggests that faith is not just a static state, but a process of engaging, exploring and discovering, of being happy - in which one actively participates. It is a metaphor that describes faith as a kind of dance in which you find your own rhythm and style by engaging with the world, with yourself and with others.

The sentence "Faith is like dancing" can be interpreted in different contexts:

Religious context: In this context, it can indicate that faith is not just a dogmatic acceptance of rules, but a personal experience and a dynamic relationship with a higher power. The dance symbolizes movement, getting involved and finding one's own expression in faith.

Philosophical context: Here it can convey the idea that faith is a personal choice and an active process of recognition and trust. The dance symbolizes movement and immersion in life, rather than just believing in a static concept.

General context: In a general sense, the sentence can mean that life, faith and action are like a dance in which one engages with the music, movement and rhythm of life and finds one's own style.

Nietzsche and the dancing god - joy instead of a religion of threat and death

To begin with, it is worth taking a philosophical sideways glance: Friedrich Nietzsche once made people sit up and take notice with some thought-provoking words. *"I would only believe in a God who knew how to dance,"* he wrote at the time. This famous sentence by the 19th-century philosopher was far more than just a shrill punch line. Nietzsche, who perceived the Christianity of his time as a joyless "religion of death", called for a God full of life, lightness and exuberance - a "dancing" God "who would be worthy of our faith at all". For Nietzsche, dancing symbolized joie de vivre, creativity and liberation from overly ossified morals. His fictional Zarathustra proclaims a God who can even laugh during sacred acts - an affront to the image of grim, immovable dogma. Accordingly, the church movement *"We are Church"* calls for a *"good news instead of a threatening message"* to be proclaimed. Figuratively speaking, this includes dancing people - including a dancing God and a dancing and adapting church.

What do we learn theologically from this? Firstly, faith that loses its joy becomes implausible. A Christianity without dance, without laughter, without lively lightness threatens to sink into "nihilism and despair". On the other hand, we must take Nietzsche's longing seriously: Behind his criticism of God is the deep intuition that genuine faith needs a playful freedom - a spark of heavenly art of living that makes us *"poets:inside our lives"*. It is precisely this joy of faith, this dance step of the soul, that needs to be (re)discovered.

Interestingly, modern Christians take up Nietzsche's impulse without sharing his bitterness. The clergyman *Wolf-Dieter Steinmann*, for example, chose the motto *"Faith means dancing"* for a morning service in 2014 and also placed the joyful God at the center.

And indeed, biblical tradition knows of such a God in action: in Jesus Christ, as sung in the hymn *"Lord of the Dance"*, God himself dances through life and even through death. The songwriter *Sydney Carter* wrote this song in 1961, "in a time when the church was still rigid and immobile- in response to this, he imagined Christ as a life-loving dancer whom nothing and no one can permanently force to the ground. *"They*

453

knocked me down, but I get up again... for I am the dancing God", it says, and: *"I live in you - but live in me too"*. This echoes exactly what Nietzsche missed: a God who celebrates life and takes believers into his dance. Those who believe in such a God find it easier to find joy.

"Dancing in the arms of God" - Madeleine Delbrêls

Not only philosophers, but also Christian seekers have drawn the analogy between faith and dance. The French woman *Madeleine Delbrêl* (1904-1964) coined the phrase: *"Faith is like dancing"*. Delbrêl, who turned from atheism to a committed Christian, understood life with God as an exhilarating dance full of devotion. In one of her prayer texts, she describes her relationship with God in beautiful dance imagery. You can sense the experience of a woman who lived her faith in the midst of everyday life and retained a tremendous lightness. *"It is up to us [...] to be happy people who dance their lives with you,"* writes Delbrêl - to be a good dancer, you don't always need to know the next step, but must be ready to follow: *"You have to follow, be happy, be light and, above all, not be stiff"*. These words paint the picture of a believer who allows God's rhythm to lead them with confidence. Those who dance with God do not anxiously *ask "where the steps lead"* after every explanation, but *"turn left and right"*, open to surprises. As with dance, it is about engaging with the moment and the partner - in this case the divine counterpart. Delbrêl sums up: All our steps in life would be meaningless *"if the music [of God] did not make a harmony out of them"*. In other words, God himself is the music that gives our lives meaning and brings the scattered dance steps - the highs and lows, successes and setbacks - together to form a meaningful whole.

This *dance metaphor* expresses a profound spiritual truth: Faith is an event between God and man, a constant engagement with one another. Just as dancers pay attention to the movements of their partners, believers listen to God's silent guidance. Delbrêl speaks of *"dancing in the arms of your love"*, in which she finds herself as if in a ballroom, completely immersed in music and rhythm. Her faith is not a dry adherence to doctrines, but a life in rhythmic relationship with God.

This visionary perspective is acknowledged in detail in the book *"Faith is like dancing"*: the thoughts quoted from Delbrêls are an example of how faith captures the heart and senses. This makes it clear that those who believe can know that they are carried by God like a dance partner - safe and yet free, guided and yet exuberant.

Everyone has dancing and faith in their blood

Dancing and faith - are these really universal human traits? The clergyman *Matthias Lüskow* thinks so. In his confirmation sermon in 2023 with the theme *"Faith is like dancing"*, he stated: *"Everyone has dancing in their blood."* What sounds thought-provoking, he explains as follows: even babies experience their "first dance" when parents cradle them in their arms - an ancient, instinctive reassurance. *"Dancing is innate to us, dancing is part of our soul,"* says Lüskow. Later in life, some people may "unlearn" or shy away from dancing, but it is originally ingrained in us. And according to Lüskow, this also applies to faith: *"As with dancing, I would say the same about faith: everyone has faith in their blood."* From the very beginning, we live with a basic trust - as children, we naturally trust that someone will nurture and comfort us - and *"we then later transfer this basic trust to God"*. When people claim that they have "no faith", something has often gotten in the way that has alienated them from God. But basically, the seed of trust still lies dormant within us. This parallel - innate dance and innate faith - is a great comfort: it means that no one is completely incapable of faith. Just as everyone has a sense of rhythm and an urge to move, everyone also carries within them the ability to engage with the divine. And dancing out of line is also an art!

If none of the guests in a small discotheque dare to go onto the dance floor, there are often just a few people standing at the bar holding on to their drink. No one dares to dance. Everyone stays in the safety of the group. Until finally someone takes heart, gawked at, smiled at and perhaps secretly envied by everyone.

What she or he dares to do! The knot has been tied. Later in the evening, the dance floor is full. Bodies bounce, sway and sway rhythmically left and right. Dancing is actually quite easy when someone else leads the way.

Sometimes it is similar in faith: we often prefer to hold on to a coffee. We talk about the weather or sports instead of courageously addressing what is necessary: when Christians opposed National Socialism and raised their voices; when we addressed things in the family that we had to settle for the better; when we finally demanded and wanted to implement in the community what was necessary and liberating for individuals and everyone.

Yes, sometimes we dare to step out - with our faith. Faith is like dancing, quite simply when others join in. We need fellow dancers who believe in our values. Then it's nice not to have to stand on the sidelines. *"So get up on the dance floor - and practice,"* emphasizes clergyman *Sebastian Sievers* in a podcast.

This realization has practical consequences: If faith, like dancing, is something originally human and good, you can build on it.

This is exactly what the book *"Deus Ex Machina - Part III"* does by inviting us to awaken and develop dormant *"religious skills"*. Faith is not presented as a rigid dogma, but as something that is innate in every person, but needs to be encouraged and trained. The texts, exercises and suggestions allow us to move from our innate spiritual longing to concrete skills that we can develop - similar to practicing the steps in dancing.

Practicing, letting go, daring - learning the dance steps of faith

If you want to dance, you have to *practise*. This truism also applies to faith. A dance seems light and free, but behind this lightness there is often discipline and training. Just as clergymembers emphasize in the service of evangelization, faith requires guidance and joint practice.

No one is born a perfect dancer; you learn steps, try them out, get corrected - until at some point you *"dance your own dance"*. It is similar with faith: without guidance and teaching (e.g. from parents, teamers, pastors, religious education), many people would lose access to God. This is exactly where the workbook for religious skills comes in: It sees itself as a training book that uses reflection questions and learning fields to guide readers in practicing faith. In twelve *"learning fields"* - from the ability to engage in dialog and empathy to self-acceptance and ethical action - skills are described that can be developed in order to live faith better.

Figure 49: God as DJ.

A spiritually luminous female figure with long white hair and a halo wears large black headphones. In front of her is a record player with a model of the solar system: Sun in the center, the planets arranged in concentric orbits around it. She gently touches the earth and other planets with her fingers, as if she were playing the music of a cosmos that encourages people to dance. In the background is a dark starry sky with shining stars and other planets. The scene of God as DJ radiates calm, wisdom and a spiritual connection to the universe.

Here are some possible applications:

- *Religious education:* Teachers can use the learning fields to encourage students to reflect on and actively live their faith.
- *Self-study:* Individuals can use the book as a guide to deepen their own religious literacy.
- *Community work:* It can serve as a basis for workshops or discussion groups to understand faith as a dynamic process.
- *Theology internship:* Theology students can use the content to develop practical approaches to religious education.

In conjunction with other teaching materials, the volume can be used as supplementary material to traditional textbooks in order to new perspectives and approaches.

And: individual quotes or questions from the book can be used as impulses for discussions or group work.

With its diverse suggestions and the lifelike metaphor of dancing, *"Faith is like dancing"* can make a valuable contribution to contemporary and skills-oriented religious education. It encourages learners to actively and confidently shape their own faith journey.

In addition to practice, it takes courage to venture onto the dance floor.

The book encourages a flexible, courageous and joyful approach to faith that goes beyond dogmatic rules: faith, like dance, requires commitment and practice. Msgr. Josef Hernoga also emphasizes in his contribution from a Catholic perspective: *"Faith also requires commitment, personal dedication and creativity. Only those who are enthusiastic about God and fascinated by Jesus Christ have 'joy in faith'".* Enthusiasm ("enthusiasm" - literally a God in us) is the motor that overcomes initial shyness.

Dancing and courage always go together: You reveal something of yourself, every movement makes you vulnerable. If you dance in front of others, you run the risk of being looked at askance - *"What's he doing there?-* and yet the joy of dancing allows you to overcome this embarrassment. In the same way, faith requires courage. In a secular environment, it often takes civil courage to profess your faith - it's easy to feel ridiculed, *"as if you'd done an expressive dance from Waldorf school"*. But those who *dance* their faith gain inner freedom from the opinions of mockers. The message is: don't let fear paralyze you. *Practice* your faith and *dare* to show it to the outside world. Just as a dancer only steps confidently onto the stage after many rehearsals, a Christian becomes courageous enough to stand up for their values in everyday life by practising them.

This shows one of the great advantages of *faith is like dancing*: Training can combine theological reflection with practical guidance on character development. This encourages people to actively shape and practice their faith - *"not just [dancing] according to foreign, dogmatic rules, but [...] self-confidently in harmony with the rhythm of [their] own life"*. This self-determination in faith - without arbitrariness, but with personally internalized conviction - is the goal of "tuning work". In the context of the previous volume of Deus Ex Machina, one could say: *everyone should find their own personal dance of faith that is also in harmony with God's great melody.*

Dance of joy - believing with body and soul

But why dance at all? What does faith gain through dance? The answer is simple: joy and wholeness. *"Dancing makes you happy,"* exclaim many young people. From the first to the last beat, dancing is pure emotion and bliss - something that even outsiders can feel. This experience can be directly transferred to faith: *"Faith also makes you happy,"* says Lüskow. It is living one's faith that gives life deeper meaning, a "common thread" in the dance of life. Those who believe find themselves - metaphorically speaking - held in a choreography that measures all of life's emotions, but ultimately leads to a fulfilled goal. Faith gives direction and hope to the dance of life.

The metaphor of dancing emphasizes above all the physicality of faith. Christian faith does not just want to take place in the head, but permeate the whole person - heart, soul and body. In the Bible, King David dances with devotion before the ark of God, regardless of his royal dignity (2 Sam 6). His famous confession: *"I will dance before the LORD"*, despite the gaze of those around him, is paradigmatic of the fact that God deserves physical expression of joy. Where faith is alive, it inspires people to sing, make music and dance *"full of devotion"*. The people of Israel did this thousands of years ago, and people around the world still experience it today in church services and church festivals. Especially in charismatic or African churches, dancing is a more natural part of praising God than in Central European churches. However, there is also a rediscovery of liturgical and meditative dance in this country. Hildegard Linn, a dance teacher for many years, has developed her own choreographies for mass and Christmas - from Kyrie and Gloria to Sanctus - and refers to the biblical symbolism of each gesture. Dances to sacred music such as the *Misa Criolla* from South America show that prayer and movement can be combined: The *pulsating rhythms are a challenge to dance to,* and those who engage with them pray with their bodies.

Dance is also valued as an experience of prayer outside of the official liturgy. In a contribution to the Catholic series *SWR4 Abendgedanken,* Marianne Krämer-Birsens gives an impressive account of how a group of elderly ladies engage in *meditative dancing* together to the music. *"Dancing is like praying" is* the title. For these women - many of whom are over 60 - the weekly dance circle becomes an oasis, a place of God's presence in the here and now. For 90 minutes, nothing else matters but harmony with the others; every step in the circle becomes a concentration on the essentials. *"Losing yourself in dance can be like a prayer. Being completely with yourself, being completely in the moment, doing it with devotion - that is prayer for me,"* writes Krämer-Birsens. This experience coincides with Delbrêl's insight: it is about devotion, letting go of all disturbing thoughts and experiencing deep joy. A dance like this *"removes all temporal and physical limitations"* - you feel young and free. At the same time, the participants draw new strength for everyday life; anger and worries are put into perspective in these moments. Apparently, not only endorphins but also spiritual energy is released here. When people pray with body and soul - be it through words, silence or dance - it appeals to them in a more holistic way than if faith were just a matter of the head. This is exactly what Msgr. Hernoga points out: Faith always involves the senses and emotions; living faith even has a healing effect on people. Dance can be a form of therapy - both physically and emotionally - and genuine faith also has a healing and meaningful effect. *Faith is like dancing* therefore emphasizes that skills such as empathy, dialogue and self-acceptance require body, mind and soul to work together. Faith should be lived *"flexibly, courageously and with joy"* - this corresponds more to the lively dance step than the rigid genuflection.

Church in motion - dance as an expression of lived faith

If faith is like dancing, the question arises: *where does the church dance?* For far too long, there has been an unwritten rule of immobility in some parts of the church - pious bodies should be quiet, hands folded and faces serious. But this attitude is changing. Pope Francis, for example, tirelessly reminds us of the *joy of the Gospel* and that Christians should not be *"sourpusses"*. Although Francis did not literally speak of dancing, his vision of a church bubbling over with joy comes close. In fact, "today's Rome", i.e. the church leadership, would do well to promote dance more consciously as an expression of faith. Liturgy can be solemn and reverent - but reverence does not exclude joy. Think of King David: his ecstatic procession before the ark was just as much a worship service as the temple sacrifice cult, only more spontaneous. So why not make room for liturgical dance where it suits the culture? In many African and Oceanic communities, it is a matter of course to dance during the offertory or the Gloria. The Roman Church could learn from these "young churches" and also allow the joy of movement in European church services without fear of losing control. Of course, tact is needed here - dancing in the chancel is not understood everywhere - but processions, rhythmic singing with body movement or meditative circle dances in prayer could be an enrichment instead of a threat.

An opening to the body would also be desirable in the training of pastors and theologians. Those who become priests or pastors learn a lot about dogmatics and liturgy, but little about bodily forms of prayer. A workshop on *"Prayer and Movement"* in the seminary for priests, a seminar on "Dance as Prayer" in theology studies - such impulses could help future clergy to overcome their fear of breaking new ground with their congregations. The French nun Sr. Geneviève Médevielle once said: "*When the spirit blows, the body must also be allowed to resonate.*

This is where pneumatology (the doctrine of the Holy Spirit) and kinesiology combine to form a holistic spirituality. The church should understand that young people today are looking for other approaches - those who offer a Taizé dance or a hip-hop moves prayer evening as part of their youth work may reach hearts more directly than just by sitting and listening.

There are already encouraging new beginnings in church practice. Dance groups, meditative dance meetings (as reported by Krämer-Birsens) or even simple movement songs in family worship loosen up the atmosphere and make you feel that you can be *happy* here. The rigid seating arrangement of the church pews becomes a stage on which everyone is invited to get involved. Where believers *learn to dance*, literally and figuratively, the congregation comes alive. A sense of community is created - people move to the same beat, laugh and lose their fear of each other. Many a prejudice that faith is boring could be debunked if it became visible from the outside how lively things can be with Christians.

The theologian and dancer Hildegard Don Bosco once remarked with a wink that Jesus' first official act after the resurrection must have been a dance of joy - but none of the evangelists dared to write this down. Even if this remains in the realm of legend, the core is true: the *joy of resurrection* actually wants to be expressed in movement. So why shouldn't we celebrate Easter with liturgical dance instead of just singing "Christ is risen"? The church of the future can become bolder and dare to *take new (dance) steps*.

Dance your faith!

In the end, we are left with the invitation that the aforementioned training book and all the quoted voices have already extended: Come to the dance floor of faith! Anyone who engages with this comparison will discover that faith really is like dancing - an interplay of leading and following, of rhythm and improvisation, of seriousness and joy. The review of *"Faith is like dancing"* shows: The book combines inspiring theological insights with very practical assistance to get faith *moving*. It emphasizes that we can only live our faith authentically if we find ourselves in it - in harmony with the beat of our lives and yet open to the beat that God sets.

Faith wins when believers *dance* and learn to dance: symbolically, by letting their faith "swing" full of trust and joy, and also practically, by understanding their body as a gift from God. A dancing believer is the opposite of a dogged fanatic - then we radiate lightness, love and courage to face life. This is exactly the kind of witness the world needs. When God's melody resounds in our hearts, we must not be afraid to respond to it with our feet. The psalmists were already convinced that God dances with us: *"Praise him with tambourine and round dance!"* (Psalm 150:4). *"Because God dances, we dance too"*, say many clergymembers. Yes, the *"dancing God"* is at our side - now it is up to us to get involved in the heavenly music. With this in mind: *"Dance your life, dance your faith!"*. For he who believes may rejoice as one who dances before God and in the light of the Holy One (GN - W/D/M). Before the love of God that sustains us, let us have the courage to express this joy - in our congregations, our prayers, our whole life. Faith is like dancing: a risk, a gift and a heavenly joy. **Amen** - or should we say: *Àmen* (in 3/4 time).

Job description / Job profile:
Popess (F/D/M – GN)

(Head of the Roman Catholic Church)

Position description

The Popess (female Bishop of Rome) is the spiritual head of the Roman Catholic Church and bears the highest leadership responsibility within the universal church. A theologically profiled, charismatic leader (f/d/m - GN) who knows he or she is called to authentically proclaim the Gospel of Jesus Christ in word and deed and to lead the Church into a future-oriented renewal will soon be sought again. This office is open to qualified persons regardless of gender, as the calling and qualification for church leadership is based on the equality of all baptized persons. The incumbent represents the universal church in ecumenical and interreligious dialogs, promotes unity in faith and stands by the faithful worldwide as a shepherd, teacher and bridge-builder.

Tasks and areas of responsibility

Leadership and teaching: The Popess exercises the supreme magisterium of the Church and develops guiding doctrinal statements on the basis of Holy Scripture and tradition. He*she upholds unity in diversity and promotes a synodal culture of discussion in which consultation, listening and a common struggle for solutions are central . This includes appointing bishops, convening world church synods and writing apostolic letters and encyclicals that provide theological guidance.

Pastoral leadership: As the highest *shepherd*, the *Popess* is responsible for pastoral care worldwide. He*she strengthens the local churches, administers sacraments (in particular the episcopal ordination of new cardinals/bishops) and bestows blessings. He is expected to promote an inclusive pastoral ministry that accepts and accompanies people from all walks of life. The Popess' ministry includes in particular the option for the poor and marginalized, the mediation of reconciliation and justice as well as the commitment to peace and human rights in the world.

Administration and representation: The *holder of* this *position* manages the Holy See and the Vatican City State with a clear sense of responsibility. He/she *heads the Roman Curia and ensures the efficient and transparent administration of the Church's goods.* *In her public role*, she *represents* the Church vis-à-vis states and international organizations and performs diplomatic tasks. In doing so, she should exemplify an authentic lifestyle of simplicity and servanthood (servus servorum Dei) that credibly reflects the Gospel.

Central areas of competence and reform

In the course of a renewed profile of activities, the following **focal points** are emphasized as central areas of competence of the papal office. The *future incumbent* should lead the way in these areas in a visionary and consensus-oriented manner:

- **Promotion of women's ordination and gender equality:** The opening of ordained ministries to women and active support for equal rights in all areas of the church is expected. The Catholic Church has already given a clear vote to allow women access to ordained ministries. The *Popees Pontiff* should take up this worldwide discourse and find theologically sound ways of recognizing and promoting the vocation of women to the diaconate and priesthood. This requires courage to review existing magisterial positions in the light of the Gospel and the signs of the times.

- **Review of compulsory celibacy and new ways of training priests:** What is required is a willingness to reassess compulsory priestly celibacy and, if necessary, to relax or abolish it. The former Pope himself recently emphasized that celibacy in the Western Church is not eternal and that the abolition of compulsory celibacy is possible in principle. The *new Popess* should be open to models of voluntary celibacy in order to make the pastoral ministry more attractive and to do justice to the various calls of life. In this context, creative approaches are needed in the training and further training of priests that integrate both celibate and married pastoral workers in order to address the pastoral shortage of priests with foresight.

- **Inclusion of same-sex couples in sacramental marriage:** The recognition and sacramental accompaniment of LGBTQIA+ people is expected as an expression of contemporary church development. The *incumbent* is to open up ways in which same-sex couples can receive the full blessing of the church - up to and including examining whether sacramental marriage can also be made possible for homosexual couples. So far, the German synodal path has decided that homosexual couples should be blessed, even if these blessings have not yet been equated with sacramental marriage. The future church leadership should continue to drive this debate forward in the knowledge that God's loving care applies to all couples who live together in faithfulness and love. This requires theological depth (e.g. in ecclesiology and sacramental theology) as well as pastoral sensitivity in order to maintain unity in diversity.

- **Development of contemporary sexual ethics (including LGBTQIA+):** Of central importance is the further development of Catholic sexual morality in line with human scientific findings and the reality of life for believers in the 21st century. The *future Popess* should initiate a reform process that recognizes the dignity and equal value of all sexual orientations and identities. Church statements that have so far excluded or discriminated against LGBTQIA+ people must be put to the test. In church reform forums, for example, it was emphasized that the recognition of the equal value of non-heterosexual orientations is urgently needed. What is expected is the ability to formulate a theologically responsible sexual ethic that combines mercy and truth and values the diversity of human love relationships. This also includes a clear rejection of so-called "conversion therapies" and a focus on the concerns of non-binary people.

- **Reform of hierarchical power structures (synodality and participation):** The office requires the competence to fundamentally renew the **church's** leadership culture. The *Popess* should reform the hierarchical structures in such a way that greater transparency, accountability and participation of all the faithful are guaranteed. In doing so, the path of synodality embarked upon by former Popes must be resolutely continued. Synodality means that bishops, priests and laity listen together to God's Spirit and share responsibility. The equality of all the baptized requires participation at all levels - in consultation and decision-making - as Bishop Bätzing also emphasized with regard to the World Synod. In concrete terms, this includes: strengthening local decision-making structures, the firm involvement of women and young people in leadership tasks, the review of the powers of the ministries and the implementation of checks and balances in church law. The *future incumbent* must create a new *culture of cooperation* in which authority is understood as service and abuse of power no longer has any place.

- **Responsibility for creation and climate protection ("Laudato si"):** Following on from the social and environmental encyclical *Laudato si'*, the *Popess* is expected to play a leading role in global climate protection. The 2015 encyclical calls for the protection of "our common home" and the promotion of a holistic ecology. In line with this message, the *post holder* is responsible for addressing the urgent climate crises and anchoring sustainable action within the church. This includes being a role model for an environmentally friendly lifestyle, motivating the faithful to act in an environmentally conscious manner and campaigning internationally for climate and environmental protection. The obligation to care for creation stems from the Christian faith; consequently, the Popess should also make this testimony of faith visible in church institutions (e.g. by promoting renewable energies, environmentally friendly building management) and in teaching (spirituality of creation, ecological conversion).

Sustainability and excellence in administration (EcoVadis & EFQM)

The Vatican is aiming for **EcoVadis** (sustainability and supply chain responsibility) and **EFQM Excellence Model** certification in the near future. This has direct relevance for the Popess' leadership role and requires specific management and change competencies:

- **Sustainability Management (EcoVadis):** EcoVadis is a globally recognized corporate sustainability rating system that helps manage ESG risks, achieve sustainability goals and improve the sustainability performance of an organization and its supply chain. For the *Popess*, this means implementing the highest standards of environmental and social responsibility in the Vatican administration and the universal church. The *incumbent* must be able to develop a comprehensive sustainability concept - from *ethical procurement* (supply chains without exploitation and environmental destruction) to the promotion of fair working conditions in church facilities and the reduction of greenhouse gas emissions (e.g. climate neutrality of Vatican City). Knowledge of international sustainability standards (e.g. *UN Sustainable Development Goals, climate protection agreements*) is just as necessary as the ability to shape change processes in a participatory manner. Forward-looking change management is required to win over employees at all levels to new environmental goals and measurably track their implementation.

- **Quality management and organizational development (EFQM):** The EFQM Excellence Model is a globally recognized framework that supports organizations in managing change and improving their performance. An EFQM-based Vatican requires *the Popess* to have a modern understanding of leadership as CEO of a complex global church organization (without losing its spiritual character). She *must formulate strategic goals based on excellence criteria - such as effective governance, stakeholder satisfaction (faithful, employees, partners) and sustainable results. In practical terms, this means introducing a continuous improvement process in the Curia, regularly evaluating the Curia's work, reducing bureaucracy and silos, and promoting a culture of transparency, efficiency and accountability.* The future incumbent should be able to transfer best practices from business and administration to the church sector where appropriate - for example in the areas of financial management, personnel development and project management. In particular, the planned EFQM certification requires the ability to set clear *quality goals*, use data and feedback to make decisions and form a learning organization that responds flexibly to global challenges.

Required job profile (qualifications and skills)

We are looking for an **outstanding personality** who meets the unique requirements profile of the papal office in terms of both theological depth and human breadth. The basic **qualifications and skills** include

- **Theological and spiritual competence:** Completed university studies in theology (licentiate or doctorate) as well as sound knowledge of the Holy Scriptures, tradition and the development of church doctrine. Deeply rooted life of faith and spiritual authenticity, recognizable by intensive prayer, closeness to the sacraments and the ability to give spiritual impulses. The person should testify to a living relationship with Christ and be able to develop theology and teaching in dialog with the *signs of the times.*

- **Pastoral experience and leadership:** Several years of leadership and pastoral care experience in the church (e.g. as a bishop, priest, *theologian* or head of a church institution). Strong pastoral skills, especially in dealing with different groups of believers worldwide - from young people to families to senior citizens. Empathy, strong communication skills and intercultural competence are essential in order to do justice to the global diversity of the church. A heart for people's needs and the ability to listen, encourage and respond to crises in a conciliatory manner are expected.

- **Social justice and charity awareness** : Proven commitment to social issues and Catholic social teaching, for example in areas such as poverty reduction, educational justice, migration or peacebuilding. The *applicant* should be sensitive to the "turning point" in society and culture and know ways in which the Church can be a credible advocate for the weak and disadvantaged. Knowledge of global humanitarian challenges and church development cooperation is an advantage.

- **Organizational and leadership skills:** Experience in the management of larger organizations or diocesan structures, ideally with an international focus. The person must be able to manage complex administrative processes and implement reform projects in the church apparatus. Skills in change management and conflict resolution are essential in order to successfully and sensitively implement the upcoming changes (women in ordained ministries, new sexual ethics, curia reform, etc.). A cooperative management style is expected that encourages employees, defines clear responsibilities and at the same time leaves room for creativity and subsidiary decisions.

- **Communication and language skills:** The *Popess* acts on the world stage - excellent rhetorical skills, pedagogical skills in communicating the faith and media competence are required. The person should be able to proclaim the Good News in contemporary language and also explain difficult church positions with empathy. Very good knowledge of several world languages (in particular Italian, English, Spanish; knowledge of Latin for liturgical matters) is desirable in order to come into direct contact with different cultures.

- **Personal integrity and spiritual authority:** Impeccable moral conduct, humility and authenticity are of central importance. The *candidate* should bear witness to the values of the Gospel through her*his way of life. A personality is required that remains steadfast, level-headed and carried by the spirit of hope, even under pressure. A pronounced capacity for judgment and wisdom to be able to make decisions on complex moral and dogmatic issues is required. The Church also expects the future head to be capable of personal renewal and to accept fraternal advice and criticism in the interests of spiritual growth.

Vision and future orientation

The *future Popess* should have a clear vision for the church in the 21st century and communicate this credibly . In a time of rapid global change - technological progress, social change, the challenges of secularization - a compass is needed that unites tradition and innovation. Here, future orientation means constantly translating the message of Christ anew into today's contexts and fulfilling the missionary mandate with joy and creativity.

This requires a deep spirit of loyalty to the traditional substance of faith, combined with a willingness to take courageous steps towards reform. The *incumbent* must strengthen the signs of hope by showing perspectives on what the church as a *community of believers* could look like in 10, 20 and 50 years' time: A church that is younger, more feminine and more diverse; that regains credibility by learning from mistakes (for example in dealing with abuse and exclusion) and consistently turning back where necessary; a church that is synodically constituted, diaconally serving and ecologically sustainable in its ministry.

Through inspiring preaching and authentic witness, the *new Popess* is expected to give people today orientation and confidence. Ultimately, what is expected is a spiritual leader who is both a visionary *and a bridge builder* - rooted in prayer and open to the world - so that the Church of Christ can continue to be a "sign and instrument" of God's love in the world

Glossary

Work assignment for the annual internship: Have an artificial intelligence create a sermon on the respective glossary keyword every day using "deep research" and comprehensive "reasoning" as well as documents collected from the Internet, private archives and libraries such as Worldcat.org, Annas-Archive.org or other document servers.

Critically evaluate the impulses for the Catholic Church and its need for reform and describe which measures can be discussed and implemented locally.

(1) **#OutInChurch:** An initiative by queer (LGBTQIA+) employees of the Catholic Church who publicly acknowledged their identity and denounced discrimination in order to initiate necessary changes.

(2) **Tuning work:** The process of finding one's own faith in harmony with the rhythm of one's own life and at the same time in harmony with God's great melody.

(3) **Adelphopoiesis (brotherly bond):** Rituals in the early Middle Ages for the liturgical blessing of same-sex, emotionally close relationships, known as "brother bonding".

(4) **Ad limina visit:** The mandatory visit of the bishops of a Conference of female, diverse and male Bishops to the Pope in Rome, which normally takes place every five years.

(5) **Disclosure of files:** The provision of church archives and documents relating to cases of abuse and the handling thereof for independent investigations and those affected.

(6) **Alfred Delp SJ:** A German Jesuit and resistance fighter against the Nazi regime, whose quote "A Christian can never be a nationalist" is cited in the text as an expression of the incompatibility of radical nationalism and Christian faith.

(7) **Amazon Synod:** A special gathering of bishops in the Vatican (2019) that addressed the challenges and pastoral needs of the Amazon region.

(8) **Concept of ministry:** The theological understanding of church ministry (e.g. priests, pastors, bishops) and its legitimacy.

(9) **Ministers:** Persons who hold an ecclesiastical office (e.g. bishops, pastors).

(10) **Apostolic visitation:** An official examination of a diocese, religious community or other ecclesiastical institution on behalf of the Pope.

(11) **Fundamental employee rights:** Fundamental rights of employees that are protected by state law (e.g. protection against discrimination, protection against dismissal).

(12) **Ascetic attitude / frugality:** A lifestyle that aims at voluntary renunciation, moderation and a reduction in consumption in favor of sharing and responsibility for creation.

(13)   **Assisted suicide:** Assisted suicide. Is fundamentally rejected by the Catholic Church.

(14)   **Treaty on the Prohibition of Nuclear Weapons (TPNW):** A treaty under international law that prohibits the possession, development, production, deployment, transfer and use of nuclear weapons.

(15)   **Reappraisal:** The process of comprehensively investigating, documenting and understanding past cases of sexual abuse in the Catholic Church and their background, including institutional failures, in order to draw lessons for the present and future.

(16)   **Call for disobedience:** A public statement by the Pastors' Initiative calling for civil disobedience against certain church rules.

(17)   **Leavers:** people who have officially left church membership, often out of protest or disappointment.

(18)   **Authentic development:** Development that is not only aimed at economic growth, but also takes into account the holistic well-being of people and the inclusion of all.

(19)   **Authentic conversion and reform:** A profound and sincere change and renewal within the church, affecting both personal attitudes and structural aspects.

(20)   **Liberation theology:** A theological direction that reflects faith from the perspective of the poor and oppressed and emphasizes social justice.

(21)   **Sermon on the Mount:** A central discourse of Jesus in the New Testament that contains ethical teachings, including the commandments on non-violence and love of enemies.

(22)   **Operational blindness:** The inability to recognize one's own mistakes, problems or outdated structures because one is too involved in the daily routine.

(23)   **Representatives of victims:** Organizations and groups of people who have experienced sexualized violence in the Catholic Church and who campaign for the rights, support and appropriate processing of the cases. They often demand a central role in dealing with these cases.

(24)   **Integrity of creation:** A theological term that describes the protection and care of the natural environment as a human duty towards God and the world.

(25)   **Relationship competence:** The ability to enter into and shape healthy, sustainable and reflective interpersonal relationships. Considered essential for effective pastoral care, especially in relationship issues.

(26)   **Episcopal chair:** special assets of bishops that are managed separately from the general diocesan finances.

(27)   **Diocese:** An administrative district of the Catholic Church under the leadership of bishops.

(28)   **Borg collective:** Fictional species from Star Trek, depicted as a cybernetic collective consciousness in which individuals lose their independence and are controlled by a central "hive mind". Used in the text as a metaphor for the desired adaptation of the seminar participants to a monolithic ideological structure.

(29) **Bundesarbeitsgemeinschaft Kirche und Rechtsextremismus (BAG K+R):** An ecumenical network that campaigns against right-wing populism, right-wing extremism and group-focused misanthropy and advises and supports church actors.

(30) **Caritas:** An international association of Catholic aid organizations that is a major employer in many countries and is subject to church labor law.

(31) **CEAMA (Conferencia Eclesial de la Amazonía):** An ecclesial conference for the Amazon region that brings together clergy and laity and is considered a model for synodal leadership.

(32) **Charisms:** Gifts and abilities given by the Holy Spirit to individual believers for service to the community.

(33) **Christian social ethics:** An area of theology that deals with the application of Christian values and principles to social, economic and political issues.

(34) **Christian Social Teaching:** The collection of principles and teachings of the Catholic Church on social, economic and political issues based on the Gospel and Church tradition.

(35) **Christian view of humanity:** The theological conviction that every human being is created in the image of God and therefore has inviolable dignity, regardless of origin, religion, sexual orientation, etc.

(36) **CIC (Code of Canon Law):** The collection of laws and norms governing the Catholic Church.

(37) **Clobber passages:** term used in queer theology for biblical passages that are often quoted in isolation and without historical context to condemn homosexuality.

(38) **Coming out:** The process of recognizing one's own sexual orientation or gender identity and communicating it to others.

(39) **Communio:** Community, a central concept in the understanding of the church as a community of believers.

(40) **Comunidades Eclesiales de Base (base communities):** Small Christian communities, often rooted in Latin America, in which believers meet at eye level and shape the local church together.

(41) **Comunidades Eclesiales de Base (CEBs):** Base communities in Latin America, small communities of believers who gather for prayer, Bible study and social engagement.

(42) **Co-responsibility (joint responsibility):** The theological principle that all the baptized are jointly responsible for the being and acting of the church.

(43) **Democratization (in the church):** Not the transfer of political democracy, but the expansion of genuine co-determination and participation in responsibility of all the baptized in the decision-making processes of the church.

(44) **German Conference of female, diverse and male Bishops (DBK):** The association of Catholic bishops in Germany.

(45) **Diaconate:** The first level of ordained ministry in the Catholic Church. Deacons assist priests and bishops and may perform certain liturgical services.

(46) **Digital native:** A person who has grown up in the digital era and has been familiar with technology and the Internet since childhood.

(47) **Dicasteries:** The most important authorities or ministries of the Vatican that assist the Pope in the governance of the universal Church (e.g. Congregation for the Doctrine of the Faith, Dicastery for Bishops).

(48) **Diocesan law:** ecclesiastical law provisions that apply to a specific diocese (diocese).

(49) **Diocesan council:** An advisory body at the level of a diocese, often with the participation of lay people.

(50) **Diocese:** Another term for diocese.

(51) **Opportunities for discrimination:** Practices in employment law that discriminate against or exclude certain groups of people (e.g. queer employees, remarried people) on the basis of their lifestyle.

(52) **Distanced baptized:** People who were baptized but later stayed away from the church, although they still formally belong to the church.

(53) **Disciplinary regulations for clergy:** A provision in canon law that provides clear sanctions against male clergy for misconduct, particularly in relation to abuse or cover-up.

(54) **Divestment:** The decision to withdraw investments or money from certain companies, sectors or funds, often for ethical or moral reasons (e.g. from companies that invest in fossil fuels).

(55) **Dogmatic boundaries:** Beliefs and doctrinal provisions that are considered binding and can form the theological basis for demarcations between denominations.

(56) **Cathedral chapter:** A body of priests that advises bishops and performs certain tasks within the diocese, often with its own finances.

(57) **Double standards:** The coexistence of public moral teaching (e.g. on sexuality) and secret, deviant behavior (e.g. secret relationships, affairs). Cited as a problem in the context of celibacy culture.

(58) **Duck and cover (in a church context):** Ironic metaphor for reflexive, passive or defensive behavior of clergy in the face of crisis or reform issues, an avoidance of conflict or uncomfortable discussion.

(59) **Dynamic vision of being a Christian:** An idea of being a Christian that goes beyond simply following rules and emphasizes an active engagement with oneself, others and the world with heart, hand and mind.

(60) **Ecclesia semper reformanda:** Latin expression meaning "the church that is always being renewed", which emphasizes the need for continuous reform in the church.

(61) **Marriage:** A lifelong and indissoluble union between a man and a woman, recognized by the Church as a sacrament (in the traditional teaching of the Catholic Church).

(62) **Sacrament of marriage:** The sacrament of marriage, which is understood as a sacred bond between a man and a woman.

(63) **Marriage ceremony:** The sacramental marriage in the Catholic Church.

(64) **Understanding marriage:** The theological and legal definition of marriage by the Church.

(65) **Unity in reconciled diversity (communion):** An ideal of the church in which unity is not enforced by uniformity, but by enduring and integrating differences in an atmosphere of reconciliation and communion.

(66) **Lone wolves:** Bishops who try to implement reforms or changes on their own, without broad support or networking within the college.

(67) **Emmaus disciples (Luke 24):** A biblical story of two disciples who wander away from Jerusalem disappointed, are accompanied by Jesus without being recognized and finally recognize him, which gives them new hope and joy. Serves as an image for the common search for happiness.

(68) **Narrow corridor:** A limited scope of action within which progressive forces within the church must operate.

(69) **De-pathologization:** The process by which certain behaviors, conditions or identities (such as sexual orientation) are no longer considered pathological or in need of treatment.

(70) **Encyclical Laudato si':** A papal circular issued by Pope Francis in 2015 that deals extensively with environmental and climate issues as well as social justice.

(71) **Episcopate:** The office of bishops.

(72) **Ethical consumption:** consumer decisions that take social, ecological and ethical factors into account, e.g. by buying fair trade products.

(73) **Eucharist / Lord's Supper:** The sacrament of the Lord's Supper in the Protestant Church and the Eucharist in the Catholic Church; joint participation in this sacrament as a sign of church communion.

(74) **EU Supply Chain Act:** A law that obliges companies to identify, prevent and mitigate human rights and environmental risks in their global supply chains.

(75) **Evangelii Gaudium:** A teaching letter from Pope Francis that begins with the "joy of the Gospel" and describes it as a source of joy for those who encounter Jesus.

(76) **External expert opinion:** An investigation, e.g. into cases of abuse or the handling thereof, carried out by a non-ecclesiastical, independent body (e.g. a law firm) to enable a more objective assessment.

(77) **Error culture:** An attitude that allows people to make mistakes and learn from them without fear of excessive punishment.

(78) **Fig leaf:** Something that only serves as a cover or alibi, but has no real substance or effect.

(79) **Feminist theology:** A theological approach that critically examines and reinterprets the Bible, tradition and church teaching from a feminist perspective in order to address inequalities and discrimination against women in the church.

(80) **Those who are distant:** People who have little or no contact with the church or who belong to other religions/worldviews.

(81) **Financial management:** The way in which financial resources are managed and used.

(82) **Meatless Friday:** A traditional Catholic practice of abstaining from meat on Fridays, often as penance or a reminder of Christ's suffering. Reinterpreted here as a possible contribution to climate protection.

(83) **Focolare Movement:** An international movement in the Catholic Church that aims for communion and dialog between Christians of different denominations and people of different faiths.

(84) **Progressive theologians:** Theologians who are committed to the further development of Catholic doctrine and practice, often taking greater account of social changes and individual realities of life.

(85) **Fratelli tutti:** A social encyclical by Pope Francis from 2020 on fraternity and social friendship, which deals with globalization, populism and nationalism, among other things, and contrasts a "culture of encounter" with the "culture of walls".

(86) **Ordination of women:** The admission of women to church offices, in particular to the priesthood or episcopate.

(87) **Joy instead of a religion of death:** a theological implication from Nietzsche's point of view that a faith without joy becomes implausible and can sink into nihilism.

(88) **Peace to this house:** The title of the new basic peace ethics text of the German Conference of female, diverse and male Bishops from 2024.

(89) **Peace ethics:** Theological and moral reflection on war and peace, violence and non-violence, based on Christian principles.

(90) **Good news:** A term for the gospel that emphasizes that the central message of the Christian faith is a message of joy.

(91) **Holistic well-being:** Development that encompasses not only economic growth, but also social, environmental and cultural aspects of human and community life.

(92) **Gaudium et Spes:** Document of the Second Vatican Council, which deals with the dignity of man and his role in the modern world and describes the conscience as the "hidden center of man".

(93) **Commandment of respect for life ("Thou shalt not kill"):** A fundamental biblical commandment that emphasizes the sanctity of human life and serves as an ethical basis for the protection of human life in road traffic.

(94) **Spiritual director:** A person who accompanies seminarians or believers on their spiritual journey, often through conversations about questions of faith, inner conflicts and conscience.

(95) **Community-oriented sheep and watchdogs of the flock:** A metaphor for active, self-confident and cooperative lay people who are not passive "sheep", but who protect and shape the church community on their own responsibility and work together with the clergy.

(96) **Common good:** The good of all members of a society, which is placed above individual interests. The church is committed to the common good.

(97) **Common good balance sheet:** An instrument for measuring a company's contribution to the common good beyond purely financial indicators.

(98) **Economy for the common good:** An alternative economic model that is not based on profit maximization, but on values such as human dignity, solidarity, justice and sustainability.

(99) **Gen Z (Generation Z):** The age group roughly born between the mid-1990s and mid-2010s.

(100) **General Relator:** An important position at a synod, responsible for summarizing the discussions.

(101) **Vicar General:** main representative of bishops in the administration of the diocese.

(102) **Generational conflict:** Tension and conflict between different age groups with different values, attitudes and expectations.

(103) **Equitable participation:** The opportunity for all members of society to participate in economic, social and cultural life and to benefit from its fruits.

(104) **Just peace:** A concept of Christian peace ethics that understands peace not only as the absence of war, but as a state of justice, reconciliation and the well-being of all.

(105) **Just war (Ius ad bellum/Ius in bello):** A traditional concept of Christian ethics that formulates conditions under which war can be morally permissible (Ius ad bellum) and establishes rules for behavior during war (Ius in bello).

(106) **Gender equality:** The principle that men and women should be treated equally and have the same opportunities and rights.

(107) **Bishops who are willing to shape things:** Clergy at episcopal level who are open to change and reform within the Catholic Church and would like to play an active role in this.

(108) **Creative clergy:** A clergy member who is willing and able to actively develop the church and its community, characterized by openness, innovative spirit, participatory leadership and courage.

(109) **Need to shape:** The urgent need to actively change and develop the structures, practices or teachings of the church in order to remain relevant and vibrant.

(110) **Separation of powers (in the ecclesial context):** The principle of introducing control mechanisms and shared responsibilities within church structures (checks and balances) to limit the concentration of power in individuals and ensure accountability.

(111) **Formation of conscience:** The process of developing and sharpening one's own moral judgment, often in comparison with teachings, traditions and personal experiences.

(112) **Freedom of conscience:** The right and moral obligation of the individual to follow his or her own carefully formed conscience, even if this may contradict official teaching (based on the Second Vatican Council).

(113) **Faith is like dancing:** The central metaphor that describes faith as a dynamic, living and active process, comparable to a dance that requires commitment, practice and dedication.

(114) **Congregation for the Doctrine of the Faith:** One of the oldest congregations of the Roman Curia, responsible for safeguarding and defending Catholic doctrine of faith and morals.

(115) **Credibility:** The capacity of the Church to be authentic and trustworthy in its teachings and practices, especially with regard to its consistency with the basic principles of the Gospel and social values.

(116) **Loss of credibility:** The loss of trust and reputation in the public eye, in this case in relation to the church, if it does not address obvious problems.

(117)　**Equality and non-discrimination:** Principles that demand that all people are treated equally and are not disadvantaged, regardless of gender, sexual orientation or lifestyle.

(118)　**Same-sex partnership/marriage:** A relationship based on love, fidelity and responsibility between two people of the same sex that is recognized by the state or the church (in some contexts).

(119)　**Equality policy implementation:** The practical implementation of measures to ensure equal treatment and non-discrimination of a group.

(120)　**Turnaround in gender equality policy:** A fundamental shift in policy and practice towards equal treatment of all people regardless of their sexual orientation.

(121)　**Gender-sensitive:** Consideration of gender equality in church structures and practices.

(122)　**Glücklichsein:** The deeper meaning of the German word "Glück", which describes a state of inner fulfillment, harmony and contentment.

(123)　**Grace theology:** From the perspective of the doctrine of God's grace.

(124)　**Golden rule:** An ethical principle that exists in many religions and cultures ("Treat others as you would like to be treated") and is cited as a common denominator in interreligious dialog.

(125)　**The image of God:** The Christian doctrine that human beings are created in the image of God, which forms the basis for the inviolable dignity of every human being.

(126)　**Idolatry (or idolatry):** The worship or deification of something other than God. In context, excessive nationalism is referred to as idolatry of one's own nation or people.

(127)　**Gray areas:** Areas within the church where certain practices or approaches are tolerated but not officially recognized.

(128)　**Basic rules of church service:** The basic set of rules that defines the conditions of employment and loyalty obligations for employees of the Catholic Church and has been reformed.

(129)　**Basic Regulations for Church Service:** The basic regulations governing the working conditions and loyalty obligations of employees of the Catholic Church.

(130)　**Principles of commercial law:** Principles of accounting and financial reporting that are customary in the economy (e.g. according to HGB in Germany).

(131)　**Full-time staff / volunteers:** People who work professionally (full-time) or voluntarily (honorary) in the church and are referred to as "ministering spirits" of the church.

(132)　**Homines Probati:** Proven people, as a group of people in general, regardless of gender, who can work practically as priests.

(133)　**Homosexuality:** Sexual orientation in which a person is emotionally, romantically and/or sexually attracted to persons of the same sex.

(134)　**Homosexual sensation:** A sexual orientation that is directed towards people of the same sex.

(135) **HuK (ecumenical working group "Homosexuals and the Church"):** A working group that takes a critical look at the church's sexual morals and advocates the recognition of same-sex relationships.

(136) **Humanist and ecological conversion:** a call to turn away from the "idolatry of money" and to focus on human life, dignity and the environment.

(137) **Human sciences:** Disciplines that study human behavior and human societies (e.g. psychology, sociology).

(138) **Vatican Council II:** A major council of the Catholic Church (1962-1965), whose documents (such as Gaudium et Spes) are often quoted, e.g. in relation to the Church as a "sign and instrument" of joy and hope.

(139) **in persona Christi:** A theological term meaning that an ordained minister acts in the person of Christ when celebrating certain sacraments (especially the Eucharist).

(140) **Indoctrination:** The systematic inculcation of a one-sided world view or certain dogmas, often using manipulation and pressure techniques to suppress critical thinking.

(141) **Informal sector:** The part of the economy that is not regulated or taxed by the government and is often characterized by insecure working conditions.

(142) **Inclusive church:** A church that welcomes and includes all people, regardless of their characteristics or background.

(143) **Inclusive understanding of the church:** A vision of the church that sees diversity as enrichment and includes all baptized people regardless of their denominational affiliation or sexual orientation.

(144) **Inculturation:** The adaptation of church doctrine and practice to the culture of a particular place or group.

(145) **Institutional homophobia:** Discrimination and prejudice against homosexual people that is anchored in the structures, rules and practices of an institution.

(146) **Institutional paralysis:** A state in which necessary reforms or changes within an institution (in this case the church) are blocked and do not make progress.

(147) **Institutional responsibility:** The responsibility of the church as an organization to acknowledge the systemic problems, to work through them, to make amends and to change structures in such a way that future abuse is prevented, over and above the individual guilt of individual perpetrators.

(148) **Integral ecology:** The concept that emphasizes the inseparable link between environmental problems and social problems and requires a holistic view of both.

(149) **Interdiocesan peer networks:** Informal associations of bishops from different dioceses or countries who meet regularly to exchange ideas and support each other.

(150) **Interreligious dialog:** The exchange and encounter between people of different religions.

(151) **Intercelebration:** The joint performance of a liturgical celebration (e.g. Eucharist or Holy Communion) by clergy of different denominations.

(152) **Isolation:** The feeling or state of being cut off from social or emotional ties. The text mentions isolation in connection with celibacy as a risk factor that can lead to loneliness and a problematic search for closeness.

(153) **John Jay Report:** Several studies conducted in the early 2000s in the USA for the US Conference of Catholic Bishops by the John Jay College of Criminal Justice investigating the sexual abuse of minors by Catholic clergy.

(154) **Critique of capitalism:** A critical examination of the basic principles and effects of capitalism, often from an ethical, social or ecological perspective.

(155) **Good Friday and Easter:** Christian days of remembrance for the death of Jesus (Good Friday) and his resurrection (Easter), which symbolize the transformation from suffering to hope and new life.

(156) **Catechism of the Catholic Church:** The official summary of the teachings of the Catholic Church.

(157) **Catholic Social Teaching:** The entirety of the Catholic Church's doctrinal documents on social, economic and political issues, beginning with Rerum Novarum (1891).

(158) **Church of fear:** A church atmosphere characterized by mistrust, control and fear of deviation.

(159) **Church of the many:** A goal of synodal renewal in which priests, bishops and laity work together at all levels.

(160) **Church of trust:** A church atmosphere characterized by appreciation, shared responsibility and the courage to explore new paths.

(161) **Church on the move:** The vision of a church that is more open to physical expressions of faith and allows dance as part of the liturgy and spirituality.

(162) **Church communion:** The full communion between churches based on agreement in matters of faith, sacraments and church structure.

(163) **Canon law:** The internal legal system of the Catholic Church, which regulates the structure, organization and rules for church offices, membership, etc.

(164) **Church Tax Council:** A body within a diocese that advises the bishop on financial matters and examines and approves the budget.

(165) **Church structures:** The organizational hierarchy and the way decisions are made in the church.

(166) **Church People's Movement "We are Church":** A Catholic reform movement that campaigns for more democracy and equal rights in the church.

(167) **Ecclesiastical labor law:** The specific labor law regulations and standards that apply to employees of the Catholic Church.

(168) **Ecclesiastical Magisterium:** The official teaching authority and doctrine of the Catholic Church, in particular by the Pope and the bishops.

(169) **Clerical culture of silence:** The tendency within the church not to speak openly about difficult or unpleasant topics, especially sexuality and misconduct, but to make them taboo, repress them or cover them up.

(170) **Clericalism:** An attitude or structure that places the clergy above the laity and overemphasizes their role and authority.

(171) **Clerics:** Clergy of the church (e.g. priests, bishops).

(172) **Climate justice:** A concept that states that climate change has a disproportionate impact on poorer countries and populations, and calls for global action to address this injustice.

(173) **Climate protection:** Measures to reduce greenhouse gas emissions and limit global warming, often seen as part of the responsibility for creation.

(174) **Climate protection concept:** A plan containing measures to reduce greenhouse gas emissions and adapt to the consequences of climate change.

(175) **Climate change:** The global, long-term change in the Earth's climate, in particular due to the increase in average temperature as a result of human activity.

(176) **Collegiality:** The principle that bishops (or, in a broader sense, other groups in the church) bear responsibility and make decisions together as a college.

(177) **Collective safe space:** A safe space created by the common attitude and actions of a group (e.g. a Conference of female, diverse and male Bishops).

(178) **Competence Center for Democracy and Human Dignity:** An institution set up by the Catholic Church to support the demand that right-wing extremists be kept away from lay positions in the church.

(179) **Conflict counseling and mediation:** Professional support to clarify and resolve conflicts between individuals or groups, especially between bishops or different camps within the church.

(180) **Public corporation:** A legal form that gives certain organizations special rights and obligations in the public sphere, as is the case with the major churches in Germany.

(181) **Artificial intelligence (AI):** Computer systems that can perform tasks that normally require human intelligence, such as learning, problem solving and decision making.

(182) **Curia (Roman Curia):** The central administrative authority of the Holy See, which assists the head of the Church in governing the universal Church.

(183) **Laity:** Baptized members of the church who are not clergy.

(184) **Laici Probati:** Proven lay people, lay persons (women and men) who are ordained on the basis of their experience and can be equated with clergy for their respective level of activity on site, also for the liturgical performance of sacraments.

(185) **Laudato Si' (2015):** An encyclical by Pope Francis that deals with environmental and social issues and introduces the concept of integral ecology.

(186) **Protection of life:** The fundamental principle in the Catholic Church that emphasizes the value and sanctity of human life from conception to natural death.

(187) **Magisterium:** The authority of the Catholic Church to proclaim and interpret teachings.

(188) **Doctrinal reassessment:** The review and, if necessary, amendment of existing church teachings.

(189) **Doctrinal preaching:** The official communication and interpretation of church doctrine.

(190) **Physicality of faith:** The emphasis that Christian faith does not only take place in the head, but should permeate the whole person - heart, soul and body.

(191) **Leadership culture:** The way leadership and decision-making are practiced in the church, including the distribution of power and responsibility.

(192) **Learning organization:** An organization that continuously adapts, experiments and learns from its experiences.

(193) **LGBTQIA+:** Abbreviation for lesbian, gay, bisexual, transgender, queer, intersex, asexual and other gender identities and sexual orientations.

(194) **LGBTQIA+ inclusion:** The inclusion and acceptance of people who are lesbian, gay, bisexual, transgender, queer, intersex, asexual or have other sexual orientations and gender identities.

(195) **Liturgy:** The entirety of the acts and forms of worship in the church.

(196) **Liturgical organization:** The way in which services and rituals are conducted in the church.

(197) **Liturgical and meditative dance:** forms of dance that are consciously used in church services or as a prayer experience to combine faith and movement.

(198) **Lord of the Dance:** A hymn by Sydney Carter that sings of Jesus Christ as the dancing God who dances through life and death and invites the faithful into his dance.

(199) **Conflict of loyalties circus:** A situation in which church actors are caught in constant conflict due to contradictory expectations (e.g. between Rome and the local church).

(200) **Torn loyalties:** The inner conflict that progressive church leaders experience when they have to mediate between official norms and the pastoral reality on the ground.

(201) **Lumen Gentium:** The dogmatic constitution on the Church of the Second Vatican Council, which, among other things, strengthened the concept of the "people of God".

(202) **Abuse of power:** The misuse of a position of power or hierarchical superiority, which in the church context is identified as a key factor in enabling sexualized violence and its cover-up.

(203) **Maria 2.0:** A Catholic reform movement that began in 2019 and is committed to full equality for women in the Church, including access to all ministries.

(204) **Mentoring:** A process in which a more experienced person (mentor) advises and supports a less experienced person (mentee).

(205) **MHG study:** A 2018 scientific study on sexual abuse of minors by Catholic clergy. The text refers to its findings regarding perpetrator profiles and systemic factors.

(206) **Minority stress:** Chronic stress caused by the stigmatization of and discrimination against members of minority groups.

(207) **Abuse commissioner of the DBK:** A commissioner appointed by the German Conference of female, diverse and male Bishops who deals with the topics of abuse and coming to terms with it.

(208) **Victims of abuse:** Persons who have experienced sexualized violence and abuse in the church by church officials.

(209) **With burning concern:** An encyclical by Pope Pius XI from 1937, written in German and critical of National Socialism and its racial ideology.

(210) **Togetherness instead of loneliness:** A topic of overcoming isolation through community and mutual support among bishops.

(211) **Monocratic:** Administration or rule in which a single person has sole decision-making authority.

(212) **Moral theology:** An area of theology that deals with the morality of human behavior and develops criteria for morally good and bad behavior.

(213) **Sustainability:** A principle in which resources are used in such a way that they serve the needs of the present without compromising the opportunities of future generations. In the Catholic Church, often in the sense of preserving creation.

(214) **Charity:** A central commandment in Christianity that calls for love and solidarity with all people, regardless of their origin or affiliation. It is mentioned as the opposite of hatred and exclusion.

(215) **Neoliberalism:** An economic system based on unbridled market thinking, profit maximization and minimal state interference.

(216) **Nietzsche and the dancing God:** reference to Friedrich Nietzsche's statement that we can only believe in a God who can dance, interpreted as a longing for a joyful and expressive God as opposed to a joyless religion.

(217) **Nuclear deterrence:** A security policy strategy in which a potential attacker is deterred from launching an attack because it fears a devastating nuclear counter-attack.

(218) **Open communion practice:** A practice that allows non-Catholics or remarried divorcees to receive the Eucharist under certain circumstances.

(219) **Open culture of debate:** A culture of discussion in which different positions can be discussed transparently, even if they are controversial.

(220) **Ecological conversion:** A change in mindset and actions that leads to a more responsible approach to the environment.

(221) **Green electricity:** Electricity generated from renewable energy sources such as wind, sun or water.

(222) **Ecumenism:** The movement and striving for unity between different Christian denominations.

(223) **Option for the poor:** A central principle of Christian social teaching, which states that Christians have a special obligation to care for the poor and vulnerable and to stand up for their rights.

(224) **Ordinariates:** administrative units in the Catholic Church that are headed by an ordinarius (e.g. bishop).

(225) **Local churches:** The local or regional parts of the Catholic Church, typically dioceses.

(226) **Pacem in terris:** An encyclical by Pope John XXIII from 1963 on peace on earth, which is considered an important point of reference for the Catholic doctrine of peace.

(227) **Palaver:** Traditional forms of consultation in African cultures that are based on intensive dialog and consensus-building.

(228) **Paradigm shift:** A fundamental change in the way of thinking or in a system (here: Catholic sexual morality) that leads to a new perspective and different practices.

(229) **Paragraph 218:** The paragraph in the German Criminal Code that regulates abortion.

(230) **Parrhesía (boldness):** A term that stands for courageous and open speech that is allowed to express everything one feels.

(231) **Participation:** The active involvement of people in decision-making processes.

(232) **Participative leadership:** A management style in which employees or members are involved in decision-making processes.

(233) **Pastoral care:** refers to the pastoral care and practical work of the church with the faithful.

(234) **Pastoral areas:** Larger pastoral care units that are created by merging smaller parish structures, often as part of structural reforms.

(235) **Pastoral trials:** Temporally or locally limited experiments with new pastoral approaches that are monitored and evaluated.

(236) **Pastoral reality on the ground:** the concrete needs, challenges and realities of people's lives in the parishes and dioceses.

(237) **Pastoral dialog:** An approach to pastoral care that aims to remain in conversation with people, even if they hold political views that differ from church doctrine. The aim is often to encourage reflection and facilitate a possible return to the church line.

(238) **Pastoral realism:** The ability of church leaders to recognize and respond to the concrete needs and circumstances of the faithful and society.

(239) **Pastoral councils:** advisory bodies in parishes, deaneries or dioceses that deal with pastoral issues.

(240) **Patriotism:** love of one's own country, which, according to church teaching, includes respect for other nations and cultures and is distinct from excessive nationalism.

(241) **Pax Christi Germany:** The German section of the international Catholic peace movement Pax Christi.

(242) **Pfarrer:innen-Initiative:** An association of priests and believers in Austria that campaigns for reforms in the Catholic Church.

(243) **Compulsory celibacy:** The canonical obligation for priests of the Latin Church to live unmarried.

(244) **Pilot projects:** Experimental initiatives or reform trials carried out on a limited scale to test their effectiveness.

(245) **Pneumatology and kinesiology:** The combination of the doctrine of the Holy Spirit (pneumatology) with the doctrine of movement (kinesiology) to describe a holistic spirituality in which the body follows the movement of the spirit.

(246) **Praedicate Evangelium:** Pope Francis' apostolic constitution on the reform of the Roman Curia, which enables greater participation of lay people, especially women, in leadership functions.

(247) **Prevention of sexualized violence:** Measures at various levels (primary, secondary, tertiary prevention) to prevent abuse, e.g. through training, rules of conduct, risk assessment and intervention.

(248) **Priestly ministry:** The second level of the ordained ministry, which authorizes the celebration of the Eucharist and the administration of other sacraments.

(249) **Primary prevention:** Measures aimed at preventing abuse in the first place, e.g. by creating safe environments, training staff and establishing a culture of mindfulness.

(250) **Primacy of conscience:** The theological doctrine that the conscience of the individual plays a paramount role in moral decision-making.

(251) **Primum non nocere:** Latin principle meaning "first do no harm", particularly relevant in a medical and ethical context.

(252) **Prophetic:** In the context of the church, this refers to the task of denouncing injustice and proclaiming a vision for a fairer world.

(253) **Psychosexual immaturity:** The lack of healthy, integrated and mature development in dealing with one's own sexuality, relationships and emotions. Cited as a risk factor associated with celibacy and abuse.

(254) **Queer:** A collective term for people whose sexual orientation, gender identity or gender expression deviates from social norms; in a broader sense also for LGBTQIA+.

(255) **Queer community:** A comprehensive term for people who are not heterosexual and/or cisgender (LGBTQIA+).

(256) **Queer Christology:** A theological approach that reinterprets Jesus Christ from the perspective of LGBTQIA+ people - understood as queer or homosexual, among other things - and critically questions what significance such an image of Jesus can have for the faith and spiritual identity of queer people.

(257) **Queer Catholics / LGBTIQIA+ Catholics:** People whose sexual orientation or gender identity is non-heterosexual or non-cisgender and who are part of the Catholic Church.

(258) **Queer employees:** Church employees who identify as lesbian, gay, bisexual, transgender, intersex or queer.

(259) **Queer-sensitive pastoral care:** Pastoral care and attitudes in the church that recognize, value and include the needs, identities and experiences of queer people.

(260) **Queer theology:** A theological approach that reinterprets and questions the Bible and theological traditions from the perspective of LGBTQIA+ people.

(261) **Accountability:** The obligation of responsible parties to be held accountable for their actions (or inactions), especially in the context of abuse and cover-ups.

(262) **Legal compliance:** Compliance with legal standards and procedures.

(263) **Right-wing populism:** A political stance or strategy that is often characterized by an emphasis on "ordinary people" as opposed to "elites", nationalism, criticism of immigration and often anti-democratic tendencies.

(264) **Rule of law:** The application of principles such as transparency, consultation, clear rules and independent control also within church procedures and decisions.

(265) **Reform of Catholic sexual morality:** The process and efforts to renew the traditional teaching and practice of the Catholic Church with regard to sexuality, partnership and family and to adapt it to current knowledge and the reality of people's lives.

(266) **Need for reform:** The need for fundamental changes in the structures, rules and culture of the church in response to the abuse scandal.

(267) **Reform efforts:** Efforts within an institution to make changes to existing rules, doctrines or practices.

(268) **Reform backlog:** A situation in which necessary structural or substantive changes are not implemented, leading to stagnation or decline.

(269) **Regens:** The leadership of a seminary.

(270) **Kingdom of God:** A central theme in the New Testament that describes the state of the world in which God's reign is realized and justice and peace prevail.

(271) **Religious competencies:** Abilities and dispositions in people that make faith possible and can be encouraged and trained, similar to practicing steps when dancing.

(272) **Repression:** Suppression or punishment of people or initiatives that deviate from the official line.

(273) **Rerum Novarum (1891):** The first major encyclical of Catholic social teaching to address the conditions of the working class.

(274) **Resilience:** The psychological resistance or ability to survive difficult life situations and setbacks without lasting impairment.

(275) **Resonance:** The ability to make a connection and be understood; in the context of the text, the ability to connect with the world in which young people live.

(276) **Retreats with collegial exchange:** Planned time-outs or retreats that offer targeted space for open dialog, spiritual reflection and mutual strengthening.

(277) **Risk aversion:** An attitude that aims to avoid possible negative consequences at all costs, even if this blocks necessary changes or innovations.

(278) **Exploitation of raw materials:** The excessive or unfair use of natural resources, often with negative social and environmental consequences.

(279) **Rome/Vatican:** Refers to the Holy See and the central administration of the Catholic Church, often synonymous with the position of Pope.

(280) **Roman norms:** Rules, instructions and doctrinal statements issued by the Vatican or the head of the Church.

(281) **Roman Catholic World Church:** The entirety of the Catholic Church worldwide, with Rome as the central seat of leadership.

(282) **Armaments policy:** Political measures and decisions relating to the manufacture, trade and use of weapons and military equipment.

(283) **Sacrament:** Holy signs and acts in the Christian church through which grace is imparted according to the teachings of the church (e.g. baptism, marriage, Eucharist).

(284) **Sacramental marriage:** The marriage between a man and a woman recognized by the Catholic Church and confirmed by a sacrament.

(285) **Sacraments:** Sacred acts in the church that are considered a sign of God's grace (e.g. baptism, Eucharist, marriage).

(286) **Shame and guilt culture:** A culture in which natural human feelings, needs or experiences (such as desire, longing, sexuality) are regarded as suspicious, sinful or shameful, which can lead to repression and a lack of integration.

(287) **Responsibility for creation:** the theological duty or mission of man to protect and preserve the world created by God.

(288) **Safe spaces for innovation:** Protected contexts (places, projects, initiatives) in which new pastoral approaches, liturgical forms or participation models can be tried out without immediate fear of sanctions.

(289) **Abortion:** The termination of a pregnancy. Is fundamentally rejected by the Catholic Church.

(290) **Pregnancy conflict counseling:** Statutory counseling in Germany for women who wish to terminate a pregnancy. Progressive voices are calling for this to be open-ended.

(291) **Pastoral care:** The care and support of believers by clergy or other church employees in matters of faith and life.

(292) **Pastoral solutions:** Practical pastoral responses to the needs of people who sometimes deviate from official rules.

(293) **Blessing:** A church act in which God's blessing is invoked on people, things or situations; often refers to the blessing of couples.

(294) **Secondary prevention:** Measures aimed at identifying borderline behavior at an early stage and intervening to prevent it from escalating.

(295) **Self-determination (sexual):** The right and ability of individuals to decide freely and autonomously about their sexuality.

(296) **Women's self-determination:** The right of women to make their own decisions about their bodies and their lives, a point that progressive voices bring to the debate on abortion.

(297) **Self-defense:** The right of an individual or state to defend itself by appropriate means against an unlawful attack.

(298) **Seminarian:** A person in training to become a priest in a seminary.

(299) **Sexual ethics:** The Church's teaching on human sexuality and sexual relationships.

(300) **Sexualized violence:** Acts of abuse of a sexual nature committed within the Catholic Church by clergy or other church employees, often by taking advantage of positions of power.

(301) **Sexual morality:** the Church's teaching on sexuality and sexual relationships.

(302) **Shalom:** A Hebrew word that means more than just peace, but also includes wholeness, well-being and inner peace.

(303) **Social market economy:** An economic model that combines a market economy with a strong social security system and state regulation.

(304) **Social framework conditions:** Social and economic factors that influence the living situation of families and pregnant women and are considered by progressive voices to be relevant for the protection of life.

(305) **Social responsibility:** The obligation of companies and politicians to assume responsibility for the well-being of society and the environment beyond the mere generation of profit.

(306) **Playful freedom:** The necessary quality of true faith that allows a certain lightness, creativity and courage of expression, similar to freedom in dance.

(307) **Spiritual depth:** An anchoring in faith and spirituality that serves as a source of strength and inspiration for shaping church life.

(308) **State truth commission:** An independent commission set up by the state to carry out comprehensive investigations into cases of abuse in institutions

(here: the church) in order to bring the truth to light and make recommendations for the future.

(309) **Permanent deacons:** A level of ordained ministry that is also open to married men. Also: the possible ordination of women as permanent deacons.

(310) **Permanent temporary solution:** A situation that exists but is not permanently secured or officially regulated.

(311) **Structural exclusion:** Systemic barriers and discriminatory practices within an institution that disadvantage certain groups.

(312) **Structural violence:** Violence that does not originate directly from individuals, but is anchored in the structures of society, the economy or politics and causes injustice, suffering or disadvantage (e.g. through unfair trading conditions, arms exports to conflict areas).

(313) **Subsidiarity:** A principle of social doctrine which states that tasks and decisions should be taken at the lowest, smallest or most local level that is capable of doing so.

(314) **Sin:** In Christian theology, an action or attitude that is considered a separation from God or a violation of God's commandments.

(315) **Synodal Council:** A planned joint advisory and governing body of bishops and laity at national level, the establishment of which was stopped by the Vatican.

(316) **Synodal path:** A discussion and reform process of the Catholic Church in Germany over several years, in which bishops and lay people are involved.

(317) **Systemic causes:** Problems that are not limited to individual persons, but are rooted in the structures, rules, cultures and power relations of an institution (here: the church) and promote misconduct.

(318) **Dance of joy:** The idea that dance (and thus also lived faith) conveys joy and happiness and makes faith a holistic experience.

(319) **Dancing in the arms of God:** A metaphor by Madeleine Delbrêl that describes the relationship with God as an exhilarating dance full of devotion, in which one allows oneself to be led by God's rhythm.

(320) **Speed limit 130:** A maximum speed limit of 130 kilometers per hour on freeways.

(321) **Tertiary prevention:** Measures taken after an offense becomes known that aim to deal with cases professionally, prevent further offenses by the offender and support the victims.

(322) **Theologians:** Scientists and scholars of theology (the doctrine of God and religion) who are mentioned in the text as important voices for reform and a critical examination of the systemic problems of the church.

(323) **Theological impoverishment:** The state in which theological discourse and the development of doctrines within the church stagnate or wither, often through the avoidance of controversial topics.

(324) **Thomas Aquinas:** An important Doctor of the Church who recognized the natural human pursuit of happiness.

(325) **Training book for religious skills:** A workbook that guides you to practice and develop faith through reflection questions and learning areas (such as dialog, empathy, self-acceptance).

(326) **Transhumanism:** A movement that aims to improve and transcend human existence through the use of technology.

(327) **Transparency:** The openness and accessibility of information about cases of abuse, processes for dealing with abuse and institutional decisions for those affected, the public and external auditors.

(328) **Practicing, letting go, daring:** steps of faith that are compared to learning to dance: Faith requires practicing (instruction, teaching), letting go (of fears, rigidity) and daring (courage to show and live faith).

(329) **Ultima Ratio:** The last resort; a means that is only used when all other options have been exhausted.

(330) **Independent Abuse Commissioner of the Federal Government:** A government agency in Germany that advocates for the interests of those affected by abuse and critically accompanies the reappraisal process in various institutions.

(331) **Universal basic salary (basic income):** A regular, unconditional income paid to every citizen or resident of a country.

(332) **Unavailability of life:** The theological view that human life is a gift from God and is not subject to the free will or control of the individual.

(333) **Ethics of responsibility:** An ethical approach that focuses on the individual's responsibility for the consequences of their actions and for the well-being of others, as opposed to rigid rules or commandments.

(334) **Association of German Dioceses (VDD):** A body that represents the common interests of the German dioceses and has its own budget.

(335) **Reconciled diversity:** An ecumenical concept that sees the unity of Christians not in uniformity, but in the recognition and appreciation of different traditions.

(336) **Crisis of confidence:** A situation in which the trust of the faithful and the public in the institution of the church has been massively shaken as a result of the abuse scandal and the way it has been handled.

(337) **Cover-up:** The deliberate concealment or disguise of cases of abuse by church officials in order to protect the institution or individuals instead of supporting the victims and clearing up the crimes.

(338) **Diversity:** Described in the text as a richness within the church and society that brings in different perspectives on happiness.

(339) **Viri Probati:** Proven men, usually married men, who can be appointed as priests (older paradigm).

(340) **People of God:** The entirety of the faithful in the Catholic Church, as described by the Second Vatican Council as a pilgrim whole.

(341) **Ethnic nationalism:** A form of nationalism that is based on the idea of an ethnically or culturally homogeneous nation and often goes hand in hand with the devaluation or exclusion of other groups.

(342) **General Assembly:** The highest authority of the Synodal Way, where decisions are made.

(343) **Priority option for the poor:** A central principle of Catholic social teaching, which states that the needs of the poor and marginalized should take priority in political and economic decisions.

(344) **Ordained ministries:** The offices in the church that are conferred by the sacraments of ordination (deacon, priest, bishop).

(345) **World Church:** The Catholic Church as a global community.

(346) **World Economic Forum Davos:** An annual meeting of leaders from business, politics, science and other fields to discuss global problems.

(347) **Remarried divorcees:** Catholics who have remarried civilly after a divorce.

(348) **Human dignity:** The idea, central to Catholic social teaching and ethics, of the intrinsic, inalienable worth of every human being.

(349) **Centralism:** An organizational principle in which decisions and power are mainly concentrated in a central body or authority, in this context in Rome/Vatican.

(350) **Central Committee of German Catholics (ZdK):** The official representation of the Catholic laity in Germany.

(351) **Celibacy:** Voluntary celibacy for the sake of the kingdom of heaven, which is still obligatory for priests of the Latin rite in the Roman Catholic Church.

(352) **Chance luck:** A meaning of the German word "Glück", which refers to random, unavailable events such as a win or the avoidance of danger.

(353) **Second Vatican Council (Vatican II):** An important council of the Catholic Church (1962-1965) that led to significant reforms and a reorientation of the Church.

List of figures

The images are generated entirely by AI:

The image of the curator in the masthead was processed using AI filters and algorithms.